SILENCE AND GUILT

AN ASSSESSMENT OF CASE LAW ON THE CRIMINAL JUSTICE AND PUBLIC ORDER ACT 1994

DAVID WOLCHOVER

Barrister, of Gray's Inn
and
HEAD OF CHAMBERS AT LION COURT (now 7 Bell Yard

With best wishes to Finchley Progressive Synagogue from the author see page 3 for the Jewish angle. David.

LONDON
LION COURT
LAWYERS
2001

First published in Great Britain 2001 by Lion Court Lawyers,
Lion Court, 7 Bell Yard, London WC2A 2JR
DX 98 LDE (Chancery Lane)
Telephone 020 7831 0636
Fax 020 7831 0719
E-mail LionCrtChambers@aol.com
www.LionCourt.co.uk

For an update go to www.7BellYard.co.uk

ISBN: 0 9540254-0-7

British Library Cataloguing in Publication Data
A CIP catalogue record for this book is available from the British Library

Typeset by Lion Court Lawyers
Printed by Biddles Ltd,
Woodbridge Park Estate, Woodbridge Road, Guildford Surrey GU1 1DA

PREFACE

Nearly six years have passed since the so-called silence provisions of the Criminal Justice and Public Order Act 1994 came into force on April 1, 1995. In the nature of any major statutory innovation, within the boundaries of legislative constraint there have emerged real conflicts of attitude amongst the judges towards the doctrinal issues involved in allowing the accused's silence to count as proof of guilt. Yet although support for the measures in the ranks of our judges is not to be discounted, a marked hostility towards the legislation (reading between the lines) has been discerned at the highest level. As will be seen at an important point in the following text, this has manifested itself in a pronouncement the effect of which has been (as was quite apparently intended) to equip defence lawyers, both those representing clients in the police station and those on their feet in front of juries, with the means to emasculate the provisions on pre-trial silence. One of the principal benefits of this book is that it furnishes defence lawyers with a coherent strategy on harnessing facilities to that end which the Court of Appeal has handed them virtually on a plate. The consequence is that solicitors in the police station are free to be as robust in advising their clients to say nothing as ever they were before the statute of 1994. It is interesting to contrast the proactive approach of those "spoiling" elements in the higher judiciary with that of the present Government. Her Majesty's Most Loyal Opposition moved to reject what became section 34 on the grounds of "high constitutional principle." Yet once enacted, concern with such principles appeared to wither on the vine. Somewhat disappointingly, no commitment to repeal the silence provisions was included in Labour's manifesto for the 1997 General Election, an omission which was on all fours with the absence of any contemporaneous commitment on the floor of either House during the debates. It is not altogether surprising, therefore, that since the Election the Government have expressly indicated that they have no plans to initiate repeal.

Considering the relatively narrow ambit of the topic, in only a few years the legislation has spawned a substantial body of appellate authority, penetrating into many (although by no means all) of the nooks and crannies of the new ediface. A number of incisive articles have examined the provisions and interpretive case learning with admirable subtlety and any book on the topic would fail to be comprehensive if it did not include extensive reference to their contributions. The original foundation and inspiration for the present work was the fifth chapter of my textbook on confessions, co-written with my long-time collaborator, fellow criminal barrister, professional neighbour, and valued old friend, Anthony Heaton-Armstrong of 9-12 Bell Yard. That chapter dealt with the silence provisions of the 1994 Act, in force for not much more than a year when the work was published by Sweet and Maxwell in 1996. The statute was then in its infancy and the chapter was soon eclipsed in utility as the accumulating results of appeal decisions began to accelerate. In a sense the same fate awaited Peter Mirfield's expanded work on confessions, the second edition of which was published in 1998. It may be that the rate of handing down appeal judgments on the topic has now sufficiently slowed to warrant a fresh analysis that can look forward to several years of validity and usefulness. I would venture to hazard that as a text dedicated exclusively to the early and recent development of the law in relation to evidential silence this treatise can rightly aspire to command the attention of practitioners and academics alike.

I must apologise for the absence of an alphabetical index. The omission was calculated. In a work concentrating on such a narrow field of law I suggest that an index would be insufficiently helpful to justify the cost and effort involved in preparing one. However, I believe that the provision of a comprehensive contents list, though not alphabetical, will assist the reader to find topics with relative ease.

Lastly, in time-honoured manner, I take the opportunity presented by this preface to acknowledge the assistance I have been given in the planning, production and marketing of this work by Joshua Dubin, of Lion Court, formerly himself active in the publishing world before coming to the Bar. I also thank others at Lion Court for their ideas and input as well as the loyal placing of their orders for the book (in anticipation; clerks exempt). My pupil Martha Knowlden proved indispensable in bringing to bear her expertise to the labour of checking and numbering the page references in the contents list and tables. I cannot forget to mention again Anthony Heaton-Armstrong, expressing my profound thanks for his co-operation on *Confession Evidence* and for his encouragement, friendship and generous praise, and I thank Neil Corre, solicitor and Higher Courts Advocate (Crime), and a collaborator on our recent work on bail, for his ideas, friendship and encouragement. I pay tribute to Mark Adler for his enormous help in showing me how to write clear English and think clear thoughts and to my fondly remembered parents for all their love and encouragement in my youth and continuing in their old age. I thank my teenage daughters Eva and Natalie for their forbearance when I have seemed more wrapped up in my writing than interested in clocking up "quality time" and I welcome into the world my young daughter Julia, as yet blissfully unaware of any obligation to read the efforts of her father's labour. I thank my in-laws in Brazil for putting up with my day-dreaming while I used my holiday with them to think through textual problems. Finally, I honour and express my love and esteem for my dear wife Ana, for whom there is no need (albeit every incentive) to enumerate reasons.

Lion Court, February 2001

CONTENTS

TABLE OF CASES

Muckian (1994) unreported, N.I.C.A., December 2, cited in [1995] Crim.L.R. 606 217
Mullen [1999] 2 Cr.App.R. 143 118, 240, 241, 242
Murdoch v. Taylor [1965] 1 All E.R. 406 203
Murphy and McKinley [1993] 4 N.I.J.B. 42 40
Murray v. D.P.P. (1993) 97 Cr.App.R. 151; (1994) 99 Cr.App.R. 398;
[1994] 1 W.L.R. 1, H.L., May 18, October 29, 1992 64, 106,
109, 110, 158, 208, 214, 218, 231, 235, 238
Murray v. United Kingdom (1996) 22 E.H.R.R.29 67, 76, 155, 156, 157, 159,
233, 234, 236, 243, 244, 245, 247
Mutch [1994] 1 All E.R. 178 204-208, 213, 214, 217
Napper [1996] Crim.L.R. 591; (1996) 161 J.P.R. 16 122, 227
Nash (1911) 6 Cr.App.R. 225 32
Naylor (1933) 23 Cr.App.R. 177 35, 37, 43, 44
Nesbeth (1991) unreported, C.A. 336/Y3/90 191
Nickolson [1998] Crim.L.R. 61, C.A. no. 97/3647/Z4 74, 75, 78, 79, 88
Nodder (1937) unreported 205
Norton [1910] 2 K.B. 496 32
Norton (1996) unreported, C.A. 96/0319/Y2, April 29 227
Okafor [1994 Crim.L.R. 221, C.A. 199
O'Neill (1950) 34 Cr.App.R. 108 202
O'Neill (1990) unreported, N. Ireland, May 17,
cited in [1991] Crim.L.R., pp..410-411 213
Oni [1992] Crim.L.R. 183, C.A. 196
Oransaye [1993] Crim.L.R. 722 199
Pall [1992] Crim.L.R. 126, C.A. 199
Park (1993) *The Times* July 30, C.A. 199
Parker (1934) 24 Cr.App.R. 2 42, 59
Parkes v. R. [1976] 1 W.L.R. 1251, P.C. 39
Pointer [1997] Crim.L.R. 676 69, 117
Practice Direction: Crown Court (Defendant's Evidence) [1995] 2 Cr.App.R. 192 188
Pratt [1971] Crim.L.R. 234 204
Purcell [1992] Crim.L.R. 806, C.A. 191
Quinn (1993) unreported, N.I.C.A, September 17 161, 166
R. v. Chief Constable of the R.U.C., ex p. Begley [1997] N.I. 278, H.L. 58
R. v. Derby Magistrates' Court, ex parte B. [1996] A.C. 487 174
R. v. Secretary of State for Trade and Industry, ex p. McCormick
[1998] *The Times*, February 10, C.A. (Civ.Div.) 10
Raghip, *sub. Nom,* Silcott, Braithwaite and Raghip
(1991) *The Times*, January 9, C.A. 134, 135
Rajcoomar [1999] Crim.L.R. 728 240
Randall (1998) unreported, C.A. 9705960 X4 75
Raphaie [1996] Crim.L.R. 812, C.A. 65
Raviraj (1987) 85 Cr.App.R. 93 32, 38
Reader (1998) unreported, C.A. 97/6342/W2 110
Rennie [1982] 1 All R.R. 385 49
Rhodes [1899] 1 Q.B. 77 203
Rice v. Connolly [1966] 2 All E.R. 649 6
Roberts [1970] Crim.L.R. 464, C.A 147
Roble [1997] Crim.L.R. 185 74, 82, 83, 174, 175, 183

TABLE OF STATUTES

TABLE OF STATUTORY INSTRUMENTS, CODES OF PRACTICE, OFFICIAL CIRCULARS, ETC

CHAPTER ONE

GENERAL PRINCIPLES

I. QUESTIONING AND THE RIGHT TO SILENCE

A. *THE HISTORICAL BACKGROUND*

(1) Pre-trial examination of the prisoner a traditional feature of Common law process

The early history of criminal justice under the Common law is marked by the reliance on unrestricted examination of the accused, both as part of the preliminary investigative process and then during the trial.[1] Indeed, the pre-trial examination was probably the first form of evidential material adduced before the petty jury, even before the stage had been reached in the evolution of trial in its recognizable modern form when proof of guilt was determined by evidence called in open forum rather than on the basis of the jury's own knowledge.[2] Custodial questioning of suspects by investigators formed such an integral part of the criminal process that it survived well into the second half of the 19th century, when the attitude of the courts turned against police questioning of arrested suspects, possibly influenced by the final ending of the examining magistrates' practice of questioning the prisoner.[3] However, the period of deprecation did not last very long. In 1964 the Judges' Rules, the guidance on interrogation of suspects propounded by a committee of judges of the Queen's Bench Division and issued to the police by the Home Office, once again sanctioned custodial questioning of suspects under caution, a licence subsequently incorporated into Code of Practice "C" issued under the Police and Criminal Evidence Act 1984 (PACE).[4]

---

[1] See generally *Wolchover and Heaton-Armstrong on Confession Evidence*, London: Sweet and Maxwell Criminal Law Library Series, 1996, *passim*

[2] For examples see *ibid.*, pp.2-3.

[3] *ibid.*, p.111.

[4] *Code of Practice for the Detention, Treatment and Questioning of Persons by Police Officers,* Code "C" of the Codes of Practice issued under s.66 of the Police and Criminal Evidence Act 1984. The Codes were originally issued in 1985 when the Act came into force (Police and Criminal Evidence Act (1984) (Codes of Practice) (No. 1) Order 1984 (S.I. No. 1937)), reissued in 1991 (Police and Criminal Evidence Act (1984) (Codes of Practice) (No. 2) Order 1984 (S.I. No. 2580) and again on April 10, 1995 by the Police and Criminal Evidence Act (1984) (Codes of Practice) (No. 3) Order 1995 (S.I. No. 450).

(2) Judicial questioning of the prisoner at the bar

The traditional practice of questioning suspects was for centuries mirrored in the criminal trial itself. Although the accused could not give sworn evidence (a prohibition which lasted until the Criminal Evidence Act 1898) this did not mean that in the earlier phase of the modern form of trial defendants were expected or allowed to remain mute. Quite the contrary, for according to Sir Thomas Smith's celebrated contemporary account of trials in the 16th century, defendants were traditionally questioned and questioned closely and vigorously both by the judge and by prosecuting advocate regardless of whether or not they had first volunteered an explanation from the dock.[5]

(3) Compulsory questioning under oath in the ecclesiastical and conciliar tribunals

Distinct from the courts of Common law the church had since the 12th century employed a form of compulsory sworn interrogatories in cases of heresy, ungodly conduct such as Sabbath breach and sexual incontinence and in matrimonial and testamentary matters. With the great theological divide which spread across Europe in the 15th and 16th centuries religious dissent grew to be identified with political opposition against the state and the Privy Council saw the utility of harnessing the canon law oath procedure in pursuance of its inquiries into secular agitation. Under the compulsory oath procedure anyone could be summoned before an ecclesiastical or conciliar tribunal on the basis of rumour alone and required to take the inquisitorial oath (called the oath *ex officio* because it could be compelled at the discretion of the inquisitor by virtue of his office). Originally, compliance was enforced by the sanction of imprisonment for the contempt of refusal. In the prerogative courts of Star Chamber and High Commission if once a suspect had complied but had then refused to give an answer, or a sufficient answer, to a specific question he might be convicted in default, *pro confesso*, as if he had confessed. In their final, most oppressive, phase, Star Chamber and High Commission could convict *pro confesso* merely on refusal to take the oath.[6]

(4) Objections to compulsory sworn questioning

The distant origins of objection to compulsory self-incrimination are obscure and have been the subject of conflicting theories.[7] Objection to the *ex officio* oath had

---

[5] *Commonwealth of England*, 1583, pp.183-201, cited by Sir James Fitzjames Stephen, *History of the Criminal Law of England*, London 1883 (3 vols.), i, pp. 325-350.

[6] See generally Leonard Levy, *Origins of the Fifth Amendment*, Camb. Mass: O.U.P. 1968.

[7] See Steven Greer, "The Right to Silence: A Review of the Current Debate," (1990) 53 M.L.R. 709, at p.710.

been raised from time to time since the Middle Ages and was originally conditional, the argument being that its imposition could only be justified on the basis of "common report."[8] By the late 16th century, however, it had come to be opposed unconditionally as a matter of fundamental principle. The protest that "no one shall be compelled to accuse himself," made its debût in 1534 dressed up in the now familiar dog Latin slogan *nemo tenetur seipsum prodere* presumably to give it a ring of ostensible Roman or Canon Law antiquity. It seems first to have been cited by the puritan John Lambert at his compulsory examination before Archbishop Warham[9] and was not infrequently coupled with the argument that when Jesus was examined by the Sanhedrin he had by implication apparently claimed a right to stand on his silence, a scriptural reference first obliquely noted by the recusant scholar William Tyndale.[10] It is known that Lambert was in close touch with Tyndale in Antwerp where Tyndale lived in exile and as a pioneer English Hebraist maintained links with rabbinical scholars.[11] For this reason, it has been conjectured that Tyndale actively sought a contemporary juridical basis for Jesus's claim, that he may have learned from his rabbinical contacts of the Talmudic precept *Ein adam meissim atsmo rasha*—"no man shall show himself as wicked," that he coined the Latin maxim as an almost direct translation (he would have been wary of citing Jewish sources expressly), identified it with the practice of Jesus, and transmitted it to Lambert.[12] The talmudic rule on confessions prohibits their use altogether in capital cases; the issue of compulsion is irrelevant.[13] But allowing for that difference the corresondence is nevertheless striking. The most notable of the "practice of Jesus" proponents was "Freeborn" John Lilburne, who cited it first before the Star Chamber and then when he attempted to stop the judges questioning him at his trial for treason a decade later in 1649.[14]

The objection by men of conscience to compulsory sworn interrogation was undoubtedly inspired by the fact that because they would not lie they knew that if required to answer under oath they would have little choice but to confess. However, where sometimes the accused might be innocent of the precise charge

---

[8] See Wigmore, "Nemo Tenetur Seipsum Prodere" 5 Harvard Law Rev. 84; Mary Hume Maguire, "The Attack of the Common Lawyers on the Oath Ex Officio as Administered in the Ecclesiastical Courts of England," in *Essays in History and Politcal Thought in Honour of Charles Howard McIlwaine* (ed. Wittke), Camb. Mass 1936, at p.199; Morgan "The Privilege Against Self-Incrimination," 34 Minn. Law Rev. 1 (1949); and see Levy, *op. cit.*, *passim*.

[9] Fox, *Acts and Monuments*, English transl. 1631, p.398; reference first identified by Maguire, *supra*.

[10] *Obedience of a Christian Man*, London 1528, 122.

[11] See Mozley, *William Tyndale*, London 1937.

[12] Wolchover, *The Descent of the Maxim Nemo Teneture Seipsum Prodere from Sanhedrin 9b*, London, 1973. For the Talmudic rule see Tractate Sanhedrin 9b in *The Babylonian Talmud* (ed. Epstein, with English transl.), London: Soncino 1935-52. For treatments on the possible Talmudic origins of the Common law precept see e.g. Norman Lamm, "The Fifth Amendment and Its Equivalent in the Halakhah," 5 Judaism 53 (Winter 1956); Horowitz, "The Privilege Against Self-Incrimination: How did it Originate?" (1958) 31 Temple Law Quarterly 121, describing Jewish thinking as exerting an indirect subterranean influence in England; Levy, *op.cit.*, Appendix.

[13] See generally Profs I. M. and Y. Rosenberg, "In the Beginning: The Talmudic Rule Against Self-Incrimination," (1988) 63 New York University Law Review 955.

[14] 4 St. Tr. 1269.

levelled there was the obvious fear that a series of ensnaring questions might produce an impression that their denials were untruthful or that they were guilty of some other related offence. Moreover, they would not have wanted to be asked questions about the involvement of associates, either for fear of being thought guilty by association, or out of a desire to protect their friends or relations.

(5) Decline of judicial questioning of defendants in common law trials

Routine questioning of the accused by the judge lasted until the immediate post Civil War period when the momentum of feeling which had built up against the *ex officio* oath procedure employed by the conciliar tribunals was turned with its abolition into an attack on the judicial habit of questioning the accused in front of the jury.[15] After the Restoration many defendants followed Lilburne's example and increasingly their claims were met.[16] However, Wigmore showed that Sir James Stephen gave too early a cessation when he said that it died out soon after the Revolution of 1688.[17] Although by then judges would refrain from questioning on demand, the practice lingered on until at least the 1700s, for as Campbell records, Lord Holt, who died in 1710, "to the end of his life . . . persevered in what we call the 'French system' of interrogation of the prisoner during his trial."[18]

The tendency of judges to engage in dialogue with the prisoner is perhaps unavoidable when the defendant is unrepresented and must himself perform the functions of advocate in his own cause. As Langbein has pointed out, so long as the prisoner was without counsel there was scarcely any possibility of distinguishing his rôle as defendant and as witness.[19] In cross-examining witnesses defendants will inevitably utter assertions which the judge must clarify by way of questioning, if for no other reason than to render the questions intelligible or unambiguous. From the Old Bailey Sessions Papers for the period from the 1670s to the mid-1730s Langbein noticed not a single case—

> ". . . in which an accused refused to speak or asserted grants of privilege or in which he makes the least allusion to a privilege against self-incrimination. Without counsel to shoulder the non-testimonial aspects of the defence, the accused's privilege would simply have

---

[15] Levy, *op.cit.*, chaps. 9 and 10).

[16] Prof. John H.Wigmore, *A Treatise on the Anglo-American System of Evidence in Trials at Common Law*, 3rd ed. Boston 1940 (10 vols.), para. 2250, note 105, for a compilation, and see Levy, *ibid.*, chap. 10).

[17] Stephen, *H.C.L.*, i, p.440; Wigmore, *op.cit.*, para. 2250, citing *Harrison* (1692) 12 *St.Tr.* 895; *Swendsen* (1702) 14 *St.Tr.* 559, 580-581; *Baynston* (1702) 14 *St.Tr.* 598, 621-625.

[18] Wigmore, *op. cit.*, para 2250, citing Campbell, *The Lives of the Chief Justices of England*, London 1849-57, ii, p.144.

[19] Prof. J.H. Langbein, "The Criminal Trial Before the Lawyers," (1978) 45 *Univ. Chicago Law Rev.* 263, at p.283.

amounted to the right to forfeit all defence and we do not wonder that he never claimed it."[20]

(6) Connection between the rule excluding involuntary confessions and the rule against compulsory self-incrimination

It has been argued that the immediate post-Restoration period provides evidence, too, of the existence of an embryonic rule excluding pre-trial confessions obtained by the threat of torture.[21] According to Hale such a rule is certainly in existence by 1676.[22] Although there is no explicit link between the maxim *nemo tenetur* and the principle of excluding pre-trial confessions obtained by extortion or inducement, whether in the 17th century or in the next, the first known references to such a principle at almost exactly the moment when defendants begin systematically to object to being questioned by the judge suggest more than mere coincidence. Wigmore, it is true, disavowed any connection, claiming that the history of the two was "wide apart, differing by one hundred years in origin, and derived through separate lines of precendents"[23] but he wrongly asserted that Hale contained no reference to a doctrine limiting the admissibility of confession on the grounds of duress or inducement.[24] No less august a body than the Supreme Court of the United States has recognised the connection, ruling that the confessions exclusion rule is controlled by "that portion of the Fifth Amendment . . . commanding that no person 'shall be compelled in any criminal case to be a witness against himself.'"[25]

It is arguable that the principle of disallowing coerced confessions and the ending of judicial questioning of the accused in court are but different applications of the same basic principle. Arguably another application of the principle was the prohibition of pre-trial questioning of suspects in custody, although admittedly inception of the ban was long delayed after the end of judicial questioning at trial and its life relatively short.

(7) Possible mixed rationale for the end of judicial questioning of the prisoner at the bar

The contrast between tentative toleration of the maxim *nemo tenetur* in the 17th century and the extent to which by the middle years of the next it was treated as a

---

20 *ibid.*

21 See *Wolchover and Heaton-Armstrong on Confession Evidence*, pp.501-503, citing *Tonge* (1660) 6 St. Tr. 225, *et seq.*

22 *Pleas of the Crown*, ii. 284, manuscript treatise ordered printed by Parliament in 1680, four years after Hale's death; published commercially in 1736, Sollom Emlyn ed.

23 *op. cit.*, para. 226.

24 *op. cit.* para. 818.

25 *Bram* v. *United States*, 168 U.S. 532 (1897), at p.542, approved in *Miranda* v. *Arizona*, 384 U.S. 436 (1966), at p.461.

fundamental tenet[26] could not furnish a better illustration of the way attitudes can change in a generation. Yet whilst it may have come to be treated among most common lawyers and judges as a point of pride its original emergence probably owed as much to a desire to deny the accused a platform for lying to the court as it did to considerations of charity. Indeed, some judges went over to gagging defendants altogether and apparently did so with a vengeance. In *Coleman* the defendant tried to establish an alibi and Scroggs C.J. asked him if he had any witnesses to prove it, but when Coleman replied that he had not, he was told he could say nothing.[27] In the words of one leading commentator it is "difficult to say whether the interrogation of the accused at his trial ended altogether because of exaggerated indulgence of his right against self-incrimination or because his word was not trusted. The latter idea, in any event, buttressed the former."[28]

(8) The suspicious nature of non-response to questioning and its coercive impact

Where questioning is conducted by a judge or official investigator, the authority of the inquisitor in the eyes of the jury will of itself be seen as imposing an obligation to answer. You do not lightly refuse to answer a questioner of such standing and, for one or other of two specific reasons, that alone will put defendants or suspects who would deny the charge under pressure to answer the questions. They may fear that if they do not answer their silence will be taken to mean that they have no innocent response to offer and that therefore it amounts to an assent to what the questions imply. On the other hand, they may fear that from their reluctance to give an innocent account, if they have one, it will raise suspicions that they know it will not withstand detailed scrutiny and that this is because it is false and that they do not have an innocent account to give which is true. When judges surrendered the tradition of questioning prisoners at the bar this removed from the criminal process a potent factor of compulsion to speak in the form of the risk of conviction if they did not. What residual obligation to speak was left hardly amounted to compulsion. Obviously, in the rare instance that a defendant abdicated a defence, remaining entirely mute and not even putting his case through cross-examination of Crown witnesses, this would make conviction by default highly likely. However, the need to raise a positive defence could hardly be classed as coercion. Furthermore, judges would only have to be able to engage in direct dialogue with defendants accused of felony where they were unrepresented, in order to clear up points of ambiguity in the questions they put to witnesses. By the middle years of the 18th century such defendants were allowed counsel for all purposes save that of making a closing

---

[26] See *Smith* v. *Read* (1736) 1 Atk. 526, *per* Lord Hardwicke L.C., at p.527.
[27] (1678) 7 St. Tr. 1, 60; see Stephen, *H.C.L.*, i, 387.
[28] Levy, *op. cit.*, p.324.

speech to the jury and from then on increasingly came to be represented.[29] When the Criminal Evidence Act 1898 allowed defendants to give evidence in their own defence that of itself placed upon them a moderate degree of pressure to exercise the right. However, what really increased that pressure was the sanctioning of adverse judicial comment on failure to go into the witness box.

(9) Prohibition on permitting silence to stand against the accused as an application of the rule against compulsory self-incrimination

Asking questions of a suspect of itself imposes some compulsion to answer because the accused is forced to give answers or run the risk of increasing the suspicion against himself. Such compulsion has existed for as long as official investigators have been empowered to question suspects. Rules of evidence which expressly allow non-response to adversarial questions to add to the prosecution case reinforce that pressure. Since there is always a risk that the statements of a suspect may have a self-incriminating effect (even though such statements are intended to be exculpatory), it follows logically that the precept against compulsory self-incrimination will be undermined if non-response is formally permitted to be held against the accused. English law, however, has not developed in accordance with such an approach. The authoritative view is that despite the legislative introduction of rules which permit an accused person's silence to be held against him "[h]e is not compelled to speak. He can still exercise his right to remain silent during police questioning or at court. The only change is that exercise of the right is no longer free of risk."[30] But surely if he "is no longer free of risk," he is compelled. *A priori*, the precept against compulsory self-incrimination does not select according to the means of compulsion, whether torture, threats, blandishment, or the risk that silence will condemn.

(10) The "right to silence"

(a) *Immunity from adverse inference*

As a matter of practice (although not of strict legal principle) triers of fact prior to the Criminal Justice and Public Order Act 1994 could not generally be given formal leave to draw any inference adverse to a defendant from the fact that when the police put the allegation to him, or had asked him questions about it, he remained silent. The protection so enjoyed by suspects was part of a group of immunities which had come to be described in England under the umbrella expression "the right to silence," or "right *of* silence." The phrase "privilege against self-incrimination"

---

[29] See Stephen, *H.C.L.*, i, p.424; Langbein, "The Criminal Trial Before the Lawyers," at pp.307-311.

[30] Lord Bingham of Cornhill, the Lord Chief Justice of England and Wales, "Silence is golden—or is it?" an address to the Criminal Bar Association on October 14, 1997.

has sometimes been used synonymously although the two expressions are logically distinguishable in that "privilege" implies the according of a special favour or concession whereas "right" denotes an interest guaranteed as an expression of basic values.[31]

An analagous immunity was applicable to the trial process itself. Neither the prosecution nor the judge was permitted to suggest that an election by the defendant to refrain from going into the witness box was indicative of guilt. (However, the form of comments which were permitted judges in summing up afforded them considerable latitude in the making of very damaging criticism dressed up in oblique language.) This immunity too was abolished by the Act of 1994.

(b) *Silence of defendants and suspects not an offence*

The rule that the accused's silence could not be invested in a formal sense with evidential significance adverse to his case was a separate immunity from the rule that a suspect generally commits no punishable offence by refusing to answer police questions. This is the out-of-court equivalent of the rule that no defendant can be forced to give evidence in his own trial by the sanction of committing a contempt of court if he declines to do so (a rule expressly preserved by section 35(4) of the 1994 Act). These are components of the general right to silence which entitles all citizens to withhold information from the authorities, an aspect of the right to personal freedom and privacy.[32] But the freedom of the defendant on trial not to co-operate is surrendered with his decision to volunteer himself as a witness in his own defence. At that point the interests of the proper administration of justice require him to answer all relevant questions and it is contumacious to refuse to do so even if the question tends to incriminate him.

(c) *The silent citizen*

Facing questions by the police potential witnesses are broadly speaking in the same position as suspects. With the abolition of the common law misdemeanour of misprision of felony (failing to report information about a felony) citizens in general bear no *legal* duty to furnish information to the police and commit no offence by refusing to do so.[33] In *Rice* v. *Connolly*[34] the appellant refused to explain his movements after being followed around by a police constable in an area in which there had been a spate of break-ins and it was held that this did not amount to the offence of wilful obstruction of the officer in the execution of his duty[35] since the citizen's only duty to answer questions put by a constable was a moral or social one.

---

[31] See Steven Greer, "The Right to Silence: A Review of the Current Debate," (1990) 53 M.L.R. 709, at p.710.

[32] See Andrew Zuckerman, "Trial by Unfair Means—The Report of the Working Group on the Right to Silence," [1989] Crim.L.R. 855; *Report of the Working Group on the Right to Silence* (ch.W.J. Bohan), Home Office C4 Division, July 13, 1989, hereafter referred to as the *Working Group Report*.

[33] Criminal Justice Act 1967, s.1, abolishing all distinctions between felony and misdemeanour; misprision of treason was preserved by s.12(6).

[34] [1966] 2 All E.R. 649.

[35] Police Act 1964, s.51(3).

It was clearly to this that Principle (a) of the Introduction to the Judges' Rules 1964 was adverting in its statement that "citizens have a duty to help a police officer to discover and apprehend offenders."

(d) *The silent witness*

The general right to silence which entitles citizens to withhold information from the executive authorities is separate from and subjugated to the special power of judicial authority to summons witnesses. But the power of the courts to override the citizen's right to silence in the interests of the proper administration of justice is compensated for by the rule that persons who are compellable as witnesses differ from defendants volunteering themselves as witnesses in that they are entitled to claim the "privilege against self-incrimination," the term conventionally used in England for the exercise of the right to silence by witnesses. Thus, although they have no right to refuse to answer relevant questions in general (such refusal constituting a punishable contempt) they are entitled to refuse to answer any question if to do so would have a self-incriminatory tendency.

(e) *Statutory powers of compulsory inquisitorial inquisition*

The general rule that it is no crime for a person suspected of an offence to refuse to answer questions put by an official inquiring into the offence is subject to a number of statutory exceptions. Various Acts of Parliament provide for the appointment of public officials to conduct inquiries into specified matters of concern, for example company insolvency and malpractice, with the power to require relevant persons (who may well be under suspicion of misconduct within the ambit of the investigatation) to submit to sworn interrogatories. Depending on the particular statute the instrument of direct compulsion to speak, exactly as in the days of High Commission and Star Chamber, will be either prosecution in a criminal court for the offence of refusing to answer or proceedings in the High Court for contempt of court. Again, depending on the provisions of the particular measure, the failure in question may be to take the oath or to affirm, to answer any and all questions, to answer particular questions, or to give false answers. Most prominent of the compulsory powers are examinations in bankruptcy or involvency, both personal or corporate, investigations into company affairs by inspectors appointed by the Department of Trade and Industry, and inquiries conducted by the Serious Fraud Office.[36]

In the nineteenth century it was held that since it was lawful to compel answers from an examinee in bankruptcy they were not entitled to claim the privilege against self-incrimination and it followed that a self-incriminatory statement extracted under compulsion in a bankruptcy examination was admissible in subsequent criminal

---

36 See, *e.g.* the Companies Act 1985, the Insolvency Act 1986, the Financial Services Act 1986, the Banking Act 1987 and the Criminal Justice Act 1987. For a very nearly comprehensive account see *Wolchover and Heaton-Armstrong on Confession Evidence*, *supra*, ch. 2, and see Archbold, 1998 ed. paras. 15-419 to 15-426 and 30-2, *et seq*. For a "family tree" of the powers in bankruptcy from the statute 1 James 1, c.15 (1603), see *Bishopsgate Investment Management (in provisional liquidation)* v. *Maxwell* [1992] 2 All E.R. 856, *per* Lord Mustill.

proceedings against the bankrupt who made the statement, provided the record was read and signed by the person.[37] Subsequent legislation made express provision for such admissibility.[38] Conversely, a number of statutes expressly prohibit the record of a compulsory examination from being used in evidence against the examinee[39] Where, however, a statute contained no provision either allowing admissibility or precluding it, the question of admissibility was to be inferred from a proper construction of the particular statute.[40]

In *Saunders* v. *United Kingdom* the European Court of Human Rights held that the use at the defendant's criminal trial of statements obtained from him in the course of a compulsory interrogation by company inspectors inquiring into the take-over of the Distillers Company by Guinness in pursuance of powers enacted by section 434 of the Companies Act 1985 had amounted to compulsory self-incrimination and as such contravened his right to a fair trial under Article 6.1 of the European Convention on Human Rights.[41] The judgment awards damages but does not overturn the applicant's conviction, which he had earlier challenged unsuccessfully in the Court of Appeal.[42] However, the Government have instituted a policy consistent with the decision.[43] In a guidance note issued by the Attorney-General to prosecuting authorities it is stated that subject to discretionary exceptions the prosecution should not normally use in evidence, as part of its case or in cross-examination, answers obtained under compulsory powers.[44] The discretionary exceptions are where the defendant who provided the answers introduces them in evidence himself and where the prosecution is based on the failure or refusal to answer, the omission of a material fact, or a lie, and the proceedings in question are those brought under the relevant Act for the failure or refusal itself, or for perjury.

The policy has now been given statutory force, as from a day yet to be appointed, by section 59 of the Youth Justice and Criminal Evidence Act 1999, which gives effect to Schedule 3 to the Act inserting appropriate amendments in all relevant statutes so as to restrict the use that may be made in criminal proceedings of answers and statements given under compulsion.

---

[37] *Scott* (1856) Dears & B. 47. The record could be authenticated by the maker: *Erdheim* [1896] 2 Q.B. 260.

[38] Starting with the Bankruptcy Act 1883, s.17.

[39] *E.g.* Theft Act 1969, s.31; Representation of the People Act 1983, s.141(2); Health and Safety at Work Act 1974, s.20(7); Supreme Court Act 1981, s.72.

[40] *Commissioners for Customs and Excise* v. *Harz and Power* [1967] 1 A.C. 760, H.L., at p.816, *per* Lord Reid.

[41] [1997] 23 E.H.R.R. 313, judgment given December 17, 1996. The judgement was followed in applications by the other three Guinness defendants (Lyons, Ronson and Parnes): *I.J.L., G.M.R. and A.K.P.* v. *United Kingdom*, E.C.H.R. Application Nos. 29522/95, 30056/96 and 30574/96, judgment September 19, 2000. See Chapter 4, *infra*, on the impact of the Convention.

[42] See *Saunders et al* [1996] 1 Cr.App.R. 463. Following the E.C.H.R. judgments the Criminal Cases Review Commission has given priority to the Guinness defendants' cases in view of the appellant Lyons' age and deteriorating health and the Court of Appeal is expediting the appeal process for the same reason: see *The Times*, January 26, and February 28, 2001.

[43] Announced in the Commons on February 3, 1998: see 35 H.C. Deb., cols 639-640. See also *R.* v. *Secretary of State for Trade and Industry ex p. McCormick* [1998] *The Times*, February 10, C.A. (Civ.Div.).

[44] Set out in *New Law Journal*, February 13, 1998, p.208.

(f) *The right to refuse answers and the power to ask them*

Subject to the limitation that a defendant volunteering himself as a witness in his own trial must answer all questions, including those tending to incriminate him, the privilege against self-incrimination (where not removed by statute) is an absolute legal right. The defendant cannot be forced by direct legal sanction to testify and silent suspects do not commit the legal offence of obstructing the police. But unlike the privilege against self-incrimination, the suspect's freedom of non-co-operation is not absolute, giving way as it does to the needs of the administration of justice through preordained procedures and in proportion to the strength of the case against him.[45] Thus, in contrast with defendants on trial, who cannot be compelled to go into the witness box, a suspect can be forced to attend interrogation if there are sufficient grounds for believing he has committed an offence. The rule that no suspect can be coerced by the threat of legal sanction to answer questions implies no duty on the part of the police to refrain from putting questions where the suspect asserts a desire to stand on his silence.

Until 1964 the power to question was restricted to that of suspects not under arrest; once a suspect had been placed under arrest the police were not generally permitted to question him. Under the regime of the Judges' Rules 1964 police powers were extended to allowing interrogation of suspects under arrest. Previously custodial interrogation was prohibited, or at least deprecated. Even before P.A.C.E. it was apparently accepted that the police were entitled to place suspects under arrest for the purpose of increasing the pressure on them to answer questions.[46] Under P.A.C.E. the police are empowered to detain a suspect where it is considered necessary in order to obtain evidence by questioning. Continuing the philosophy of the 1964 Rules P.A.C.E. allows the police to carry on with questioning a suspect after he has indicated that he does not wish to answer. It also permits further detention (within the time limits laid down by P.A.C.E.) for the purpose of re-interview after a lapse of time. Although the effect of these rules and practices was that a suspect might be detained longer because of his silence, this was not generally considered to be a sanction which negated the right to silence.[47]

B. *DEBATE ON WHETHER SILENCE SHOULD COUNT TOWARDS EVIDENCE OF GUILT*

(1) Abolition or retention of the right to silence: the four stances

Participants in the debate on abolition of the right to silence have been identified as falling into four categories.[48] Lined up against the right to silence are utilitarian and

---

45 See Zuckerman, [1989] Crim.L.R., at p.856.

46 *Mohammed-Holgate* v. *Duke* [1984] 1 All E.R. 1054.

47 See Roger Leng, *The Right to Silence in Police Interrogation: A Study of some of the Issues Underlying the Debate*, R.C.C.J. Research Study No. 10, 1993, p.1.

48 Greer, 53 M.L.R., at p.718. See generally Morgan and Stephenson (eds.) *Suspicion and Silence*, London 1994, and see also Wood and Crawford, *The Right of Silence*, Civil Liberties Trust, 1989. For

exchange abolitionists; in support are symbolic and instrumental retentionists. The arguments deployed in the debate are discussed under specific topic heads in the next section.

(a) *Utilitarian abolitionism*

In the early period of the debate on the right to silence the abolitionist argument was dominated by utilitarian abolitionism, the position held by Jeremy Bentham and characteristic of the "frankly . . . utilitarian" view of the majority of the Criminal Law Revision Committee (C.L.R.C.).[49] Bentham's unreconstructed utilitarian approach to the law of evidence in the criminal justice process is that accuracy of outcome is the exclusive objective of the judicial trial and that its pursuit should not be impeded merely in order to preserve values external to proof, except in the interests of avoiding or reducing delay, vexation and expense[50] Since, under pure utilitarianism, the rights of defendants are considered extraneous to the processes of proof the doctrine sees the right to silence as having no contribution to make in the quest for an accurate outcome. Pure utilitarians therefore argued for abolition of the right to silence without any compensatory replacement by other safeguards for defendants.

(b) *Exchange abolitionism*

The main weakness of the utilitarian abolitionist case has been seen as its failure to provide empirical evidence that the accuracy of outcome will not be prejudiced by abolition. It has not, in other words, been able to demonstrate that the right to silence does not prevent wrongful convictions. In the face of the considerable resistance to abolition a modified abolitionist approach emerged. Exchange abolitionism, as the name implies, seeks abolition of the right to silence in exchange for granting other rights to defendants which will go to preventing miscarriages of justice. Foremost amongst these is the right to have a legal adviser present at police interviews. According to Greer:

> "Some closet utilitarians may also be found in the exchange abolitionism camp, not because they have been converted to the notion

---

a view not unsympathetic to abolition see C. Williams, "Silence in Australia: Probative Force and Rights in the Law of Evidence," [1994] 110 L.Q.R. 629.

[49] The C.L.R.C. had proposed abolition of the right to silence in their 11th report, *Evidence (General)*, Cmnd. 4991, June 1972, *passim*; proposal so described by the Royal Commission on Criminal Procedure (ch. Sir Cyril Phillips), report, Cmnd. 8092, January 1981, para. 1.26.

[50] Bentham, *Rationale of Judicial Evidence*, ed. J.S. Mill, Hunt and Davis, London 1827, Garland reprint, New York 1978. See also Twining, *Bentham and Wigmore: Theories of Evidence*, London 1985. The C.L.R.C. followed Bentham in asserting that all relevant evidence should be admissible: para. 14. Vexation to judge and jury from an excess of evidence, or undue delay and expense, may justify exclusion of evidence in the interests of "preponderant collateral convenience," for "even evidence, even justice itself, like gold, may be bought too dear": *Rationale of Judicial Evidence*, Garland reprint p.482. Bentham accepted that no harm could come from the exclusion of evidence tainted with collateral inconvenience if there was other, sufficient evidence in the case: *supra*, p. 504. G. Menlowe has argued that this doctrine of exclusion may be applied to evidence of silence: "Bentham, Self-Incrimination and the Law of Evidence," [1988] 104 L.Q.R. 286, cited in Greer, 54 M.L.R., at p.719.

of defendants' rights, but because they may consider that acceding to rights discourse is the most effective way of achieving the abolition of the right to silence in the post-P.A.C.E. era."[51]

An early expression of exchange abolitionism was the approach of the minority of the C.L.R.C. in arguing that implementation of the Committee's proposals for abolition should be postponed pending introduction of the routine tape-recording of police interviews with suspects.[52] The introduction of tape-recording under P.A.C.E.[53] gave this argument considerable impetus when the debate was revived at the end of the 1980s.

(c) *Symbolic retentionism*

Symbolic retentionists, whilst conceding that it may be of little real value to suspects, favour retention of the right to silence because of its symbolic significance. They argue that attempts by the police to use the right to silence as a means of re-asserting a sense of authority should be resisted in order to keep police powers within proper limits.[54]

(d) *Instrumental retentionists*

Instrumental retentionists maintain that the right to silence is a vital part of an accusatorial criminal justice process and that since its abolition will facilitate the obtaining of convictions this will lead to an increase in the chances of innocent people being wrongly convicted with no obvious gains for law enforcement.[55] The instrumental basis for retention avoids resort to the argument that it is intolerable *per se* to hold a man's silence against him and to those sentimental "[p]retences for exclusion" of the accused's compelled testimony castigated by Bentham, namely, *inter alia*, the "old woman's reason" that "'tis hard on a man to incriminate himself," the "fox-hunter's reason" for allowing the fox his "length" and a fair chance of escape, the idea of confounding interrogation with torture, and the reference to unpopular institutions, *i.e.* the idea that compulsory interrogation should be spurned because it had been employed by the Inquisition, Star Chamber and High Commission.[56] Instrumental retentionists would specify two conditions which need to be met before any procedure intended to protect the innocent from wrongful

---

[51] *ibid.*

[52] 11th report, para. 52.

[53] Enacted under s.60, P.A.C.E. Act.

[54] See Greer, 53 M.L.R., at pp.719 and 724; Dixon, "The Right to Silence: Politics and Research," paper presented at the Conference of the Society for the Reform of the Criminal Law: *Investigating crime and apprehending suspects: police powers and citizens rights,* Sydney, Australia, March 19-23, 1989; Bottomley, Coleman, Dixon Gill and Wall, "Safeguarding the Rights of Suspects in Police Custody," paper presented to the British Criminology Conference, Bristol Polytechnic, July 17-20, 1989.

[55] Prof. I. Dennis argued that "none of the claims which have driven the reform of the right to silence have any very secure foundation": "The Criminal Justice and Public Order Act 1994: The Evidence Provisions," [1995] Crim.L.R. 1, at p.14.

[56] *Rationale of Judicial Evidence*, ed. J.S. Mill, Hunt and Davis, London 1827, IX, 4, c.III.

conviction can legitimately be abolished, even in exchange for other alternatives which allegedly perform the same function. First there must be clear evidence that the innocent suspect is not in fact protected as the procedure in question is supposed to do, or that it is open to excessive abuse by the guilty as a way of evading just conviction. Second, the proposed alternatives should be at least as effective in guarding against wrongful conviction.[57]

(2) The supposed natural inclination of the innocent to speak out

For many people it is an irresistible axiom that the natural reaction of the innocent on being confronted by someone in authority with an accusation of wrongdoing, is to protest their innocence. The C.L.R.C. expressly based their proposal for abolition on such an assumption.[58] Failure to react according to the supposed natural inclination of the innocent may therefore be indicative of guilt, although not necessarily so. The axiom goes back at least as far as Bentham's famous aphorism on the rule prohibiting defendants from being judicially interrogated:

> "Innocence never takes advantage of it. Innocence claims to the right of speaking, as guilt invokes the privilege of silence."[59]

The urge of the innocent to deny a charge at the first opportunity is such a naturally and universally compelling one, it is contended, that it is not law—the risk of an adverse inference from silence—which is liable to compel the innocent suspect to proclaim his case so much as human nature itself. The state of the law, in other words, will be irrelevant in *ordering* the responses of suspects. An evidential rule allowing silence to be indicative of guilt would merely be descriptive of, and flowing from, the law of human nature. If the natural urge of the innocent is to declare their innocence, the argument runs, a defendant who, as a suspect, behaved contrarily to the natural ways of the innocent—by remaining silent—can hardly be prejudiced if the jury are told what they already know as a matter of instinct—that he did not react according to the ways of the innocent.

(3) Arguments against the natural inclination theory

There are two main arguments against treating silence as capable of indicating guilt.

---

[57] Greer concluded that the point had not been reached (if it ever could be) where the provision of other pre-trial safeguards such as access to legal advice could compensate for abolition: *supra*.

[58] 11th report, para. 37.

[59] *Treatise on Evidence*, p.241.

(a) *The instrinsic objection: the reticence of the meek*

The first argument involves an intrinsic objection to the validity of the axiom that the natural urge of the innocent is to deny an allegation when officially informed of its existence. The axiom assumes that the generality of mankind is by nature vocal. This is clearly and palpably not the case but the provenance of such an assumption is not difficult to find. Judges, lawyers, politicians and policemen are either born self-confident or have learned to affect the manner of it and many seem unable to empathise with others of a meeker cast of character. The assumption may have been reinforced by the fact that nowadays the "humble" tend to speak up for themselves more than they used to; in an age of incessant exposure to the diverse influences of television ordinary citizens are becoming increasingly better equipped with verbal skills. The skills they possess they are inclined to use and so, perhaps not surprisingly, it tends to be forgotten that many people nevertheless remain timorous and tongue-tied, particularly in the presence of authority figures. Such people may be naturally reticent to speak about themselves, and it may not occur to them to do so unless they are asked a direct question. Even when faced with questioning, the meek may so lack confidence in themselves that innocent or guilty they may gratefully prefer to stay silent, *if offered the option*. But by the same token experience shows that most people are sufficiently intimidated by the "inherently coercive nature of custodial interrogation"[60] that they will give answers even if told that they need not and against their preferred inclination.

(b) *Extrinsic objections*

The second argument is that apart from the *intrinsic* counter-factor of reticent personality there may be *extrinsic* reasons for silence consistent with innocence. In other words, there may be motivations for silence which stem more "from basic structural features of the criminal justice process rather than from personal predilections of the suspect."[61] The Criminal Law Revision Committee (C.L.R.C.) acknowledged a number of possible innocent explanations: a defendant might be too shocked by the accusation to state his defence or too embarrassed to do so, for example because he was with a prostitute at the time, or he might prefer to remain silent than reveal the guilt of someone else, possibly a relative, close friend or confederate.[62] Stultifying shock on being faced with suspicion is obviously distinct from reticence but fundamental timidity may have been what the C.L.R.C. were driving at when they gave shock as a possible reason for muteness. The reasons given by the C.L.R.C. were dismissed at the time of the 11th report as fanciful[63]

---

[60] *Miranda* v. *Arizona, supra.*

[61] McConville and Hodgson, *Custodial Legal Advice and the Right to Silence*, Royal Commission on Criminal Justice Research Study No. 16, 1993, p.195.

[62] 11th report, para.35.

[63] See Prof. Rupert Cross, "The evidence report: sense or nonsense—a very wicked animal defends the 11th report of the Criminal Law Revision Committee" [1973] Crim.L.R.329; and Glanville Williams, "The tactic of silence" (1987) 137 *N.L.J.* 1107)

although there is now some empirical evidence to suggest that the desire to protect others may be the motivation for silence in a not insignificant number of cases.[64]

It has been suggested that the general attitude of suspects towards the police may determine whether they stay silent and that silent suspects are more likely to hold attitudes hostile to the police.[65] Exercise of the right to silence may have been no more than an indication of the lack of public confidence in the police, at least in particular districts, and this may be an important factor in explaining the high incidence of suspects staying silent in many districts in Northern Ireland.[66] Whether any real advantage is likely to be gained from proffering such an explanation may be doubtful. In the English case of *McGuinness* evidence was adduced that the accused's "experiences and background had taught him to be reluctant to answer" police questions.[67] The existence of a history of offending which such an assertion would seem to imply is likely to negate any advantage in terms of explaining away the accused's silence.[68] Abolition of the right to silence is likely to make hostility to the police in effect a ground for conviction and may diminish public confidence still further, with an increased likelihood of silence and an exponential increase in convictions accordingly.

The Royal Commission on Criminal Justice (R.C.C.J.) gave as additional reasons, outrage (although it is not clear why this should stifle speech as against stimulating it unless they meant temporary apoplectic aphasia) and a reasoned decision to wait until the allegation has been set out in detail and there has been an opportunity to receive considered legal advice.[69] Research carried out on behalf of the Commission by McConville and Hodgson revealed that some suspects refused to answers questions in fact as a "protest" against not being given a proper indication of why they were under suspicion, or as a tactic to obtain such information.[70] They demonstrated further that whilst some suspects were advised to remain silent because their advisers were concerned that they might be led to make some inadvertent incriminating statement others, interestingly, were advised to remain

---

64 See R. Leng, *The Right to Silence in Police Interrogation: A Study of some of the Issues Underlying the Debate*, Royal Commission on Criminal Justice Research Study No. 10, 1993, p.20.

65 Dixon, "The Right to Silence: Politics and Research," paper presented at the Conference of the Society for the Reform of the Criminal Law: *Investigating crime and apprehending suspects: police powers and citizens rights*, Sydney, Australia, March 19-23, 1989.

66 Greer, 53 M.L.R., at p.727. Certainly distrust of the police has frequently been put forward in N. Ireland trials as a reason for silence. See *Averill* v *United Kingdom*, E.C.H.R. application no. 36408/97, June 6, 2000, *The Times*, June 20, 2000 (defendant professed a policy of never speaking to the police).

67 [1999] Crim.L.R. 575. In *Argent* [1977] 2 Cr.App.R. 27, atp.33, Lord Bingham C.J. acknowledged that one reason for silence might be that the accused was "suspicious of the police."

68 See Birch, "Suffering in Silence: A Cost-Benefit Analysis of Section 34 of the Criminal Justice and Public Order Act 1994," [1999] Crim.L.R. 769, at p.777.

69 Report, Cm. 2263, July 1993, Chap. 4, para. 13. In *Argent* [1997] 2 Cr.App.R. 27, at p.33, Lord Bingham C.J. said of the jury: "Sometimes they may conclude that it was reasonable for the defendant to have held his peace for a host of reasons, such as that he was tired, ill, frightened, drunk, drugged, unable to understand what was going on, suspicious of the police, afraid that his answer would not be fairly recorded, worried at committing himself without legal advice, acting on legal advice, or some other reason accepted by the jury."

70 *op. cit.* pp.90-93.

silent as a defensive strategy by an adviser who lacked experience in handling police interviews.[71]

It should be stressed that non-coöperation or protest motives for silence are qualitatively different from a conscientious belief in the right to silence as a matter of principle impelling an insistence upon exercising it.

Silence can never be the same as speech. It is the very converse of positive evidence. Its meaning can only be deduced circumstantially and obliquely and whether it is neutral or self-incriminatory depends on guesswork based on the subjective preferences of the trier of fact. With so many potential explanations for silence consistent with innocence it may be said to be arbitrary and dangerous to permit it to be used to prove the defendant's guilt when the true reason may just as easily be an innocent one. Not discounting any of these reasons for silence proponents of abolition of the right to silence would nevertheless argue that if the defence rely on any of them they can always put it forward. If the defendant elects to give evidence, offers an account which he did not give to the police and can give a convincing reason for not having done so it may be argued that he will suffer no disadvantage. A mild objection to this is that even if there is a good reason for having stayed silent it may be quite difficult for an unsophisticated person to give a coherent account of the explanation. But defendants are often called upon to give difficult explanations for their behaviour and juries almost certainly make allowances for manifest inarticulacy.

A more problematic objection concerns cases in which the defendant elects not to give evidence. For example, the prosecution case may be relatively weak and the defence may prefer to adopt the approach of offering no evidence and putting the prosecution to proof. Alternatively, it may be decided, for example where there is a strong alibi, to call the evidence in support of it but not to call the defendant himself. In either sort of case the defendant's silence both when questioned by police and at trial might be regarded as suspicious. How is the suspicion to be allayed if the defendant does not give evidence? In cases in which the approach is that of putting the prosecution to proof there is no tactical problem for the defence. Where the prosecution case is weak criticising the defendant for his silence would almost certainly prove counter-productive since defending counsel would be able to overturn the criticism as a transparent attempt to divert attention from the strong arguments which the defence were able to marshall in favour of acquittal. In cases in which a defence is adduced through evidence although not that of the defendant the absence of a sworn explanation of why the defendant chose not to answer police questions may to some extent be offset by the skill of defending counsel in conjecturing with the jury various possible reasons without, of course, offending against the strictures of the Court of Appeal in *Cowan*.[72] Indeed, advocacy might prove a much more persuasive instrument for deflecting suspicion of guilt than where the defendant goes into the witness box with a reason which under cross-

---

[71] *ibid.*, pp.93-97.

[72] *Cowan; R.* v. *Gayle; R.* v. *Ricciardi* [1996] Q.B. 373; [1996] 1 Cr.App.R. 1. See Chapter 3.

examination is exposed as implausible. This is but one aspect of the general problem of the tactical assessment of whether or not to call the defendant.

(4) The constitutional argument

Against allowing the accused's silence to be held against him is the argument that there is a fundamental inconsistency of principle in requiring the onus of proof to be discharged by the prosecution without any assistance from the accused and yet in enabling the prosecution to use the accused's silence both in the face of police questioning and at trial as a part of their case.[73] It was this unavoidable truth which explains why, in the words of the Royal Commission on Criminal Procedure, opponents of the C.L.R.C.'s original scheme had "stood aghast at this proposal, and loudly, often emotionally, protested that the Committee was treating the matter in much too narrow and limited a sense, and that in reality the right of silence formed a vital issue in the whole constitutional relationship in a free society between the individual and the state."[74] Adoption of the C.L.R.C. scheme was opposed by a majority of the R.C.C.P. on the ground that it would detract from the burden of proof fundamental to the adversarial system by creating psychological pressure to answer questions that might be based on unsubstantiated suspicion rather than on hard evidence.[75] A decade after the R.C.C.P., the R.C.C.J. was appointed with a specific remit to consider the right to silence and the majority opposed abolition on the basis of the fundamental importance of the burden of proof coupled with the absence of any solid evidence that hardened criminals routinely escaped conviction by reliance on silence under questioning.[76] It was considered that increasing the chances of convicting a few guilty defendants was not worth the risk of convicting innocent defendants who might either be driven to admit guilt falsely under questioning coerced by the pressure of the fear of adverse comment on silence or whose silence might wrongly be taken by the jury as an indicator of guilt.

---

[73] See the *Working Group Report*, para 29.

[74] *ibid*., para. 1.27. For the Opposition's position during Commons debate on the 1994 legislation see p.45, *infra*.

[75] Report, paras. 4.37 and 4.52. The majority's position was strongly influenced by research evidence suggesting that the right to silence was rarely exercised: *ibid*., para. 4.43 and see P. Softley, *Police Interrogation: An Observational Study in Four Police Stations*, R.C.C.P. Research Study No. 4, H.M.S.O. 1980.

[76] Report, Chap. 4, para. 18. There was no evidence that silent suspects were more likely to be charged or convicted but some evidence that silence was less infrequent in serious offences, suggesting a possible correlation with professional criminals: see *infra* and see Leng, *The Right to Silence in Police Interrogation: A Study of some of the Issues Underlying the Debate*, R.C.C.J. Research Study No 10, H.M.S.O. 1993.

(5) Depriving the police of opportunities to investigate

In favour of allowing the accused's silence to be treated as capable of supporting the prosecution case it is contended that in a significant number of cases it would otherwise be impossible for the police to carry out an effective investigation without at an early stage asking suspects to explain the conduct which had brought them under suspicion. With very few exceptions, to prove a criminal offence there must be evidence of guilty knowledge or intent. It might be possible to infer this from the circumstances of the offence but in many instances it could only be obtained by asking an accused to explain the conduct in question. It is said to be important that in such cases innocent suspects should provide explanations for the facts alleged against them as soon as practicable. This is to enable suspects either to exonerate themselves or to direct attention towards the guilty (or both), and to provide the police with a fair and reasonable opportunity of investigating the suspect's account. By refusing to answer questions and thus depriving police of the investigative opportunities presented by interview a significant number of experienced or professional criminals were in the past supposedly able to avoid being charged or, if charged, to escape conviction. The initial aim of these suspects might have been to avoid being charged but if they were charged and indicted then by concealing their defence until the trial, when it might have been be too late for the police to investigate it properly, they could prevent a defence from being exposed as concocted. This was the tactic of the "ambush defence."

The validity of these arguments has been subjected to empirical scrutiny in various research projects.[77] Those favouring retention of the rule against allowing silence to be treated as strengthening the prosecution case have argued that there is little evidence to support the idea that the right to silence had been abused since the implementation of P.A.C.E. and they criticised the Government for not commissioning further research before deciding on the need for change.[78] As already mentioned, pre-trial disclosure would be a sufficient antidote without abolishing the right to silence at the interrogation stage.

(6) Professional criminals, terrorists and the weak and vulnerable

One of the chief planks of the abolition case has been the contention that the right to silence provides a shelter for professional criminals, an argument adopted by the C.L.R.C.[79] Although the Committee provided no empirical evidence to support their suspicions some evidence has since been obtained that suspects with previous convictions and those charged with serious offences are more likely to stay silent

[77] For a summary see *Wolchover and Heaton-Armstrong on Confession Evidence*, *supra*, pp.630-633.

[78] *Working Group Report*, para. 50.

[79] 11th report, para. 21.

than other types of suspect. The details are given later in Part I, below. It has already been mentioned that there is some evidence of a high incidence of the systematic practice of maintaining silence among terrorist suspects.

Even supposing there is a tendency for professional criminals to exploit the right to silence there are two problems with abolition in the interests of depriving them of a shelter from conviction. First, even where silence was permitted to be probative, seasoned criminals might well have an instinctive appreciation of the fact that in most cases it was likely to be less harmful than giving answers which could not but prove self-incriminating. In other words, abolition of the right to silence would be likely to make very little difference in the rate of professional criminals staying silent but even if there were a marginal decrease in silence this would be likely to be gained at the expense of a very serious potential increase in the wrongful conviction of weak and vulnerable suspects.

A rule allowing adverse inferences to be drawn from a suspect's silence could not be implemented without abolishing or, at least, altering, the traditional caution. The suspect would need to be warned of the possible adverse consequences of silence, that the keeping back of an explanation until later might mean that it was less likely to be believed. The retentionist argument is that since such a warning would provide a basis in practice for the imposition of increased pressures on suspects to answer questions put by the police there would be an increased risk that some suspects, particularly those who were intellectually weak or emotionally vulnerable, might give damaging answers which were unreliable. It has been authoritatively suggested that the way the old caution—

> ". . . was delivered or the manner of its phrasing seemed to present the right to silence as an option that the suspect was not seriously expected to entertain."[80]

The retentionist argument is that during questioning police interrogators would be likely to overplay the consequences of staying silent just as in the past they have underplayed the right to say nothing.[81]

(7) Alteration by P.A.C.E. of the balance in favour of suspects

(a) *General*

In support of abolition it was argued that suspects were taking advantage of a principle of the criminal justice system left over from a past era when there were far fewer safeguards to protect the defendant than there are today. Those taking this

---

[80] Baldwin and McConville, *Courts, Prosecution and Conviction*, Oxford: Clarenden Press, 1981, p.138.

[81] See Zuckerman, [1989] Crim.L.R., at p.862.

exchange abolitionist position may have been prepared to concede[82] that the courts had in the past paid lip service to values embodied in the Judges' Rules whilst hardly ever acting to remedy breaches, even when these were deliberate and common. They may well have been prepared to accept that the existence of the Judges' Rules enabled the courts to maintain the illusion that the law provided adequate safeguards for the protection of suspects during interrogation (such as the right to legal advice) whilst, at the same time, the failure to enforce the Rules adequately gave the police the necessary freedom to overcome the suspect's reluctance to speak. But whatever the failings of the old regime, it was argued, present day protective procedures were adequate enough to prevent abolition of the right to silence from weakening the position of the innocent and the vulnerable.

Under P.A.C.E. and its codes of practice suspects now enjoy access to free legal advice and benefited from the requirement for all interviews at the police station to be tape-recorded. The basic assumption of exchange abolitionism is that, provided defendants' other legitimate interests are adequately catered for, only the guilty will try to hide behind silence in the police station.[83] One of the main criticisms raised by the police was of the effect of the presence of a solicitor on interviews with suspects (especially professional criminals) which they contended was making the conduct of interviews more difficult and less likely to lead to admissions. It was this concern which led directly to the Home Secretary's re-opening of the debate in his Police Foundation lecture in July 1987.[84]

It has been argued[85] that the safeguard for suspects under P.A.C.E. which has been of more relevance to the right to silence than any other is the stringent set of limitations on the duration of pre-charge detention; according to some police officers, suspects who know they cannot be held indefinitely are the most likely to remain silent. But it has also been noted[86] that exchange abolitionists have not sought to argue that the right to silence should be traded in for more relaxed pre-charge detention periods. To do so would be politically untenable because it would be tantamount to an admission that the mere fact of being locked in a police cell can exert strong pressure in favour of co-operation.

The weakness in exchange abolitionism is the assumption that access to legal advice and other safeguards remove any legitimate reasons which an innocent suspect might otherwise have for preferring to remain silent.[87] Possibly the chief argument against exchange is that the bestowing of the benefits of legal advice and tape-recording are irrelevant to the issue of abolition because they were part of the balance of police powers and suspects' rights carefully worked out by the R.C.C.P. which included the maintenance of the right to silence in its existing form.[88]

---

[82] Following *ibid.*, at p.858.
[83] Greer, 53 M.L.R., at pp.719-720.
[84] *Working Group Report*, para. 32.
[85] Dixon, *op.cit.*, p.12, and see Greer, 53 M.L.R., at p.270
[86] *ibid.*
[87] *ibid.*
[88] *ibid.*, para. 34.

(b) *Legal advice*

On the specific question of legal advice retentionists were wary of the value of the right to legal advice at the police station, given the existence of evidence that the police were active in dissuading many suspects from exercising it or otherwise resorted to various ploys (*e.g.* reading suspects' rights too quickly or omitting to mention that legal advice was free) designed to obtain ostensible waiver.[89] But even where a solicitor was consulted research conducted on behalf of the R.C.C.J. has shown that the quality of advice and representation in the event received is often disappointing. Furthermore, it was argued that although in the case of *Samuel*[90] the Court of Appeal narrowed the discretion of the police to the point where access to legal advice could be denied only if the police could demonstrate that a named solicitor was corrupt, the court was still allowing evidence obtained in breach of the requirement to permit access and that while it continued to do so there was little incentive for the police to comply. The question of the availability of legal advice raises the difficult question of whether it can be fair to draw an adverse inference if the suspect has followed the advice of the solicitor or legal representative to refrain from answering questions. This is considered later.

(c) *Tape-recording*

The tape-recording of an interview may be no guarantee against injustice since there is some evidence of police interrogators steering suspects away from attempts to articulate an exculpatory account.[91] Furthermore, it was argued, tape-recording was changing the nature of police questioning, enabling it to be much more sophisticated and more pressure to be put on suspects.[92]

(8) The argument that abolition will reduce incentives to obtain confessions

Proponents of abolition point out that prior to the new legislation the law placed undue pressure on the police to obtain a confession because that was often virtually the only way open to them to prove key elements of an offence. Thus, they argued, if silence could be taken into account against the defendant together with other evidence this would reduce the present emphasis on confession evidence and the police would not press so hard to obtain one. This seems to boil down to saying that suspects can be spared the inconvenience and discomfort involved in traditional police methods of seeking confession by the simple device of making silence itself the confession. It remains unclear what benefit there is for defendants if the price of being saved from the unpleasant experience of interrogation is the risk of the much

---

[89] Sanders, Bridges, Crozier and Mulvaney, *Advice and Assistance at Police Stations and the 24 Hour Solicitor Scheme*, Lord Chancellor's Department, 1990.

[90] [1987] 87 Cr.App.R. 232.

[91] See Leng, *op.cit*.

[92] *Working Group Report*, para. 34.

greater unpleasantness of being convicted on silence. But even if silence does not quite add up to a confession, making it incriminatory may actually be the route to a false confession. Many suspects who feel obliged to talk out of fear that their silence will otherwise be held against them may give confused replies which create the impression of lying, or they may even be tempted to resort to expedient lies in the first instance. Faced on further probing with an ostensible demonstration of their untruthfulness they may assume that conviction is now inevitable and that the only hope of mercy is to make a show of remorse by going through the motions of confession.

(9) Fabricated silence

The use by the police of the suspect's silence as a substitute for confession leads directly on to an objection raised against abolition that it will create a positive incentive for the police to concoct silence.[93] Thus, even though the suspect may have intimated to the police the nature of his defence, an unscrupulous officer may wish to suppress it and thus gain for the prosecution the benefit of the defendant's alleged self-incriminatory silence. There is some evidence, referred to above, of a tendency on the part of the police—it may be no more than unconscious—to brush over defences raised by suspects.

(10) Controlling the jury's instincts

Although it was supposed that under the common law a jury could not *formally* be invited by prosecuting counsel, or given leave by the judge, to treat the accused's silence when confronted with an allegation as indicative of guilt there was nothing to stop any jury from reaching this conclusion if they chose to. The absence of any such control has been disparaged in graphic terms:

> "How can it be said that the inferences drawn by a jury will be more detrimental to a defendant under the limiting and carefully controlling language of the instruction here involved than would result if the jury were left to roam at large with only its untutored instinct to guide it, to draw from the defendant's silence broad inferences of guilt?"[94]

On the other hand, damage limitation is no justification for sacrifice of principle:

---

[93] However, the C.L.R.C. did not regard this possible danger as a good enough reason for leaving the law unreformed: 11th report, para. 31.

[94] Dissenting opinion in *Griffin* v. *California*, 380 U.S. 609 (1965), at p.621.

> "What the jury may infer, given no help from the court, is one thing. What it may infer when the court solemnises the silence of the accused into evidence against him is quite another."[95]

Under the traditional system a jury would be warned that they were not to hold against the defendant his silence in the police station. Proponents of abolition argued that although a stern instruction of this kind might have gone some way towards inhibiting the jury from following their instincts it afforded no absolute bulwark against the jury drawing wholly unmerited inferences of guilt from silence. It was argued that the only way of ensuring that the jury were adequately reigned in would be to allow adverse inferences but to give detailed instructions on how they should approach the task of applying the licence. The counter-argument is that the completely effective way of ensuring that the accused's silence when questioned does not prejudice him is to conceal the fact of his silence from the jury. If silence is no evidence it need not be mentioned. Yet research carried out under the old procedure revealed that in four fifths of cases where the defendant had been silent the jury learnt of it from the evidence in the course of the trial.[96] Since defendants could have had little reason for revealing to the jury that they had given a "no comment" interview this must have been elicited by the prosecution, presumably because it was supposed implicitly to help their case.

II. THE NATURE OF SILENCE

A. *DEGREES OF SILENCE*

In the context of pre-trial questioning of the defendant *qua* a suspect it is obvious that silence does not only mean a complete abstention from speech. In six out of seven of the following categories of silence capable of having incriminatory significance it is partial:

- (i) a refusal to protest innocence and to answer *all* substantive questions (*i.e.* those having relevance to the inquiry);
- (ii) no protest of innocence but some substantive questions answered;
- (iii) a simple denial but no elaboration by way of intimating a specific line of defence and no substantive questions answered (an "inscrutable" denial[97]);
- (iv) a denial with no elaboration but some substantive questions answered;

---

[95] Majority opinion in *ibid.*

[96] Zander and Henderson, *The Crown Court Study*, R.C.C.J. Research Study No. 19, H.M.S.O. 1993, cited in main report Chap. 4, para. 5, note.

[97] Term adopted by Leng, *op.cit.*

(v) a denial with partial elaboration (*i.e.* omitting some material aspects), answering all substantive questions asked, but questioning not comprehensive in covering all aspects of the case;
(vi) a denial and full intimation of defence, but no substantive questions answered;
(vii) a denial and full intimation of defence and some substantive questions answered.

B. *FROM SILENCE TO GUILT: DIRECT AND INDIRECT INFERENTIAL ROUTES*

There are two distinct ways in which the accused's silence before trial may be held against him. According to the first it will be treated as more or less directly probative of guilt on the basis of the argument that from silence in the face of an accusation, or a weak and inadequate rebuttal, it is reasonable to apply the maxim *qui tacet consentit* (silence gives assent) and to infer that the accused was tacitly accepting the truth of the charge. It has been suggested that, alternatively to "tacit admission," silence may imply a "consciousness of guilt"[98] but since this supposedly manifests itself in silence because the accused has no innocent answer, it is really only another way of saying that the allegation is tacitly accepted as true and is not an alternative at all.

It seems doubtful in the extreme that silence on being confronted with an accusation entirely unsupported by other evidence of the accused's guilt could ever be sufficient to convict in the way that a confession might. The issue in most of the common law authorities on implied admission was whether silence in the circumstances was capable of providing corroboration of other evidence.

The second basis on which silence may be held against the accused does not directly establish guilt in the way that silence can amount to tacit admission. Rather, it involves the silence weakening, or harming, other defence evidence[99] without actually furnishing direct evidence of guilt in itself. It does so by undermining a specific line of defence in due course proffered at trial. The reasoning which impels the inference of guilt is that if the assertion relied on by the accused at trial had been true he would have mentioned it to the police, that as he failed to mention it, the assertion must be untrue, and that as his defence is false, he must be guilty.[100] There are two alternative bases for drawing this inference. One is that of late invention: that the story only occurred to the accused after he was taxed with the accusation in interview and charged. The other is that whilst the story had already formed itself in the accused's mind at the time of the interview he appreciated that it required further

[98] Rosemary Pattenden, "Silence: Lord Taylor's legacy" (1998) 2 *International Journal of Evidence and Proof,* 141 (hereafter 2 E. & P.), at p.142, following J. Heydon and M. Ockleton, *Evidence: Cases and Materials*, 4th ed., London: Butterworths, 1996, p.143, and P. Mirfield, *Silence, Confessions and Improperly Obtained Evidence*, Oxford: O.U.P. 1997, p.239.
[99] Pattenden, 2 E. & P., p.142.
[100] See Sir Bernard MacKenna [1972] Crim.L.R. 605, at p.613.

preparation (such as checking against facts not yet confirmed or known, priming of witnesses, or general polishing), that it would therefore not stand up to detailed questioning at that stage or might subsequently be exposed as false, that the accused knew this would happen because his defence was bogus, that he had no defence, and that he was in fact guilty.

The principle of drawing an adverse inference from late account primarily goes to the credibility of the defence proffered at trial. But it may also be relevant to the issue of tacit acceptance in that an unexplained delay in furnishing an assertion or explanation consistent with innocence may reinforce an inference that the original silence indicated tacit acceptance of the truth of the allegation. The principle of authorising an inference of guilt from late account is the basis of section 34 of the Criminal Justice and Public Order Act 1994, which permits such an inference to be drawn from the failure of the defendant when questioned to mention any fact relied on in subsequent proceedings.

C. *EMPIRICAL RESEARCH*

(1) The general pattern

From a number of research projects on police interrogation a consistent pattern has emerged in which only a relatively small proportion of suspects either remained completely silent or otherwise said nothing of substantive significance and the police have not therefore been seriously handicapped in this respect. In a review undertaken for the R.C.C.J. David Brown examined the relevant research and concluded that past studies, as well as the research one for the Commission, adopted differing definitions of silence as a response to questioning or the levelling of suspicion, varied in the extent to which their samples were representative of police forces generally, and, where they relied on data collected by the police, may have exaggerated the extent of the incidence of silence.[101] He estimated that, outside the Metropolitan Police District between 6 per cent and 10 per cent of suspects were silent to a greater or lesser extent, while within the M.P.D. the equivalent proportion was between 14 per cent and 16 per cent. The number of those who refused to answer any questions at all was estimated at 5 per cent at most in provincial police force areas and 9 per cent at most in the M.P.D.

Prior to the of the English legislation in 1994 some evidence had emerged of the impact of the equivalent Northern Ireland provisions enacted by the Criminal Evidence (Northern Ireland) Order 1988. Under the Northern Ireland (Emergency Provisions) Act 1973 scheduled offences (*i.e* those having a potential terrorist connection) are tried by a judge without a jury. In such "Diplock trials" the judges'

[101] *The Incidence of Right to Silence in Police Interviews: The Research Evidence Reviewed*, Home Office Research and Planning Unit, unpublished, cited in R.C.C.J. report, Chap. 4, para. 15 and note 4. Research conducted on behalf of the R.C.C.P. showed only rare exercise of the right to silence: P. Softley, *Police Interrogation: An Observational Study in Four Police Stations*, R.C.C.P. Research Study No. 4, H.M.S.O., London 1980.

reasoning is on record and it is therefore known that inference from silence (whether during questioning or at trial) had made a difference in 40 cases (5 per cent) from the time the order was introduced until 1993.[102] One quarter of these cases were regarded as unsafe by Amnesty International and British and Irish Rights Watch.[103] But this figure did not show if the measures had been effective in inducing significantly more suspects to become more forthcoming with the police than was formerly the position. In fact, conviction rates actually went down after 1988[104] although the material significance of this remains unclear. It might be argued that the increasing number of acquittals could be taken as indicative of more *innocent* suspects deciding to put their innocent accounts on record and being believed.

The impact of the evidential silence provisions of the Criminal Justice and Public Order Act 1994 has been the subject of Home Office research. By comparing the results of a field research study carried out by Tom Bucke and David Brown after the Act came into force with a similar study conducted by Phillips and Brown before the law was changed, it has been possible to learn whether the Act has modified the behaviour of suspects in interview to any significant degree.[105] For the post-Act study observation was conducted in the custody areas of 13 police stations with observers present every day between 9 am and midnight for a period of three weeks. A total of 3,950 detainees passed through police custody during the observation period. A self-completion questionaire was also given to the police officer responsible for each case in the observation sample, and 12,500 custody records were analysed from 25 police stations (500 custody records at each station). The fieldwork period ran from the middle of August 1995 until the end of February 1996. In the study by Phillips and Brown on the régîme prior to the Act 10 per cent of suspects refused to answer all questions, 13 per cent refused some questions and 77 per cent answered all questions. In the study carried out by Bucke and Brown after the 1994 Act came into force the figures were 6 per cent, 10 per cent and 84 per cent. The reduction in suspects refusing all questions and those selectively answering questions, with the corresponding rise in suspects answering all questions occurred across all police stations included in the two studies. The reduction in the use of the right of silence in police interviews indicated by these studies has been characterised as "signficant"[106] but whilst this may be correct in the sense of being "statistically significant" (as distinct from being too small to fall outside the margin of error) it is arguable whether the shift is of very much practical signficance. Under

---

102 Revealed by the B.B.C.'s *File on Four* programme, edition of October 26, 1993, transcript, p.12.

103 *ibid.*, p.13.

104 *ibid.*, p.12.

105 Bucke and Brown, *In police custody: police powers and suspects' rights under the revised PACE codes of practice*, Home Office Research Study No. 174, December 1997; C. Phillips and D. Brown (assisted by P. Goodrich and Z. James), *Entry into the Criminal Justice System: a survey of police arrests and their outcomes*, Home Office Research and Statistics Directorate report; both studies summarised and compared in *Research Findings*, No. 62, Home Office Research and Statistics Directorate 1997. The provisional findings were originally reported in *The Daily Mail*, October 26, 1996. Relatively little change was found in the proportion of suspects making confessions before and after the reforms (Phillips and Brown: 55 per cent; Bucke and Brown: 58 per cent).

106 *Research Findings*, No. 62, *supra*, p.1.

the 1994 Act special warnings can be given when suspects refuse to account for incriminating objects, marks or substances (section 36) or for their presence at a particular place (section 37). The research found that such warnings were given to 39 per cent of suspects exercising silence (7 per cent of all suspects interviewed) and that having been given a special warning a majority of suspects either refused to provide an account or gave one which was considered by officers to be unsatisfactory; only in a relatively small proportion of cases did a special warning result in a satisfactory account being given.[107]

(2) Silence and legal advice

The assumption that suspects are more likely to stay silent when they obtain a legal adviser at the police station than when they do not is borne out by research. Thus a study by Williamson and Motson revealed that when suspects had access to legal advice they were silent in 33 per cent of cases compared with less than 5 per cent where advice had not been available.[108] Other research revealed that whilst some suspects were advised to remain silent because their representatives were concerned that they might be led to make an incriminating statement inadvertently, others were advised to remain silent as a defensive strategy by an adviser who lacked experience in handling interviews.[109] It is interesting to note that the two Home Office studies carried out by Phillips and Brown and by Bucke and Brown indicate that the reduction in the use of silence after the 1994 Act came into force was greatest among suspects receiving legal advice.[110] The rather obvious suggestion has been made that this may be the result of legal advisers warning their clients about the consequences of remaining silent under the new provisions.[111]

(3) Experienced professional criminals

It had been an important plank of the abolitionist case that professional criminals who knew their way around the system customarily exploited the right to silence to obtain an unmerited acquittal. However, the research evidence neither confirms nor refutes the suggestion that of the small minority of cases in which suspects remained silent, that minority included a disproportionate number of professional criminals. On the other hand, there was some evidence to suggest a correlation between the

---

[107] Having been given a section 36 special warning 70 per cent gave no account, 11 per cent gave what was considered to be an unsatisfactory one and 19 per cent gave a satisfactory one. Of those who were given a section 37 warning the figures were 77, 10 and 13 per cent.

[108] "The Extent of Silence in Police Interviews," in S. Greer and R. Morgan (eds.) *The Right of Silence Debate*, Bristol 1990.

[109] McConville and Hodgson, *Custodial legal advice and the right to silence*, R.C.C.J. Research Study No. 16, H.M.S.O. 1992.

[110] See *Research Findings*, No. 62, *supra*, p.3.

[111] *ibid.*

incidence of silence and three variables which taken together may be loosely associated with active criminality on an occupational footing: gravity of the offence under investigation; previous record; and presence of a legal adviser. The study by Williamson and Motson, for example, revealed that suspects were silent in 23 per cent of serious cases but in only 8 per cent of trivial ones. Of those who were silent 21 per cent had a criminal record while only 9 per cent of those who answered questions had a record. The researchers pointed out that request for a solicitor may be more common amongst seasoned offenders who, having already decided to stay silent, appreciate the tactical advantage of being "advised" by a solicitor to say nothing.

(4) Terrorism and the Northern Ireland experience

It was conjectured that the Criminal Evidence (Northern Ireland) Order 1988 would not be effective in inducing more suspects to talk, at least to begin with, because suspects to whom it was intended to apply (those supposedly involved in terrorism) were the very persons who would probably wait and see how the judiciary would apply it.[112] How far it has produced change is not clear. Because the judges' reasoning is on record it is known that inference from silence (whether during questioning or at trial) has made a difference in 40 defended cases (5%) since the order was introduced.[113] One quarter of these cases are regarded as unsafe by Amnesty International and British and Irish Rights Watch.[114] But this figure does not show if the measures have been effective in inducing significantly more suspects to become more forthcoming with the police than was formerly the position. In fact, conviction rates have actually gone down since 1988[115] although the material significance of this is not clear. It might be argued that the increasing number of acquittals could be taken as indicative of more *innocent* suspects deciding to put their innocent accounts on record and being believed.

(5) Test of the supposition that the use of silence obstructs the police

(a) *General*

The supposed need for curtailment of the right to silence was based on the assumption that it is advantageous for the police that the defendant should offer a false denial rather than remain silence. This is because the obstructive guilty suspect is better able to shield his guilt through silence rather than through lies. A false

112 J.D. Jackson, "Curtailing the Right of Silence: lessons from Northern Ireland," [1991] Crim.L.R. 404, at p.413.

113 B.B.C. Radio Four, *File on Four*, October 26, 1993, transcript, p.12

114 *ibid.*, p.13.

115 *ibid.*, p.12.

denial provides opportunities for the exercise of interrogation techniques and further investigation which are not available if the suspect remains silent. In his study for the R.C.C.J. Roger Leng found that the supposed benefits to the police of defendants answering questions—the opportunity to break down the defence or refute it by further investigation—accrued in only a small minority of cases.[116] He examined 94 cases in which the suspect gave an innocent account but failed to convince the police although they took no further action to prosecute. In 75 per cent of the sample the account was inscrutable in the sense that nothing was asserted which was capable of being investigated or tested and the police gained no advantage from the fact that the suspect chose to answer questions rather than remain silent. A number of such cases involved the classic explanation for the possession of stolen goods that they had been obtained from a "man in the pub" known only by his first name. Further questioning would elicit a generalised description of no real assistance to the police from which the mystery man might be identified. In other cases there was no obvious means of faulting the account offered. In a further 21 per cent the account was capable of further investigation. However, by comparison, of nine no further action cases in which the suspect relied on the right to silence at some stage it appeared that in 6 cases the suspect could have answered the allegations by an effectively inscrutable denial or defence. In these cases there would have been no particular disadvantage for the investigation. But in 3 cases there was a realistic prospect that the investigation might have benefited from the suspect answering questions.

(b) *Ambush defences*

As the supposed problem of late mention was closely associated with that of the so-called ambush defence research by Long embraced that question too. His definition of an ambush defence included the following ingredients: raised for the first time at trial and taking the prosecution by surprise; based on a fact or explanation which could have been given during interrogation; hampering the prosecution by making its investigation impossible or more difficult by lapse of time or by allwing insufficient time for the preparation of the prosecution case in the light of the new defence; the defence is false. Although a true defence which is not dislosed until trial may inconvenience the prosecution the central focus of the debate on the right to silence was the avoidance of unmeritorious acquittals and research therefore excluded defences which were true. A defence will not be an ambush merely because the defendant fails to nominate the appropriate legal category of defence provided the essential facts on which it is based are intimated. The denial of an offence would amount to an ambush if the defendant fails during interrogation to support it with a fact asserted at trial, for example, whilst denying intent he fails to mention that his perception of the consequences of his actions had been occluded by the effect of taking drugs. Even where a defence is raised for the first time at trial it would not be considered an ambush if the suspect were not given sufficient

[116] *supra.*

information about the suspicions against him to indicate the relevance of the facts on which his defence was later based, he were not given an opportunity to put the factual basis of his defence in interview, or he was subjectively unaware of the potential for raising a defence. Leng found that the extent of concern about ambush defences was misplaced but that there was evidence to suggest that in a small number of cases in which the prosecution was faced with a supposedly unexpected defence, the root cause was failure by the police to allow a suspect to explain his proposed defence in interview with the consequence that they deprived themselves of the opportunity of further investigation. True ambush defences were very rare and did not always succeed. In only a very small proportion of cases would curtailment have any impact in enhancing the prospects of convicting the guilty, and then to only a limited extent.

(6) Impact of silence on charge and conviction

The research findings lend no support to the supposition that suspects who remained silent were less likely to be charged or less likely to be convicted. In fact, most of those who were silent in the police station either pleaded guilty later or were subsequently found guilty. A study by Moston, Stephenson and Williamson revealed that although silence had no affect on the liklihood of a suspect being charged where the evidence was clearly strong or clearly weak, where it was on the borderline silence appeared to make a charge more rather than less likely.[117]

[117] Moston, Stephenson and Williamson, "The effects of case characteristics on suspect behaviour during questioning," (1992) 32 *British Journal of Criminology*, 23; "The incidence, antecedents and consquences of the use of the right to silence during police questioning," (1993) 3 *Criminal Behaviour and Mental Health*, 30; *Police Investigation Styles and Suspect Behaviour, Final Report to the Police Requirements Support Unit*, University of Kent Institute of Social and Applied Psychology, published in *Criminal Behaviour and Mental Health*, 1993.

CHAPTER TWO

SILENCE BEFORE TRIAL

I. COMMON LAW

A. *TACIT ADMISSIONS*

(1) Principle of silence as assent

There are many different situations in which suspicious circumstances appear to demand an explanation, the failure to provide which may warrant an inference of guilt. For example, under the doctrine of "recent possession" the failure by a person to give an innocent explanation for the possession of goods recently stolen has been taken as strengthening the inference that the he is guilty of stealing them or has guilty knowledge in relation to a charge of dishonestly handling them.[1] Again, silence has been regarded as strengthening the inference, drawn from the trespassary presence of the defendant in someone else's house, that he was there with an intent to steal.[2] Other examples are provided by the burden imposed by the numerous statutes on defendants to furnish an innocent explanation for proven facts.

In the 19th century the consensus of judicial opinion was that the failure to answer an accusation or question when an answer could reasonably be expected might provide some evidence in support of the accusation.[3] The principle was expressed by Lord Atkinson in *Christie* early in the present century:[4]

> "The rule of law undoubtedly is that a statement made in the presence of an accused person, *even upon an occasion which should be expected reasonably to call for some explanation or denial from him*, is not evidence against him of the facts stated save so far as he accepts the statement to make it, in effect, his own. . . . He may accept the statement by word or conduct, action or demeanour, and it is the function of the

---

[1] *Schama; Abramovitch* (1914) L.J.K.B. 396; *Aves* (1950) 34 Cr.App.R. 159; *Seymour* [1954] 1 All E.R. 1006; *Raviraj* (1987) 85 Cr.App.R. 93.

[2] *Wood* (1911) 7 Cr.App.R. 56. See also *Kelson* (1909) 3 Cr.App.R. 230 and *Nash* (1911) 6 Cr.App.R. 225.

[3] See *Burdett* (1820) 4 B. & Ald. 95, 161-162; *Boyle* v. *Wiseman* (1855) 10 Ex. 647; *Bessela* v. *Stern* (1877) 2 C.P.D. 265; *Wiedemann* v. *Walpole* [1891] 2 Q.B. 534 (failure to reply to written allegation); *Mitchell* (1892) 17 Cox C.C. 503, 508; *Corrie and Watson* (1904) 20 T.L.R. 365, 68 J.P. 294; *Bernard* (1908) 1 Cr.App.R. 218, 219; *Norton* [1910] 2 K.B. 496. See also Phillips Arnold, *Evidence*, 10th ed., 1852, vol. 1, 334, cited in *Chandler* [1976] 1 W.L.R. 585, at p.589.

[4] [1914] A.C. 545, at p.554.

jury which tries the case to determine whether his words, action, conduct or demeanour at the time when a statement was made amounts to an acceptance of it in whole or in part."

The words in emphasis make it clear that silence can amount to acceptance by the accused of the statement made in his presence. If silence can be treated as evidence of an acknowledgement of guilt ought it to be treated as being capable of corroborating other evidence? On the question of whether silence could corroborate other evidence the authorities were in conflict.[5]

(2) Detailed allegation put by interested private individual

In *Cramp*[6] a conviction for administering a noxious thing with intent to induce miscarriage was upheld where the jury had ben directed that the appellant's silence upon being accused by the pregnant woman's father could be corroboration. Significantly, the father had also confronted him with the bottle of juniper and pills said to have been supplied to her for the illegal purpose. That factor was distinguished in *Tate*,[7] in which the appellant made no reply when formally charged by a police officer with the sodomy of a 16-year-old youth who, on the Crown's case, had consented and was therefore an accomplice. Quashing the conviction the court conceded that in some cases the absence of an indignant repudiation of a charge might be some corroboration of it, but not in the circumstances of the present case. There had, observed the court, to be something more than a mere charge, as in *Cramp* where the father had in his possession the evidences which might reasonably be expected to call forth a reply from an innocent man.

(3) Analysis of the old cases on allegations put by the police

Absent from the report of *Tate* in the *King's Bench Reports* series but cited in the *Law Times* version is another point which is of significance. Giving judgment, Lord Alverstone C.J. is quoted as declaring:

> "We are far from saying that evidence of non-denial cannot be corroboration, for in some cases the absence of indignant denial would amount to that, but non-denial of a formal charge made by the police is not, *or may not be*, on the same footing."[8]

---

[5] For the analysis in the text see originally Wolchover, "Guilt and the Silent Suspect," *New Law Journal*, March 24, 1989, p.396; March 31, p.428; April 7, p.484; and April 14, p.501.
[6] (1880) 14 Cox C.C. 390.
[7] [1908] 2 K.B. 680.
[8] 99 L.T. 620, at p.621, emphasis supplied.

The passage is ambiguous. Lord Alverstone may have meant that while he thought that in principle non-denial of a formal charge made by the police was probably on a different footing from that when a private person levelled a charge he was undecided on the point. On the other hand, he may have meant that in some cases it was on the same footing and that in others it was on a different footing.

If non-denial to a charge by a policeman is always on a different footing from that by a private person this could only have been the case if there was some factor *necessarily* placing charge or accusation by the police in a category apart from charge by a civilian. Such a factor might be the premise that intervention by the police marks the start of proceedings beyond which point silence could never be held against the defendant. If Lord Alverstone was undecided as to whether or not it was on a different footing in principle he was leaving open the possibility that it might be on the same footing. But since for reasons given below it could not invariably be on the same footing, we are effectively brought to the second interpretation—same footing in some cases; different footing in others. The use of the indicative ("is not") with a subjunctive in the alternative ("or may not be") seems to convey a sense of the *usual* and the *exceptional*: in most cases non-denial in response to a policeman would be on a different footing from that in response to a charge levelled by a private individual but in a few cases it would be on the same footing. On this reading the key distinguishing factor cannot have been the basis on which *Tate* was distinguished from *Cramp*—the absence of detail in the statement of the charge. It must be one specific to the nature of a charge put by a police officer if such a charge is generally to be on a different footing from charge by a private person. Absence of detail in conveying an allegation was not a requirement or a characteristic of police practice.

The factor which most readily comes to mind in commonly precluding silence from being held against the defendant was the giving of the traditional caution. It would plainly be unfair to hold a man's silence against him if he had been told he need say nothing in reply because he would have been entitled to assume that he would not be in any way worse off if he stayed silent than if he spoke. Conversely, if, exceptionally, there had been no caution, the absence of an indignant denial might amount to corroboration. The distinction between the usual and the exceptional is exactly reflected in the fact that whilst police officers making an arrest or informing suspects of a charge usually gave the caution as a matter of prudence, they did not at that time necessarily or invariably give one and were certainly not required to do so.[9] In *Tate* there is no reference to any caution having been administered but the court nevertheless held that the accused's silence could not furnish corroboration. In order to reach this decision they resorted to distinguishing the facts from those in *Cramp* by stressing the point about the absence of detail in the statement of the charge. It happens to be exactly on this

[9] A caution was not required to be given on arrest until the introduction of P.A.C.E. Code C in 1985: see p.196, *infra*. For advice in 1906 (two years before *Tate*) on when to give the caution see p.47, *infra*.

basis that *Feigenbaum*,[10] in which there is also no reference to any caution being given, may be reconciled with *Tate*. Upholding conviction the Court of Criminal Appeal decided that the jury had been properly directed that the appellant's silence when arrested and told of the allegation was capable of corroborating the evidence of three boys whom he allegedly paid to commit thefts as to which he was charged with being an accessory. In fact, the arresting constable had recited to the appellant more than merely a bald nominal statement of the charge; he had stated not only the boys' names but repeated their allegations in a good deal of detail.

An inadequate account of the judgment in *Whitehead* set out in the *Criminal Appeal Reports* may, interestingly, have been the source of error in subsequent decisions.[11] A police officer served on the appellant a summons for carnally knowing a female of 15, read it to him, and cautioned him. The appellant replied that he did "not want to say anything about it now." The jury were directed that this could be corroboration and that it was for them to say whether a respectable man would at once deny the charge. The headnote in the *Criminal Appeal Reports* states that "[i]t is not corroboration of incriminating evidence that the accused did not deny the charge or was silent about it." Yet there is plainly nothing in the brief text of the judgment of Lord Hewart C.J. to suggest the endorsement of any such proposition. All that is attributed to Lord Hewart is the bald description of the above remarks as a misdirection, coupled with the comment that it went further than anything in *Tate*.[12] (The significance of this observation is presumably that, as in *Tate*, the accused was given a bare statement of the charge but that in that case there had been no embellishment citing the notional reaction of a respectable man.)

By contrast, the much fuller account of *Whitehead* in the *King's Bench Reports* reveals the true ratio of the decision.[13] In giving judgment quashing the appellant's conviction, Lord Hewart is reported to observe:

> "To say that silence after [the usual caution] may be treated as corroboration of the evidence of the prosecutrix appears to us to be a misdirection. It goes beyond anything that was said in *Tate*."

Thus it is the essence of the decision that it would be wholly misleading to tell a person that he was under no obligation to say anything if his resulting silence could formally be held against him all the same.[14] There is nothing intrinsically wrong about silence when faced with a charge corroborating other evidence, when an indignant rebuttal might reasonably be expected. It is just that a caution makes it

---

[10] [1919] 1 K.B. 431.

[11] (1928) 21 Cr.App.R. 23.

[12] *supra*.

[13] [1929] 1 K.B. 99, at p.102. The summing up was also regarded as defective in that it may have conveyed a suggestion that by virtue of what was assumed to have been an original allegation to the mother, the girl could be deemed to have corroborated herself.

[14] The ratio thus follows a strain of reasoning adopted in two late account cases which stress the caution as the factor preventing silence from being held against the defendant: see *Naylor* (1933) 23 Cr.App.R. 177 and *Leckey* (1944) 29 Cr.App.R. 178.

inappropriate to hold the silence against the defendant. This is the factor which, as argued above, probably underscored Lord Alverstone's thinking in *Tate*.

If the account of the decision in *Charavanmutto* set out in the *Criminal Law Reports*[15] is any guide Lord Hewart appears to have been led into error by confining the reading of his own judgment in *Whitehead* to the unsatisfactory *Criminal Appeal Reports* version. On being charged with indecent assault upon two boys the appellant replied "I reserve my defence." Although "not treated as corroboration under the name of corroboration," the remark was stressed in summing up as something which might help the jury in assessing the evidence of the boys (who were present as accomplices but for whom, in any case, corroboration was desirable). Giving judgment Lord Hewart said: "It would be unfortunate if the jury thought that mere silence of the accused might amount to corroboration, for it is well settled since the decision in *Whitehead* . . . that it could not be." Yet *Whitehead*, of course, settled no such thing. There is no reference in the report to any caution being administered, and it might be argued that the decision is authority for saying that the principle that silence cannot corroborate (or, at least, be held against the defendant) applies independently of the caution. But *Charavanmutto* is the expression of an erroneous reading of *Whitehead* and must be regarded as wrongly decided.

The cumulative effect of this error had a bearing on the later case of *Keeling*,[16] an indictment for carnal knowledge of an 8-year-old girl whose unsworn evidence required corroboration. Under caution the appellant had been told by a policeman that there was a warrant out for his arrest on the charge, which the officer specified, and the appellant replied "I know what you mean, but not likely." When formally charged later and cautioned he replied "I have got you, nothing to say." Before the committing justices, in answer to the statutory caution, he said "I am not guilty. I am going to say nothing." He gave no evidence at trial. The jury were directed that they could find the necessary corroboration in the appellant's conduct from first to last after the accusation had been made. As to his reaction on arrest the trial judge suggested that if the words "not likely" were taken in their ordinary sense they meant that it was not at all likely that anybody would do such a thing. In the view of the Court of Criminal Appeal this was intended to imply, in effect, that it was a weak and inadequate denial, but the court observed, with undoubted preference, that on another view the words were a colloquial way of giving an emphatic denial. In essence it could not even begin to be corroborative and the issue was not, despite their preliminary contra-indication, "whether an insufficiently strenuous denial can afford more corroboration against the prisoner than the absence of any denial at all."[17] (As to the defendant's silences after charge and committal respectively, the court stressed the unfairness of holding a person's silence against him if he had been cautioned.)

---

[15] (1930) 22 Cr.App.R. 23.
[16] (1942) 28 Cr.App.R. 121.
[17] *ibid.*, at p.125.

Referring to *Whitehead* and to *Charavanmutto*, and to another case, *Naylor*,[18] the court suggested that on some future occasion it might have to be considered whether *Feigenbaum* was to be regarded as having been overruled by those cases. Quite whether this justifies the terse caption "*Feigenbaum* doubted" in the prefatory note is debateable. In any event, the reasoning which they gave in support of any reservations which they might have harboured over *Feigenbaum* is, to say the least, obscure. In *Naylor* the appellant prior to committal at the police court was cautioned and made a bald denial. In summing up the judge commented that an innocent man would surely give some explanation of why he was innocent and give the prosecution time to make inquiries, even with a solicitor advising silence. The court in *Keeling* pointed out that Lord Hewart in his judgment in *Naylor* had laid stress on the caution as the factor which precluded the appellant's failure to give such an explanation from being held against him, and stated that *Naylor* followed *Whitehead*. So saying, they appear to have been acknowledging their appreciation of the true ratio of the latter decision, *i.e.*, that it was the caution which stopped the appellant's silence from being held against him. Confusingly, the court also stated that *Charavanmutto* followed *Whitehead*, which manifestly it does not, being an eccentric judgment.

Despite these difficulties of interpretation and reconciliation, it is possible to distil from the line of decisions here considered a seam of principle which may be expressed in the following propositions. (1) The making of a charge may raise the expectation of an indignant denial, the failure to give which may signal acceptance of the charge and hence furnish corroboration. (2) According as greater detail of the charge is given, so the expectation of a denial increases. (3) No such implication can arise where the charge was coupled with a caution. (4) Since a caution is usually administered when a charge is made by police, it will be unusual for non-denial of a charge made by the police to be corroborative. (5) In that sense non-denial to charges made by police may be on a different footing from that when a charge is made by other persons (*Tate*, *Law Times Reports*), but when a charge is made by police exceptionally without the giving of a caution, non-denial may be corroborative (*Feigenbaum*; but *Charavanmutto* wrongly decided).[19]

That *Feigenbaum* was doubted in *Keeling* was assumed by the Privy Council in *Hall* v. *Regina*,[20] an appeal from Jamaica in which the Board expressly repudiated *Feigenbaum*. The police found drugs in a two-roomed dwelling which, according to the report, the appellant, absent at the time of the search, was said to occupy with two women, his co-accused. One of the women told the police the drugs belonged to the appellant. Shortly afterwards he was brought to the premises and made no reply when the police told him under caution of the woman's accusation. On this evidence the magistrate convicted him of possession and his original appeal was dismissed on the ground that his silence when told of the woman's accusation could be regarded

[18] (1933) 23 Cr.App.R. 177.

[19] Zuckerman was plainly incorrect, therefore, in extrapolating a finite rule that silence could not amount to corroboration: (1973) 36 M.L.R. 509, at p. 510.

[20] (1970) 55 Cr.App.R. 108.

as an acknowledgment by him of its truth. Holding this to be wrong, Lord Diplock observed:[21]

> "It may be that in very exceptional circumstances an inference may be drawn from a failure to give an explanation or a disclaimer, but in their Lordships' view silence alone on being informed that someone else has made an accusation against him cannot give rise to an inference that the person to whom the information is communicated accepts the truth of the accusation. This is well established by many authorities, such as *Whitehead* . . . and *Keeling* . . . Counsel has sought to distinguish these cases on the ground that the accused had already been cautioned and told in terms that he was not obliged to reply. Reliance was placed on the earlier case of *Feigenbaum* . . . But if the inference ought not to be drawn in ordinary circumstances (while it may be drawn in very exceptional circumstances) it cannot be that there is any rule of law which prevents it being drawn; it must be because in ordinary circumstances the inference would not in fact be a reasonable one. The correctness of the decision in *Feigenbaum* was doubted in *Keeling*. In their Lordships' view the distinction sought to be made is not a valid one and *Feigenbaum* followed. The caution merely serves to remind the accused of a right which he already possesses at common law. The fact that in a particular case he has not been reminded of it is no good ground for inferring that his silence is not in exercise of the right, but was an acknowledgment of the truth of the accusation."

The distinction drawn here between ordinary and exceptional circumstances is reminiscent of the earlier cases. Yet, in *Hall*, the basis of the distinction is quite changed, with the Board repeating earlier errors on the ratio of *Whitehead* and failing to address themselves to the confusion revealed in *Keeling*. Their repudiation of *Feigenbaum* was therefore insufficient to set aside the corpus of earlier decisions, the thrust of which (*Charavanmutto* apart) is to stress the caution as the main factor in determining whether silence can be taken as tacit acceptance of the truth if the allegation. In any event, despite the Board's undoubted authority, their opinion could not be binding on the English courts. Furthermore, it is arguable that the decision in to overturn the appellant's conviction was highly merciful. It could probably have been supported on the strength alone of his occupancy of the premises and the consequent presumption of control over the drugs. (Although the report supplies no details beyond stating that Hall "was said" to occupy the dwelling, if he had given the police and court another address the resulting dispute would inevitably have been mentioned.)

In *Mann*[22] the appellant's reaction to over half the questions puts to him by the police was either to remain silent, shake his head or reply "no comment" and it was

[21] *ibid.*, at p. 112.

[22] (1971) 56 Cr.App.R. 750, C.A. See also *Raviraj* (1987) 85 Cr.App.R. 93, C.A.

held to be proper to allow the whole series of exchanges to go before the jury. However, it was suggested that if the appellant had failed to respond to any of the questions it might well be, on the principle in *Hall*, that the evidence of the abortive dialogue ought not to be admitted. A less sympathetic view of *Hall* was taken in *Chandler*[23] in which the Court of Appeal rejected Lord Diplock's opinion that the caution reflected the principle that in ordinary circumstances an inference of guilt could not properly be drawn from the defendant's silence when accused or questioned. The defendant was suspected of involvement in a conspiracy to defraud, but on grounds which, the Crown conceded on the appeal, were insufficient by themselves to sustain a case against him. He was questioned by police and before being cautioned gave replies to some questions but refused replies to others. Following the caution he continued in the same vein to answer some questions, refusing to answer others. The jury were directed that it was open to them to decide that the series of answers indicated guilt. It was held that this was to short-circuit the intellectual process which had to be followed in accordance with *Christie*.[24] The issue to which the jury's attention should have been directed was whether the defendant's silence amounted to an acceptance by him of what the interviewing officer had said and only then whether guilt could reasonably be inferred from what he had accepted. However, the essential thrust of the decision is that an acceptance of the truth of an allegation may properly be inferred from the defendant's silence when that allegation is put by police. The appeal was allowed because, the court stressed, even if the direction had been in accordance with *Christie*, those facts which it might be inferred the defendant had tacitly accepted provided no safe foundation for an inference that he was a member of the conspiracy.

For obvious reasons it would hardly have been proper to allow an adverse finding from the defendant's comprehensive silence after caution. Where, however, having been cautioned the defendant opted to answer questions selectively, this might have given evidential significance to those which remained unanswered, because the contrast was capable of suggesting that the selective non-response was attributable not to an assumption engendered by the caution that he could remain silent without cost but to an embarrassed inability to furnish satisfactory replies to those questions he chose not to answer.

(4) Even terms and presence of a solicitor

In considering whether it would be proper to infer tacit acceptance of an accusation the Court of Appeal in *Chandler* cited an important condition enunciated by Cave J. in *Mitchell*:[25]

---

[23] [1976] 1 W.L.R. 585. See also *Parkes* v. *R.* [1976] 1 W.L.R. 1251, P.C.
[24] [1914] A.C. 545.
[25] (1892) 17 Cox C.C. 503, at p.508.

> "Undoubtedly, when persons are speaking on even terms, and a charge is made, and the person charged says nothing, and expresses no indignation, and does nothing to repel the charge, that is some evidence to show that he admits the charge to be true."

This passage was described in the 4th edition of *Cross on Evidence*,[26] as "a broad principle of common sense," a view with which the court in *Chandler* concurred.[27] Exploring the meaning of the expression "even terms" Lawton L.J. said:

> ". . . we are of the opinion that the defendant and the detective sergeant were speaking on equal terms since the former had his solicitor present to give him any advice he might have wanted and to testify, if needed, as to what had been said. We do not accept that a police officer always has an advantage over someone he is questioning. Everything depends upon the circumstances. A young detective questioning a local government dignitary in the course of an inquiry into alleged local government corruption may be very much at a disadvantage. This kind of situation is to be contrasted with that of a tearful housewife accused of shoplifting or of a parent being questioned about the suspect wrongdoing of his son."[28]

Chandler contrasts with the position in *Mitchell* itself in which an allegation was made by a dying woman from whom evidence was being taken in the presence of the accused and her solicitor. The formality of the occasion clearly ruled out any contradiction as inappropriate, particularly as the accused was relying on her solicitor to act as her spokesman. This would not have been the position at a police interview. Of course, under the régîme of the Judges' Rules (extant at the time of *Chandler*) the interviewing of a suspect by police could not have imbued total non-response with evidential significance even where the interview was conducted with a solicitor in attendance. Such an interview, if properly conducted, would have been prefaced with a caution, which would clearly have precluded any inference of tacit admission. Under the then existing Judges' Rules régîme the potential impact of *Chandler* was of narrow scope. The making of an arrest did not of itself require the giving of an otherwise disabling caution and if the pronouncement of arrest involved a certain amount of detail then the suspect's non-response to the pronouncement could have furnished evidence of acceptance of the truth of the "charge," *but only* if a solicitor acting for the defendant was at that stage in attendance. In most instances

[26] p.189.

[27] *supra*, at p.590. In *Horne* [1990] Crim.L.R. 188, C.A. the defendant was found by police hiding and thereafter made no reply when the man he was accused of wounding said "Take that bastard away, he's the one who glassed me." It was held that in circumstances where some protest or denial might have been expected a jury were entitled to take account of the fact that the accused had said nothing. This therefore also appears to be an "even terms" case.

[28] *ibid*. *Cf. Murphy and McKinley* [1993] 4 N.I.J.B. 42, at p.59, where the Northern Ireland Court of Appeal described the "contentious part of the judgment in *Chandler*" (that the solicitor's presence put the suspect on even terms with the police officer) as *obiter*, and expressed reluctance to extend the common law any further.

this would not have been the reality although non-response might imply an admission where, for example, a suspect went to the police station in the company of his solicitor and was arrested without a caution and the solicitor asked the arresting officer in the presence of his client to summarise the grounds for the arrest. Again, the suspect might have had his solicitor in attendance at his home or place of business or employment in anticipation of the police coming there to arrest him or he might have been arrested by arrangement at his solicitor's office. Another example might be where during the course of an ongoing and complex inquiry the investigating officer held a meeting with a suspect and his solicitor for the exclusive purpose of informing them, as a matter of courtesy and common fairness, that a firm allegation against the suspect was now on the table. However, the purpose of the encounter would not have been to arrest the suspect nor to question him or otherwise do anything to invite a response. In these situations there might have been some scope for an adverse inference although conceivably this could be averted by evidence that the solicitor had previously advised his client to say nothing on the not unreasonable basis that he, the solicitor, would "handle" the situation, in effect the position in *Mitchell* where the solicitor was acting as spokesman.

Another marginal scenario in which *Chandler* might have had some impact was where a person against whom reasonable grounds for suspicion had yet to crystalise was being interviewed as a potential witness, with his solicitor present. It might be imagined that at a certain point he gave an answer the effect of which was dramatically to provide compelling grounds for suspicion, so strong in fact that the officer immediately arrested him, clearly explaining why. Indeed, the answer may have been so telling that without more it furnished sufficient evidence to prosecute. For that reason perhaps, but in any event, the officer refrained from cautioning him as he did not intend at that stage asking any further questions, pending consultation with a senior officer. Under *Chandler* and until P.A.C.E. the non-response in this illustration might well have provided evidence of tacit admission.

With the changes brought about first of all by P.A.C.E. and then subsequently by the Criminal Justice and Public Order Act 1994, *Chandler* will now have little or no application.

(5) Failure to reply to written allegation

The failure to reply to an allegation in writing may in certain circumstances amount to an admission. In *Wiedemann* v. *Walpole*[29] the Court of Appeal said that there were business and mercantile cases in which the court had taken notice that in the ordinary course of business if a person "states in a letter to another that he has agreed to do certain things, the person who receives the letter must answer it if he

---

[29] [1891] 2 Q.B. 534, at pp.537-538, *per* Lord Esher M.R. (plaintiff's evidence of breach of promise of marriage held incapable of corroboration by defendant's failure to reply to her letter alleging such a promise).

means to dispute the fact that he did so agree." In *Edwards*[30]the Court of Appeal said that although this principle applied in criminal cases the courts must be very wary of admitting evidence of written allegation and non-reply. The appellant was indicted for incitement to racial hatred by aiding the publication of a comic journal which contained racially offensive matter and the prosecution relied on a letter written to the appellant referring to the comic as "your idea and your work" and an unfinished reply found in his typewriter, containing no reference to the comic. In fact, the court doubted whether the letters had been properly admitted, but held that the jury would inevitably have reached the same conclusion if they had been excluded. It has been suggested that it would be rare for a court to be satisfied that the failure to reply was capable of amounting to an acknowledgment of the truth of the accusation, given the disinclination of many to reply to letters.[31]

B. *COMMENT ON FAILURE DURING QUESTIONING TO MENTION A FACT RELIED ON AT TRIAL*

The cases considered so far concern the extent to which failure to deny an allegation can be treated as an admission of its truth. Silence as assent contrasts with the indirect route of reasoning from silence to guilt, by way of the belatedly mentioned fact. On this aspect of the topic of silence the authorities deal with the extent to which judges are permitted to comment adversely.

It has been pointed out[32] that the "problem" of the ambush defence has been accorded a central place in the modern abolitionist case usually with scant regard to the existing common law solution. Convictions have always been upheld when the judge has commented that by the accused's failure at committal stage to reveal the defence raised at trial, or a fuller account of it, he has deprived the police of the opportunity to investigate it.[33] Even the bald direction that when considering the weight to be given to the accused's evidence in court the jury may take into account his failure to give his story earlier, without the rider that the police have been deprived of an opportunity to check it, has been sanctioned.[34] In other words, "a fishy story is all the worse for being stale."[35] On the other hand, where the defendant made a bald denial at the police court after caution and the comment did not merely refer to the police being handicapped but involved the suggestion that an innocent

---

30 [1983] Crim.L.R. 539.

31 R. May, *Criminal Evidence*, 3rd ed., London: Sweet and Maxwell, 1995, p.215.

32 See Greer, "The Right to Silence: A Review of the Current Debate," (1990) 53 M.L.R. 709, at p.713.

33 *Moran* (1909) 30 Cr.App.R. 25 (alibi; at police court defendant stated he was away at the time; commented that if he had gone on to say he had been at a certain place police would have investigated); *Parker* (1934) 24 Cr.App.R. 2 (co-defendants disclosed their alibis at police court; observed that comment necessary in fairness to them); *Littleboy* (1934) 24 Cr.App.R. 192 (alibi, but at police court defence reserved).

34 *Ryan* (1966) 50 Cr.App.R. 144.

35 *Hinton* v. *Trotter* [1931] S.A.S.R. 123, at p.127, *per* Napier J., cited by Greer, 53 M.L.R., at p.713.

man would have given some explanation, *even with a solicitor advising silence* (thus affording the prosecution time to inquire) the conviction was quashed.[36] Indeed, when the comment had involved stressing comparison with the notional behaviour of the innocent convictions were usually quashed. Thus, in *Leckey*, an indictment for murder in which the defence involved a partial alibi, the defendant replied to the police after caution "I was with the girl [but] have nothing to say until I have seen a solicitor" and three times in the summing-up it was suggested that an innocent man would have denied the murder.[37] The decision was described by Humphreys J. in *Gerard* as the high water mark of those cases in which a conviction was quashed because of a comment by the judge about an observation by the accused on arrest.[38] Humphreys J. presumably had in mind the gravity of the charge and the strength of the evidence. Curiously, however, convictions were not always overturned where the comment involved equating silence with guilt. In *Gerard* itself the defendant was stopped in possession of a lorry load of spirits and ran off. After his arrest later but before police had knowledge that the spirits were stolen he was asked at the police station under caution to explain his possession of them and replied, "What I have to say I will say to the court." His conviction was upheld despite the comment that if innocent it was curious that he had made that statement when not yet charged and had merely run away because he had lost his head. In *Sullivan*,[39] the defendant refused to answer when questioned by customs officers about the smuggling of watches. A comment that whilst the defendant was absolutely entitled to say nothing an innocent man would be anxious to answer was held to be a misdirection, but the proviso was applied. It is with some justice that in *Gilbert*[40] the Court of Appeal noted the impossibility of reconciling all the decisions. However, they reaffirmed the rule that a jury must not be invited to conclude that the defendant is guilty because the defence raised went unmentioned until the trial.

Where the comment involved no explicit link between silence and guilt, the tendency was to turn a blind eye to the damaging effect of its oblique meaning. Thus, in *Tune*,[41] an indictment for fraudulent conversion, the defendant on being cautioned made a statement in which he admitted having been shown by the police various documents but gave no explanation and at the end said "I can fully explain the whole question, but would prefer to have legal advice before doing so in writing." In summing up, the judge observed: "Could not that have been said without legal advice?" Giving judgment on appeal, Humphreys J. said:

> "We have been asked to say that that was a misdirection in the sense that it was inviting the jury to form some adverse conclusion from the fact that the applicant did not give an explanation. It was nothing of the

[36] *Naylor, supra.*

[37] *supra.*

[38] (1948) 32 Cr.App.R. 132. See also *Whitehead, supra*; *Naylor, supra*; *Davis* (1959) 43 Cr.App.R. 215; *Hoare* (1966) 50 Cr.App.R. 166.

[39] (1967) 51 Cr.App.R. 102.

[40] (1977) 66 Cr.App.R. 237.

[41] (1944) 29 Cr.App.R. 162.

sort. It was merely a comment that what the applicant was saying, if it was true, was something that did not require any legal advice."

A further example of this reasoning is *Ryan*,[42] in which Melford Stevenson J. observed:

> "It is, we think, clear . . . that it is wrong to say to a jury 'Because the accused exercised what is undoubtedly his right, the privilege of remaining silent, you may draw an inference of guilt;' it is quite a different matter to say 'this accused, as he is entitled to do, has not advanced at an earlier stage the explanation that has been offered to you today; you the jury may take into account when you are assessing the weight that you think it right to attribute to the explanation.'"

This passage was memorably described by Sir Rupert Cross as "gibberish"[43] and the Court of Appeal subsequently characterised it more politely as expressing a distinction without a difference, the second statement merely being an "oblique" way of expressing the first.[44] On the other hand, there is no doubt that the distinction can be justified on the basis that a belated explanation, as a matter of strict logic, is not necessarily tantamount to the absence of one that is genuine.[45]

In at least two of the successful appeals involving the suggestion that only the guilty take refuge in silence, the court laid stress on the fact that there had been a caution and on the argument, therefore, that as the accused had been informed that he was not obliged to say anything, it would be a trap for him if the jury were to be invited to draw an inference from his silence.[46] But in the opinion of the C.L.R.C. there was now no doubt that the rule that an invitation to draw an inference of guilt from the accused's silence was a misdirection existed independently of any caution.[47] For this view they sought reliance on two authorities. One was the opinion of Lord Diplock in *Hall* v. *R.*, already cited. The other was *Ryan*. The appellant, a railman, was found by police in a goods wagon in suspicious circumstances. When challenged by the officers and before any question of his being cautioned arose he appears to have replied "Are you making it up?" or words which, in the opinion of the court, amounted to a total denial. At his trial he claimed to have been tidying up, after finding that various articles had been disturbed. His appeal based on misdirection was dismissed for the reason set out in the passage quoted earlier. Noting that the judgment contained no reference to any caution the Committee

---

42 *supra*.

43 [1973] Crim.L.R. 329, at p.333.

44 *Gilbert*, *supra*, at p.244.

45 Thus Zuckerman, *supra*, at p.511, was strictly correct to redeem the distinction as more than mere gibberish, although it would be a charitable view of the comment, indeed, that it was other than a barely concealed attempt to signal in favour of an inference of guilt.

46 *Naylor*, *supra*; *Leckey*, *supra*. *Cf. Gerard*, *supra*, in which it is assumed that the giving of a caution was not regarded as having constituted a trap.

47 para. 29.

suggested that, had the court construed the comment as meaning that the jury might infer guilt from the accused's failure to tell his story, they would have held it to have been a misdirection.[48] The Committee noted that the headnote to *Ryan* suggested the reason why the judge's comment was upheld was that it was "coupled with an indication that the defendant was under no obligation to give any explanation." But they pointed out that in most, if not all, of the recent cases where a comment was held to have been a misdirection it had been coupled with a similar indication. *Ryan* is a case of comment on late explanation, not one in which silence could be taken as assent to an accusation (the response, after all being a denial). In the late explanation cases a direct invitation to infer guilt has almost always been held to be misdirection, even without a caution, presumably because it assumes too much.[49] By contrast, a caution did not necessarily preclude some measure of criticism, as the decision in *Tune*,[50] discussed earlier, attests.

C. *IMPACT OF THE CAUTION*

(1) Cautioning and tacit admission

Chandler superceded the opinion of commentators such as Miller[51] who assumed that the principle behind *Cramp* and other cases, that silence could be taken as an admission, had no application when the accusation was made by a police officer, or in his presence. Miller was following the C.L.R.C., who limited their proposals to questioning by police or other professional investigators on the grounds that the common law already allowed for the drawing of adverse inferences in the case of questioning "for example, by the victim of the offence or a member of his family, by an eyewitness or by a person having no interest in the case [or] where the accused was not being questioned but was taxed with his conduct by somebody who knew or strongly suspected that the accused was the offender."[52]

In extending the even terms principle to embrace confrontation by the police questioner *Chandler* saw off that distinction. The only factor which would universally have operated to preclude an inference of tacit admission from the silence of suspects questioned by the police was the giving of the traditional form of caution. In strict logic, to say to a suspect "you are not obliged to say anything but anything you do say may be given in evidence" does not *necessarily* make it unfair to draw an inference against him if he stays silent. If it is a natural compulsion for an innocent man to protest his innocence, being advised that he is not obliged to speak is unlikely to put off an innocent suspect. The caution may convey no more than that the suspect commits no criminal offence by staying silent or that no sanction having

48 *ibid.*
49 The notable exception is *Gerard, supra*.
50 (1944)29 Cr.App.R.. 162.
51 [1973] Crim.L.R., at p.344.
52 para. 34.

specific tangible consequences (such as the refusal of bail) may legitimately be deployed to compel answers, rather than implying also that there is no need to worry about any risk of his silence being ultimately viewed with suspicion. However, the traditional words of the caution might have been taken to suggest that the suspect would be none the worse off if he remained silent. A suspect who wanted to deny the allegation but also had coherent and defensible reasons for staying silent would therefore have been led into a trap if he decided to keep silent for those reasons, believing as a result of the caution that he would not be prejudiced by his decision, and the jury were then invited to draw inferences against him as a result.

In the light of *Chandler* Lord Diplock's statement in *Hall* that the caution merely served to remind the suspect of a right enjoyed under common law was now seen to be accurate only in a limited sense. It was now only true to say that the caution meant that there was no criminal offence of refusing to answer and no legitimate powers vested in the police to hold out the prospect of hardships or benefits as a means of compelling speech. It did not reflect a rule prohibiting the accused's silence from being held against him since the common law clearly provided for the contrary. Thus, in the light of *Chandler* the caution was seen to have become an impediment to the application of the principle that the accused's silence was capable of being indicative of guilt. The caution was now seen in effect to afford a wider margin of protection for the suspect than the common law strictly bestowed.

(2) Origin of the caution

Cautions came into being as a concomitant of the emergence of the rule excluding involuntary confessions but it is uncertain when they were first used. According to the compilers of an "Historical Memorandum" furnished by the Home Office to the 1929 Royal Commission on Police Powers and Procedure, the word "caution" as applied to a form of warning by an examining magistrate "is found as early as 1730 in circumstances suggesting that it was then well understood."[53] In 19th and 20th centuries case reports there are distinguishable two forms of caution, which might be called the full and the partial. The first advises of a right to say nothing, but warns that anything said will be recorded and may be used in evidence. The partial consists simply of the second part of the full caution.[54] The magisterial habit of cautioning was self-imposed; it did not come about through judicial enjoinder. Langbein has shown that until a comparatively late time the examining magistrate also often performed the function of prosecuting advocate at trial.[55] The examining magistrate *cum* advocate would therefore be keenly aware of the consequences if a

[53] Report, Cmd. 3297, para. 64, and Appendix 4, referring to minutes of evidence to the Commission.

[54] *E.g.*, *Drew* (1837) 8 C. & P. 140; *Furley* (1844) 1 Cox 76; *Harris* (1844) 1 Cox 106; *Brackenbury* (1893) 17 Cox 628. See *Wolchover and Heaton-Armstrong on Confession Evidence*, para. 4-025.

[55] *Prosecuting Crime in the Renaissance*, Camb. Mass. 1974, pp. 45-54. See also Stephen, *History of the Criminal Law*, i, pp.222-223.

confession were not held to have been voluntary: he would be present in court to suffer a personal affront if it were excluded. The Home Office researchers must have been correct when they stated that—

> "... the caution was introduced for the purpose of ensuring that the prisoner's statement was voluntary and of establishing to the satisfaction of the court that the prisoner knew that he was under no obligation to make a statement or to incriminate himself."[56]

In 1848 the caution was formalised into the procedure of the preliminary hearing.[57] But by this time the preliminary hearing was a judicial proceeding and no longer part of the investigative process. Having in the meantime taken over from the magistracy the function of original investigation the police adopted the habit of cautioning suspects, although there was little uniformity of practice and there did not begin to be any until the publication of Vincent's *Police Code* in which Hawkins J. contributed a preface in the form of an Address to Constables. After deprecating the questioning of suspects who had been arrested or were about to be arrested, he went on to state that an officer "ought not, by anything he says or does, to invite or encourage an accused person to make any statement without first cautioning him ..."[58] The Address to Constables hardly amounted to a comprehensive code of practice on cautioning and a marked lack of uniformity continued. Then, in October 1906, Lord Alverstone C.J. received a letter from Charles Rafter, the Chief Constable of Birmingham, requesting his advice. It seemed that on the same circuit one judge had censured a member of Rafter's force for having cautioned a prisoner, whilst another judge had criticised a constable for having omitted to do so. Lord Alverstone consulted the other judges of the King's Bench Division and sent the following reply:

> "There is, as far as I know, no difference of opinion whatever among the judges of the King's Bench Division upon the matter. The practice which has been definitely followed, and approved for many years, is that whenever a constable determines to make a charge against a man he should caution him before taking any statement from him. Whether there is any necessity for a caution before a formal charge is preferred must depend upon the particular circumstances of the case: no definite rule can be laid down. In many cases a person may wish to give an explanation which would have exonerated him from any suspicion, and he ought not to be prevented from making it. On the other hand, there

---

[56] 1929 Report, para. 64. See also Devlin *The Criminal Prosecution in England*, London 1960, p.32; Abrahams, *Police Questioning and the Judges' Rules*, p.9; and MacKenna, [1972] Crim.L.R. 605, at p.609.

[57] Indictable Offences Act 1848, 11 & 12 Vict. c.42.

[58] There was no inconsistency between this passage and the general disapproval of the questioning of prisoners if the passage is taken to refer, not to questioning, but to the practice of specifying in detail the reason for the arrest.

> are cases in which it would be the duty of the constable to caution the person before accepting any further statement from him, even though no charge has actually been formulated.[59]

In the next few years similar requests for advice were received from other parts of the country and, accordingly, in 1912, in the wake of conflicting rulings and dicta the first four of the Judges' Rules were formulated and approved by the judges of the King's Bench Division at the request of the Home Secretary. In 1918 a further five rules were drafted and approved and the whole nine were then circulated by the Home Office to all chief officers of police and to the criminal courts.[60] The Judges' Rules were fundamentally reformulated in 1964, with a sanction given for the questioning of persons under arrest.[61] So a habit which had originated informally gradually became honoured by time and eventually achieved sufficient standing to be regarded by the judges as obligatory, albeit expressed to be so in extra-judicial pronouncements. So regarded it was then transformed into a creature of administrative decree, without any legislative support whatsoever.

Whilst the caution seems, then, to have begun life as an instrument by which investigating justices sought to safeguard the admissibility of the accused's examination, by the middle of the 20th century it was seen, on the highest authority, to possess an altogether more momentous quality. Thus, in the perception of Patrick Devlin:

> "The real significance of the caution is that it is, so to speak, a declaration of war. By it the police announce that they are no longer representing themselves to the man they are questioning as the neutral inquirer whom the good citizen ought to assist; they are the prosecution and are without right, legal or moral, to further help from the accused; no man, innocent or guilty, need thereafter reproach himself for keeping silent, for that is what they have just told him he may do."[62]

But that the caution had humbler origins and purposes was identified by Lord Widgery C.J. during the Lords debate on the C.L.R.C.'s eleventh report.[63] Citing the 19th century authorities, he stated that the first edition of the Judges' Rules "of about 1906 or 1908" had been laid down "with what we would now regard as considerable presumption." The caution did not reflect a rule of law bestowing any general immunity from an adverse inference.

---

[59] The episode is related in the 1929 report, para. 182, and Appendix 10.

[60] *ibid*, and para 185. The whole nine are conveniently set out in *ibid.*, para. 182, note, and in Devlin, *op. cit.*, Appendix, p.115. A corrective circular, H.O. 536053/23, was issued by the Home Office on June 24, 1930 and eight supplementary rules on the taking of statements, approved by the Lord Chief Justice, were issued in circular H.O. 238/1947 on November 22, 1947.

[61] *Judges' Rules and Administrative Directions on Interrogation and the Taking of Statements*, Home Office F.2 division, Circular H.O. 31/1964, January 1964, re-issued in circular 89/1978, June 1978.

[62] *The Criminal Prosecution in England*, p.31.

[63] 338 H.L. Deb. 1564, at col. 1626, February 14, 1973.

(3) The lost opportunity for administrative abolition

In the light of *Chandler* the caution reflected no rule of common law prohibiting inferences of guilt from silence and it was only the requirement for the caution in its traditional form which precluded the proper drawing of such inferences. Prior to the enactment of P.A.C.E. the Home Office, had they thought of it, could have promulgated a new form of caution to take account of the state of the authorities on tacit admission, in particular *Chandler*. Prior to *Gilbert*, a year later, such an alteration could also have removed any doubt in cases of late mention about the legitimacy of expressing criticism not involving an express license to infer guilt. Alteration would have required no legislative intervention whatsoever. (Although conceding that there was no need to provide in their draft Criminal Evidence Bill for abolition of the caution the C.L.R.C. thought that as it had become so much a part of police interrogation procedure, it was desirable to include a declaration of the absence of any legal requirement for one.[64]) Alteration would not even have required any reference to the judges although in the light of the observation by Lord Lane C.J. in *Rennie*[65] that it was time to allow inferences to be drawn from the accused's silence such a change would probably have been encouraged by them. But P.A.C.E. eliminated the scope for such a simple step. With little substantial alteration the cautioning structure of the 1964 Judges' Rules was incorporated into Code C, paragraph 10, although an important innovation was the requirement to administer a caution on arrest whether or not it was intended to question the arrested person. The Code was issued by the Home Secretary under the power conferred by section 66 of the Act and, in accordance with section 67, the Code (and any re-issued version) could only be brought into operation by an order made by statutory instrument authorised on a resolution of both Houses of Parliament. The Code was therefore now a creature of statute and could not be changed administratively. Paragraph 10 of Code C is discussed in detail later, with consideration given both to its original, 1985, form (as incorporated in the 1991 revision) and to the 1995 version, revised to include the new form of caution which was drawn up in accordance with the provisions of Part III of the Criminal Justice and Public Order Act 1994.

II. THE CRIMINAL JUSTICE AND PUBLIC ORDER ACT 1994

A. *THE LEGISLATIVE BACKGROUND*

Not more than a century had passed after the judges finally abandoned their old habit of questioning prisoners at the bar when Jeremy Bentham extolled the virtues

[64] 11th report, para. 43.
[65] [1982] 1 All E.R. 385.

of compulsory interrogation.[66] But the debate on whether pressure should be placed on suspects to speak to the police did not take up centre stage until it was revived in 1972 with publication of the C.L.R.C.'s Eleventh Report.[67] The Committee's proposals, which were the origin of sections 34 and 35 of the Criminal Justice and Public Order Act 1994, provoked an immediate outcry. In the words of the R.C.C.P. nearly a decade later, "[b]oth within and outside Parliament a formidable body of professional and lay opinion stood aghast"[68] and no action was taken by the Government to implement the proposals.[69] Interest in the topic eventually waned and, despite occasional efforts to keep the issue on the agenda,[70] to there seemed little likelihood that the proposals would be revived, particularly as a majority of the members of the R.C.C.P. had come out firmly against any alteration in the law.[71] But the debate was renewed in 1987 when Mr Douglas Hurd, the Home Secretary, gave a lecture at the Police Foundation in which he argued the need for change[72] and

---

[66] See *supra*.

[67] Report, paras. 28-52 and draft Criminal Evidence Bill, cl. 1. Proposal foreshadowed by Sir Norman Skelhorn Q.C. in 1965, cited *ibid*, at para. 30; Cross, "The Right of Silence and the Presumption of Innocence—Sacred Cows or Safeguards of Liberty?" (1970) 11 J.S.P.T.L. 66; Lord Parker C.J., *The Times*, April 8, 1971; Lord Widgery C.J., *ibid.*, July 17, 1971, *Observer* July 18.

[68] Report, Cmnd. 8092, 1981, para. 1.27. For the Lords debate on the proposals see 388 H.L. Deb., col. 1546 *et seq.* contemporary memoranda published variously by such bodies as Justice, Society of Conservative Lawyers, Society of Labour Lawyers, National Council for Civil Liberties, National Council for the Care and Resettlement of Offenders, Release Lawyers Group, and the Criminal Bar Association, whose 1973 paper was adopted by the Bar Council. For academic treatments see *e.g.*, Sir B. MacKenna, [1972] Crim.L.R. 605; Sir Rupert Cross, [1973] Crim.L.R. 329; C.J. Miller, "Silence and confessions: what are they worth?" [1973] Crim.L.R. 343; and A.A. Zuckerman, (1973) 36 M.L.R. 509. For a selection of reactions to the 11th report during 1972, both before and after publication, see *The Times*, April 8, (report of warning of dangers sounded by N.C.C.L., N.A.C.R.O., David Napley on behalf of the Law Society's standing committee on criminal law, Dick Taverne Q.C., M.P., Shirley Williams M.P.); letter, R. Paget, M.P. supporting abolition, *ibid.*, April 10; "Rules of the Criminal Process," editorial, *New Law Journal*, April 13, pp.573-575; letter, T. Smyth, Gen. Sec., N.C.C.L., *The Times*, April 14; report of lecture by Sir L. Radzinowicz, director, Institute of Criminology, Cambridge, *ibid.*, April 27; *ibid.*, June 12 and 15 (efforts by N.C.C.L. to promote opposition); P. Crowder, Q.C., M.P. and I. Lawrence, *The Conviction of the Guilty*, Conservative Political Centre, June 1972; *The Times*, June 21 (lecture by Robert Mark to Royal Society of Medicine); letter in reaction, B. Payton, *ibid.*, June 23; *ibid.*, June 28 (publication of report, reactions and leader); *ibid.*, June 30 (letters); *ibid.*, July 1 (reported views of Lord Hailsham, the Lord Chancellor); *Sunday Times*, July 2 (analysis and reactions); letter, Prof. R. Dworkin, *The Times*, July 3; *ibid.*, July 6 (reaction by Society of Labour Lawyers and Law Society, and letter, J.B. Wheatley of the London Criminal Courts Solicitors' Association); letter T. Smyth, *Sunday Times*, July 9; letter, J. Hutchinson Q.C., and B. Wigoder, Q.C., and letter, O. Lovibond, *The Times* July 10; *ibid.*, July 10 (further reactions, Magistrates' Association, Bar Council); *Sunday Times* August 6 (report about C.B.A. memorandum); *The Times*, August 7 (report about N.C.C.L. memorandum); letter, Henry Cecil, *ibid.*, August 21; *ibid*, September 23 (Liberal Party Assembly reaction); *ibid.*, September 29 (N.C.C.L. campaign); letter, Edmund Davies L.J., *ibid.*, 29 September; letter, Dr Manfred Simon, former President of a Chamber of the Court of Appeal of Paris, *ibid*, October 10; *Guardian*, December 11 (summary of reactions); letter, Prof. Glanveille Williams, Q.C., *The Times*, February 22, 1973. For a survey of reactions see M. Zander, *Law Soc. Gaz.*, October 7, 1974.

[69] See *The Times*, September 23, 1972 reporting Government deferment of decision on implementation.

[70] *E.g.* Sir Norman Skelhorn Q.C., D.P.P., taking part in Durham University Debating Society, see *Observer*, February 1, 1976.

[71] See Report, para. 4.53 and for discussion leading to this conclusion see paras. 4.47-4.52.

[72] See *The Guardian*, July 31, 1987.

this triggered various public calls for abolition from the police.[73] Wedged between the hammer of police discontent and the anvil of liberal resistance, the Government seemed uncertain how to pitch their initiative.[74] Mr Hurd's argument that change was necessary was self-contradictory, in that his main suggestion was to "introduce" the practice of informing the jury that the defendant had remained silent throughout interview. This was evidently thought to be a more diplomatic way of proceeding than a full-blown scheme of allowing silence to substantiate proof. But in fact the practice had always been followed, a state of affairs which did not prevent the error being cited without either comment or correction in a report subsequently commissioned by the Home Office.[75] To demonstrate that they were serious about tackling the "problem" of the right to silence the Government needed to find a valid "solution" capable of winning wide acceptance. For a time they considered a strategy of merely extending the existing arrangements for alibis and expert opinion by requiring universal pre-trial defence disclosure. The purpose of such a scheme, to which bodies such as the Law Society were prepared to lend their support,[76] would have been to prevent the springing of ambush defences during the trial, when it is too late for the police to investigate them.

Although by the end of 1987 it was reported that the strength of opposition to the more ambitious approach of allowing silence to count as evidence of guilt was such that the Government had been persuaded to leave well alone[77] the Home Secretary in May 1988 announced in the Commons the appointment of a working party (the Working Group on the Right of Silence) to consider the details of a legislative scheme for England and Wales.[78] It was made clear that the Working Group were being asked to advise on how to change the law, not whether or not in principle some change was justified.[79] They reported in July 1989.[80] Meanwhile, on October 20, 1988, Mr King, the Northern Ireland Secretary of State, announced to the Commons in a written answer that a draft Order in Council had been laid before Parliament to restrict the right to silence in Northern Ireland.[81] On the same day and by means also of a written answer Mr Hurd announced that similar legislation would eventually be enacted for England and Wales once the Working Group had

---

[73] See *e.g.* Peter Imbert, national press, September 16, 1987, and see also *The Guardian*, September 22, 1987 (Police Superintendents' Association).

[74] See the *Report of the Working Group on the Right to Silence* (Chairman W.J. Bohan), Home Office C4 Division, July 13, 1989, para. 2. See also contemporary national quality press (including *The Independent* (*I*) and legal press references.

[75] *Working Group Report*, para. 1.

[76] *ibid.*, para. 2.

[77] G. Williams, "The Tactic of Silence," *New Law Journal*, November 27, 1987, p.1107.

[78] Setting up announced in the Commons on May 18, 1988, written response to Mr Kenneth Hind M.P., 133 H.C. Deb., col. 466. See also *Working Group Report*, para. 2; *The Guardian*, May 19, 1988; *New Law Journal*, May 27, 1988, p.358. and progress of work referred to in *The Daily Telegraph*, October 10, 1988.

[79] See *Working Group Report*, para. 50.

[80] See note 78, *supra*.

[81] 138 H.C. Deb., col. 996.

reported,[82] an announcement which rather defeated the object of waiting for the report.

Modelled in part on changes which had been introduced in the Republic of Ireland by sections 18 and 19 of that country's Criminal Justice Act 1984 the Criminal Evidence (Northern Ireland) Order 1988 was swiftly enacted, and came into effect in December 1988.[83] When introducing the proposed Order to the Commons Mr King referred to the belief that terrorists were trained to maintain silence under questioning and he stated that of all persons detained in the province in connection with serious crime including terrorism, about half apparently refused to answer any substantive questions.[84] Mr King's widely reported announcement coincided with the trial of three persons for conspiring to murder him. Two had refused to answer police questions and all three had declined to give evidence and their subsequent appeal against conviction was allowed on the ground that in the light of Mr King's remarks, as well as public comments by Lord Denning, the jury should have been discharged.[85] The decision was reported to have caused serious doubts at the Home Office on the wisdom of removing the right to silence in England and Wales[86] and in July 1990 the Government indicated that they would not be seeking to introduce legislation on the right to silence either in the current or subsequent Parliamentary session.[87] With the appointment of the Royal Commission on Criminal Justice in 1991 Home Office plans were effectively put in abeyance. When the Commission reported in 1993 the majority followed the 1980 Royal Commission and came out against abolition of the right to silence.[88] In the light of their doing so the Home Office plans seemed likely to be shelved. Nevertheless, within a short time of publication Mr Michael Howard, the Home Secretary, speaking at the 1993 Conservative Party Conference, disregarded the opinions of the two Royal Commissions and announced a new legislative programme.[89] The silence

[82] Statement of intentions in response to a written Question from Tim Devlin M.P., 138 H.C. Deb., cols. 983-984, October 20, 1988.

[83] S.I. No. 1987 (N.I. No. 20); order enacted on November 14, and brought into force on December 15, 1988. See J.D. Jackson, "Curtailing the Right of Silence: lessons from Northern Ireland," [1991] Crim.L.R. 404, at pp.404-405. For criticism of the way the Order was introduced, see Standing Advisory Commission for Human Rights, *Report for 1987-89*, H.C. Paper 394, 1989; Ashworth and Creighton, "The Right to Silence in Northern Ireland," in *Lessons from Northern Ireland* (eds. Hayes and O'Higgins) Belfast 1990. For background to the introduction of the Order, see J.D. Jackson, "Recent Developments in Criminal Evidence," (1989) 40 N.I.L.Q. 105 and "Developments in Northern Ireland" in *The Right of Silence Debate* (eds. Greer and Morgan), Bristol Centre for Criminal Justice 1990. For recent developments in Northern Ireland see Jackson, "Curtailing the Right of Silence: lessons from Northern Ireland," [1991] Crim.L.R. 404; "Inferences from silence: from common law to common sense," (1993) 44 N.I.L.Q. 103; *The Right of Silence Debate: The Northern Ireland Experience*, Justice 1994; "Intepreting the Silence Provision: The Northern Ireland Cases," [1995] Crim.L.R. 587.

[84] See 140 H.C. Deb., cols. 183-187, November 8, 1988.

[85] *Cullen, McCann and Shanahan* (1990) 140 N.L.J. 629.

[86] *Law Soc. Gaz.* May 2, 1990.

[87] *The Guardian*, July 5, 1990.

[88] Report, chapter 4.

[89] For reportage and editorial comment see national press, October 7, 1993, and correspondence, *The Times*, October 14 and December 29. Announcement foreshadowed in remarks attributed to Mr David Maclean, Minister of State at the Home Office with responsibility for criminal justice: see *The Times*, June 7, 1993.

provisions of the resulting Criminal Justice and Public Order Act 1994 came into force on April 10, 1995,[90] reproducing those in the Criminal Evidence (Northern Ireland) Order but amending the Order, where there were differences, to conform almost entirely to the 1994 Act.[91]

It is of some significance to mention the response of the Labour Party to the silence proposals when they were being considered in Parliament. During Commons Second Reading on the Bill which became the 1994 Act the Shadow Home Secretary moved an amendment to prevent adverse inferences from being authorised in respect of the stage prior to interview at the police station unless the accused had been informed of the right to legal advice and had been given an opportunity to consult a solicitor in private.[92] Although Labour was therefore pursuing the pragmatic approach of seeking to limit the width of the proposed legislation this did not mean that their opposition to abolition was not fundamental and unqualified. It was not merely a question of raising objections to curtailment in the absence of adquate safeguards. This was made clear by the Shadow Home Secretary:[93]

> "[T]he issue of the right to silence, as it is called . . . is part of the more general principle that a person has a right under British law not to incriminate himself. The prosecution must prove guilt, and there is a presumption of innocence—those are fundamental principles of our law . . . [E]ven if, technically, the right to silence remains, there will be in effect strong practical pressure on those who are accused to talk. That is a change in those fundamental principles of law. I do not say that fundamental principles of law can never change, but they should yield only if there is a clear benefit, and no detriment which outweighs the value of the principle. Our conclusion, along with that of the Royal Commission on Criminal Justice, is that this has not been demonstrated, and that the case for changing the fundamental principles in this way has not been made. We go further, and say that it is more than merely *a matter of high constitutional principle*. There is a serious and substantial risk that, in the manner in which the Government have proceeded, we will not merely fail to convict more of the guilty, but that we are in danger of convicting more of the innocent. . . . I believe that the single most extraordinary feature of the Government's proposals—what makes them chilling in their degree of political, rather than judicious, motivation—is that they do not seek simply to abolish the right to

[90] Brought into effect by the Criminal Justice and Public Order Act 1994 (Commencement No. 6) Order 1995 (S.I. 1995 No. 721).

[91] Sched. 10, para. 61, of the 1994 Act. It has been suggested that the English legislation owes its existence not so much to a considered choice between opposing views as to the political incentive to assimilate Northern Ireland law and its English counterpart, with which the former had been "glaringly out of line," and so render it "considerably less conspicuous": Birch, [1999] Crim.L.R., at p.772.

[92] Amendment No. 4 to cl. 29. Labour appear not to have appreciated the extremely marginal extent to which the Bill applied to silence outside the police station.

[93] 241 H.C. Deb., cols. 261, 262, 264 and 281, emphasis supplied.

> silence in a limited or controlled way or under certain conditions. Rather, they abolish it completely, in all circumstances and without any apparent additional safeguards whatever. . . . Surely, even if we differ on the question of principle—whether the right to silence should be curtailed, and I do not believe that it should—it is wrong to abrogate the right without establishing any safeguards against abuse, given past experience and the judgment of the Royal Commission. . . . It is not as if there is any strong evidence that abolition will transform the criminal justice system—that is not even the Government's case. Indeed, I was astounded when I came across the Minister's words in Committee [stating that the Government were not looking for recognisable changes in rates of conviction[94]]. I should have thought that that would be the one justification for the clause. Abrogation of an otherwise fundamental principle of British law can be justified in circumstances in which one could say that there is a fundamental problem that can be dealt with only in that way. We will press the amendments to a vote, first because we do not believe that the Home Secretary has adequately justified the abolition of an important fundamental principle of British law—a constitutional principle upon which people are entitled to rely. Our second reason is that the Government proposal, without any proper safeguards, will go further than anyone has ever recommended on the abolition of the right to silence."

These words demonstrates that Labour's resistance to the measures was deep-rooted and uncompromising. There was no question of any fudging of the issue by horse-trading in order to obtain concessions. The speech has been quoted at length because its maker was Tony Blair. As the basis of his opposition to the scheme was a matter of "high constitutional principle" it might have been expected that when Labour came to office steps would have been taken to repeal the legislation. However, the position of the Labour Government in 1998 was that they had "no immediate plans" to do so.[95]

The 1994 Act makes provision for adverse inferences to be drawn from both the silence of the suspect at the investigative stage of a criminal case and, in section 35 (equivalent to Article 4 of the Criminal Evidence (Northern Ireland) Order 1988), from his refusal to give evidence. The latter is dealt with in Part III below. The silence provisions of the Act primarily deal with two classes of silence before trial: (a) failure of the suspect to mention a fact on which the defence rely in subsequent proceedings (section 34(1) and (2), equivalent to Article 3 of the Order) and (b)

---

94 Standing Committee B, *Official Report*, February 1, 1994, col.401.

95 Letter to the author from the Home Office Procedures and Victims Unit (V. Pugh), ref. C/97 13/14/1, January 7, 1998. It has yet to be seen whether the Home Office will be spurred on to repeal section 34 by the influential opinion of Birch that it exacts too great a cost, first because it consumes too much judicial time both at trial and on appeal, second because it is a headache for the conscientious jury and a tool which the slapdash, incompetent jury may wreak injustice, and third because the gains in terms of cogent evidence are likely to be slight: [1999] Crim.L.R., at p.772-773.

failure to explain (a) objects, substances or marks physically associated with the suspect (section 36, equivalent to Article 5 of the Order) and (b) presence at a particular place (section 37, equivalent to Article 6). The Act preserves the Common law in relation to the admissibility of the evidence of silence of an accused as a reaction to the making of an accusation, the effect of which is to permit silence to be taken as potential evidence of tacit admission of an allegation voiced by a private citizen (Common law saving, section 34(5)). In conjunction with, and essential to the implementation of, the Act is the alteration of the wording of the caution to suspects, brought about by the issuing of the latest, third, edition of P.A.C.E. Code C. The statutory provisions do not apply in relation to a failure or refusal which occurred before the commencement of the Act.[96]

In keeping with the original scheme of the C.L.R.C. the Northern Ireland Order permitted the relevant silence to be treated as capable of amounting to corroboration. The 1994 Act abolishes the corroboration warnings and various specific requirements for corroboration[97] and contains no provision for relevant silence to count as corroboration. In conformity with the 1994 Act the Northern Ireland Order has been amended to remove the corroboration provision.[98]

B. *THE MAIN PROVISION: FAILURE TO MENTION FACTS RELIED ON AT TRIAL*

(1) Legislative text of the main provision

Section 34 of the Act deals principally with the effect of the accused's failure, when questioned by the police or upon being charged, to mention a fact relied on by the defence in subsequent proceedings. It provides, *inter alia*:-

> "(1) Where, in any proceedings against a person for an offence, evidence is given that the accused—
>
> (a) at any time before he was charged with the offence, on being questioned under caution by a constable trying to discover whether or by whom the offence had been committed, failed to mention any fact relied on in his defence in those proceedings; or
>
> (b) on being charged with the offence or officially informed that he might be prosecuted for it, failed to mention any such fact,
>
> being a fact which in the circumstances existing at the time the accused could reasonably have been expected to mention when so questioned, charged or informed, as the case may be, subsection (2) below applies.

---

[96] s.34(6).

[97] s.32, accomplice warnings; s.33, sexual offences.

[98] See Anthony F. Jennings, "Resounding Silence," *New Law Journal*, May 17, 1996, p.725, n.4.

(2) Where this subsection applies—
   (a) a magistrates' court inquiring into the offence as examining justices;
   (b) a judge, in deciding whether to grant an application made by the accused [for dismissal of charge following notice of transfer in a case of serious fraud or of a violent or sexual offence involving a child under fourteen[99]]; and
   (c) the court in determining whether there is a case to answer; and
   (d) the court or jury in determining whether the accused is guilty of the offence charged,

   may draw such inferences from the failure as appear proper.

(3) Subject to any directions by the court, evidence tending to establish the failure may be given before or after evidence tending to establish the fact which the accused is alleged to have failed to mention.

(4) This section applies in relation to questioning by person (other than constables) charged with the duty of investigating offences or charging offenders as it applies in relation to questioning by constables; and in subsection (1) above 'officially informed' means informed by a constable or any such person."

(2) Ancilliary provisions

(a) Committal, transfer and sending forthwith

As originally enacted section 34(2)(a) made provision for the drawing of such inferences from the failure as appeared proper by a magistrates' court in deciding whether to grant an application for dismissal made by the accused under section 6 of the Magistrates' Courts Act 1980 (application for dismissal of charge in course of proceedings with a view to transfer for trial). The reference in section 34(2)(a) to proceedings with a view to transfer for trial related to the transfer procedure which under section 44 of the 1994 Act was to have replaced the function of examining magistrates acting in committal proceedings. The section was subsequently repealed by measures which introduced a modified form of committal proceedings involving no provision for the *inter partes* cross-examination of live evidence.[100] Legislation has now been enacted to abolish committal proceedings in the case of indictable

[99] The paragraph relates to applications under s.6 of the Criminal Justice Act 1987 for dismissal of a serious fraud charge in respect of which notice of transfer has been given under s.4 of that Act, and applications under Sched. 6, para. 5, to the Criminal Justice Act 1991 for dismissal of a charge of violent or sexual offence involving a child in respect of which notice of transfer has been given under s.53 of that Act.

[100] Criminal Procedure and Investigations Act 1996, s. 47 and Sched. 1. Under s.34 as originally enacted provision was made in subs. (7) for the section to be applied in committal proceedings pending implementation of the measure in s.44 replacing such proceedings with transfer for trial. Subs. (7) was repealed by CPIA 1996, s.44(4).

only offences and to replace them with a procedure by which prosecutions for such offences are simply "sent forthwith" to the Crown Court (in effect summary or instant transfer without consideration of evidence).[101] The measure was tried out in a number of pilot schemes prior to being implemented nationally on January 15, 2001. As in transferred cases of serious fraud or violent or sexual offences involving children defendants are permitted to apply to a judge of the Crown Court for dismissal,[102] but the 1994 Act has not been amended to include provision for the drawing of inferences on the occasion of such applications. This may have been oversight or it may have been a recognition of the fact that in practice there is little scope for such inferences to be drawn in the context of applications for dismissal.

(b) *The "offence charged"*

Section 38(2) provides that the reference in section 34(2) to the "offence charged" includes a reference to any other offence of which the accused could lawfully be convicted on that charge. Accordingly, where, for example, a court could determine the validity of a transfer, decide whether a prima facie case has been established, or return a conviction in respect of an offence other than that charged or indicted the failure or refusal in question may be relevant in that particular adjudication.

(c) *Failure or refusal insufficient in itself for a conviction*

Section 38(3) provides that no one may have proceedings against him transferred to the Crown Court for trial, have a case to answer or be convicted of an offence solely on an inference drawn from a failure or refusal to which section 34(2) relates. Similarly, section 38(4) provides that where there has been a notice of transfer in a case of serious fraud or in the case of an offence of violence or sex involving a child under fourteen a judge must not refuse an application for dismissal if the charge is based solely on an inference drawn from such a failure or refusal.

(d) *Refusal of access to a solicitor*

Section 34 has been amended from a day yet to be appointed by the insertion of a new subsection (2A) providing that where the accused was at an authorised place of detention at the time of the failure subsections (1) and (2) do not apply if he had not been allowed an opportunity to consult a solicitor prior to being questioned, charged or officially informed that he might be prosecuted.[103]

---

[101] Crime and Disorder Act 1998, s.51

[102] *ibid.*, Sched. 3, para. 2.

[103] Inserted by the Youth Justice and Criminal Evidence Act 1999, s.58(1) and (2). The amendment applies only to proceedings instituted on or after the commencement date for the new section but so applies whether the relevant failure or refusal on the part of the accused took place before or after that date: s.67(4) and Sched. 7, para. 8. For further consideration see, *infra*, p.158. Section 38(2A) provides that in s.34(2A) "authorised place of detention" means (a) a police station or (b) any other place prescribed for the purposes of that provision by order made by the Secretary of State, and the power to make an order under s.38(2A) shall be exercisable by statutory instrument which shall be subject to annulment in pursuance of a resolution of either House of Parliament.

(e) *Section 34 does not preclude the operation of existing statutory powers to exclude evidence as inadmissible or of any exclusionary discretion*

Nothing in section 34 prejudices the operation of a provision of any enactment which provides (in whatever words) that any answer or evidence given by a person in specified circumstances shall not be admissible in evidence against him or some other person in any proceedings or class of proceedings (however described, and whether civil or criminal).[104] Further, nothing in the section prejudices any power of a court, in any proceedings, to exclude evidence (whether by preventing questions being put or otherwise) at its discretion.[105] The effect of the first of these provisions would seem to be to ensure section 34 places no impediment on the power of any court to invoke section 76 of P.A.C.E. in order to exclude evidence, for example, of an interview containing a relevant failure. The second measure would have the same effect in relation to the discretion under section 78 to exclude an interview containing a relevant failure.

(3) The general legislative effect

(a) *Did section 34 change the law of England?*

Section 34(1) and (2) broadly enact the C.L.R.C.'s original scheme.[106] The Committee's perception of what they were seeking to achieve always lacked consistency. They had referred at length to their assumption that the common law already permitted silence to be taken as an acknowledgment of guilt when the accusation was levelled by a private individual, though never when put by a police officer or other professional investigator.[107] Yet it was unclear why they expounded on that distinction when they were proposing measures dealing with failure to mention to police facts relied on in subsequent proceedings and were not seeking to make provision for tacit admission by silence in the face of official or professional investigation. (Had they done so they would not in the event have been making any change in the law, as a survey in depth of the authorities would have revealed.)

In a leading contemporary critique of the C.L.R.C.'s Eleventh Report it was asserted that the Committee's scheme undoubtedly changed the law of England.[108] Whether, at the time, this was a valid statement is debateable. It had long been acceptable to make comments critical of the defendant for failing to mention to the police or at the magistrates' court a line of defence relied on at trial. Wherever failure at the "police" court to mention the defence raised at trial involved an unfavourable comparison by the judge with the supposed behaviour of an innocent

---

[104] s.38(5). The reference to giving evidence is a reference to giving evidence in any manner, whether by furnishing information, making discovery, producing documents or otherwise: *ibid*.

[105] s.38(6).

[106] Draft Criminal Evidence Bill, cl. 1(1).

[107] Report, para. 34.

[108] Zuckerman, (1973) 36 M.L.R., at p.512. In *R.* v. *Chief Constable of the R.U.C., ex p. Begley* [1997] N.I. 278, H.L., the Northern Ireland legislation was described by counsel as having "transformed the landscape of a criminal trial."

person the conviction was quashed.[109] Notably, however, two appeals concerning a failure to mention the defence to investigators were unsuccessful, one being *Gerard,* in which the comparison was not disavowed,[110] the other where the proviso was applied.[111] In other decisions concerning failure to mention to police the subsequent trial defence the court simply avoided the issue by pretending that the obviously damning comment was not saying in terms that an innocent person would have revealed his defence.[112] Subsequently, in *Gilbert,*[113] the Court of Appeal acknowledged that the authorities were in conflict but sought to reaffirm the principle that the jury were not to be invited to conclude that the defendant was guilty because the defence raised went unmentioned until the trial. Whether this actually amounted to ending the conflict of authority is to be doubted, as the court were simply disavowing the decision of an earlier bench of equivalent status. The 1972 proposal would have adopted the permissive thinking in *Gerard* rather than changing the law as such and, despite *Gilbert*, the 1994 Act did no more.

(b) *Inference may comprise part of the prima facie case*

Section 34 follows the scheme of the C.L.R.C. in expressly permitting the failure to be taken into account for the purpose of determining whether the prosecution have erected a *prima facie* case. Supporting the Bill in the House of Lords Lord Taylor, the Lord Chief Justice, said:

> "The intitial burden on the prosecution is to establish a prima facie case which must be done by evidence other than the mere silence of the defendant. Unless that is done, there is no case to answer and none of the provisions as to comment on silence would come into play."[114]

Similarly, Lord Lowry, the Chief Justice of Northern Ireland, at an earlier stage in the debates, assumed that "a prima facie case will always be the prerequisite of the new drill."[115] These impressions on the working of the section do not reflect its express terms, although the C.L.R.C. recognised that the application of the provision in determining a case to answer would be very limited.[116] It will almost exclusively depend on the extent to which a relevant fact is relied on in the course of cross-examination of a prosecution witness and, as one commentator has observed,[117] "[t]he reality is that silence will seldom be of use in determining if a defendant has a

---

109 *Moran* (1909) 30 Cr.App.R. 25; *Parker* (1934) 24 Cr.App.R. 2; *Littleboy* (1934) 24 Cr.App.R. 192.

110 *Gerard* (1948) 32 Cr.App.R. 132

111 *Sullivan* 1967) 51 Cr.App.R. 102. Where the ground of appeal was upheld but the court decided that no miscarriage of justice had occurred they would "apply the proviso" to s.2(1) of the Criminal Appeal Act 1968.

112 *Tune* (1944) 29 Cr.App.R. 162; *Ryan* (1966) 50 Cr.App.R. 144.

113 *Gilbert* (1977) 66 Cr.App.R. 237.

114 555 H.L. Deb., cols. 519-520, May 23, 1994.

115 554 H.L. Deb., col. 397, April 25, 1994.

116 Eleventh Report, para. 39.

117 Jennings, "Resounding silence," at. p.766.

case to answer. A defence submission of no case to answer will rarely rely upon a fact advanced by the defendant before trial and reliance upon the fact will invariably occur in the course of the defence case after a prima facie case has been established." As far as establishing the prima facie case is concerned, the opinion of another commentator, that silence under the section can probably establish *mens rea*, offset poor quality identification evidence and excuse the absence of forensic evidence[118] may be a counsel of alarm, although it may be more pertinent to the position at the end of the evidence.

(c) *Overall predicted impact of the section*

It is true that in most of the English appeal decisions on section 34 there was a strong prosecution case aside from the issue of silence,[119] and Northern Ireland Diplock court judges often stress that the evidence was quite adequate to convict without it.[120] This has led one commentator to observe that the "danger" of evidence of silence in such cases lies not in a wrongful conviction but that misapplication of section 34 will result in the quashing as unsafe of an otherwise respectable conviction[121] and that even if the conviction is upheld this will be at a considerable cost to the public purse.[122] In contrast it may happen that a weak prosecution case will be propped up by the defendant's silence as a result of a failure to exercise proper control over the jury and a verdict attributable in strong measure to their disapproval of the defendant's tactics.[123]

It is to be noted that although section 34 is not restricted in its application to suspects who remain silent in interview it has most commonly been invoked where defendants have refused to answer some or all of the interviewer's questions.[124]

(4) Application of section 34

(a) *Formal preconditions for invoking the section*

It was the Government's stated intent that the Act should apply only in "carefully defined circumstances."[125] These are contained in the statutory text and in

118 Pattenden, "Inferences from Silence," [1995] Crim.L.R. 602, at p.607.

119 See, *e.g. Condron* [1997] 1 Cr.App.R. 185; *Argent* [1997] 2 Cr.App.R. 27; *Bowers* [1998] Crim.L.R. 817; *Daniel* [1998] Crim.L.R. 818; *Taylor* [1999] Crim.L.R. 77.

120 See, *e.g. Mathers and Hillen* (1993) unreported, C.A. (N.I.), September 1; *McKee* (1991) unreported, Crown Court in Northern Ireland, October 14, both cases cited by Birch, "Suffering in Silence: A Cost-Benefit Analysis of Section 34 of the Criminal Justice and Public Order Act 1994," [1999] Crim.L.R. 769, at p.774, n.30.

121 *ibid.*, citing *Moshaid* [1998] Crim.L.R. 420 ("Although the evidence available to the Crown appears to have been powerful, this conviction is unsafe": quoted from transcript).

122 Birch, *supra*, at p.774, citing *Bansul* [1999] Crim.L.R. 484

123 Birch, *supra*, at p.774, citing *Hart and McLean* (1998) unreported C.A. No. 9703362 W4, April 23. Pattenden has described silence as the "evidential poly-filler for cracks in the wall of incriminating evidence which the prosecution has built around the accused": "Inferences from Silence," [1995] Crim.L.R. 602.

124 Birch, *supra*, at p.775. In *Condron* [1997] 1 Cr.App.R. 185, the advice given by the court dealt only with the typical "no comment" interview.

125 554 H.L. Deb., col. 383, April 25, 1994, Earl Ferrers.

Argent[126]Lord Bingham C.J. set them out in a list of six formal conditions to be met before the jury may draw an inference under the section:—

(1) There had to be proceedings against a person for an offence.
(2) The alleged failure had to occur before a defendant was charged.
(3) The alleged failure had to occur during questioning under caution by a constable, or any other person within section 34(4).
(4) The questioning had to be directed to trying to discover whether or by whom the alleged offence had been committed.
(5) The alleged failure by the defendant had to be to mention any fact relied on in his defence in those proceedings.
(6) The fact the appellant failed to mention was a fact which, in the circumstances existing at the time, he could reasonably have been expected to mention when so questioned.[127]

Lord Bingham stressed that it was for the jury to resolve these factual preconditions,[128] a declaration which Dr Pattenden has argued departs from the traditional division of function between judge and jury, according to which the judge decides any question, legal or factual, determinant of the admissibility of evidence.[129] But *Argent* is not saying that the Act removes from trial judges their basic supervisory function of screening evidence in order to decide if a necessary fact has been adduced. If any question is raised by the defence as to the existence of a particular factual pre-condition for drawing an inference required by the statute, a *voir dire* must assuredly be conducted to determine if there is *prima facie* evidence of the existence of the factual pre-condition, because if there is no such evidence, there would be no basis for drawing an inference from silence and no reason therefore to allow the evidence of the silence to go before the jury. If such *prima facie* evidence is adduced, then the issue will go to the jury. In this sense it is true that the test is different from the very rigorous one for the admissibility of a confession under section 76(2)(b) of P.A.C.E. (the obtaining of a confession in consequence of any thing said or done which was of a nature likely, in the circumstances existing at the time, to render unreliable *any* confession the accused might make in consequence thereof must be proved to the satisfaction of the trial judge byond reasonable doubt before either the confession or the fact of its existence can be adduced before the jury.) However, the standard of proof of the traditional "voluntary" precursor test of confession admissibility was always a special case.

---

[126] *Argent* [1997] 2 Cr.App.R. 27

[127] The Working Group had recommended the incorporation in the statute of specific guidelin es for determining the applicability of condition (6): report paras. 63 and 65 and Appendix D. For full discussion of the condition see p.77, *infra*.

[128] [1997] 2 Cr.App.R., at p.32. In *Gill* (2000) *The Times*, August 17, C.A. No. 9907637 X1, the appellant's conviction was quashed because, *inter alia*, the judge failed to direct the jury clearly that the six conditions triggered a discretion, not a duty, to draw an inference, and failed to give them clear directions in accordance with the fifth and sixth conditions.

[129] (1998) 2 E. & P.141, at p.156.

Dr Pattenden may believe that Lord Bingham could have done more to prevent inferences from being drawn in doubtful cases but, as will be seen later, he has deployed a subtle hand in going as far as it may have been politic to go in neutralising the impact of the Act whilst appearing to observe its terms. Indeed, noting in *Argent* that the overall fairness of the trial was the responsibility of the judge, to whom it was open to give the jury guidance on the approach to the evidence, the Lord Chief Justice enthused that there would "certainly" be circumstances in which a judge could warn a jury against drawing inferences and his lukewarm attitude to the statute could not have been signalled in plainer language when he went on to say that "Parliament in its wisdom had seen fit to enact section 34."[130]

(b) *Questioning of non-suspects inapplicable to section 34*

Sections 34(1) and (2) restrict relevant silence before charge to that of suspects "on being questioned under caution . . ." In its original draft the Bill did not require the questioning to be "under caution" and this followed the scheme of the Working Group and of the C.L.R.C. The original wording was considered by Lord Taylor, the Lord Chief Justice, as too widely drawn—

> "It would have allowed comment at trial not only on the silence of a suspect but also of someone who at the time of the questioning was regarded only as a potential witness—for example, during routine house-to-house inquiries. That would have been oppressive."[131]

The words "under caution" were therefore inserted by the Government at Lord Taylor's suggestion.[132] The amendment had the incidental benefit of deftly incorporating in the section the safeguard addressed in other more cumbersome amendments requiring the defendant to be warned of the consequences of silence, as a condition for drawing an inference.[133] The caution would be in the terms formulated for the revised P.A.C.E. Code C.

The section assumes that there are reasonable grounds for suspicion because otherwise there would be no caution. However, this may not necessarily be the case and an interesting problem may arise from the possibility that prior to arrest the interviewer, straining to be fair, administers a caution although not yet in possession of evidence furnishing the necessary reasonable grounds for suspicion warranting a caution. According to the strict letter of section 34 the foundation for an inference is

---

130 [1997] 2 Cr.App.R., at p. 32. Another hint as to Lord Bingham's attitude to the legislation emerged from *Bowden* [1999] 1 W.L.R. 823, at p.827, when he said that even though proper effect must be given to the adverse inference provisions, as they "restrict rights recognised at common law as appropriate to protect defendants against the risk of injustice they should not be construed more widely than the statutory language requires."

131 556 H.L. Deb., col. 1399, July 7, 1994 (3rd Reading).

132 *ibid.*, col. 1400.

133 Commons amendment No. 252: see 3rd Reading, 241 H.C. Deb., col. 260, April 13, 1994; Lords amendment No. 32 (Lord Campbell of Alloway): see 3rd Reading, 556 H.L. Deb., col. 1386; amendment No. 37 (Lord Ackner): *ibid.*, col. 1418, July 7, 1994.

laid, that is questioning under caution. However, it may be doubted whether the draftsman intended that it should be be open to draw an adverse inference where the caution was strictly unnecessary because of the lack of reasonable grounds for suspicion. Otherwise officers, ostensibly moved by an overabundance of "fairness," might be to tempted to preface all preliminary pre-arrest questioning with a caution regardless of whether they in fact had any grounds for suspicion, in order to justify an adverse inference.

(c) *Questioning of free suspects under caution outside the police station*

In response to the amendment inspired by Lord Taylor various counter-amendments were moved in both Houses of Parliament to remove the possibility of any inference being drawn from a failure to give relevant information prior to the suspect's arrival at the police station, where the twin safeguards of tape-recording and access to a solicitor were available.[134] However, fortified by Lord Taylor's opinion that the court of jury should be permitted to take account of a suspect's failure to give relevant information "at or near the scene of a crime" the Government rejected them.[135] This was therefore to adopt the C.L.R.C.'s original scheme, in turn recommended by the Working Group who regarded it as essential to allow adverse inferences to be drawn from the silence of suspects prior to arrival at the police station in order to deprive them of the chance of thinking up a plausible explanation. Yet it was a curious anomaly in the thinking of the Working Group that whilst they adopted the basic C.L.R.C. scheme under which the failure to mention a fact later relied on had to be in the context of questioning if an adverse inference were to be drawn from the failure they mistakenly assumed that the police were in general forbidden to interview the suspect prior to his arriving at the police station and having the opportunity to consult a solicitor.[136] For suspects under arrest (or those whom an officer had decided to arrest) this did not become the rule until the 1991 revision of Code C, a prohibition which had not been anticipated in 1989 when the Working Group reported.[137]

Where outside a police station a person falls under suspicion but the officer has not yet decided to arrest him there is nothing to prevent the suspect from being interviewed under caution. (This is consistent with Code C11.1 which prohibits questioning outside the police station of persons who have been arrested or whom the police have decided to arrest.) Since it was the intention behind the Act that the

---

[134] Commons amendments No. 4 and 252: see 241 H.C. Deb., cols. 260 and 261; Lords amendment No. 37: see 556 H.L. Deb., col. 1418.

[135] 556 H.L. Deb., col. 1399, July 7, 1994; 248 H.C. Deb., col. 325, October 19, 1994, David Maclean, Home Office Minister.

[136] Report, para. 73. They may have believed that although there was no express prohibition on questioning of arrested suspects outside the police station in the original version of Code C it was actually implicit since the Code was designed to ensure that arrested suspects were protected by the right to a solicitor and tape-recording, facilities only available at the police station. Such an interpretation was belied by the weight of authority: see *Wolchover and Heaton-Armstrong on Confession Evidence*, p.183.

[137] They may have been intending to recommend that adverse inferences might be drawn from the silence of suspects who were being questioned under caution *prior to* arrest or in furtherance of the proper and effective conduct of a search under Code C10.1 and 11.1A in the 1991 and 1995 versions.

suspect should not have an opportunity without cost for delaying any explanation until he can think up or polish up a plausible story it is in these circumstances that the suspect's failure prior to arrest to mention a fact relied on in proceedings may count against him. Supporting the Government Lord Taylor gave as the classic sort of example in which an inference might reasonably be drawn that where a man found in the garden of a house with a bag of tools remains silent when asked under caution to account for himself but at trial explains that he is a carpenter who had gone to the wrong address.[138] In the view of one commentator section 34 is intended to deal with circumstances "which objectively and inexorably call for an explanation from the suspect and which clearly fall short of an arrest situation," the situation in Lord Taylor's example being one which in the commentator's view obviously "calls out" for an explanation at the scene.[139] Under the Act an inference may be drawn if the fact was one which in the circumstances existing at the time the suspect might reasonably have been expected to mention. It is not clear whether in pre-arrest street encounters an expectation can only be reasonable if it is "inexorable".

In any event, the scope for the drawing of adverse inferences in these circumstances is likely to be narrow. There will be no tape-recording of the exchanges and unless the interview is being conducted by prior arrangement, for example at the suspect's home or place of work, it is unlikely that a suspect will have his solicitor in attendance to keep notes and offer support. (Suspects who are stopped in the street by police searching for the perpetrator of a very recent robbery rarely happen to have their solicitor with them at the time.) It is significant that in *Argent*[140] Lord Bingham C.J. acknowledged that good reasons for making no comment might be the fear that what was said would not be fairly recorded or a desire to say nothing before taking legal advice. Furthermore, it is envisaged that in street encounters the police would not be asking many questions of a suspect before deciding to make an arrest, so that the scope for alerting him to relevant matters which required explanation would be narrow. (On the other hand, it might be thought that the carpenter in the garden would hardly need to be told why his conduct was suspicious in order for him to be expected to give an account of himself on the spot.)

(d) *Questioning elsewhere than at a police station (or other authorised place of detention) of suspects under arrest or whom the police have decided to arrest*

Although the Government clearly intended the legislation to embrace failure to mention a fact later relied on where the failure occurred prior to the arrested suspect's arrival at the police station, the scope of circumstances in which subsections 34(1) and (2) will bite on such failure will be rather marginal. This is because under those subsections adverse inferences are restricted to failure *on being questioned under caution* and Code C11.1 provides that a suspect who is under

---

[138] 555 H.L. Deb., col. 520, May 23, 1994.

[139] Jennings, "Resounding Silence," *supra*, p.726, citing *Murray* v. *D.P.P.* (1993) 97 Cr.App.R. 151, H.L., at p.160, *per* Lord Slynn of Hadley.

[140] [1997] 2 Cr.App.R., at p.33.

arrest or whom it has been decided to arrest must not in general be interviewed about the offence for which he is under arrest, or is about to be arrested, except at the police station or other authorised place of detention (where all the relevant safeguards apply, notably opportunity for access to a solicitor and tape-recording of interviews) or outside the police station in certain defined categories of special urgency.

Where questioning properly takes place in the latter, exceptional, sort of case but the defendant's response is one of silence, the scope for the drawing of adverse inferences is likely to be narrow. There will be no tape-recording of the exchanges nor any opportunity to take legal advice and Lord Bingham's reasons for saying nothing, *i.e.* the fear of not being accurately recorded or a desire to say nothing without first taking legal advice, will be applicable here too.[141]

If the police wrongly conduct questioning of a suspect under arrest outside the police station, for example under the pretext of asking questions in the course of a search, or if they deliberately defer making an arrest in order to avoid the protective requirements of Code C[142] the resulting answers or significant silence would presumably be liable to exclusion under section 78 of the Police and Criminal Evidence Act 1984 in the normal way.[143]

There is a weight of authority that questioning for the purposes of P.A.C.E. is not less an interview for its brevity or apparent informality and an admission obtained by one question, which was itself a response to a spontaneous remark by the accused, has been held to constitute an interview.[144] It will follow that one question asked after an arrest will be improper and the fact that it was asked and the accused made no response will be liable to discretionary exclusion.

(e) *"Validation interviews" (P.A.C.E. Code C11.2A)*

The problem with allowing even the relatively limited scope for the suspect's silence outside the police station to count against him is that it affords the police the convenient opportunity of making a false allegation that the suspect failed to mention an exculpatory fact later relied on. At the police station the suspect's silence can be tape-recorded but with no tape-recording outside the police station the danger of false attribution of silence is manifest. The danger was stressed with much force by Lord Taylor who was instrumental in securing the innovation in Code C of what he termed a "validation interview."[145] Building on a recommendation of the Royal Commission on Criminal Justice, paragraph C11.2A of the 1995 edition

---

141 *ibid.*

142 In *Maynard* (1998) unreported, C.A. 97/3255/W3, April 2, the Court of Appeal deprecated tactical deferral designed to circumvent P.A.C.E. safeguards. See also *Khan* [1993] Crim. L.R. 54, CA; *Raphaie* [1996] Crim.L.R. 812, CA; *Batley* v. *D.P.P.* (1998) *The Times*, March 5, D.C. If a police officer "persists in his questioning, beyond the point it is necessary for his purpose at that time, it may be that the protection of the Code is invoked": *Weekes* (1993) 97 Cr.App.R. 222, at p. 227, C.A.

143 See *Argent* [1997] 2 Cr.App.R. 27, at p.31, *per* Lord Bingham C.J.

144 *Ward* (1994) 98 Cr.App.R. 337. See generally *Wolchover and Heaton-Armstrong on Confession Evidence*, pp. 166-168.

145 556 H.L. Deb., cols. 1400 *et seq.*, July 7, 1994 (3rd Reading).

provides that at the beginnning of an interview carried out in a police station, the interviewing officer, after cautioning the suspect, must put to him any significant statement or silence (i.e. failure or refusal to answer a question or failure or refusal to answer it satisfactorily) which occurred before the start of the interview, must ask him whether he confirms or denies that earlier statement or silence and whether he wishes to add anything.[146] This will not, of course, prevent false attribution but it will afford a subsidiary advantage, as Lord Taylor argued:[147]

> "Inferences will be susceptible of being drawn from silence at the scene of the crime but only after compliance with a requirement to validate what was said or not said at the first formal interview in the police station. If there is a conflict of evidence, or allegation of malpractice, then this will be identified as a material issue at that very early stage in accordance with one of the Royal Commission's key objectives: that the issues should be highlighted as early as possible."

In other words, the admissibility of the earlier significant silence will be put at risk by the failure to comply with C11.2A.

(f) *Silence upon pronouncement of arrest*

Since the mere pronouncement of the formalities of arrest is clearly not "questioning under caution" sections 34(1) and (2) create no licence to draw an adverse inference from the failure of the suspect on arrest to mention a fact relied on at trial. Common law principles on the effect of silence are preserved by section 34(5). Had the time-hounoured form of caution been retained for use on arrest it is arguable that this might have meant that on the authority of such decisions as *Tune*[148] and *Ryan*[149] it would have continued to be acceptable for adverse comment short of an express invitation to infer guilt to be made on the defendant's failure at the point of arrest to mention a fact relied on at trial, even if it were shortly afterwards mentioned during questioning at the police station. (Necessarily, the fact which the arrested person might have been expected to mention, and on failure to do which might have been made the subject of adverse comment, would have been limited to an intimation of the bare bones of the defence.) Granted that informing the suspect on his arrest that he may be prejudiced by his failure *when questioned* (that is, later) to mention a fact relied on at trial is not additionally saying, at least technically speaking, that he can remain silent *now* without damaging any defence he raises at trial. However, stressing the consequences of a failure later (specifically at the questioning stage) implies a contrast with the position now and is likely to induce a belief that the suspect can safely opt to say nothing *for the time being.* To permit adverse comment on silence at arrest (albeit short of an express invitation to

---

[146] As originally urged by Wolchover and Heaton-Armstrong, *N.L.J.*, March 23, 1990, at p.408.
[147] 556 H.L. Deb., at col. 1400, 3rd Reading.
[148] (1944) 29 Cr.App.R. 162.
[149] (1966) 50 Cr.App.R. 144.

infer guilt), on the authority of the earlier cases, would therefore render the new form of caution misleading and unfair. Moreover, even had the old form of caution been retained for arrest, it would probably also now fall foul of the Human Rights Act 1998 for a court to follow the decisions in *Tune* and *Ryan*.

(g) *Silence on being charged*

Section 34(1(b) provides for inferences to be drawn from the accused's failure, on being charged with an offence or officially informed that he might be prosecuted for it, to mention a fact relied upon in proceedings for the offence. There are two concerns which potentially arise out of this. The police are not obliged to interview persons detained for inquiries under P.A.C.E. and a court may have to determine whether, there having been no interview, it is appropriate to permit an inference to be drawn from the defendant's silence when charged. It has been suggested that in exercising its discretion the court would take in account the fact that the defendant had been denied an opportunity to deal with allegations in detail and would deprecate a deliberate attempt to invoke section 34 in relation to charge by refraining from conducting an interview.[150]

The second potential concern arises from the fact that defendants are often formally charged in the absence of a solicitor and it has been argued[151] that an adverse inference drawn from silence at the point of charge would fly in the face of the right to legal advice and the decision of the European Court of Human Rights in *Murray* v. *United Kingdom*.[152] There may be some merit in this complaint because, as distinct from the P.A.C.E. prohibition on interviews in the absence of a legal representative where one has been requested[153] there is no P.A.C.E. rule prohibiting the police from charging a detained person in the absence of a solicitor where consultation with a solicitor has been requested.

(h) *Initial non-mention of fact mentioned in subsequent interview*

It may happen that a suspect on being questioned under caution in the street prior to arrest makes no mention of a particular fact on which he later relies at his trial, but then, on being interviewed formally at the police station, mentions it for the first time. It seems logical to assume that the earlier failure cannot be redeemed by the later mention, provided that it would have been reasonable to expect the fact to have been mentioned at that earlier stage.

(i) *Non-mention in police station interview of fact mentioned on arrest*

As distinct from delayed mention it may be that on initial detention in the street the defendant mentioned the relevant fact, but then on being questioned in the police station declined to answer. In Northern Ireland the provision equivalent to section

---

150 Jennings, "Resounding Silence," *supra*, p.726.

151 Raised by Michael Mansfield Q.C. and Anthony F. Jennings, "The right to silence in criminal proceedings," Practical Research Papers, Sweet and Maxwell, 1997, p.7.

152 (1996) 22 E.H.R.R. 29; see generally Chapter 4.

153 Code C6.6.

34 has been held to apply to such a case,[154] an approach which coheres with the prevailing view of the Court of Appeal[155] that it may be a proper infererence from silence that the defendant wished to avoid subjecting his account to critical scrutiny. However, in England it has been held that in such a situation section 34 does not apply,[156] although the decision in question predates the stage by which it had become settled that that particular inference was a permissible one.

(j) *Section 34 applies even where fact relied on comes as no surprise to the prosecution*

If the primary purpose of the section is to encourage suspects to intimate important facts relevant to their defence at an early stage in order to allow the police an opportunity of investigating it the section arguably ought not to be invoked where the fact withheld until trial comes as little surprise to the prosecution. In a Northern Ireland trial it was contended that the provision was intended to combat ambush defences and therefore could have no application where it was obvious from the outset that a defence of innocent presence near the scene of the crime was likely to be raised.[157] The submission was rejected and not renewed on appeal. This is consistent with the section having a wider purpose than that of facilitating the investigation. Thus, if the purpose of the section is to encourage defendants to submit their account to early scrutiny and to penalise defendants who are reluctant to do so, it should be immaterial whether or not the prosecution were able clearly to anticipate the defence case.

(k) *Questioning where police consider sufficient evidence exists for a successful prosecution: not questioning by "constable trying to discover whether or by whom the offence had been committed;" alternatively questioning excluded for impropriety*

The effect of Code C11.4 and 16.1 together provide that where the police consider that there is sufficient evidence to bring a successful prosecution, they must not delay charging a person in order to interview him, even if the reason for the delay is to afford him an opportunity to provide an explanation.[158] This was the view of the Court of Appeal in *Coleman, Knight and Hochenberg*[159] in which the police

---

[154] See *Averill* (1997) unreported, N.I.C.A., January 3, in which the appellant made an exculpatory statement on arrest but remained silent during the thirty seven interviews which followed.

[155] See p.75, *infra*.

[156] *Mason* (1996) unreported, C.A., April 2.

[157] *Fox and Sullivan* (1996) unreported N.I.C.A., July 2.

[158] C11.4 provides: "As soon as a police officer who is making enquiries of any person about an offence believes that a prosecution should be brought against him and that there is sufficient evidence for it to succeed, he should ask the person if he has anything further to say. If the person indicates that he has nothing more to say the officer shall without delay cease to question him about that offence . . ." C16.1 provides: "When an officer considers that there is sufficient evidence to prosecute a detained person, and that there is sufficient evidence of a prosecution to succeed and that the person has said all that he wishes to say about the offence, he should without delay . . . bring him before the custody officer who shall then be responsible for considering whether or not he should be charged. . . ."

[159] (1995) unreported C.A. 94/4814/X4.

considered that there was sufficient evidence to prosecute the defendant for fraudulent trading but that since they had been unable to trace him and had not yet heard his side of the story they interviewed him (as they told him) in order to give him an opportunity to say all that he wished to say about the allegation. Questioning in breach of this principle is not caught by section 34 because it is not questioning by a "constable trying to discover whether or by whom the offence had been committed." In *Pointer*[160] undercover police officers at a nightclub bought Ecstasy from the appellant who had been observed either supplying or discussing its supply on five occasions. The nightclub was raided and the appellant was arrested. He was interviewed and on legal advice answered no questions. The judge permitted the jury to be told of the fact that a no comment interview had taken place but not the details of the questions. On the *voir dire* the interviewing officer stated that before the interview he believed he had sufficient evidence for a prosecution to succeed and it was submitted that the jury ought not to have been told that a no comment interview had taken place. The Court of Appeal expressed the view that asking a person whether he has anything further to say in accordance with C.11.4, or conducting or continuing an interview in breach of that provision and C16.1, was not questioning for the purpose of discovering whether or by whom an offence has been committed within section 34 (1)(a). Accordingly, no adverse inference might be drawn under subsection (2) if the accused had failed to mention a fact subsequently relied on. However, the appeal was dismissed because the judge had directed the jury that it would not be right to draw any adverse inference and the conviction was not therefore unsafe.

The state of affairs in which the police have evidence sufficient for a prosecution to succeed is obviously distinct from that where the available evidence merely establishes a prima facie case.[161] It remains unclear which standard the Court of Appeal were applying in *Gayle*.[162] The appellant, an alleged crack-cocaine dealer, made sales to undercover officers, was arrested and interviewed, on legal advice answered no questions and at trial raised duress as his defence. The Court of Appeal professed to follow *Pointer* in quashing the conviction on the ground that the appellant should not have been interviewed as the police recognised that there was already by then sufficient evidence to prosecute and no adverse inference ought to have been permitted to be drawn. In *McGuinness*[163] it was held that C11.4 and C16.1 do not automatically apply to prohibit an interview where the evidence is merely sufficient to establish a prima facie case and that the question whether there is sufficient evidence for a prosecution to succeed must involve some consideration of any explanation given by the suspect, or of the fact that no such explanation has been forthcoming. A similar decision was reached in *Ioannou*.[164] In *Van Bokkum*

---

160 [1997] Crim.L.R. 676.

161 See *Wolchover and Heaton-Armstrong on Confession Evidence*, pp.193-196.

162 [1999] Crim.L.R. 502; (1998) 148 N.L.J. 1445; C.A. 975542Z5, February 17.

163 [1999] Crim.L.R. 318; C.A. 97/8570/W5. See *Criminal Law Week* 99/16/4 for criticism of the decision.

164 [1999] Crim.L.R. 586.

and others[165] the Court of Appeal said that in so far as *Gayle* could not be explained on its own facts they preferred the reasoning in *McGuinness* and *Ioannou*. However, the decision in *Gayle* is justifiable in terms of C11.4 and C16.1 if by "sufficient evidence to prosecute" the court assumed that the police believed that they had sufficient evidence to prosecute *successfully*. That this may well have been the court's thinking can be inferred from an assumption that the police would not normally be likely to level a charge in a serious case unless they were confident of success. It is on this basis that *Gayle* may not necessarily be in conflict with the later decisions. The reasoning in those cases is not the less compelling for the fact that, as has been noted, the court was not referred to *Coleman* and did not consider section 37(1) and (7) of the P.A.C.E. Act 1984, obliging a custody officer to determine whether there is sufficient evidence to charge, and if he so determines, to charge the defendant.[166]

Consideration of whether there is evidence sufficient for a successful prosecution is subjective so that if in the officer's judgment such evidence does not exist the Code provisions will not have been breached and section 34 may apply. Thus an officer whose mind is more open to persuasion can comply with P.A.C.E. and thereby keep alive the possibility of adverse inferences.[167] However, this does not mean that the court is bound to accept the officer's assertion and comparison may validly be made with an objective standard in order to determine if the officer's avowed opinion was genuine. There is a theoretical check on the subjective view of the interviewing officer in that the custody officer bears the duty of determining the sufficiency of evidence to charge and, if he considers that there is such sufficiency, to proceed to charge.[168] However, although the duty is apparently a continuing one, the impossibility in practice of maintaining a permanent watch on developments from minute to minute, means that an interviewing officer will enjoy a relatively free hand to decide when it is proper to terminate the interview.

(l) *Defence disclosure statement*

In *Hart and McLean*[169] the Court of Appeal suggested that the defence might be deemed to be relying on a fact contained in a written statement prepared in consultation with a solicitor and lodged with police after a formal "no comment" interview had concluded. Clearly, for section 34 to apply, the statement would have to be relied on in proceedings, that is, where it was adopted by the defence in the course of any submissions. It is open to question whether a defence disclosure statement required by the Criminal Procedure and Investigations Act 1996 to be served on the prosecution and on the court might amount to a statement of facts relied on for the purposes of section 34. It has been argued that since it merely

165 (2000) unreported C.A. 199900333/Z3, *et seq*., March 7.

166 Anthony F. Jennings, "Recent developments in the law relating to the right to silence," *Archbold News* June 9, 1999, 5, at p.7.

167 Birch, [1999] Crim.L.R., at p.781.

168 P.A.C.E. Act, s.37(7).

169 (1998) unreported, C.A. 23/04/1998, April 23; [1998] 6 *Archbold News* 1.

provides advance notification of the defence which will be called, permitting different inferences if a different defence is put forward it should not be available to the prosecution to bolster up their case.[170] If a statement could be used to that end it would in many cases prevent the defence from making no case submissions. In any event, the Director of Public Prosecutions has given a public undertaking that defence statements will not be used for the purposes of section 34.[171]

(5) Nature of proper inferences

(a) *Problems in identifying proper inferences*

Beyond sanctioning "such inferences as appear proper" section 34 offers no definition of the nature of the possible inferences which Parliament may have had in mind. Obviously, the Act primarily contemplates adverse inferences; it would hardly have required legislation to licence favourable ones. A limited sense in which an inference may be said to be adverse is that it diminishes the credibility of the defendant's exculpatory assertion in consequence of its lateness. On the other hand an inference may be more ambitious, conceivably involving a finding that by failing to tender the exculpatory account given at trial the suspect was tacitly accepting the truth of the allegation.[172] The Judicial Studies Board specimen direction may have sanctioned the more permissive approach.[173] The jury are told that they may take the silence into account as "some additional support" for the prosecution case, presumably implying direct support as distinct from indirect support by way of undermining the credibility of the defence facts. Direct support can only occur by an inference of tacit admission.

Broadly, the approach of the courts has been to allow the jury a free hand in construing silence, provoking criticism for encouraging speculation under the guise of applying common sense.[174] A worse criticism is that the licence to speculate is one-sided. A variety of possible reasons for silence consistent with innocence may explain the defendant's silence and from the general burden of proof the Court of Appeal has extrapolated the rule that the jury must be instructed that they may draw

---

170 See Phillip Plowden, "Silence at the police station," *New Law Journal*, October 30, 1998, at p.1600.

171 Addressing the joint British Academy of Forensic Sciences and Criminal Bar Association seminar on disclosure, December 1, 1999.

172 It has been noted that no consensus exists between commentators on whether the section is confined to the issue of credit or allows a direct inference of guilt: Mirfield, *Silence, Confessions and Improperly Obtained Evidence*, Oxford 1998, at p.258.

173 See Birch, [1999] Crim.L.R., at p.776.

174 See *e.g.* S. Easton, "Legal Advice, Common Sense and the Right to Silence," (1998) 2 E. & P. 109 (suggesting that the common sense approach of a jury is likely to be "unreliable, impressionistic and unsystematic") and E. Cape, "Sidelining Defence Lawyers: Police Station Advice after *Condron*," (1997) 1 E. & P. 386 (arguing that juries are being encouraged to speculate about the defendant's motives "frequently in the absence of any evidential basis to support a particular conclusion").

an adverse inference only if no favourable explanation rationally presents itself.[175] However, this safeguard may be more cosmetic than beneficent, since the defence are precluded from presenting possible alternatives other than evidentially. On the other hand, the direction may provide compelling support for the defence once an innocent explanation is adduced which is met by no counter-evidence. In such a case the combination of explanation and direction may prove too strong for an inherently speculative adverse inference. This seems to be the encouraging direction heralded by *Mountford*.[176] The appellant's answer to a charge of possession of Class A drugs with intent to supply was that they were in the possession of W, in whose flat the appellant was staying, and that the appellant was merely the prospective purchaser of drugs for his own use. His explanation for non-disclosure of this at interview was that he did not wish to "land W in trouble," having not yet at that stage been told that W was blaming him. The trial judge told the jury that it was open to them to decide whether to take account of the failure as some additional support for the prosecution's case. It was held that it was wrong for them to be "left to make what they could" of section 34 because there was no evidence on which they could rationally reject the appellant's reason for not mentioning the fact without first rejecting the truth of the fact itself, that W was guilty and the appellant was not. In other words, the section 34 issue begged the very question it was intended to resolve, that of the appellant's guilt.[177] The conundrum involved here has been neatly encapsulated in relation to trial silence by Jackson:

> ". . . no matter how strong the evidence, the court or jury is in a position to draw the 'proper' inference from silence only where it knows the reason for silence. Without knowledge of that reason, it would only seem safe to draw an inference of guilt where the trier of fact is already convinced of guilt on the basis of existing proof beyond reasonable doubt. But the inference then becomes merely an *ex post facto* rationalisation of what the trier of fact is already convinced of, and the provision becomes redundant."[178]

Since many, if not most, explanations for silence might be thought to be incapable in themselves of refutation, it was perhaps understandable that in *Hearne*[179] the Court of Appeal said that applying *Mountford* generally would have the result of emasculating the section and defeating the very purpose of section 34. To avoid being bound by *Mountford*, therefore, the court held that it was not necessarily to be considered to have general application, that it had been concerned with its own very

---

175 See *e.g. Condron* [1997] 1 Cr.App.R. 185 (as to which see generally, *infra*, p. 103); *Argent* [1997] 2 Cr.App.R. 27; *Daniel* [1998] Crim.L.R. 818. See also Birch, [1999] Crim.L.R., at p.776.

176 [1999] Crim.L.R. 575.

177 The decision was followed on virtually identical facts in *Gill* (2000) *The Times* August 17, C.A. No. 9907637, judgment July 21.

178 "Intepreting the Silence Provisions: The Northern Ireland Cases," [1995] Crim.L.R. 587, at p.600.

179 (2000) unreported, C.A. 99/4240/Z4, May 4, at para. 11.

particular facts and that it could not have been intended to have application in the present case. A comparison between the facts in *Mountford* and those in the present case may reveal the basis of the court's thinking. In *Mountford* the explanation given by the accused for not having mentioned at interview the fact relied on at trial was precise, explicit and straightforward and appeared incapable of being faulted without a finding that the defendant was guilty. In *Hearne*, an indictment for cocaine importation, the defence raised at trial was that the appellant believed he was merely involved in tobacco smuggling from the continent but he explained that he had not advanced this in interview because he realised by then that he had inadvertently involved himself in something much more serious and was afraid to put forward his defence. This was not developed further although possibly he was hinting that he had anticipated that proffering the tobacco explanation would invite further questions and would inevitably lead him into implicating other persons, so incurring the risk of reprisal. It is difficult to see any such risk in his expanding at trial on the basis for his fear. However, he appears not to have done so and it therefore remained conjectural and obscure. The reason the court gave for treating *Mountford* as inapplicable to *Hearne* was that although, as was assumed to be the case, the tobacco smuggling explanation must have been found to have been recently invented this:—

> ". . . did not of itself lead inevitably to the conclusion that the appellant was guilty of the offence. There may have been some other available explanation, perhaps disreputable, which was not offered either at interview or at trial."

Yet this could equally be said to apply to *Mountford* and fails to provide a distinguishing rationale. However, a rationale which does work is that an explanation is capable of rejection without reference to the issue of guilt if it is inherently improbable, obscure or vague, as in *Hearne*, or rebuttable by other evidence[180] (as where, on facts identical in all other respects to those in *Mountford*, the prosecution are in a position to prove that the appellant had been told that W was blaming him[181]). In many if not most cases the proffered explanation will not be susceptible to contradiction and the jury can only be sure that it is false if other evidence proves guilt. The example *par excellence* which comes to mind is staying silent on legal advice and *Mountford* would seem to be on all fours in this respect with observations considered later in *Argent*.[182]

We may now turn to considering specific adverse inferences which the courts have recognised.

---

[180] See J. Richardson, *Criminal Law Week*, 99/19/4.

[181] Birch, [1999] Crim.L.R., at p.778.

[182] [1997] 2 Cr.App.R. 27, see *infra*, at p.151, *et seq*.

(b) *Initial suggestion that an adverse inference is confined to that of subsequent fabrication*

In *Condron and Condron*[183] Stuart-Smith L.J., giving the judgment of the Court of Appeal, said that it was desirable to direct the jury that if, despite evidence offered to explain the defendant's silence on being questioned after caution, they concluded that the silence could only sensibly be attributed to the accused having subsequently fabricated the account relied on, they might draw such an adverse inference. This was an adaptation of the fifth of five essential directions which Lord Taylor C.J. had held in *Cowan*[184] should be given in relation to trial silence (three of the other four of which it was said in *Condron* should also be given in relation to section 34 silence). The compass of Stuart-Smith L.J.'s application of the fifth essential to section 34 cases initially occasioned an assumption that the only adverse inference capable of being drawn under section 34 was that the fact in question was not mentioned at interview because it was fabricated later. In the words of one commentator,[185] *Condron* was "for a while . . . clutched at by practitioners" in arguing that any other potential inference was inadmissible and they were fortified in this approach by the fact that the restrictive view was adopted in *Roble*[186] and *Nickolson*[187] and reiterated by Stuart Smith L.J. himself in *Samuel (David)*.[188]

In *Condron* the court conjectured that it would be open to the defence to attempt to rebut an inference of late invention by calling the accused's solicitor to give evidence that the accused had stated the relevant facts to him at the police station, and this would not involve a waiver of the privilege of lawyer-client confidentiality.[189] Had late invention been the only permissible inference that might be drawn this would have meant that a solicitor could pre-empt the operation of section 34 simply by taking from the client at the police station a contemporaneous proof setting out the account later given at trial and then confirming at trial that that version had been put forward prior to the interview.[190]

(c) *Inference that defendant was unwilling to subject his account to critical scrutiny*

Despite its clear enunciation in at least three reported appeal cases the restrictive approach was not consistently followed. In *Daniel*[191] the Court of Appeal held that a proper inference was not confined to that of subsequent fabrication. In an appropriate case, it would also be appropriate to direct the jury that if they concluded that the accused's reticence could only sensibly be attributed to his

183 [1997] 1 Cr.App.R. 185.

184 [1996] Q.B. 373.

185 Philip Plowden, "Silence at the police station," *New Law Journal*, October 30, 1998, 1598, at p.1599.

186 [1997] Crim.L.R.185.

187 [1998] Crim.L.R. 61, C.A. 97/3647/Z4.

188 (1997) unreported, C.A. 97/1143/Z2, May 12.

189 [1997] 1 Cr.App.R., at p.197, relying on *Wilmot* (1989) 89 Cr.App.R. 341 and confirmed in *Bowden* [1999] 1 W.L.R. 823, at p.827. See further, *infra*, p.176.

190 See D. Wright, "The Solicitor in the Witness Box," [1998] Crim.L.R. 44, at p.45; Plowden, *supra*; Pattenden, (1998) 2 E. & P., at p.161.

191 [1998] 2 Cr.App.R. 373.

unwillingness to be subjected to further questioning, or that he had not thought out all of the facts, or that he did not have an innocent account to give, they might draw an adverse inference. The court pointed out that the dicta in *Condron* were "apt to cover a reluctance to be subject to questioning and further enquiry"[192] but, as Mansfield and Jennings have astutely observed,[193] the court, in spite of examining *Condron* in some detail, did not refer to the passage in the judgment of Stuart-Smith L.J. in which he said:

> "However, it should be borne in mind that the inference which the prosecution seek to draw from failure to mention facts in interview is that they have been subsequently fabricated."[194]

The court also failed to consider *Nickolson* and its confirmation of this point.[195] In *Randall*[196] Evans L.J., without referring either to *Condron* or to any of the other cases on the same point, said that it was a permissible inference from silence on questioning under caution that an accused had already made up his account on the day of his interview, but did not wish it to be subjected to critical questioning and information.

The departure from *Condron* crystallised in *Beckles and Montague*[197] in which the Court of Appeal said that the remarks in *Condron* were made because it was a case dealing with an allegation of recent fabrication but that there was nothing in it to confine section 34 to cases of recent fabrication. The court added that were the position otherwise one of the purposes of section 34, namely the encouragement of speedy disclosure of genuine defences, would be defeated. The same approach was adopted in *McGuinness*[198] and in *Taylor.*[199]

In a further commentary by Jennings alone[200] it was pointed out that in none of the cases departing from *Condron* was the court aware that in *Samuel (David)*[201] Stuart-Smith L.J. said that the effect of *Condron* was that—

> ". . . the jury should be satisfied that the only explanation for failure to mention important facts in interview which were subsequently to be relied upon in evidence is that the evidence is a recent fabrication, and if the only sensible explanation of the failure to mention it is that it is a

[192] *ibid.*, at p.383.
[193] Mansfield and Jennings, *supra*, p.6.
[194] [1997] 1 Cr.App.R. 185, at p.197.
[195] See Mansfield and Jennings, *supra*, p.7.
[196] (1998) unreported, C.A. 9705960 X4.
[197] (1998) unreported, C.A. 97/4261/Z4, May 7.
[198] [1999] Crim. L.R. 318, C.A. 97/8570/W5.
[199] [1999] Crim.L.R. 75 (murder; alibi of drug dealing elsewhere given to solicitor at time of interview; held it was for the jury to determine appellant's motivation in withholding it from police).
[200] Anthony F. Jennings, "Recent developments in the law relating to the right to silence," *Archbold News*, June 9, 1999, 5, at p.7.
[201] (1997) unreported, C.A. 97/1143/Z2, May 12.

recent fabrication, then the jury can properly draw the inference against the accused."

Not content to confine their criticism of the broader approach to its breach of precedent, Mansfield and Jennings venture to offer, with some ingenuity, a substantive justification for the *Condron* position. They point out that section 34(1)(a) speaks of a failure "to *mention* any fact," as opposed to failure to provide details of any fact and although expressed tersely the undoubted thrust of their argument is that the section in terms imposes no obligation to furnish the police with material in sufficient detail to render it capable of being subjected to critical examination and scrutiny during the interview. The section can therefore contemplate no inference of a motive to avoid such an exercise. The argument may be coupled with the submission of the commentators[202] that the intention of the section is to create an obligation to disclose only matters of importance subsequently relied upon and they cite in support examples of the type of facts which the C.L.R.C. had in mind, all of which were facts central to a defence, such as alibi or consent in a rape case.[203] Moreover, they note that Lord Taylor C.J. said at Committee stage on the Bill that the section did not apply to "any old fact."[204]

In contrast with the perspicacity of the main argument Jennings in his later commentary adds the somewhat opaque suggestion that the line of authorities culminating in *Beckles* confused the motivation for refusing to answer questions with the inference that can be drawn from such a refusal,[205] a distinction the relevance of which it must be said remains elusive, at least to the present writer.

The argument advanced by Mansfield and Jennings provides an explanation as to why Stuart Smith L.J. appeared to restrict the nature of an adverse inference to late fabrication when the "fifth essential" in *Cowan* stipulated that the jury were to be told that if, despite any evidence relied on to explain the defendant's refusal to go into the witness box or in the absence of any such evidence, the jury concluded the silence could only be attributed to the defendant's having no answer, *or none that would stand up to cross-examination*, they might draw an adverse inference.[206] Clearly the situation at interview differs markedly from that at trial when the defendant would be expected, in the witness box, to face cross-examination in detail. If the correct analysis of section 34 is that the suspect is only obliged to disclose the bare bones of his defence, he would not be obliged to face questioning in detail at that stage and so would not have a motive for avoiding it.

---

202 Mansfield and Jennings, p.3.

203 *Evidence (General)*, 11th report, June 1972, Cmnd. 4991, para. 33.

204 555 H.L. Deb., col. 520, May 23, 1994. See further p.96, *infra*.

205 [1999] 5 *Archbold News*, at p.8.

206 The idea of an explanation which would not stand up to scrutiny appears to have originated with Lord Mustill in *Murray* v. *D.P.P.* (1993) 97 Cr.App.R. 151, at p.155.

(6) Determining whether in the circumstances existing at the time the accused could reasonably have been expected to mention the fact relied upon in his defence

Where the accused relies upon a particular fact in his defence, having made no mention of it when questioned under caution, charged or given notice of possible prosecution, it is the fundamental requirement of section 34 that an adverse inference may not be drawn against the accused for not having mentioned the fact at that stage unless it is one which in the circumstances existing at the time he could reasonably have been expected to mention.[207] As stated earlier it is for the jury to resolve this question.[208] Whether the accused could reasonably have been expected to mention the fact is dependent on a number of considerations.

(a) *Subjective test*

It has already been observed that the avowed purpose behind the legislation was to prevent professional criminals from exploiting the criminal justice system by sheltering behind the right to silence. Speaking in the House of Lords in support of the silence provisions in the Bill Lord Taylor said that they were "not directed towards the vulnerable or towards the common run of first offenders,"[209] and this is reflected in the structure of section 34 and in the way it has been applied. Thus, according to Pattenden, the reference in the section to the term "the accused" points to a subjective test,[210] an interpretation followed by Lord Bingham C.J. giving guidance in *Argent*[211] on the approach to be adopted in determining whether the fact which the accused had failed to mention when questioned under caution was a fact which, in the circumstances existing at the time, he could reasonably have been expected to mention when so questioned. In Lord Bingham's view the relevant time was the time of questioning and account had to be taken of all the relevant circumstances existing at the time. The expression "in the circumstances" ought not, he said, to be construed restrictively; matters such as time of day, the defendant's age, experience, mental capacity, state of health, sobriety, tiredness, personality and legal advice were all part of the relevant circumstances. These were only examples of the things which might be relevant. When reference was made to the accused, attention was directed not to some hypothetical reasonable accused of ordinary fortitude but to the actual accused with such qualities, knowledge, apprehensions and advice as he was shown to have had at the time. They were questions for the jury to resolve in the exercise of their collective common sense, experience and understanding of human nature.

---

207 The precondition does not apply to ss.36 or 37. It has been suggested that this is because it is "considered reasonable *per se* to expect a person found in the relevant circumstances to respond": P. Mirfield, *Silence, Confessions and Improperly Obtained Evidence*, Oxford University Press, 1997, p.262. See also R. Pattenden, (1998) 2 E & P 141, at p.150, n.65.

208 See *supra*, p.61, citing *Argent* [1997] 2 Cr.App.R. 27, at p.32.

209 555 H.L. Deb., col. 521, May 23, 1994.

210 [1995] Crim.L.R., at p.604.

211 [1997] 2 Cr.App.R. 27, at p.33.

(b) *Awareness of the fact not mentioned*

It is self-evident that for an adverse inference to be drawn under section 34 the accused must have been aware of the existence of the fact on which he is relying in his defence and, as the Working Group recommended[212] the jury must clearly be instructed to consider whether the accused had such knowledge before they can draw an inference against him from the fact that he made no mention of it. So, for example, where the defendant on being questioned raised alibi, stating that he was at a certain public place at the material time, but made no mention of the fact that a certain witness called at the trial had seen him there, it would be necessary to establish whether or not, on the facts of the sighting, the accused for his part would have been aware of the witness's presence on the same occasion. (In cross-examination of the witness it may emerge that the accused must have seen him—perhaps the witness avers it was a mutually acknowledged encounter—and this may give the lie to the accused's protestations to the contrary.)

(c) *Unawareness of incriminating fact requiring explanation*

A fact relied on by the accused in his defence may serve to furnish an explanation of the facts upon which the allegation is based. It is important to distinguish the situation in which the accused does not mention an exculpatory fact (amounting to such an explanation) until his trial because he does not become aware of its existence until that stage (for example, the fact that there is a witness to his alibi) from the situation in which the accused proffers an explanation of incriminating facts for the first time only at his trial because those facts were not known to him at the time he was questioned under caution, not because he did not become unaware of the exculpatory fact until the trial stage. The nature of the excuse for silence in both situations is the same—lack of awareness—but in the one case it is the exculpatory fact which is not known, whereas in the second case it is ignorance of the incriminating facts which make the explanation pertinent.

That it is absurd (rather than that it can be reasonable) to expect the accused to have given an explanation for some incriminating fact the existence of which was not at the time known was acknowledged in effect by the Court of Appeal in *Nickolson*,[213] an indictment against the appellant for indecently assaulting his step-daughter. In interview he was told by police that they would be looking for evidence of seminal staining but they did not mention staining on the child's nightdress, because at that stage none had been detected. Denying at trial any indecency the appellant admitted masturbating in the child's bedroom and in the bathroom and in chief suggested that she might have picked up staining from the lavatory seat. The judge suggested to the jury that that explanation could reasonably have been mentioned in the interview and gave a section 34 direction. It was held that this was erroneous because at the time of the interviews it was not known that there was seminal staining on the nightdress, which was why the appellant was not asked to

212 Report, para. 65 and Appendix D.

213 [1999] Crim.L.R. 61, C.A. 97/3647/Z4, originally reported as *N.* See also *Bowers* [1998] Crim.L.R. 817; 163 J.P. 33.

explain it. (It was also held that at no stage in his defence did the appellant assert a fact. His proferred explanation in evidence was not and could not be construed as a fact.) In the circumstances there was a real possibility that his conviction was secured in part by the drawing of an adverse inference following an erroneous direction.

Another decision in point is *B.(M.)*[214] The appellant was convicted of three counts of raping his "quasi-stepdaughter" and two counts of unlawful sexual intercourse involving her schoolfriend. In interview he had been asked if he knew why the complainants should have made up allegations of rape and, and said he did not. In her evidence the quasi-stepdaughter said she hated him because he was living with her mother, because he was coming between her and her mother and because her mother was not putting her first. In his evidence the appellant conceded said he did think that she was jealous of the relationship but it was held that the judge had been wrong to direct the jury that they could draw an adverse inference from the fact that the appellant had failed to mention the motive in interview. It was submitted on his behalf that in interview he was being asked to speculate and was not being asked a question as to any fact relied on in his defence but in the view of the Court of Appeal this was not a complete answer. Adopting the commentary of Professor Birch in her commentary on *Nickolson* in the *Criminal Law Review* the court pointed out that if the appellant did not know that the complainant was jealous of the relationship at the time of the interview, he could not have been expected to mention it as a "fact." On the other hand, if at the time of the interview he did know that the complainant bore him a grudge, and his knowledge was based on some specific incident such as a heated argument over discipline, then such a motive would be based on fact and he could reasonably have been expected to mention it. In the judgment of the court there had been no attempt to explore with the appellant when it was that he first realised that the complainant might have a motive of jealousy and hatred[215] and so there could be no basis for an inference. Accordingly, the jury should have been directed to draw no adverse inference from the fact that the appellant had not mentioned the jealousy motive in interview.[216]

(d) *Appreciation of relevance of exculpatory fact*

It is not merely the accused's awareness of the inculpatory fact which will determine whether it is reasonable to expect him when questioned to have mentioned a counter-fact or to have proferred an explanation for incriminating facts. That question will also depend on the accused's appreciation of the relevance of the counter-fact or explanation to the incriminating fact and although in many, if not most, cases this may be assumed in some cases the association may have been far from obvious.

---

214 (1999) unreported C.A. 98/06635/X4, November 4.

215 The prosecution certainly had some basis for pursuing the issue in cross-examination of the appellant because the complainant had said in evidence that she had entered the bedroom while the appellant and her mother were having sexual intercourse and had called her mother a slag and a tart.

216 *McGarry* [1999] 1 Cr.App.R. 377.

(e) *Appreciation of the importance of mentioning the relevant fact*

Not only must the suspect clearly appreciate the relevance of the fact in question but must also appreciate the importance of mentioning it and this may require him to be given some form of caution. Of course, if it is a natural impulse for the innocent to mention facts relevant to their defence it follows that there will be no need to warn them of the prejudicial consequences of failing to do so. According to the axiom on which the new legislation is based the innocent suspect will naturally feel impelled, subject to the existence of counterveiling factors, to state any fact which he knows to be relevant, and this will be irrespective of any such warning. But without any warning that silence might be harmful to his case, the innocent suspect's natural urge to protest his innocence (and any material fact) may be outweighed by inhibiting urges equally if not more instrinsic to his nature, for example a shyness of authority figures, or by any number of extrinsic factors, for example a desire to protect a third party or a dislike of the police. Without such a warning it would be unfair to hold his silence against him because it might have been attributable to a belief that he could opt for silence at no cost.

(f) *The question of non-disclosure by the police of relevant matters*

In some cases the accused may clearly know of the incriminating fact which it would be reasonable to expect him, if innocent, to deny, giving the reasons, or to explain, and his appreciation of the relevance of an exculpatory fact to the inquiry may be obvious and need not be explained to him by the police. In other cases, there may be incriminating facts of which it is by no means certain he is aware, or his appreciation of the relevance to the allegation of some exculpatory fact within his knowledge may in other cases depend on the clarity with which it is drawn to his attention. In such cases the police may have to give the details.

The Working Group believed that to expect the police to disclose to the suspect details of their case, particularly when dealing with serious offences, might be highly damaging. The Government agreed.[217] As the Working Group pointed out,[218] the only disclosure which, at the time of their report, the police were obliged to make was that in accordance with Code C requiring the custody officer to inform a suspect of the reason for his detention before he was interviewed.[219] (Since 1995 Code D on identification has provided that a copy of the record of the description of the suspect as first given by a potential witness must be provided to the suspect or his solicitor before any procedures under the code are carried out.[220] Of the submissions received by the Working Group in favour of requiring the police to show more of their hand before they could reasonably expect a suspect to be more forthcoming suggestions ranged from telling the suspect why he was being

217 See Earl Ferrers, 555 H.L. Deb., col. 260, July 7, 1994 (3rd Reading).
218 Report, paras. 90-91.
219 C3.4. See *Wolchover and Heaton-Armstrong on Confession Evidence,* chap. 2, p.289.
220 D2.0.

questioned without giving any detail of the evidence against him so far available to giving him a written summary of the evidence against him.[221]

In the event, the statute as enacted contains no guidelines and adopts the Working Group scheme in imposing on the police no requirement to disclose to the suspect details of the case as a pre-condition for the drawing of inferences from his silence.[222] In the Commons at Third Reading an amendment was unsuccessfully moved to make it a condition for the application of section 34(1) and (2) that "the accused was told in ordinary language prior to being questioned by a constable about the offence . . . the facts available to any constable at the time supporting the accused's involvement in the offence."[223] At Lords Committee stage Lord Ackner unsuccessfully moved an amendment to similar effect, the terms of which made it a condition of the application of subsections (1) and (2) that "prior to the questioning or charge or notification of possible prosecution the person is informed of the purpose and nature of the questions he is asked."[224] For the Government, Earl Ferrers dismissed the explicit inclusion of the condition as unnecessary since the safeguard was implicit in the requirement of section 34(1) that the fact later relied on had to be one "which in the circumstances existing at the time the accused could reasonably have been expected to mention, when so questioned . . ."[225] There is certainly merit in this argument. Even without any explicit requirement to convey the relevant particulars of the offence, where the suspect is questioned in detail about the offence it is likely that the relevance of all the material points will be brought to his attention through the medium of the questions. If the police omit to touch on some aspect of the case which later proves relevant the suspect's silence on that matter could not reasonably be held against him unless it is found that he must have been aware of its relevance in spite of the police omission to deal with it. There will be some points the relevance of which the accused could not possibly have appreciated whilst in other cases there may be points the relevance of which must have been manifestly obvious to him from the course of the questioning or from the circumstances. The difficulty will lie in borderline cases, as to which Earl Ferrers suggested, "If the suspect failed to grasp what the police were driving at, and that is why he did not mention a point, he can of course make this perfectly clear at the trial."[226] A suspect may well have been aware of the relevance of a fact later relied upon in spite of the absence of any reference to it by the police during questioning. Indeed, there may be many circumstances in which the assumption can reasonably be made that the defendant did not need an express reference to the point by the police investigator in order to appreciate its relevance. Whether this was the case may be a matter for the jury to consider. For the avoidance of doubt and in order to increase the probability that the Act will bite, it will generally be prudent for the

221 Report, para. 90.
222 *ibid.*
223 Amendment No. 252, 241 H.C. Deb., col. 260, April 13, 1994 (3rd Reading).
224 554 H.L. Deb., col. 443, April 25, 1994 (2nd Reading); 555 H.L. Deb., cols. 496 and 498, May 23 (Committee stage); 556 H.L. Deb., col. 1390, July 7 (3rd Reading).
225 *ibid.*, col. 1396.
226 *ibid.*, col. 1395.

police to alert the suspect to the relevance of all the salient issues in the case. However, the application of the Act to a fact not mentioned by the defendant in interview but later relied on is not conditional on the police canvassing the issue in interview. It will follow *a fortiori* that the Act imposes on the police no requirement to disclose *all* the evidence that they have against an accused, as a condition for it to apply in relation to a particular fact not mentioned by the accused until trial. This issue has now been considered by the Court of Appeal in decisions which are discussed below.

After the 1994 Act came into force it was argued in Northern Ireland that unless there was full disclosure, the witness could not know whether there was a case that called for an explanation.[227] It has now been established that under section 34 there is no principle which justifies the defendant not answering questions in interview because of non-disclosure by the police and therefore no such principle precluding an adverse inference in such circumstances. In *Argent* the police made only partial disclosure of the evidence before questioning the appellant about a murder. The Court of Appeal dismissed the argument that no section 34 inference should have been drawn but did stress that one of the factors which a jury had to take into account in determining whether it was reasonable for a defendant to have remained silent in interview was the question whether a defendant had sufficient information to be able to put forward the facts on which the defence was based.[228]

The same point was made in *Roble*.[229] In reaffirming the principle that it was for the jury to determine whether the accused could reasonably have been expected to mention facts upon which he relied on in his defence, the Court of Appeal suggested that, although such considerations did not arise on the facts of the case, there might be good reasons for silence where, for example, the interviewing officer had disclosed little or nothing of the nature of the case against the defendant, and so the solicitor could not usefully advise the client. However, non-disclosure will not always furnish a good reason for non-participation in an interview, as the decision in *Kavanagh*[230] shows. The appellant was convicted of robbing an elderly lady in her home. His fingerprint and palm print were found inside her front door and in evidence at his trial he explained that he must have left them there when he had called at her home on an earlier occasion for an entirely innocent purpose. At the time of the interview the police had disclosed that his prints had been found in the house but they would not reveal where and for this reason and another his solicitor had advised him to make no comment in the interview. The trial judge ruled that the question whether this constituted a good reason not to draw an inference against the appellant was a matter for the jury and in referring in his summing up to the defendant's assertion that he had not answered questions because he had been so advised on the basis that he had not been told the whereabouts of the fingerprints the judge asked—

---

[227] *Murray* v. *D.P.P.* (1993) 97 Cr.App.R. 151.
[228] [1997] 2 Cr.App.R. 27, at pp.35-36.
[229] [1997] Crim.L.R. 449.
[230] (1997) unreported, C.A. 9503897/Z2, February 7. See also *Griffin* [1998] Crim.L.R. 418.

> "Does that mean he could not reasonably have been expected to mention his whereabouts on 28th July? Does that mean he could not reasonably have been expected to mention his innocent visit to [the victim's address]?"[231]

On appeal the defence criticised this comment in that it posed questions rather than gave directions but the Court of Appeal found no sustainable argument that the judge's remarks in relation to inferences under section 34 were other than appropriate and adequate. In the words of Rose L.J. "the reasonableness or otherwise of the police approach was pre-eminently a matter for the jury to consider, when deciding the wider question of the reasonableness of the defendant's failure to disclose material matters."

Silence in interview was not actually in issue in *Imran and Hussein*,[232] although the decision clearly has serious implications for the advice to be given by solicitors on whether the client should stay silent or answer questions. The appellants were video-taped during an attempted robbery but the police chose not to reveal the existence of the tape before the interview and after the appellants had given their accounts the tape was played to them and they were invited to explain the discrepancies. It was held that the police were not bound to disclose prior to interview all the evidence that they had assembled against an accused and that the trial judge was correct in saying that it would be "totally wrong to submit that a defendant should be prevented from lying by being presented with the whole of the evidence against him prior to the interview." The court made the somewhat banal point that the police should not actively mislead the defendant and also suggested that a legal adviser taken by surprise could always intervene to stop the interview while appropriate consultation with the client is held in private. These somewhat lame concessions do not spare the decision from involving a most unfortunate challenge to the right of suspects to receive proper legal advice, and the contrast with the spirit of *Roble* is stark. It may be tempting to conceal the existence of certain evidence in order to allow suspects to incriminate themselves by lying. However, the approval of such an attitude ought not to be adopted at the expense of undermining the right to fully informed legal advice. A solicitor can hardly be expected to give proper advice unless he has the benefit of the whole picture on which to give it; to deprive the solicitor of that information is to deprive the suspect of the right to proper legal advice. The essential advice in question is whether to say nothing or to answer (by way of denial or confession). Formerly, where solicitors could not be sure of having received full disclosure they would advise silence because it would not be possible to advise the client on the strengths of the case and therefore whether or not it would be worth making an immediate full confession in order to gain full credit in mitigation. It has been pointed out that the rôle which the solicitor use to have, bargaining for disclosure with silence as the fall-back position,

---

231 The comment is reminiscent of that by the trial judge in *Tune* (1944) 29 Cr.App.R. 162, except there the proffered excuse was that the appellant wanted to speak to a solicitor first (see *supra,* p.43).

232 [1997] Crim.L.R. 754, C.A.

has been completely eroded.[233] Since the 1994 Act now puts pressure on solicitors to advise clients to answer questions in interview the very least that should be guaranteed is that the advice is based on as complete a picture of the facts as it is possible to furnish so that the solicitor does not become the unwitting instrument of the prosecution. In *Imran and Hussain* a preliminary viewing of the tape might well have resulted in the appellants being advised to confess with the consequence that they might have pleaded guilty instead of protracting the proceedings with a self-defeating and time-wasting trial. (On the other hand, it might be observed that the incriminating nature of the video-tape coupled with the evidence of their lies did not apparently deter the accused from contesting the charge.)

The justification given by Rougier J. in *Imran and Hussain* for rejecting any duty on the police to grant disclosure as a condition for seeing the activation of section 34, that the defendant should not be prevented from lying by being presented with the whole of the evidence against him prior to interview, was coupled with the statement that the rules of disclosure did not apply at the investigation stage and that it was unrealistic to suggest that the police had to play cricket under the rigorous set of rules while the suspect can play under no rules whatever. One pre-eminent commentator, otherwise critical of the Act, was not troubled by the argument, suggesting that in the context of what amounted in the particular case to an unrealistic request for full disclosure it was not as "ominous [or] alarming" as might seem if quoted in isolation.[234] It is certainly true that the scheme of mutual discovery embodied in the Criminal Procedure and Investigations Act 1996 for trial is not mirrored in any statutory rules of disclosure for the investigation stage. However, the absence of formal rules of disclosure hardly affords a convincing justification for placing a suspect in a worse position than he would be at trial when often the most decisive moment for an accused occurs during the investigation. If a defendant on trial must not be induced to lie by the withholding of relevant evidence why should suspects not be protected by the same principle?

(g) *Substantial grounds for making an accusation*

For it to be reasonable to expect the accused to have mentioned a fact in question there must surely have been substantial grounds for suspecting him of guilt. The expectation that a relevant fact will be mentioned arises from the supposition that it is the natural response of the innocent to defend themselves. But on the assumption that the innocent are naturally impelled to do so the strength of that impulse would be proportionate to the strength of the accusation. The stronger the evidence, the greater will be the expectation of a defensive response. Conversely, it might be considered to be the perfectly natural reaction of a person on being told of the existence of an unsubstantiated rumour about him to treat it "with the contempt it deserves," that is, as not worthy of a reply. Thus, for an accused's silence to be

233 Birch, [1999] Crim.L.R., at p.779, citing Dixon, "Common Sense, Legal Advice and the Right of Silence," [1991] P.L. 233. Birch suggests that there is not much more an adviser can now do than bluff in the hope of obtaining reasonable discovery: [1999] Crim.L.R., at p.780.

234 Birch, [1999] Crim.L.R., at p.779.

imbued with evidential significance against him there would *at the very least* have to be reasonable grounds for *suspecting* him of guilt before it could be said that there was any expectation of a response. The Act gives evidential significance to omissions during questioning under caution. Under section 34(1) the failure to mention a fact relied on in subsequent proceedings can be significant when the defendant is questioned under caution, that is when supposedly under suspicion based on reasonable grounds. The statutory intent therefore is to permit an inference to be drawn against the defendant from a failure to mention at the level of reasonable suspicion, rather than in the first place at the next determinable notch above reasonable grounds for suspicion on the conceptual scale of weight, that is, possession of evidence establishing a *prima facie* case. (To have imposed the latter standard would not have involved a contradiction in terms. As we have seen, unrestricted questioning under caution can continue despite the acquisition of a *prima facie* case, since Code C11.4 permits suspects to be questioned under caution until the stage is reached at which the questioner believes that a prosecution should be brought and that a prosecution will succeed.)

The question has already been raised as to the impact of questioning under caution on section 34 where the caution is not strictly warranted because the interviewer is not yet in possession of evidence furnishing the necessary reasonable grounds for suspicion.[235] It would seem unlikely that the draftsman can have intended to licence an adverse inference where the caution was not in fact warranted because of the lack of reasonable grounds for suspicion. In *Argent* the Court of Appeal suggested that the trial judge had "overstepped the bounds of his judicial function" in directing the jury that no inference should be drawn where the appellant had apparently been interviewed initially on the strength of one anonymous phone call.[236] However, they must have been influenced by the fact that the judge had held the appellant's arrest to be lawful, so presumably grounds for suspicion did exist.

The basic problem with allowing inferences to be drawn in relation to a stage when there is yet comparatively little evidence is proof by process of boot straps. In the words of one commentator:

> "There would seem to be real risk of injustice . . . if a firmer prosecution case is constructed using evidence supplied by [the accused] under pain of inferences, at a time when very little evidence was in the bag. And if a firmer case is constructed without help from [the accused], there would seem a real risk that a jury will draw adverse inferences if it subsequently appears that crucial facts were withheld, not appreciating (or not accepting) that [the accused's] decision to wait and see if a prima face case was constructed was an acceptable tactic. Closer judicial control of the section might have alleviated these difficulties, but control has been sacrified on the altar of simplicity."[237]

---

[235] See p.62, *supra*.
[236] [1997] 2 Cr.App.R. 27, at p.29.
[237] Birch, [1999] Crim.L.R., at p.780.

(7) Tacit admission inferred from failure to mention

In the case of investigative stage silence sections 34(1) and (2) do permit an inference of tacit acceptance of the allegation, but only by an indirect route of reasoning and effectively only where the failure is to proffer any defence (as in a "no comment" interview). From such a failure it may be inferred that if the defence now relied on were true it would have been put forward at interview; since it was not proffered at that stage it was not then in the defendant's mind; it was not in his mind because it was invented later; at the interview he proferred no defence because none had occurred to him; none had occurred to him because he had no defence; he had no defence and by staying silent was acknowledging the truth of the allegation. But the essential condition is that there must have been a failure to mention the defence relied on at the trial. Without that condition there can be no inference of tacit admission under the two subsections.

(8) Facts relied on

(a) *Evidential assertion only or non-evidential challenge?*

Section 34 will not apply unless the defendant relies on a fact but it provides no definition of "fact." Is the term meant to be restricted to a witness box avowal of some historical event or state of affairs or is there a wider scope in contemplation, the mere assertion or suggestion of a fact put by or on behalf of the defendant in cross-examination of a prosecution witness or in argument?[238] Preferring the narrower meaning, that a triggering fact must be adduced in the form of evidence in the "technical sense," one commentator[239] has cited the view of the Criminal Law Revision Committee that a relevant fact would be "any definite statement made by a *witness* at the hearing and supporting the case for the defence."[240]

That a fact for the purposes of section 34 will not include a non-evidential assertion put to a witness in cross-examination appears to be the implication of the following passage from the judgment of Rose L.J., the Vice-President of the Court of Appeal, Criminal Division, in *Bowers*:[241]

> "A fact relied on may, in our judgment, be established by the accused himself in evidence, by a witness called on his behalf, or by a prosecution witness, in evidence in chief or in cross-examination."

---

238 The wider intepretation was advocated by Jackson, "Interpreting the Silence Provisions: The Northern Ireland Cases" [1995] Crim.L.R. 587, at p.590.

239 Mirfield, *Silence, Confessions and Improperly Obtained Evidence*, Oxford 1998, at pp. 252-253.

240 Eleventh Report, para. 33, emphasis supplied. This unambiguous restriction to evidential facts seems to render unwarrantable Birch's view that the Committee's definition "stops short of the clear statement of principle required: [1999] Crim.L.R., at p.782, n.76.

241 (1998) 163 J.P. 33; *The Times*, March 13, C.A. 97/2213/Y4.

If this definition is all-embracing it would exclude non-evidential assertions put to a prosecution witness in cross-examination. However, the definition may not have been intended to be exhaustive and the wider meaning certainly appears to have been favoured in *Hart and McLean*[242] in which the Court of Appeal suggested that reliance on a fact during the prosecution case could occur where the defence involved putting, in cross-examination of prosecution witnesses, a positive case on behalf of the defendant, *perhaps supported by documents*. Yet the court were clearly not implying that production of documents was a necessary condition for reliance to be established. In the absence of any finite statement from the Court of Appeal the ambit of the definition may therefore be regarded as undecided.

The weakness of the wider interpretation is arguably that it goes further than is necessary to give effect to the purpose of the section, which is to prevent the defendant from achieving an evidential advantage by adducing previously undisclosed and therefore potentially untested facts; if no such advantage is gained from merely suggesting a fact (or explanation) an adverse inference will be unnecessary.[243] Yet the argument fails to recognise that occasionally a significant tactical (as opposed to evidential) gain may be achieved merely through putting a contrary fact to a prosecution witness without necessarily adducing it in evidence later. Moreover, restricting the meaning of a fact to an evidential statement is likely to produce a significant anomaly where section-triggering reliance is contingent on the outcome of a particular line of cross-examination. Although such a condition was implied in *Bowers*, in the earlier case of *McLernon*[244] it was explicit. At submission stage the defence had relied on the defendant's belated written statement to police but the Northern Ireland Court of Appeal conjectured that another way in which the defence could be said to rely on a fact before the close of the prosecution case was where defence counsel suggested to a prosecution witness in the course of cross-examination a fact which assisted the accused *and the witness accepted it.* However, this would be precisely to contradict the purpose of the legislation which can hardly have been intended to bite where a fact favourable to the defence was conceded. If the fact is accepted by the witness and there is no basis for the prosecution resiling from the answer, the fact is no longer in issue and it cannot matter when it was first mentioned by the defendant."[245] In the words of one commentator, "[i]t is difficult . . . to envisage how an adverse inference could be drawn against a defendant from a fact elicited from a prosecution witness in circumstances where the prosecution are unable to challenge the truthfulness of the fact."[246]

---

242 (1998) unreported, C.A. 9703362 W4, April 23.

243 *ibid.*, at p.782.

244 [1992] N.I.J.B. 41, N.I.C.A., April 1, 1992, cited in Jackson, "Interpreting the Silence Provisions: The Northern Ireland Cases," [1995] Crim.L.R. 587, at pp.589-590.

245 See *Wolchover and Heaton-Armstrong on Confession Evidence*, para. 5-088.

246 Anthony Jennings, "Recent developments in the law relation to the right to silence," *Archbold News*, June 5, 1999, 5 at p.6.

(b) *Suggesting an hypothetical explanation*

When we speak of suggesting some fact to a witness this may be no more than a polite or diffident means of asserting it, or, as insinuation, its intent may be more hostile. Either way, it will be tantamount to an avowal by way of challenge, which, as we have seen, may or may not be capable of triggering the section. There is, however, a clear distinction between the suggesting of a fact in the sense of putting it to a witness in cross-examination and the tentative suggestion of an exculpatory explanation for facts which the prosecution contend proves guilt circumstantially. That a mere hypothesis consistent with innocence and unsustained by any factual avowal will not activate the section appears to have been the approach of the Court of Appeal.[247] In *Nickolson*,[248] the facts in which were set out earlier, the court pointed out that for an explanation to be caught by the section it had to be factually based. The section had to be confined to its express terms and the provision at trial of an explanation which was no more than something in the nature of a theory, a possibility or speculation did not constitute a fact. It has been hinted that the defendant's suggestion that the staining on the nightdress might have come from the lavatory seat may have gone beyond an hypothetical conjecture, amounting in reality to an assertion of fact.[249] In *Nickolson* the court noted the contrast between the expression "fact relied on" in section 34(1)(a) and the reference to "something which you later rely on" in the words of the caution administered to suspects under Code C10.4. The pronoun "something" would seem to be synonymous with "fact" rather than, say, an explanation but the exact statutory wording was avoided in the caution apparently in the forlorn hope of making it more intelligible.[250]

(c) *Testing evidence without intentionally establishing facts*

The Northern Ireland courts developed a distinction between cross-examination establish-ing a positive fact and that designed to show that a witness was lying or mistaken.[251] If the advocate stepped over the wrong side of the line, the provisions would be triggered. However, even here there is a potential semantic problem. A deficiency in evidence exposed or underlined by cross-examination or argument is arguably a "fact." The implications of this under section 34 are that if the defendant makes no comment on the obvious shortcomings in a witness's description of the culprit when the police read it over to him in interview and if a demonstration by his counsel as to the *fact* of that weakness amounts to reliance on a fact within the meaning of the Act this could mean that the simple fact of the defendant's "failure" to point it out to the police might paradoxically compensate for the weakness

---

[247] Birch describes the approach as "largely implicit:" *ibid*.

[248] [1998] Crim.L.R. 61, C.A. 97/3647/Z4, see *supra*, p.78. See also *Hart and McLean* (1998) unreported, C.A. 9703362 W4, April 23, and.*B.(M.)* (1999) unreported, C.A. 98/06635/X4, November 4.

[249] Birch, [1999] Crim.L.R., at p.783. Had that been accepted s.34 would still have been excluded because the existence of the stain was unknown at the time of the interview: see *supra*, p.78.

[250] See Birch, [1999] Crim.L.R., at p.783, citing R. Munday, "Inferences from Silence and European Human Rights Law," [1996] Crim.L.R. 370, at p.389.

[251] See E. Rees, *Counsel*, March/April 1995, at p.22.

highlighted by the demonstration. Yet it seems inconceivable that the Act can have been intended to have such an effect. "Fact" for present purposes can hardly include a *state of comparison or contrast* between conflicting evidential assertions.

(d) *Mere putting to proof is not reliance on a fact.*

Although section 34 may conveniently be described as penalising silence no sanctions are imposed by it on silence as such, however suspicious. If no facts are relied on at trial the section will have no application no matter how incriminating the interview silence might appear to the jury to be in the light of the evidence put to the suspect during questioning.

Putting a fact to a witness in cross-examination may amount to reliance for the purpose of the section (as to which see below). However, there is plainly a difference between that and probing the strength of the prosecution case without suggesting any fact on which the defence rely. It was perhaps stating the obvious when, during Lords Committee stage on the Bill, Lord Taylor C.J. pointed out:

> "If a defendant maintains his silence from first to last, and does not rely on any particular fact by way of defence but simply puts the prosecution to proof, then [section 34] would not bite at all."[252]

In *Devine*,[253] a Northern Ireland appeal case, it was held that merely probing the prosecution case, without suggesting any fact on which the defence relied would not be caught by the equivalent Northern Ireland legislation. The principle has since been affirmed by the English Court of Appeal[254] although it has been pointed out that a defendant cannot automatically preclude the drawing of an adverse inference by not giving evidence.[255]

That mere silence in interview without reliance during the prosecution case on a given fact may not be taken into account for the purposes of determining whether there is a case to answer was well illustrated by the judgment of the Court of Appeal in *Hart and McLean*.[256] A sloop arrived in Cornwall with a large quantity of cannabis resin on board and developed engine trouble. It was alleged that the appellant came down from London to "baby-sit" the smugglers. The main evidence against him was a piece of paper bearing telephone numbers linked to numbers called by the smugglers. The appellant gave a no comment interview on legal advice. It was submitted that there was no case to answer and the trial judge revealed that he would have upheld the submission were it not for the inferences to be drawn from the appellant's silence in interview under section 34. It was held that

---

252 555 H.L. Deb., col. 519, May 23, 1994.

253 (1992) unreported, N.I.C.A., May 13, cited in Jackson, "Interpreting the Silence Provisions: The Northern Ireland Cases," [1995] Crim.L.R. 587, at pp.589-590, and in Edward Rees,"The Right to Silence—to be Continued . . . ," *Counsel*, March/April 1995, at p.22. See also *Lamont* (1992) unreported, N.I.C.A., December 14, cited in Birch, [1999] Crim.L.R., at p.775, n.34.

254 *Moshaid* [1998] Crim.L.R. 420; *Bowers* [1998] Crim.L.R. 817; 163 J.P. 33, C.A. 97/2213/Y4.

255 *ibid.*

256 (1998) unreported, C.A. 9703362 W4, April 23.

in the present case he had been in error in rejecting the submission on account of the appellant's silence. Although section 34 entitled the court in a case to which the section applied to take failure to answer questions into account when determining a submission of no case, the subsection itself only applied where, when questioned, a defendant failed to mention any fact relied on in his defence, being a fact which in the circumstances existing at the time the accused could reasonably have been expected to mention. The appellant having relied on no facts, the section had no application. (It was further held that the judge had misapplied the section in his directions to the jury and the conviction was quashed, and a retrial ordered, because the other evidence, although just sufficient to constitute a prima facie case, was not very strong and the jury's verdict might well have been influenced by the direction.)

If a defendant is initially silent and then in a later interview puts forward a positive account it is assumed that if the defence case during proceedings merely involves putting the prosecution to proof the section would not apply for the purposes of a submission of no case even if the later account afforded a full defence.

(e) *Other channels of reliance*

It has been noted that in *Bowers*[257] the Court of Appeal stated that a fact relied on might "be established by the accused himself in evidence, by a witness called on his behalf, or by a prosecution witness, in evidence in chief or in cross-examination." It has been seen that restricting the meaning of "fact relied on" to an evidential statement is liable to produce to anomaly where such a fact is elicited by cross-examination of a prosecution witness. Similarly, complications are likely to be occasioned where a fact relied on arises from examination-in-chief of a prosecution witness or cross-examination of the defendant or defence witnesses.

(i) Fact adduced by prosecution witness in evidence in chief. Although *Bowers* sanctions reliance on facts adduced by a prosecution witness in chief, in the words of one commentator[258] "reliance cannot be assumed simply because the fact, if believed, tells in [the defendant]'s favour." There must clearly be some positive avowal of reliance. Thus, if a prosecution witness makes an assertion of fact during examination in chief and the defence seek to rely on that fact in arguing in favour of a no case submission, the defendant's silence at interview, or upon being charged, in relation to that fact (where it could reasonably have been expected to be mentioned by him at that stage) may be taken into account by the court in rejecting the submission. It is difficult to envisage a case in which this might occur but a hypothetical example may be instructive. Suppose in a case where identification is in issue a prosecution witness called to give evidence on a matter collateral to the issue of identification unexpectedly volunteers in chief an alibi for the defendant, although the defendant has not himself raised alibi. If during a submission of no case based on the weakness of the identification evidence the defence make no reference to the alibi volunteered by the prosecution witness, it will be irrelevant in terms of section 34. If, however, they seek to reinforce the argument going to the

[257] (1998) 163 J.P. 33; *The Times*, March 13, C.A. 97/2213/Y4.
[258] Birch, [1999] Crim.L.R., at p.784.

weakness of the evidence of identification by relying as a makeweight on the volunteered alibi, *Bowers* would appear to allow the failure to mention it to strengthen any evidence in favour of identification (provided the defendant could reasonably have been expected to mention the alibi at interview). If, in other words, a piece of exculpatory evidence which the defendant has not sought to adduce has fallen into his lap and he has the temerity to use it in reinforcing his submission based on the weakness of the identification evidence this may serve to support, instead of weakening, the identification. The effect will be that the alibi is self-cancelling if relied on. It is difficult to imagine that section 34 could ever have been intended to achieve such a result.[259] (On the other hand it is arguable that since the alibi evidence is not relevant in determining the existence of a case to answer it is incapable of being relied upon.)

(ii) Cross-examination of defendant. *Bowers* establishes that a fact can be relied on for the purposes of section 34 if it is elicited by cross-examination of the accused or of defence witnesses.[260] It has been suggested that by analogy with the authorities under the Criminal Evidence Act 1898, section 1(f)(ii), an adverse inference may be drawn if the defendant in the course of cross-examination volunteers new information but not if the defendant accepts an exculpatory fact held out by the cross-examiner in the hopes of trapping him.[261] This distinction appears to have been applied in the Northern Ireland case of *Fox and Sullivan*.[262] The defendant maintained silence in interview and, apparently in an attempt to get round the statutory provisions, answered only one question in chief, denying involvement in the murder, and only raised his defence of innocent presence in cross-examination. The trial judge, Lord Hutton C.J., rejected the argument that Article 3 of the 1988 Order (the provision corresponding to section 34) did not apply to the facts adduced in this way, on the ground that "any fact relied on his defence" includes a "central and important fact relied on by the accused under cross-examination, particularly where that fact would have been elicited in a normal examination in chief but defence counsel deliberately chose not to elicit it."

(f) *Assertion made outside a "no comment" interview: whether it can be a "fact" available for reliance*

Prior to a formal "no comment" interview or perhaps afterwards at a comparatively late stage in the original inquiry, for example, at the moment of being

---

259 *Cf.* the example given by Birch, *ibid.*, of evidence supporting a provocation defence volunteered by a prosecution witness in chief on which the defence studiously refrain from placing explicit reliance knowing that it must be put by the judge in accordance with *Cambridge* [1994] 1 W.L.R. 971. She submits this could not amount to reliance.

260 See *ibid*.

261 See Birch, [1999] Crim.L.R., at p.784. Section 1(f)(ii) subsection permits retaliatory cross-examination of the accused as to character where the nature of the defence involves casting imputations on the character of prosecution witnesses but the authorities preclude this where the imputation is elicited for the first time by a question asked in cross-examination of the accused: *Jones* (1909) 3 Cr.App.R. 67; *Beecham* [1921] 3 K.B. 464; *Baldwin* (1925) 18 Cr.App.R. 175; *Eidinow* (1932) 23 Cr.App.R. 145.

262 (1996) unreported, Crown Court in Northern Ireland. Reliance was conceded on appeal: N.I.C.A., March 14, 1997.

charged, it may happen that the defendant makes an exculpatory assertion. Alternatively, it may happen that after formal interviews have concluded, he lodges with the police a written statement prepared in consultation with a solicitor in attendance at the police station. Then, without giving evidence the defendant seeks at trial to adopt the statement through non-evidential representation (from the dock if defending himself or through counsel). Can the adoption at trial amount to reliance on a fact from the failure to mention which in the interview an adverse inference might be drawn? In *Hart and McLean* the Court of Appeal stated that there might be reliance for the purposes of section 34 where "the defendant has chosen to refuse to answer questions when initially interviewed but some time later, after consulting with his solicitor, has produced a prepared statement or has given later answers."[263] It is assumed that the court was referring to reliance on the extra-interview account by way of purported adoption at trial, whether during a no case submission or during closing arguments to the tribunal of fact.

If an utterance or statement is wholly self-serving (*e.g.*, consisting of alibi) it will generally be inadmissible as evidence of the truth of its contents and although such a statement may be led by the prosecution as evidence of reaction no reliance for the purposes of section 34 may be placed on it by the defence, because it is not evidence of the facts which it asserts.[264] Accordingly, it has been contended[265] that insofar as the Court of Appeal may have been referring in the example they gave to wholly self-serving statements it was misconceived. That the fact could and should have been mentioned in interview does not affect the defendant adversely if at trial it cannot be weighed in the balance on the defendant's behalf (and as the statement is not evidence, the judge should direct to that effect, so that the defendant derives no evidential benefit). Where, however, the statement is "mixed," for example a claim that the defendant acted in self-defence, it is argued that the self-serving parts may provide evidence of the facts stated and the defendant's reliance on the statement may be liable to import section 34.

(9) Determining a case to answer by reference to the failure to mention a fact relied on at trial

(a) *Impact of reliance on no case submission*

In determining whether there is a case to answer a court may take into account the failure by the accused during questioning under caution or at charge stage to

---

[263] (1998) unreported C.A. No. 9703362 W4, April 23. See also *McLernon* [1992] N.I.J.B. 41, C.A., April 1 (M remained silent during interviews over several days but shortly afterwards volunteered a statement when in prison), discussed by Jackson, [1995] Crim.L.R., at pp.589-590, Mirfield, *Silence, Confessions and Improperly Obtained Evidence*, Oxford 1998, p.252, and Birch, [1999] Crim.L.R., at p.775, n.37, and p.785.

[264] Mirfield, *op.cit.*, at p.252, noting that the point was missed in *McLernon*, *supra*. See also Birch, [1999] Crim.L.R., at p.785, noting the same of *Hart and McLean*, *supra*.

[265] See Birch, [1999] Crim.L.R., at p.785, n.94.

mention a fact relied on by the defence in the proceedings.[266] In following the C.L.R.C.'s scheme in this respect, the 1994 Act departs from the scheme of the Working Group which was restricted to allowing inferences to be drawn only for the purposes of determining whether the accused was guilty.[267] In fact they never even addressed the implications of making "failure to mention" part of the prima facie case, an omission which, it has been suggested, was the result of their erroneous assumption that the Criminal Evidence (Northern Ireland) Order 1988 made no provision for silence to be used to establish a *prima facie* case.[268] In the case of a retrial there will be little difficulty in applying the provision because the defence may have adduced evidence of a fact during the first trial which had not been previously mentioned and the prosecution may lead as part of their case in the retrial the adducement by the defence of that fact in the first trial and of the failure originally to mention it to the police. But the legislation is clearly intended to be of more general application than to retrials.

One reason why the Act makes failure to mention a fact later relied on relevant for the purpose of deciding whether there is a case to answer was suggested by the Royal Commission on Criminal Procedure.[269] If it could not be used for that purpose—

> ". . . the guilty person who knew the system would be inclined to sit it out. If his arrest had been on reasonable suspicion only and this were not enough to make a *prima facie* case, he would lose nothing and gain everything by keeping silent, since he would not be prosecuted if no other evidence emerged. If the police had got sufficient evidence to mount a case without a statement from him, it would still be to the guilty suspect's advantage to keep to himself as long as possible a false defence which was capable of being shown to be such by investigation. It might just be believed . . . despite the fact that [adverse comment would be made]."

Whether defendants are likely to be seriously incommoded or not by a rule permitting failure to mention to be treated as part of the *prima facie* case will depend on whether the fact not mentioned until trial is construed narrowly for the purposes of section 34 as evidence, or in a broader sense, as an assertion put to a prosecution witness in cross-examination irrespective of whether the assertion is adopted by the witness. Even if the wider interpretation applies the accused is not necessarily compelled by the provision to reveal his defence at an early stage or otherwise have his failure to do so treated as part of the *prima facie* case. The accused is not necessarily "forced to come forward with evidence or have his silence turned into

[266] s.34(2)(c).
[267] Report, Appendix D.
[268] Zuckerman, [1989] Crim.L.R., at p.864; Working Group Report, para. 84.
[269] Report, para. 4.50, and see Zuckerman, [1989] Crim.L.R., at p.863.

evidence against him."[270] To illustrate this proposition, it is worth comparing three different hypothetical cases. The first demonstrates how the potential evidential impact of silence can put pressure on a suspect, but in a way which is not decisive or even significant for the purposes of determining whether a *prima facie* case has been established. A defendant is charged with an unprovoked assault on the basis of clear and unchallenged evidence of identification. His account involves self-defence although he does not put it forward to the police when originally questioned. He is obliged to put his case in cross-examination of the victim and eye-witnesses and his failure originally to mention it could, under the wider interpretation of "fact" in section 34, be taken into account for the purpose of determining if there is a case to answer. But the power would be academic in this example because there is obviously sufficient evidence quite apart from the silence.

The second example is one in which the weakness of the identification evidence might make the additional factor of the suspect's belated explanation decisive in assessing whether a *prima facie* case has been established. However, the nature of the defence may allow it to be put to the victim or any eyewitnesses in such a way that no admission of identity is implied. Thus, suppose the evidence of identity of the assailant is weak, being based on a description which is unchallenged and on some circumstantial factors. The defendant's instructions are that he is indeed the man who struck the blow, but that he did so as the result of misinterpreting a certain gesture by the complainant as the prelude to an attack. The complainant might have flinched, for example. It would be feasible for the defence, with some care, to cross-examine without declaring or revealing their case and without, therefore, being seen to rely on a fact not previously disclosed. Thus, the victim might be asked if he happens to remember his exact body movements immediately before the blow was struck. The odds are that he will not be able to remember and if he says he cannot remember there is no obligation on the defence to put specific gestures to him.

In the third case the evidence of identity may be weak, but may be just enough to support a case to answer. There is no way of knowing how the tribunal will find. The defendant's instructions are that he was indeed the man involved but was acting in self-defence on the basis that the "victim" was unequivocally the aggressor. In this delicate situation counsel may decide to leave his options open by not putting the client's version to the prosecution witnesses. (If he was uncomfortable being wholly silent about any possibility of self-defence, he could always suggest to the victim that he had "information" that the victim had in the first instance attacked the other man—without identifying him.) If a no case submission fails a decision can then be taken whether to proceed by the muted approach of putting the prosecution to strict proof on the matter of identity or, if that is regarded as too risky, alternatively calling the defendant to give his version of events. If the second course is chosen, the prosecution could always seek leave to call rebutting evidence. Criticism might be made of the defence for not putting their case to the witnesses in the first instance but the sting could always be taken out of this by asserting that

[270] *ibid.*

responsibility lies with the defendant's legal representatives. In any event it will not have been necessary to rely on self-defence before close of the prosecution case and, accordingly, it will not be apparent that there has been any failure to raise self-defence before the hearing. The defendant's silence would not therefore be a factor which could strengthen the identification evidence.

Since failure to mention a fact relied on during police questioning can be a component of the *prima facie* case it is clear that reliance is not restricted to that by the accused in giving or calling evidence.[271] The relevance of lateness in the asserting of a fact is that it tends to cast doubt on the credibility of the assertion. If the fact were true the defendant would have volunteered it at the first opportunity, so the supposition has it. But here the credibility is not that of the defendant *qua* witness under oath, because the credibility of his defence is under scrutiny before he goes into the witness box or calls other evidence. Rather it is the issue of his credibility in asserting a fact through the medium of cross-examining a prosecution witness. Whether that failure will have relevance for the purpose of section 34 will depend on whether or not the rule is that the fact must accepted by the prosecution witness.

(b) *Preliminary process involving no live evidence*

In the schemes of the C.L.R.C. and of the Working Group it was proposed that failure to mention a fact could be taken into account by a magistrates' court in deciding whether to commit an accused for trial. This was also originally proposed in the Criminal Justice and Public Order Bill. However, abolition of committal proceedings and their replacement by "transfer proceedings" was later included in the Bill and duly enacted. Subsequently, the provisions for transfer were replaced by a modified form of committal process involving no live evidence (and therefore no cross-examination) but in which the defence were entitled to make no case submissions in writing.

In contrast with trial, it is difficult to envisage circumstances in which an identifiable failure could ever have emerged for the purpose of adjudicating on an application for dismissal of a transferred case. Even if committal proceedings had not been abolished and the original scheme maintained of permitting a failure to mention to be taken into account for the purposes of considering whether there should be a committal for trial it would in reality seldom if ever have arisen that a fact not mentioned during interrogation or at charge would be relied on at committal. In committal proceedings there was no obligation to put the defence during cross-examination and the usual practice was not to do so, a fact recognised by the C.L.R.C.[272]

No element of live evidence with provision for cross-examination or the adducement of defence evidence was to be involved in the form of transfer proceedings as originally enacted (but never brought into effect before abolition). Similarly, there is no involvement of live evidence in the modified form of

---

271 Sir Ivan Lawrence, 3rd Reading, 241 H.C. Deb., cols. 268-269, April 13, 1994.

272 Eleventh Report, para. 36.

committal proceedings at present in force for either way offences and for the majority of indictable only cases and none upon applications for dismissal of transferred cases of serious fraud and violent and sexual offences concerning children. (As noted earlier, no provision is included in section 34 for inferences to be drawn upon an application for dismissal of an indictable matter sent forthwith to the Crown Court.) Supposing that the accused is questioned by the police on two occasions and during the second such interview makes a factual assertion not mentioned during the first interview. The assertion foreshadows the defendant's instructions. Although the defence may make a "no case" submission during committal proceedings or before judge following transfer of a case of serious fraud or a violent or sexual offence involving a child, it is difficult to envisage in what circumstances the defence might be said to rely on the later self-serving assertion. It has no relevance in the submission and even if the defending advocate were to announce that the defence "relied" on it such reliance would have no bearing at that stage. In a second, more straightforward, example, suppose the written statement of a prosecution witness contains an important fact exculpatory of the accused, say an alibi, which the defendant could reasonably have been expected to mention to the police but did not. The defence purport to use the fortuitous alibi in support of a no case submission on identification but as in the first example the alibi is surely irrelevant. If the other evidence of identification is so weak as to be tenuous (warranting a ruling that the case should stop) the fact that the defendant never mentioned it in interview and only prayed it in aid for the first time in argument can hardly be construed as an evidential makeweight. Sections 34(2)(a) and (b) would seem, therefore, to be superfluous.

(10) The fact mentioned: "bare bones" or details of the defence case?

Presumably a fact relied on, the failure to mention which the section penalises, means precisely that, namely a fact relevant to the defence case and significant enough for the defendant to be relying on it for that purpose, and not, in the words of Lord Taylor C.J. speaking during the Parliamentary process, "any old fact."[273] The Criminal Law Revision Committee thought the term "fact" meant "any definitive statement made by a witness at the hearing and supporting the case of the defence"[274] although the examples they cited, alibi and consent in rape,[275] suggested that they had in mind broad statements of the nature of the defence case rather than details. In *McGarry*,[276] an indictment for inflicting grievous bodily harm, the appellant had said nothing at a first interview, and at a second he volunteered the "bare bones" of a defence of self-defence but otherwise replied "No comment" throughout the rest of the interview. Prosecuting counsel charitably accepted that he

---

[273] 555 H.L. Deb., col. 520, May 23, 1994.
[274] Eleventh Report, para. 33.
[275] *ibid.*, para. 28.
[276] [1998] 3 All E.R. 805.

had said enough for section 34 not to apply and the judge agreed. However, the judge left it open to the jury to draw their own inferences and the appeal was allowed because it was held that he should have given an old-style direction under the preserved common law and not left the jury to wonder whether adverse inferences were permissible when in law they were not.

In spite of the opinion of prosecuting counsel and the trial judge in *McGarry* it is open to question whether intimating the bare bones of a defence can be enough to avoid section 34, particularly where the defence case involves a significant amount of detail.[277] In *Averill*[278] the bare statement of a defence was held not to preclude the drawing of inferences if relevant details were withheld. There is certainly nothing in the language of section 34 to exclude from its application any non-disclosure of details where the defendant was forthcoming on the essence of the defence.

(11) No conviction (or prima facie case) may be based on an inference drawn solely from a failure to mention

Supposedly affording defendants protection from injustice is the provision of section 38(3) ensuring that a defendant will not have a case to answer or be convicted on an inference drawn solely from his failure, during questioning under caution or on being charged, to mention a fact relied on in subsequent proceedings.[279] Strictly, the explicit prohibition on a prima facie case being based solely on a failure to mention is redundant, since such a rule is implicitly subsumed in the rule that no conviction may be based solely on such a failure.

Despite its oblique wording section 38(3) presumably contemplates that there shall be no conviction or prima facie case where apart from the failure to mention there is no evidence against the accused. What exactly does the expression "no evidence" mean? When advocates speak of "no evidence" in making a no case submission they are generally understood to be using a form of rhetorical shorthand to argue that insufficient evidence has been adduced to establish a prima facie case. They are not necessarily asserting that there is no evidence whatsoever; they may well be conceding that there is some evidence warranting suspicion. The expressions not a "shred," or not a "scintilla," of evidence (the latter meaning a minute particle or atom[280]) are merely emphatic versions of "no evidence." Section 38(3) is plainly not applicable to a situation in which there is some evidence apart from the failure (albeit insufficient in itself to establish a prima facie case) because section 34 allows the failure to be taken into account for the purpose of determining a prima facie case; otherwise section 34 and section 38(3) would be mutually contradictory. Section 38(3) clearly relates to cases in which there is literally not a scintilla of evidence against the accused: those cases in which there is either no evidence at all

277 Birch, [1999] Crim.L.R., at p.781.
278 (1997) unreported, N.I.C.A., January 3.
279 Emulating Art. 2(4) of the Criminal Evidence (Northern Ireland) Order 1988.
280 *Shorter Oxford English Dictionary*.

of the fact of a crime or no evidence connecting the accused with a provable offence committed by some unidentified person.

Whether the provision is of any practical benefit is doubtful.[281] It is inherent in the Act that, apart from one special circumstance, no prosecution can be *opened* at trial on the basis of a failure to mention since at that stage there will have been no proceedings as yet during which any "reliance" (*i.e.* on a fact not mentioned to the police) will have emerged. (Defence statements have been excluded for the purpose of section 34 by declaration of the current Director of Public Prosecutions.[282]) The possible exception is a re-trial, which might be opened on the basis that the defendant had failed under the Act to mention a fact relied on in the first trial (meeting the requirement of "proceedings"). Had old style committal proceedings been retained, reliance during cross-examination on a fact not mentioned to the police might also have provided material for opening (although in the nature of committal proceedings so rarely as to be virtually never). In contrast to the opening, it is at the *close* of the prosecution case that section 38(3) does have some potential application, but only in the marginal situation in which a predicted case has entirely evaporated leaving only the failure to mention evinced through cross-examination. However, it is almost inconceivable that in this situation any judge would be likely to find a case to answer solely on the basis of a failure to mention a fact relied on in cross-examination.[283] At Committee stage in the Lords, Lord Wigoder aptly remarked:

> "I was more than a little astonished to hear the noble and learned Lord the Lord Chief Justice refer to [section 38(3)] as being in some way a significant protection for a defendant in showing, apparently, how fair the Government are determined to be. The clause provides that if there is no evidence against a defendant except that he was on some occasion silent, he cannot be convicted of a criminal offence. That is hardly an astonishing proposition or a very welcome proposition. It is hardly to be regarded as a concession that a charge of robbery with violence can be brought against someone and the prosecuting counsel can get up and say, 'We have no connection between this defendant and this crime except one day a village policeman stopped him and asked him whether he was doing something or other and the defendant looked at him in an astonished way.' On that evidence, according to [section 38(3)] that man cannot be convicted of robbery with violence. I should jolly well think not."[284]

---

281 The rule elaborated by the European Court of Human Rights that under the European Convention on Human Rights no case may be based solely *or mainly* on silence would seem to be more realistic and useful. provision: see Chapter 4.

282 See *supra*, p.71.

283 See Zuckerman [1989] Crim.L.R., at p.863.

284 555 H.L. Deb., col. 526, May 23, 1994. In other words, s.38(3) "is a statement of the painfully obvious": Prof. D. Birch, "Suffering in Silence: A Cost-Benefit Analysis of Section 34 of the Criminal Justice and Public Order Act 1994," [1999] Crim.L.R. 769, at p.774.

In *Doldur*[285] the Court of Appeal, applying *Cowan*[286] to cases under section 34, said that the effect of the rule in section 38(3) was that it was necessary to remind the jury that they could not convict on adverse inferences alone[287] but that they must have evidence, which could include defence evidence as well as prosecution evidence, and which, when considered together with any adverse inference they thought proper to draw, enabled them to be sure of the truth and accuracy of that evidence and in consequence, of guilt.

(12) Pre-trial defence disclosure

In the late 1980s the Government had apparently wavered as to the extent to which legislation should be taken in curtailing the right to silence. The choice lay between, on the one hand, the full-blown scheme proposed by the C.L.R.C. in 1972 and, on the other, measures limited in scope to a requirement for pre-trial defence disclosure in the interests of eliminating the supposed problem of ambush defences. The Working Group recommended a watered-down version of the C.L.R.C. scheme (failure to mention a fact later relied on not to be relevant in determining whether a *prima facie* case had been established, see *post*) coupled with measures for pre-trial defence disclosure. The Criminal Justice and Public Order Act reverts to the full C.L.R.C. scheme and contains no measures for pre-trial disclosure, the Government having recognised the need for such measures but deferring legislation pending consideration as a separate issue.[288] Since these had originally only been proposed as a soft alternative to full curtailment of the right to silence they seem to have been regarded as of only limited additional value to implementation of the full scheme. In fact, whilst failure to comply with a rule designed to force disclosure between transfer of the case to the Crown Court and the trial might have marginally reinforced an adverse inference from the suspect's silence at the investigative stage, compliance might equally, on the other hand, have served to weaken such an inference. It is easy to see that the accused's manifest willingness to enter before trial a properly formulated defence might have strengthened the suggestion that the only reason for his having remained silent at the investigative stage was to await an opportunity to take fully considered—as against rushed or hastily tendered—legal advice. In any event, the Common law already permitted adverse judicial comment on the failure at committal to intimate the defence run at trial and the Act specifically preserves Common law principles.[289] One commentator has expressed the view that the Working Group's proposed method of enforcing the obligation of disclosure through the strategy of comment and inference confuses a sanction aimed

285 (1999) *The Times*, December 7, C.A.

286 [1996] Q.B. 373.

287 In *Gill* (2000) *The Times*, August 17, C.A. No. 9907637 X1, the appellant's conviction was quashed because of the judge's failure, *inter alia* to give this direction.

288 See Earl Ferrers, 555 H.L. Deb., cols. 533-534, May 23, 1994 (Committee stage.) The disclosure regime was subsequently enacted by the Criminal Procedure and Investigations Act 1996.

289 s.34(5)(b).

at compliance with a rule of court and questions of evidential evidence.[290] The normal sanction for non-disclosure is the power to disallow a defence not previously disclosed. Enforcement is a separate issue from the question whether its breach is of probative weight.

(13) Timing of adducement of pre-trial silence

Where it is alleged that at a certain stage prior to the moment at which the accused was charged or officially informed that he might be prosecuted for an offence he failed to mention a fact relied on in proceedings against him for the offence the court will need to determine when in the proceedings it becomes appropriate to give evidence of that failure. Section 34(3) purports to deal with this issue but its meaning and application appear to be uncertain and confused, not to say obscure. It provides—

> "Subject to any directions by the court, evidence tending to establish the failure may be given before or after evidence tending to establish the fact which the accused is alleged to have failed to mention."

Two potential problems arise from this. In the first place, there is the difficulty over the wording of the subordinate clause. Evidence tending to establish a fact not previously mentioned is distinct from a fact relied on during the cross-examination of a prosecution witness. If a witness affirms an assertion put in cross-examination that will become "evidence." If not, the fact would seem to be excluded from the embrace of the subsection until it is supported by evidence led by the defence. This is in spite of the rule that for the purposes of determining whether the prosecution have adduced a *prima facie* case a court may take into account defence reliance in cross-examination upon a fact not mentioned at the appropriate investigative stage. If the fact relied on during cross-examination fails to become "evidence" as a result of the witness rejecting it, the prosecution would not be authorised by section 34(3) to lead the evidence of failure before the close of their case. On this basis the subsection would arguably be inconsistent with section 34(1).

The second possible difficulty is that section 34(3) authorises the adducement of the silence *before* (as well as after) the adducing of evidence tending to establish a fact which the accused is alleged to have failed to mention. But how can it be known for certain whether such evidence is going to be given? For example, supposing the accused has given a no comment interview. It will enjoy no evidential value under section 34(1) unless and until some positive averment of fact is made by way of raising a defence. Logically, therefore, it ought not to be led until after that has happened. Yet the subsection allows the evidence of failure to be led in advance of the evidence tending to establish the fact not mentioned at the investigative stage.

---

[290] Zuckerman, [1989] Crim.L.R. 855, at p.859, referring to report, para. 110.

There is, however, a simple solution to these apparent problems of interpreting the application of section 34(3). Since it permits the evidence of the failure to be given before evidence is adduced of the fact upon which the defence rely, being a fact not mentioned at the investigative stage, the subsection provides the statutory basis for contingent adducement of the evidence of failure irrespective of whether any exculpatory fact is subsequently sought to be relied upon by the defence. In other words, the subsection gives the prosecution the statutory power, subject to court directions to the contrary, to lead as a matter of routine no comment interviews as a part of their case. The reasoning behind this power would seem to be that if the defence do subsequently seek to rely on some exculpatory fact, they will have lost nothing from the jury knowing that that fact was not mentioned in interview. Conversely, if the defence case should happen to involve no more than putting the prosecution to proof the fact that the jury will have learnt that the accused made no comment when questioned by the police will not prejudice his position because it will have represented a consistent approach throughout the case.

Although for these reasons adducement in the first instance of the whole of a no comment interview would be unlikely to involve unfairness to the accused to any marked extent, the Court of Appeal suggested in *Condron* that where it is not yet known what, if any, facts the defence will be relying on, the evidence of silence to be adduced should be limited to—

> ". . . [t]he fact that after the appropriate caution the accused did not answer questions or made no comment. Unless the relevance of a particular point has been revealed in cross-examination [of prosecution witnesses], it would not seem appropriate to spend time at this stage going through the questions asked at interview."[291]

The obvious thinking here is that where the defence is restricted to putting the prosecution to proof the reciting to the jury of a series of questions implicating the defendant in the offence, to which he simply remained mute, might cause them to give disproportionate weight to the truth behind the questions. Out of an abundance of caution, therefore, they are best not recounted, it would be argued. In *Argent*, however, Lord Bingham was plainly unworried that any such prejudice would be significant, expressing no disapproval of the fact that at a stage in the trial when the judge was ignorant of what the accused's defence would be a police officer was permitted to give evidence of an interview in which the appellant had given negative responses.[292]

---

291 [1997] 1 Cr.App.R.185, at p.196, *per* Stuart Smith L.J.

292 [1997] 2 Cr.App.R. 27, at p.30. Dr Pattenden has observed that trial judges are unlikely to find this inconsistency helpful: (1998) 2 E & P, at p.159.

(14) Judge may authorise an adverse inference at own motion

Even though the prosecution have not sought to rely on an adverse inference from silence judges may nevertheless give a section 34 direction of their own motion. This principle was upheld in the somewhat suprising decision of *Khan*.[293] The appellant's defence of duress had been alluded to but not fully deployed in interview. In the circumstances, prosecuting counsel considered that it would not be fair to cross-examine her on the basis that she had not mentioned her defence in interview, and accordingly she was not asked to explain the point, her counsel did not deal with it in his speech and no representations were made to the judge on the applicability of section 34. In summing up, however, the judge directed the jury that if they concluded that she had no good reason for failing to explain her defence, they could draw an adverse inference. At the request of counsel, he subsequently told the jury that the point had not been put by the Crown or dealt with in defending counsel's speech. The Court of Appeal deprecated the judge's failure to raise with counsel, if only as a matter of courtesy, the fact that he intended to direct the jury that they might draw inferences. However, it was held that it was within the judge's discretion to leave the issue to the jury. The way in which this decision was apparently rationalised was that since it was unlikely that counsel would have wished to recall the defendant and there was nothing he could have said about it in his speech had the judge raised his intentions at the end of the evidence there was no basis on which the judge could have been deterred from giving his direction. Thus, in effect, no harm had been done. It remains unclear how this argument saved the appellant from the injustice of being deprived of the opportunity to deal with the question of inferences and how it can have been reasonable to drawn an adverse inference in these circumstances. How it could have been known to the court that counsel would have declined to recall his client or that there was nothing he could have said about the issue in his speech, are matters which remain obscure. Had counsel decided not to recall the appellant to deal specifically with the issue such a decision would have been understandable enough, since calling the appellant for this purpose alone at that late stage might well have attracted disproportionate attention to the point. Additional support for the decision seems remarkably to have been found in the proposition that the onus lies on defending counsel to make submissions that an adverse inference should not be drawn.

(15) Directions to the jury where adverse inferences permissible

(a) *Essential directions*

In *Cowan* the Court of Appeal cited with approval the Judicial Studies Board specimen direction on the inferences which the jury might reasonably draw under section 35 of the Criminal Justice and Public Order Act 1994 when the defendant

[293] [1999] 2 *Archbold News* 2, C.A. 96/03965/Y4.

was absent from the witness box, and they listed five points which it was essential to make to the jury.[294] In *Condron and Condron*[295] the court stressed the importance of giving directions to the jury in relation to the inferences which might be properly be drawn under section 34 from the defendant's failure to answer questions after caution, along the same lines as those which had been given in *Cowan* in relation to the defendant's trial silence. Necessarily only four out of the five essential points expounded in *Cowan* were applicable to failure to answer questions under caution. The following are the four which were applicable to questioning under caution:

- the burden of proof remains on the prosecution throughout to the standard required;
- the defendant is entitled to remain silent as of right and by choice and the right to silence remains;
- an inference from failure to answer questions cannot on its own prove guilt;
- if despite any evidence relied upon to explain his silence or in the absence of any such evidence, the jury conclude the silence can only sensibly be attributed to the defendant's having no answer [or none that would stand up to cross-examination,] they may draw an adverse inference.

As has already been mentioned the inference in square brackets in the last of these—the "fifth essential" in *Cowan*—was not expressly referred to in *Condron*, although it was later recognised as being permissible in the context of section 34.

(b) *The "fifth essential"—direction that an adverse infererence is permissible if silence can "only sensibly be attributed" to the defendant's having no answer or none that would stand up to questioning*

The significance of the "fifth essential"—the direction that an adverse infererence is permissible if silence can "only sensibly be attributed" to the defendant's having no answer or none that would stand up to questioning—must be viewed against the background of the facts in *Condron*, the actual decision of the Court of Appeal, and the subsequent decision in the case by the European Court of Human Rights.

The appellants were a married couple living in a council flat adjacent to a flat occupied by C, their co-accused. Over a four-day period the police maintained an observation, from the second day of which the appellants and C, were video-recorded. It was alleged that whenever C had a purchaser and knocked on the back window of.the appellants' flat, wraps of heroin prepared by the appellants for sale would be handed from the balcony of their flat to someone leaning out of the back window of C's flat. The appellants were seen to pass various items to C including a plastic bottle for smoking crack cocaine and silver foil for smoking heroin. On one particular occasion a man was seen at the back window of the appellant's flat

[294] [1996] Q.B. 373. See Chapter 3.
[295] [1997] 1 Cr.App.R. 185.

handing what looked like a cigarette packet to the second appellant who was on her balcony. She went into her flat, then re-emerged and returned the packet to the man. At the conclusion of the observation the appellants were arrested for being concerned in the supply of diamorphine and for possession of diamorphine with intent to supply and in their flat were found 16 wraps of heroin and a further quantity of heroin. Also allegedly found in the flat was a polythene sheet used to make wraps. At the police station the appellants' solicitor noted that the first appellant, who seemed to be in the early stages of withdrawal, was unfit to be interviewed, but the Force Medical Examiner, formed the view that although an opiates addict with symptoms and signs of withdrawal he was thinking clearly and able to answer questions and was fit for interview. The second appellant also showed withdrawal symptoms but in the opinion of the F.M.E. was thinking clearly and able to answer questions. During interviews the solicitor expressed concerned that his clients were unfit to be interviewed and in distress and that the second appellant in particular was having difficulty concentrating on what he was saying to her. Both appellants stated that they understood the caution and were advised that if during the interview they felt unwell they should say so and the interview would be stopped. At no stage during interview did either of the appellants request this, even though at one point in the interview of the first appellant the solicitor specifically suggested that this might happen., but the first appellant expressly stated that he did not want the interview to stop. Both appellants gave a no comment interview.

The defence applied to have the interview excluded on the ground that the appellants were suffering from drug withdrawal symptoms and that since the solicitor had therefore considered them unfit to be interviewed and had advised them in good faith not to answer, no adverse inference could be drawn. The judge accepted that the solicitor genuinely believed that the appellants were unfit to be interviewed and might prejudice their defence through the incoherence of any answers they might give. However, he rejected the application on the basis that the doctor had considered them fit to be interviewed, that they were thinking clearly and were able to answer questions, and that both appellants had stated in response to direct questions that they understood the charges against them and the possible repercussions of failing to answer questions.

The line of defence which they both raised in the witness box at their trial was that they were addicts and that the heroin found in their flat had been for their own personal use, having been purchased in bulk by the first appellant on the evening before their arrest. They denied that heroin was ever supplied in the way or for the purpose alleged by the prosecution or at all. They claimed that the polythene sheet had been planted in their flat by the police after they had been brought to the police station. When asked about the incident in which the second appellant was seen receiving and then returning a packet to the person in C's flat, the appellants explained that the packet contained either cigarettes or money, while the second appellant stated that it was simply an exchange of a packet of cigarettes. They said that other items had been passed this way since it was easier than having to go along the walkway of the front of each flat. For his part C gave evidence that the appellants had never given him heroin and referred to his frequent borrowing as a neighbour, with communication via the balcony. When he was arrested he was told he would not get bail and this made him angry and "bloody minded" so he decided not to help the police by answering their questions. Both appellants attributed the fact that they had made no comment in interview to their solicitor's advice that they were not in a condition to do so, given their withdrawal from heroin. The solicitor gave evidence and, having said that the basis of his advice was his perception of one of his client's fitness for interview, was asked in cross-examination: "Coming down to the specifics of the allegation, he was in a sufficiently lucid state to be able to explain to you why it was that he had taken drugs, and to repeat that in interview." The solicitor claimed privilege and the judge upheld the objection.

In summing up to the jury the judge closely followed the then current J.S.B. specimen direction on the application of section 34 dating from October 1996, the relevant terms of which were as follows:

> "If he failed to mention [the fact relied on] when he was questioned, decide whether in the circumstances which existed at the time, it was a fact which he could reasonably have been expected then to mention. . . . The law is that you may draw such inferences as appear proper from his failure to mention it at that time. You do not have to hold it against him. It is for you to decide whether it it is proper to do so. Failure to mention such a fact at that time cannot, on its own, prove guilt, but depending on the circumstances, you may hold that failure against him when deciding whether he is guilty, that is, take into account as some additional support for the prosecution's case. It is for you to decide whether it is fair to do so."

As far as it went, the Court of Appeal approved this direction but took the view that it failed to go far enough. In the court's view, it would have been "desirable" for the judge to have adopted the fifth essential laid down in *Cowan* for trial silence by directing the jury that if despite any evidence relied upon to explain his silence or in the absence of any such evidence, they were to conclude that the silence could only sensibly be attributed to the defendant's having no answer they might draw an adverse inference. (As already mentioned, the court did not incorporate into the formula the inference that the accused had no answer that would stand up to cross-examination.) However, the omission did not render the convictions unsafe, the court held, because in their view there was substantial, almost overwhelming, evidence of drug supply by the appellants. Moreover, the acquittal of C, the co-accused, who had similarly remained silent in interview, demonstrated, in the court's view, that the jury must have attached little significance generally to the fact of silence.

In *Condron* v. *United Kingdom* the European Court of Human Rights (E.C.H.R.) upheld the contrary position—that it was more than merely "desirable" to give the

Cowan fifth essential direction.[296] Citing the earlier E.C.H.R. case of *Murray* v. *United Kingdom*[297] the court noted that the domestic law and practice of the United Kingdom attempted to strike an appropriate balance between the exercise by an accused of his right to silence during police interview and the drawing of an adverse inference from that fact at a jury trial.[298] Access to legal advice in the police station and at the interview was in the court's view, a "particularly important safeguard for dispelling any compulsion to speak which may be inherent in the terms of the caution" and the fact that an accused was advised by his solicitor to maintain silence had to be given appropriate weight by the domestic court.[299] Although in his summing up the trial judge had dealt with the applicants' explanation for their silence, the effect of giving the relevant specimen direction at the time without the addition of a *Cowan* direction "left the jury at liberty to draw an adverse inference notwithstanding that [they] may have been satisfied as to the plausibility of the explanation."[300] In the court's view it was impossible to ascertain what weight, if any, the jury gave to the applicants' silence and, unlike in *Murray* v. *U.K.*, in which the defendant had been tried without a jury by an experienced Northern Ireland "Diplock" judge who was required to give reasons for his verdict, the jury's thinking was not susceptible to review on appeal.[301] It was thus all the more compelling to ensure that they were properly advised on how to address the issue of the applicants' silence.[302] The E.C.H.R. did not accept that the fact that the co-accused, who also remained silent during his police interview, was acquitted indicated that the jury attached little weight to the applicants' silence in convicting them.[303] The Court of Appeal had taken into account the weight of the evidence against the applicants but had had no means of ascertaining whether or not the applicants' silence played a

---

[296] Application no. 35718/97, May 2, 2000, para. 61. The court stated that "as a matter of fairness, the jury should have been directed that if it was satisfied that the applicant's silence at the police interview could not sensibly be attributed to their having no answer or none that would stand up to cross-examination it should not draw an adverse inference." It is doubtful if the apparent reversing of the onus of proof implicit in this purported paraphrasing of the fifth essential was other than inadvertent.

[297] (1996) 22 E.H.R.R. 29.

[298] *Condron* v. *U.K.*, para. 58.

[299] para. 60. See also *Averill* v. *U.K.*, E.C.H.R. application no. 36408/97, June 6, 2000, paras. 57-58; [2000] Crim.L.R. 682; *The Times*, June 20, 2000; *Magee* v. *U.K.*, E.C.H.R. application no. 28135/95, June 6, 2000, para. 39; *The Times* June 20, 2000. The significance of legal advice recognised by the E.C.H.R. coheres with the view of Lord Bingham C.J. in *Argent* [1997] 2 Cr.App.R. 27, at p.36 (see *infra*, at p.184). Referring in effect to the trial judge's rejection of the application to exclude the evidence of silence on the basis that the doctor had considered the appellants fit to be interviewed, the E.C.H.R. regarded the question of fitness for interview and that of lucidity for the purposes of comprehending the consequences of silence as separate issues: para. 60.

[300] para. 61. The court presumably meant by this that even though the jur y may have accepted that the solicitor's advice was capable of providing a plausible enough reason for the accused's silence, the omission of the fifth essential left them free nevertheless to conclude in the event that the true reason for the silence was that having no answer or wishing to avoid being questioned the accused conveniently sought refuge behind advice fortuitously given. (Presumably the court cited the *Cowan* direction with both possible inferences because the Court of Appeal now recognised as relevant to section 34 cases the alternative inference that the accused had no answer that would stand up to cross-examination.)

[301] para. 62.

[302] *ibid.*

[303] para. 64.

significant role in the jury's decision to convict and accordingly were in no position to assess properly whether the jury considered this to be conclusive of their guilt.[304] Conversely, the E.C.H.R. could not exclude the possibility that the jury might have accepted the defence to the charges, for example, that the police had planted incriminating evidence in their flat, and they did not accept that the evidence against the applicants was as overwhelming as the Court of Appeal considered.[305] In the court's view it was in any event a speculative exercise which only reinforced the crucial nature of the defect in the trial judge's direction and its implications for review of the case on appeal.[306] The formula of direction employed by the judge could not be said to reflect the balance which it was necessary to strike between the right to silence and the circumstances in which it was permissible to draw an adverse inference from silence, including by a jury.[307] The imperfection in the summing up could not be remedied on appeal, any other conclusion would be at variance with the fundamental importance of the right to silence, a right lying at the heart of the notion of a fair procedure guaranteed by Article 6 of the European Convention for the Protection of Human Rights and Fundamental Freedoms, and the applicants did not receive a fair hearing within the meaning of Article 6.1 of the Convention.

Although modified in February 1997 supposedly to take account of the judgment of the Court of Appeal in *Condron*, the Judicial Studies Board's specimen direction (subsequently updated in May 1999 to reflect *Argent*[308]) plainly falls short of expressing the fifth essential in the final sentence of the current version:

> "The defendant, as part of his defence, has relied upon [. . .]. But [the prosecution case is][he admits] that he did not mention this when he was [questioned before being charged with the offence][charged with the offence][officially informed that he might be prosecuted for the offence]. The prosecution case is that in the circumstances, and having regard to the warning which he had been given, if this fact had been true, he could reasonably have been expected to mention it at that stage, and as he did not do so you may therefore conclude that [it has since been invented][it has since been tailored to fit the prosecution case][he believed that it would not then stand up to scrutiny]. If you are sure that he did fail to mention [. . .] when he was [questioned][charged][informed that he might be prosecuted] it is for you to decide whether in the circumstances it was something which he could reasonably have been expected to mention at that time. If it was, the law is that you may draw such inferences as appear proper from his failure to do so. Failure to mention [. . .] cannot on its own prove guilt. But, if you are sure that quite

[304] para. 63.
[305] para. 64.
[306] *ibid.*
[307] para. 61.
[308] [1997] 2 Cr.App.R. 27.

regardless of this failure, there is a case for him to meet, it is something which you are entitled to take into account when deciding whether his evidence about this matter is true, that is, you may take it into account as some additional support for the prosecution's case. You are not bound to do so. It is for you to decide whether it is fair to do so. There is evidence before you on the basis of which the defendant's advocate invites you not to hold it against him that he failed to mention this fact when he had the opportunity to do so. That evidence is [. . .]. If you think this amounts to a reason why you should not hold the defendant's failure against him, do not do so. On the other hand, if it does not in your judgment provide an adequate explanation, and you are sure that the real reason for his failure was that he then had no innocent explanation to offer in relation to this aspect of the case, you may hold it against him."[309]

It is noteworthy that in *Gill*[310] the Court of Appeal, citing *Condron v.U.K.*, quashed the appellant's conviction where the judge had failed, *inter alia*, to direct the jury in unequivocal terms that only if they rejected the explanation for silence and concluded that the failure could only sensibly be attributed to the defendant's having no answer or none that would withstand cross-examination, could they then consider whether to draw an adverse inference. Apparently following the E.C.H.R. the court held that the jury might have been left with the impression that they could and should draw an adverse inference irrespective of the plausibility of the explanation and, without proper directions, they might have drawn an adverse inference without being satisfied of the various essentials.

(c) *Direction that adverse inference from failure to mention cannot on its own prove guilt*

As to the essential direction that an inference from failure to answer questions cannot on its own prove guilt it has already been pointed out that in *Doldur*[311] the Court of Appeal said that the effect of the rule in section 38(3) was that it was necessary to remind the jury that they could not convict on adverse inferences alone but that they must have evidence, which could include defence evidence as well as prosecution evidence, and which, when considered together with any adverse inference they thought proper to draw, enabled them to be sure of the truth and accuracy of that evidence and in consequence, of guilt.

---

309 Adapted from the text printed in *Archbold*, 2000 ed. Its updating in May 1999 was disclosed in *Condron* v. *U.K.*, para. 34. That it had been updated in February 1997 to reflect the C.A. judgment in *Condron* was referred to in Jennings, Ashworth and Emmerson, *Silence and Safety: The Impact of the Human Rights Law*, [2000] Crim.L.R. 879, at p. 880, note. 10. The current terms are understood to be under review in the light of *Condron* v. *U.K.*: see *ibid.*, p.881, note 13.

310 (2000) *The Times*, August 17.

311 (1999) *The Times*, December 7, C.A. See *supra*, p.99.

(d) *No requirement for jury to be satisfied that a prima facie case has been adduced as a condition for drawing an inference under section 34*

In *Cowan*, which concerned the drawing of an inference under section 35 of the 1994 Act from the failure of the accused to give evidence, the Court of Appeal had approved the J.S.B.'s specimen direction that in a section 35 case the jury "must be satisfied that the prosecution have established a case to answer before drawing any inferences from silence."[312] This condition was subsequently imported into the specimen direction on section 34 requiring there to be a case for the defendant to meet before an adverse inference could be drawn.[313] The direction was peculiar in introducing a constraint on the application of the section which is plainly at odds with its express terms allowing the failure to be taken into account for the purpose of determining whether there is a case to answer. It has been suggested[314] that the direction was intended to limit the effect of the section in the light of *Murray* v. *U.K.*[315] but that a more appropriate application of the judgment would have been that silence could not be the sole or the main basis for a conviction. Importantly, the direction was disavowed by the Court of Appeal in *Doldur*.[316] The appellant argued that the trial judge had failed to direct the jury that before they could draw an adverse inference under section 34 from the appellant's failure to give an explanation in interview which he later relied on at trial, they had to be satisfied that there was, on the prosecution evidence, a case to answer.[317] The submission clearly confounded the different functions of the two sections. The failure of an accused to give evidence necessarily only arises where a case to answer has been adduced to the satisfaction of the trial judge. *Cowan* requires the jury to revisit the judge's decision and only if they come to the same view will it be permissible for them to draw an inference. An inference under section 34, by contrast, is not conditional on the adducement of a prima facie case; rather, the inference can make up a deficit in the prima facie case. This seems to have been the thrust of the reasoning of the Court of Appeal in rejecting the ground of appeal in question (although allowing it on another ground). Giving judgment, Auld L.J. said that a direction in relation to section 35 was to be distinguished from one concerning section 34, because with section 35 the jury was necessarily confined to a consideration of the prosecution evidence. With section 34, a jury would almost always be required to consider the

---

312 See Chapter 3 for a full discussion of the direction.

313 "But, if you are sure that quite regardless of this failure, there is a case for him to meet, it is something which you are entitled to take into account when deciding whether his evidence about this matter is true, that is, you may take it into account as some additional support for the prosecution's case."

314 By Jennings, the contributing editor to *Archbold*, at para. 15-404.

315 (1995) 22 E.H.R.R. 29.

316 (1999) *The Times*, December 7, C.A. Curiously, this has apparently not deterred judges in a number of first instance cases from being induced to adopt for s.34 directions the language of Lord Bingham C.J. referring, in *Birchall* [1999] Cr.L.R. 311, to s.35 inferences, that there must be a "sufficiently compelling" case to call for a response: see Jennings, Ashworth and Emmerson, [2000] Crim.L.R. at p. 882, note 24.

317 The assertion in question was that it was an associate and not the appellant who had kicked the victim and had been wearing a red jacket described by witnesses as having been worn by the person kicking the victim.

defence as well as prosecution evidence because it was the contrast between the earlier silence and later reliance on the defence which could give rise to the inference. With section 34 there was no logical basis for confining the jury to a consideration of the prosecution case and evidence when directing them on drawing adverse inferences from silence. After the jury had determined at the close of the prosecution case whether there was a case to answer on the prosecution evidence if accepted by them, it was not for the jury to reconsider that question but to determine whether they accepted the truth or accuracy of that evidence. They could then take into account an adverse inference they thought proper to draw in order to determine whether they were sure of guilt.

In *Condron* v. *U.K.*[318] the applicants, relying on *Murray* v.*U.K.*, sought to challenge the trial judge's direction on the ground that it omitted a reference to the requirement that the prosecution must establish a *prima facie* case before an adverse inference might be drawn. The applicants conceded that the point had not been taken before the Court of Appeal, maintaining that they would have stood little prospect of success. The U.K. Government argued that having regard to the facts that the Court of Appeal accepted the main ground for challenging the direction and that the law in this area was evolving at the time of the appeal, the applicants should have included the issue in their grounds of appeal. The E.C.H.R. considered that it did not have to take a stand on the issue having regard to its finding on the main defect relied on by the applicants.

(e) *Importance of identifying relevant facts from which to draw a proper inference*

It has already been mentioned that in *Condron*, *supra*, the Court of Appeal expressed the view that the judge did not go far enough in directing the jury that it was a matter for them to decide whether any adverse inference should be drawn against the accused from their failure to mention certain facts at interview. It will follow from this, as has since in fact been held, that where it is ruled open to the jury to draw an adverse inference the judge should identify the relevant facts in respect of which such an inference may arise.[319]

(f) *Importance of complying with standard directions*

In *Abdullah (Ghilwan)*[320] the Court of Appeal applied to section 34 the guidance which the court gave in *Birchall*[321] concerning the question of compliance with specimen directions on adverse inferences under section 35 from the accused's failure to give evidence. In *Birchall* Lord Bingham C.J. said that although the court was reluctant to countenance the view that the direction to the jury called for the mouthing of a number of mandatory formulae, and that departure from a prescribed

318 E.C.H.R., application no. 35718/97, May 2, 2000.

319 *Reader* (1998) unreported, C.A. 97/6342/W2, April 7, following *Condron* [1997] 1 Cr.App.R. 185. See also *Gill* (2000) *The Times*, August 17, C.A. (conviction quashed because, *inter alia*, the jury had not been given clear directions on identifying the relevant precise fact).

320 [1999] 5 *Archbold News* 3, C.A. 98/02542/Y2.

321 [1999] Crim.L.R. 311.

form of words would by no means always justify the upsetting of a jury's verdict, nevertheless standard directions were devised to serve the ends of justice and the court must be astute to ensure that these ends were not jeopardised by a failure to give directions when they were called for. The drawing of inferences from silence was a particularly sensitive area. Many respected authorities had voiced the fear that the silence provisions of the 1994 Act might lead to wrongful convictions. It seemed possible that the application of those provisions could lead to decisions adverse to the United Kingdom in the European Court of Human Rights in Strasbourg under Articles 6.1 and 6.2 of the European Convention on Human Rights unless those provisions were the subject of carefully framed directions to juries.

(g) *Directions on the silence of a co-accused*

Where the guilt or innocence of two or more defendants stands or falls together, it may generally be desirable to direct the jury that they should not hold the silence of one defendant in interview against the other defendant(s): *McClean and McClean*.[322]

(16) Procedural options where defence oppose an adverse inference

(a) *General considerations*

The basic rationale for drawing an inference of guilt from the suspect's silence is the axiom that innocent people wrongly accused of crime are naturally inclined to protest their innocence. The well known response to this supposition is that there are a variety of possible reasons why an innocent suspect might be inclined to remain silent in the face of police inquiries, for example: inherent reticence (shyness); shock or dumbfoundedness at the accusation; bewilderment, poor memory or comprehension of the circumstances and a cautious preference for deferring discussion of the matter until after careful reflection; a reasoned decision to wait until the allegation has been set out in detail and there has been an opportunity to consider it with the benefit of legal advice before answering any questions;[323] a preference for concealing embarrassing facts or improper conduct amounting to a defence; a desire to protect a close friend or relative; fear of reprisal by persons to the fact of whose guilt the suspect is privy without being complicit; rejection of the accusation by silent contempt; distrust of the police or antipathy towards them. Coupled with each of these reasons may be the additional factor of restricted cognitive ability, which may preclude the suspect from understanding the meaning and effect of the new form of caution and from appreciating therefore the risk involved in opting for silence for any innocent reason. (Failure to understand the

---

[322] [1999] 4 *Archbold News* 1, C.A., 98/01354/R2; 98/01609/S2.

[323] Research conducted for the R.C.C.J. found that in almost 50 per cent of the cases observed in which silence was advised, the dominant reason was a lack of knowledge of the police case: see McConville and Hodgson, *Custodial Legal Advice and the Right to Silence* R.C.C.J. Research Study No 16, H.M.S.O. 1993.

earlier, more cumbersome, version of the new caution employed in Northern Ireland was a common experience there.[324])

With so many potential reasons for explaining away silence consistent with innocence it is arguable that an adverse inference should not be too readily drawn. However, the reality is that the foundation for most exculpatory explanations for silence will need to be laid by evidence from the defence, usually from the defendant. In *Argent* it was said that "the jury may conclude, after hearing all that the defendant and his witness may have to say" that no inference should be drawn against the accused under section 34.[325] It has been suggested that there is an implication in this, perhaps unintentional, that an explanation for silence will not be considered unless supported by evidence *from the defence*.[326] Conversely, Lord Bingham may have meant to imply no more than that exculpatory material will almost invariably come from the defence. In the absence of evidence, counsel's conjecture at the final speech stage, even if it were permissible, would hardly be the most forceful means of trying to win acceptance of the explanation by the tribunal of fact. In practice, silence by the accused at interview would need to be explained by the accused, or a material defence witness, in the witness box. But there will be at least two favourable inferences which would not require evidence from the defendant and may be drawn by presumption. Of all the possible innocent or neutral explanations which might be advanced for a suspect remaining silent under questioning almost certainly the best defence against an adverse inference ought to be that it was on legal advice. This is discussed in section H, below. The second inference which should generally be drawn in favour of the accused is that a person suffering from severe mental illness or mental handicap could not be expected to have appreciated the potentially harmful implications of silence however carefully this might have been explained.

(b) *Direction where defence proffer exculpatory explanation for silence*

Where the defence seek to proffer an innocent reason for the defendant's not having mentioned during questioning a fact relied on at trial this must obviously be dealt with by the judge in summing up. The Judicial Studies Board's specimen direction states:—

> "There is evidence before you on the basis of which the defendant's advocate invites you not to hold it against him that he failed to mention this fact when he had the opportunity to do so. That evidence is [. . .]. If you think this amounts to a reason why you should not hold the defendant's failure against him, do not do so."

---

324 See Justice report, *The Right of Silence Debate*, *supra*, pp.13-14.
325 [1997] 2 Cr.App.R., at p.33, *per* Lord Bingham C.J.
326 Pattenden, (1998) 2 E. & P., p.160.

(c) *Exclusion of evidence of silence*

Where the defence are adducing or suggesting an exculpatory reason explaining why the defendant did not mention during questioning a fact relied on at trial the very least that may be expected from the judge is a careful direction to the jury. But their aspirations may be bolder; they may be hoping to establish that there is no basis for an adverse inference in the particular circumstances and to demonstrate therefore that the evidence of silence is irrelevant or prejudicial and should be excluded. Giving guidance in *Condron and Condron*[327] on the procedural approach to be adopted in such a case Stuart-Smith L.J. said that there was no hard and fast procedure and that each case must be determined on its own facts. Uncontroversially, he envisaged that a court might exclude the evidence of silence under section 78 of the P.A.C.E. Act where the interview in question had been conducted in breach of the relevant code.[328] Apart from this, where on an application to exclude evidence, the judge—

> ". . . is being asked to hold, in effect, that it would be perverse of a jury to draw an adverse inference . . . except in clear cases, where, in effect, it would be perverse for the jury to draw an adverse inference . . . the judge is likely to consider that the question why the accused did not answer is one for the jury. . . ."[329]

A similar although arguably slightly more permissive approach was sanctioned by Lord Bingham C.J. in *Argent*:

> "We can readily accept that there will be some situations in which a judge should rule against the admissibility of evidence [from which the jury could draw inferences under section 34]. For example (and only way way of example), the judge might so rule in the case of an unlawful arrest where a breach of the Codes had occurred, or if the situation were one in which a jury properly directed could not properly draw an inference adverse to a defendant. Again, such a situation might arise if, in application of section 78, the judge concluded that the prejudicial value of evidence outweighed any probative effect it might reasonably have. However, save in a case of such a kind the proper course in our judgment is ordinarily for a trial judge to allow evidence to be given and direct a jury carefully concerning the drawing of inferences."[330]

It is assumed that exclusion in the second example (jury properly directed cannot properly draw an adverse inference) is synonymous with exclusion where such an inference would be perverse. However, the perversity (that is, unreasonable nature)

---

327 [1997] 1 W.L.R. 827, at p.836.
328 *ibid*. For code breach see more generally p.123, *infra*.
329 [1997] 1 Cr.App.R. 185, at p.196.
330 [1997] 2 Cr.App. R. 27, at p.29.

of an adverse inference would seem to be distinct from an inference drawn from silence the prejudicial effect of which was likely to outweigh its probative value. The prejudiciality versus probative test of exclusion does not contemplate the absence of probative value, merely the danger of overvalue. One commentator has argued that it is less rigorous than that of perversity and that the conflict between *Condron* and *Argent* needs to be resolved.[331] However, it seems most unlikely that the tribunal presided over by Stuart-Smith L.J. would have quarrelled with the inclusion of the prejudiciality versus probative test and it was conceivably omitted from the judgment by no more than oversight. In practice it tends to be a difficult obstacle for the defence to surmount anyway.

The approach of the Court of Appeal in defining the limits of control to be exercised by trial judges over the admissibility of evidence of silence has been described as an extremely restrictive one, the exclusionary function having been marginalised, supposedly in keeping with Parliament's intention that in the vast majority of cases it is the tribunal of fact which should be left to consider whether to draw inferences.[332] The restrictive policy of the courts is exemplified, it is argued, by their refusal to sanction exclusion where, for example, the accused was silent on legal advice, where the police failed to disclose the evidence in their hands, or where they questioned the accused on wholly inadequate evidence.[333] Yet, these are issues of fact and judgment relevant to the question whether it is reasonable to expect the defendant to have spoken and are matters properly within the jury's province if the legislation is not to lack teeth. The attitude of the Court of Appeal has not been inconsistent on this aspect of the silence provisions with its parsimonious policy on exclusion in general.

Not only has the Court of Appeal emphasised that exclusionary rulings are exceptional but the court has gone further in stressing that only in exceptional cases would it be appropriate to entertain exclusionary applications at all, that is by holding a *voir dire*, the customary method of the trial-within-the-trial by which judges make determinations when the admissibility of evidence is challenged. Thus, in *Condron* Stuart-Smith L.J. said:

> "If the objection is simply that the jury should not be invited to draw any adverse inference it will seldom be appropriate to invite the judge to rule on this before the conclusion of all the evidence. Only in the most exceptional case . . . could it be appropriate to make such a submission before the introduction of the evidence by the Crown."[334]

---

331 See Pattenden R., "Silence: Lord Taylor's legacy" (1998) 2 E. & P. 1 41, at pp.146-147.

332 See Birch [1999] Crim.L.R., at p.778: "As though to arm themselves in advance against arguments that section 34 is too complex, the judges of the Court of Appeal of England and Wales set about stripping it down to essentials from a very early stage." See Pattenden, (1998) 2 E. & P., at pp.146-147; and E. Cape, "Sidelining Defence Lawyers: Police Station Advice After *Condron*," (1997) 1 E.&P. 386, at p.388.

333 Birch, *supra*, at pp.778-779.

334 [1997] 1 Cr.App.R. 185, at p.196. It is not clear if there is any distinction between "not inviting the drawing of an adverse inference" and "inviting the jury not to draw an adverse inference," the

The court was evidently referring in the second sentence to exclusion of the evidence of silence because there could be little purpose in making a submission before the introduction of the evidence in question if it were not for the purpose of securing exclusion. By way of criticising the restriction of exclusion to exceptional cases it has been argued that if the admissibility of a confession, an express admission of guilt, is normally determined on the *voir dire*, the same procedure should surely apply when the admissibility of evidence capable of giving rise to an implied admission of guilt is contested.[335] As a debating point the argument is diverting but unconvincing. First of all, no comment interviews conducted in breach of the codes may be scrutinised on a *voir dire* in exactly the same way as statements to the police obtained in breach of the codes and since P.A.C.E. most applications on the *voir dire* for exclusion of statements are for code breach. Secondly, the special procedural rules for dealing with coerced confessions, and now embodied in section 76 of the P.A.C.E. Act, have evolved *sui generis*, and there is no logical basis for applying them to the generality of instances of silence, the admissibility of which is not being challenged on the ground of coercion.

The real difficulty with entertaining the holding of a *voir dire* only in exceptional cases lies not in any disparity with confessions exclusion but in a more fundamental problem. The only basis upon which the defence could argue that the judge should refrain from inviting the jury not to draw an adverse inference from silence is where it would be unreasonable of them to do so or where the prejudicial effect of the silence outweighed its probative value. However, in that event the evidence ought to be excluded, and it would be insufficient to direct the jury to draw no adverse inference. Either it is perverse to draw an inference (or at any rate unsafe to do so: prejuciality outweighing probative value), in which case the evidence ought to be excluded (and not merely dealt with by way of a direction to the jury), or it is not perverse or unsafe, in which case there would be no basis for not leaving the issue to the jury. In other words, if there is any prospect that it may be perverse or unsafe to draw an adverse inference the defence should be allowed an opportunity to seek its exclusion before the existence of the silence is led before the jury.

Yet *Condron* says that trial judges ought normally to wait until all the evidence has been called before determining whether or not an adverse inference is proper, thereby ruling out a *voir dire*. The reticence to sanction the routine holding of a *voir dire* reflects a prediction that in most conceivable instances the defence will be unable to lay a foundation for the argument that an adverse inference will be perverse or unsafe.[336] Although there was an undoubted place for the *voir dire* in cases of silence, albeit in exceptional cases only, the trial judge in *Kavanagh*[337] apparently reached the conclusion that in no circumstances would it ever be appropriate for a judge to hold a *voir dire* for the purpose of ruling whether or not

point being that whilst the latter may have a counter-productive effect the former seems to convey studiously saying nothing about the silence which may damage the accused.

[335] R. Pattenden, (1998) 2 E & P, at p.159, note 133.

[336] As where, *e.g.*, the accused was silent on legal advice, where the police failed to disclose the evidence in their hands, or where they questioned the accused on wholly inadequate evidence.

[337] (1997) unreported, C.A. 9503897/Z2, February 7.

there was material to go before the jury from which they could draw section 34 inferences. The Court of Appeal stated that the assumption was incorrect. In their view the passage quoted above from the judgment of Lord Bingham in *Argent* demonstrated that in exceptional circumstances, but only in exceptional circumstances, should a judge rule, having heard evidence on the *voir dire*, as to whether or not inferences were capable of being drawn and as to the evidence which should go to the jury in support of the drawing of such inferences. In *Kavanagh* it was submitted that the fact, first, that the appellant was at the time of his arrest a heroin addict in a state of withdrawal and, second, that the decision of the police not to tell the appellant or his solicitor where precisely in the house the fingerprints had been found, were exceptional circumstances which impelled the conducting of a *voir dire*. It was held, however, that although the judge was wrong to work on the assumption that in no circumstances would it be appropriate for a *voir dire* to be conducted he was not wrong in the instant case to decline to hold one. In any event, the court further held, even on the assumption that the judge should have conducted a *voir dire* and had then heard the evidence in relation to the two grounds on which it was claimed that the appellant adopted his solicitor's advice to make no comment in his interview, it was inevitable that he would have ruled that neither or them, separately or together, was a reason for precluding the jury from hearing the evidence of the silence. In the court's view if the fact that an accused was a heroin addict in a state of withdrawal were of itself a reason for not providing information relevant to his defence, that would be to drive a coach and horses through the Act. Further, the question whether or not the approach of the police in not disclosing the location of the fingerprints was a reasonable one was pre-eminently a matter for the jury to consider when deciding the wider question of the reasonableness or otherwise of the appellant's non-disclosure of his defence.

(d) *Jury directions on non-material silence*

In cases which are found on the *voir dire* not to fall within the exceptional category or in which the judge declines to hold a *voir dire* on the basis that no proper foundation has been laid for examining the question of exclusion, it may happen that material emerges during the trial before the jury on the basis of which it may be appropriate to rule that no inferences ought to be drawn under section 34 from the defendant's silence. Of course by that stage it will be too late to exclude the evidence of silence from the jury. Short of discharging the jury, therefore, (an improbable though theoretically possible outcome) the only option open is to direct them to draw no inferences from the evidence of the defendant's silence. Another way of expressing this is that the silence is "withdrawn" from the jury, by which is meant that they are instructed to ignore it. The existence of a residual discretion to give such a direction was recognized by the Court of Appeal in *Argent*[338] in which Lord Bingham C.J. applied to investigative stage silence the principle previously enunciated in *Cowan* that the judge enjoys a discretion "to advise the jury, or even

338 [1997] 2 Cr.App.R. 27, at p.33.

to direct the jury, that they ought not to draw any adverse inference from the defendant's failure to give evidence."[339] The existence of a discretion is also implied in the passage which was quoted above from the judgment of Stuart-Smith L.J. in *Condron*, when he said—

> "If the objection is simply that the jury should not be invited to draw any adverse inference it will seldom be appropriate to invite the judge to rule on this before the conclusion of all the evidence."

However, Lord Bingham cautioned that the discretion was to be used only sparingly:—

> "Only rarely would it be right for the judge to direct the jury that they should, or should not, draw the appropriate inference."[340]

In other words, it is not, generally speaking, open to the trial judge "to admit the evidence but exclude the inference."[341]

Where the judge does determine that the jury should not draw an adverse inference it was held in *McGarry*[342] that he should specifically direct them not to do so. The Judicial Studies Board has provided a specimen direction to this effect.[343] Where the judge rules that no proper inference may be drawn from the fact that the defendant made no comment through his interview and gives the jury a positive direction not to draw an adverse inference, it is debateable how far this will neutralise any prejudice which might have been caused by the giving in evidence of the non-material silence. The Court of Appeal has shown confidence that prejudice can be eliminated by suitable directions. In *Griffin*[344] a summary of questions asked during a no comment interview was read out to the jury at the close of the prosecution case, and a summary was then given to the jury. When the judge summed up he made it clear that no adverse inference should in fact be drawn. The appeal was unsuccessful because it was held that even if there had been prejudice suffered by the defence, it was put right by the clear direction not to draw any inference.

The question whether the failure to give a *McGarry* direction would render a conviction unsafe in the light of Article 6 of the European Convention on Human

---

339 *Byrne* (1995) unreported, C.A., November 21, *per* Lord Taylor, paraphrasing his own words in *Cowan* [1996] Q.B. 373, at p.380. Pattenden makes the cogent point that no indication has been given as to when a judge should "direct," as opposed merely to "advise:" (1998) 2 E. & P., at p.148.

340 [1997] 2 Cr.App.R., at p.33.

341 Birch, [1999] Crim.L.R., at p.779. In *Condron* [1997] 1 Cr.App.R. 185, at p.196, the court instanced the hypothetical exceptional case of a defendant of very low intelligence and understanding who had been advised to say nothing by his solicitor.

342 [1999] 1 Cr.App.R. 377, C.A. See also *B.(M.)* (1999) unreported C.A. 98/06635/X4, November 4.

343 J.S.B. specimen direction no. 44. See *Archbold*, para. 15-404.

344 [1998] Crim.L.R. 418. See also *Pointer* [1997] Crim.L.R. 676; *McGarry* [1999] 1 Cr.App.R. 377.

Rights was considered by the Court of Appeal in *Francom and others*.[345] Although, in the opinion of the court, the judge was not compelled to do so, she had agreed to direct the jury that they should not draw any adverse inference from the fact that the appellants made no mention to the police of matters which they relied on at trial. The trial was conducted by all parties on that understanding and counsel for one of the appellants actually told the jury that the judge would direct them to draw no adverse inferences from the appellants' silence. However, she failed to give such a direction in accordance with *McGarry* and no counsel invited her to make a correction. On appeal prosecuting counsel's explanation for not alerting the judge to the oversight was that the tone in which she had given her direction relating to the appellants' interview summaries was such that he considered that she was indicating that no adverse inference should be drawn[346] (although, curiously, at another point in their judgment the court referred to prosecuting counsel's admitted failure to notice the omission[347]). Giving judgment, the court pointed out that the statutory test of "unsafeness" in section 2(1) of the Criminal Appeal Act 1968, as amended by section 2(1) of the Criminal Appeal Act 1995, was not identical to the issue of unfairness in Article 6 of the Convention,[348] a distinction which the court noted had been recognised by the E.H.C.R. in *Condron* v. *U.K.* and by the Court of Appeal in *Davis, Rowe and Johnson*.[349] However, in the court's view, following variously *Condron* v. *U.K.*, *Mullen*[350] and *Davis,Rowe and Johnson*, the term "unfair" was to be given a broad meaning favourable to the defendants, not limited to the safety of the conviction itself and encompassing the entire prosecution process.[351] It had been urged for the appellants that the position in *Francom* was exactly the same as that considered in *Condron* v. *U.K.* because the court did not know what could have influenced the jury's decision.[352] In the judgment of the court, the test which had to be applied was—

> ". . . whether, notwithstanding what is, in this case, a non-direction, we are satisfied that no reasonable jury could have come to a different conclusion from that which was reached by this jury if they were properly directed. This approach not only means that there must be a lack of safety, it also means there must be no unfairness because the

---

345 (2000) *The Times*, October 24; C.A. 99/3936/W5, *et seq*.

346 Transcript para. 49. Thus she reminded the jury that the first appellant gave no comment replies to some of his interviews because, as he said, the police kept going on over the same questions and he did not like the way the questions were asked, and two other appellants gave "no comment" interviews on their solicitor's advice: see *ibid*., para. 40.

347 *ibid*.

348 *ibid*., para. 43.

349 (2000) *The Times*, July 17; C.A. 99/2239/41/S3.

350 [1999] 2 Cr.App.R. 143.

351 para. 43.

352 para. 45.

> non-direction or misdirection must not affect the defendant's right to a fair trial."[353]

In the court's judgment the trial was fair within the meaning of Article 6.1 and the conviction was safe. Importantly, they acknowledged that the only way in which the jury could have obtained the impression that inferences might be drawn from the appellants' silence and that they did not have a right to silence was from the fact that the jury were told the terms of the caution. In the view of the court, however, this had to be be kept in proportion in the context of a long trial and a long summing-up and having regard to the fact that the appellants were not believed,[354] the latter a rationalisation which appears perhaps not wholly devoid of *petitio principii*.

(e) *Exculpatory reasons must be proffered evidentially*

In *Cowan*[355] it was submitted that without the need for evidence, defending counsel could properly advance reasons or excuses for the accused's trial silence which might justify the court not drawing or the jury being directed not to draw an adverse inference. The Court of Appeal rejected the argument, stressing that there must be an evidential basis for not drawing an adverse inference from the defendant's having declined to give evidence and that the rule against advocates giving evidence dressed up as a submission applied to preclude them offering conjectural reasons why the defendant had not been called.[356] In *Condron*[357] the court said that the principles in *Cowan* applied to silence at the investigative stage, and the prohibition against advocates suggesting reasons for silence in lieu of evidence would apply therefore to silence at that stage.

Dr Pattenden has noted that these rulings follow a pattern of recent decisions in the Court of Appeal which together have created a new kind of defence evidential burden irreconcilable with the traditional axiom that an accused can contest a criminal charge without calling evidence, the so-called "frozen" defence.[358] Thus, with the abolition of mandatory corroboration warnings in cases involving accomplices and certain sexual offences[359] it was held in *Makanjuola*[360] that a cautionary direction to the jury about the evidence of these categories of witness will now only be given in the discretion of the trial judge where an evidential basis had been laid and that an evidential basis does not include mere suggestions by cross-examining counsel. Earlier, in *Bateson*, it was held that in addressing the jury on a lie told by the accused defending counsel was not entitled to "conjure explanations out of the air" but that any such explanation had to be supported by

---

[353] para. 50, following an interpretation of *Condron* v. *U.K.* originally suggested by Jennings, "The death of silence or safety?" C.B.A. newsletter June 2000, 3, at p.4.

[354] para. 50.

[355] [1996] Q.B. 373.

[356] *ibid*., at p.383, *per* Lord Taylor C.J.

[357] [1997] 1 Cr.App.R. 185, at p.194.

[358] (1998) 2 E. & P., at pp.156-158.

[359] Criminal Justice and Public Order Act 1994, s.32.

[360] [1995] 3 All E.R. 730, at p.733, *per* Lord Taylor C.J.

evidence, although not necessarily from the defendant.[361] There must now been supporting evidence before reasons for doubting the incriminating effect of circumstantial evidence can go to the jury at the instigation of the defence. This contrasts with a *Lucas* direction by the judge about possible innocent reasons for lies, which does not require an evidential foundation.[362] As Dr Pattenden tellingly observes, why the judge but not defence counsel, can make speculative suggestions to the jury has not been explained.[363]

Clearly the rule requiring the prosecution to negate every hypothesis consistent with the accused's innocence[364] does not go so far as "to allow the defence to submit at the end of the prosecution's case that the Crown had not proved affirmatively and beyond a reasonable doubt that the accused was at the time of the crime, sober, or not sleepwalking or not in a trance or black out."[365] However, within the constraints of that qualification—

> "It has always been the practice of defence counsel to invite the jury to speculate about innocent explanations for the prosecution evidence: this is what the notion of testing the prosecution is all about."[366]

The effect of the introduction of a defence evidence requirement is, in Dr Pattenden's words, a subtle subversion of the burden of proof neither foreseen by Parliament nor compelled by the Criminal Justice and Public Order Act 1994.[367] The attitude of Lord Taylor C.J. in *Cowan* and of the Court of Appeal in *Condron* stands in stark contrast to that of Lord Bingham C.J. in *Bowden*[368] when, referring to the issue of legal professional privilege, he said that even though proper effect must be given to the adverse inference provisions, as they "restrict rights recognised at common law as appropriate to protect defendants against the risk of injustice they should not be construed more widely than the statutory language requires." The prohibition on non-evidential conjecture by the defence has produced a fundamental inbalance between prosecution and defence advantageous to the prosecution. Where the defendant is silent at interview, raises a specific defence at trial through witnesses, but does not give evidence at trial and does not otherwise call evidence to explain why he failed to intimate his defence at interview it is open to the prosecution to invite the jury to draw an inference adverse to the defendant. There is only one adverse inference capable of being drawn. that the defendant is guilty. It is based on the presupposition that the innocent will naturally be impelled to proclaim

---

361 (1991) *The Times*, April 10, C.A. The court said that any evidence, whether from the prosecution or from other defence witnesses, would suffice, and not merely that from the defendant, as the trial judge had wrongly ruled.

362 *Lucas* [1981] Q.B. 720; *Goodway* [1993] 4 All E.R. 894.

363 (1998) 2 E. & P., at p.157, n.117.

364 *Hodge* (1838) 2 Lew. C.C. 227.

365 *Hill* v *Baxter* [1958] 1 Q.B. 277, at p.284, *per* Devlin J.

366 Pattenden, (1998) 2 E. & P., at pp.159-160.

367 *ibid.*, p.159.

368 [1999] 1 W.L.R. 823, at p.827.

their innocent explanation at the earliest opportunity. However, although this is an *assumption*, in the absence of any explanation as to why the accused said nothing the reason can never really be *known.* An adverse inference is therefore a presumption of guilt based on no more than conjecture and this is the fundamental drawback of the legislation. This shortcoming has been exacerbated by judicial pronouncement. Whereas the jury may not be invited by defending advocate to speculate *in favour* of the defendant by conjecturing innocent reasons as to why he might have remained silent, they are allowed to be invited by the Crown (and the judge) to make assumptions *against* the defendant. This is an inequity which was not inherent in the 1994 Act but which has been introduced judicially to slant prosecutions still further against defendants.

(f) *Rebuttal*

Where the defendant adduces an innocent explanation for his silence in interview or for failing to mention a fact later relied on, the judge may be called upon to consider any application by the Crown to call evidence in rebuttal, and the admissibility of any such evidence.[369]

(g) *No general requirment for judges to direct the jury as to possible exculpatory reasons for silence*

The attitude of the Court of Appeal towards the issue of the defendant's silence contrasts very remarkably with the way trial judges are expected to deal with evidence of the accused's *lies*. In *Lucas*[370] it was held that the judge must warn the jury not to infer guilt from the fact that the accused had lied unless satisfied that the lie is deliberate, relates to a material issue, and arises from a consciousness of guilt. Giving judgment, Lord Lane C.J. said that "the jury should in appropriate cases be reminded that people sometimes lie, for example, in an attempt to bolster up a just cause, or out of shame or out of a wish to conceal disgraceful behaviour from their family."[371] In certain respects there is a close correspondence between silence and lies, as Dr Pattenden has aptly demonstrated:

> "Silence and lies have a lot in common: both are a means of avoiding saying something. In the former case by saying nothing, in the latter case by saying something that is false. Both derive their evidential force, if any, from the motive behind the accused's evasive behaviour. Because motives can never be known for certain, both silence and lies are therefore also forms of evidence prone to ambiguity."

With such an abundance of potential reasons for explaining away silence consistent with innocence it is arguable that an adverse inference should not be too readily drawn. In view of the analogous relationship between lies and silence it might have

369 See Birch, [1999] Crim.L.R., at p.785.
370 [1981] Q.B. 720.
371 *ibid*, at p.724.

been supposed that, following the lead given by *Lucas,* judges would have been similarly enjoined to give full directions on possible exculpatory reasons for silence, as Dr. Greer urged should be done:—

> "[T]he criminal burden of proof implies a presumption, albeit a rebuttable one, in favour of an innocent interpretation. It is unrealistic to attempt to prohibit juries from ever allowing verdicts of guilty to be influenced by the fact that the accused said nothing to the police or refused to testify in court. What can and should be done is to require judges to outline possible innocent reasons for the accused's silence. . . . The basic principle should be that, in trials on indictment, judges should be obliged to point out to jurors that silence in response to the police (with or without legal advice) and in the courtroom may be entirely innocent. . . . Possible grounds for an innocent exercise of the right to silence . . . should be . . . listed by trial judges."[372]

However, although there was nothing in the Criminal Justice and Public Order Act 1994 to prevent the Court of Appeal from instructing judges to give warnings analogous to those in the case of lies, it has eschewed such a course. In *Cowan* Lord Taylor C.J., referring to trial silence, stated that the court did not "think it incumbent on a judge or appropriate for him to embark or invite the jury to embark on possible speculative reasons consistent with innocence which might theoretically prompt a defendant to remain silent."[373] Presumably it is only evidentially supported reasons which the judge is bound to deal with in summing up but nothing has been said by the Court of Appeal obliging judges to give sympathetic weight to such reasons or to discourage them from treating such reasons in dismissive language. The divergence of approach from that in regard to lies could not be more stark.[374] As Dr Pattenden has pointed out, "appropriate cases" in the *Lucas* direction have not been confined to those in which there is evidence that supports an innocent explanation for the lie, a judicial warning being standard practice.[375] She notes the possible significance of the fact that the accused is not formally cautioned about the consequences of lying, as in the case of silence.[376]

---

[372] 57 M.L.R., at pp.729-730.

[373] [1996] Q.B. 373, at p.386. *Cowan* was applied to investigative stage silence in *Condron* [1997] 1 W.L.R. 827.

[374] *Cf. Napper* (1996) 161 J.P.R. 16, at p.23, in which Lord Taylor C.J. denied that *Cowan* was in any way inconsistent with the standard direction on lies set out in *Lucas*. See also [1996] Crim.L.R. 591.

[375] (1998) 2 E. & P., at p.154, citing *Goodway* [1993] 4 All E.R. 900, at p.902.

[376] (1998) 2 E. & P., at p.154.

(17) Code breach

The Working Group recommended that under their scheme juries ought to be instructed to consider, *inter alia*, whether the defendant had the benefit of various safeguards, for example, being cautioned on the consequences of silence, access to legal advice and the safeguards afforded to juveniles and the mentally ill or handicapped.[377] In summing up on the issue of the code breach it would doubtless become conventional practice to tell the jury that they should take the breach into account when considering what inferences, if any, to draw from the defendant's silence. But there may be no logical basis for such an invitation. Whilst some aspects of an interrogation can affect the evidential significance of silence the absence of procedural fairness is not always reflected in lower probative value. Thus, if the suspect is not told that he is suspected of having been in one place, it can hardly be of probative value that he omitted to mention he was in another place. But an interrogation may be wholly unfair and yet elicit reliable answers or probative silence, as where he is improperly refused a solicitor. A direction to discount probative significance cannot adequately deal with many aspects of the procedural unfairness.[378]

The exclusionary discretion under section 78 of P.A.C.E. will clearly be available to exclude evidence of the suspect's silence in the event that questioning is sullied by Code C breaches. Zuckerman has argued that this is unlikely to prove an adequate safeguard because if the probative value of silence is unaffected by the non-observance of procedural requirements it would be hard to expect judges to use their discretion to exclude it.[379] This reservation perhaps gives too little credit for the performance of trial judges under P.A.C.E. On the other hand, he points out that the Working Group, who themselves envisaged the use of the exclusionary discretion, expected the emphasis to be placed on probative force rather than on the nature of the procedure:[380]

> "In rare cases it may be material for the court to hear precisely how the suspect's failure to answer particular questions fitted in with the rest of the interview, but usually we would expect the court to concentrate on the *explanation* given for silence rather than the precise context in which it was exercised."

The Court of Appeal has held that where the defence are contending that evidence of silence should be excluded because of police malpractice or breaches of the PACE Code such an application should normally be taken on the *voir dire* before the jury hears the evidence.[381] In *Argent*[382] Lord Bingham C.J. said:—

---

377 Report, para. 65.
378 See Zuckerman, [1989] Crim.L.R., at p.861.
379 *ibid.*
380 *ibid.*, at pp.861-862, citing report, paras. 81 and 91, and para. 88.
381 *Condron* [1997] 1 Cr.App.R. 185, at p187; *Argent* [1997] 2 Cr.App.R. 27, at p.31.

"We can readily accept that there will be some situations in which a judge should rule against the admissibility of evidence [of the accused's silence]. For example (and only by way of example) the judge may so rule in the case of an unlawful arrest where a breach of the Codes has occurred . . ."

Since this is only an example it is assumed that unlawful arrest is not a prerequisite of exclusion for code breach.

C. *STATUTORY SAVING OF COMMON LAW PRINCIPLES RELATING TO TACIT ADMISSION*

Section 34(5) of the 1994 Act provides that the section does not—

"(a) prejudice the admissibility in evidence of the silence or other reaction of the accused in the face of anything said in his presence relating to the conduct in respect of which he is charged, in so far as evidence thereof would be admissible apart from this section; or (b) preclude the drawing of any inference from any such silence or other reaction of the accused which could properly be drawn apart from this section."

One of the inferences which arguably might properly be drawn from a failure to mention a fact relied on in later proceedings is that if the failure arises in the context of total silence it may be evidence that the defendant was accepting the validity of the allegation at large. But such an inference could only be drawn under the provisions of section 34(1) and (2) where a fact was asserted at trial which had not been mentioned during questioning under caution or when the defendant was charged. However, the defendant may be totally silent when questioned or charged, raising at trial no defence nor relying on any fact which it can be said he might reasonably have been expected to mention at the investigative stage. In short, he may be content to proceed by putting the prosecution to proof. In preserving the Common law it is necessary to examine whether section 34(5) in these circumstances permits silence at the investigative stage to constitute evidence against the accused. The subsection obviously preserves the Common law on tacit admission in the face of an allegation made by a private individual, as enunciated in such authorities as *Cramp* and *Christie*.[383] In theory it would also have the effect of preserving the Common law on tacit acceptance of an allegation put by a police officer. This would be to keep intact the principle in *Chandler*[384] and so much of the principles as can be deduced from the case learning analysed at the beginning of

---

382 [1997] 2 Cr.pp.R. 27, at p.31.
383 See pp.32-33, *supra*.
384 [1976] 1 W.L.R. 585.

Chapter 2. A number of those authorities addressed the question of whether the suspect's silence could amount to corroboration. With the general abrogation by the Act of the corroboration rules it should be pointed out that where tacit admission can be inferred those authorities will be relevant to the question of whether silence may be taken into account in deciding if a *prima facie* case has been established.

Although the Common law is theoretically preserved in permitting a finding of tacit admission to be made from the defendant's non-response to an allegation put by a police officer, the circumstances in which such a finding is possible, already very narrow before P.A.C.E., have been further whittled down to the point at which there is now hardly any scope in practice for the principle to be applied. As observed earlier, before P.A.C.E. there was no requirement to administer a caution on arrest, so that an arrest without a caution might give rise to a finding of tacit admission, provided that the defendant had his solicitor present. After P.A.C.E. made the caution an obligatory concomitant of arrest there remained very little scope for such a finding. The old form of caution rendered it unfair to the accused if his silence following a caution could be taken to amount to an admission of the truth of the allegation because in that case the suspect would have been led into a trap. Since neither questioning under caution nor now arrest could provide a context for tacit admission there were very few occasions when the stating of an allegation (a) without an accompanying caution and (b) in the presence of a solicitor (the "even terms" condition laid down in *Chandler*) could furnish such a context. One example which was suggested earlier was where during the course of an developing inquiry into complex facts the investigating officer holds a meeting with a suspect and his solicitor for the exclusive purpose of informing them, as a matter of courtesy and common fairness, that a firm allegation against the suspect has now crytallised. Another example might be a casual encounter in the village High Street between a police investigator, on the one hand, and the suspect and his solicitor, on the other, when the officer tells them, for their information, that an allegation has been made against the suspect although at this stage no action is to be taken against the suspect.[385]

It may be asked why the new form of caution, instead of maintaining an obstacle in the way of an inference of tacit admission, does not rather remove the element of a trap since it warns the suspect of risks involved in silence. Why should not the existing caution when given on arrest, for example, provide a foundation for an inference of tacit admission from the defendant's silence at that point? The answer seems clear enough. First, the terms of the caution warn the arrested person of risks associated with silence *when questioned*, an exercise which is not normally permitted outside the police station[386] and which will therefore be undertaken only later. It follows that as to the immediate present the traditional element of the caution applies, with the consequence that any inference of tacit admission must be ruled out on the basis that otherwise the caution would constitute a trap.

---

[385] A variation on the example suggested by Lord Wigoder at Lords Committee stage on the Criminal Justice and Public Order Bill, 555 H.L. Deb., col. 526, May 23, 1994.

[386] Code C.11.1.

The second reason why the new form of caution ought to preclude an inference of tacit admission is that its terms refer to the risks involved in delaying the presentation of facts by way of defence. Notably it makes no declaration of any risk that silence now may give rise in any event to an inference of admission of the truth of the allegation, even if no facts are relied upon later which are not first mentioned at the questioning stage. If tacit admission were permitted to be inferred from silence on arrest a caution which confined its warning to the possible weakening effect of delay on the credibility of a defence fact would be likely to draw attention away from, in fact even conceal, what would otherwise be a more directly incriminating implication of silence, namely tacit admission. The caution would be misleading and unfair.

D. *SPECIAL ASPECTS OF INVESTIGATIVE STAGE SILENCE LIABLE TO HAVE AN INCRIMINATORY EFFECT REGARDLESS OF ANY DEFENCE OFFERED AT TRIAL*

At Common law the presence on the accused of any object, mark or substance and the presence of the accused at a place connected with the crime has always been capable of furnishing circumstantial evidence of guilt. The 1994 Act allows the accused's failure to provide an explanation for any of these circumstances to stand as an additional element of circumstantial evidence. These measures were not in the original C.L.R.C. scheme but were inspired by sections 18 and 19 of the Republic of Ireland's Criminal Justice Act 1984, subsequently enacted as Articles 5 and 6 respectively of the Criminal Evidence (Northern Ireland) Order 1988. The provisions allow adverse inferences to be drawn from the accused's failure or refusal to explain an object, substance or mark on or otherwise physically associated with his person, or a failure or refusal to explain his presence at a particular place. The inferences allowed resemble those in tacit admission cases rather than those allowed under the general provision on failure to mention a fact later relied on. The failure or refusal to explain the suspicious mark, *etc*. associated with the suspect's person or to explain his or her presence at a particular place, unlike the failure contemplated in the general provision, is statutorily deemed capable in its own right of being taken as an admission that the consequent suspicion of guilt is justified. It is not the factor of delay in furnishing an explanation which serves to increase the evidence against the defendant. It will also be noted that there is no express reference in these provisions to the need for the circumstances to be such that the accused could reasonably have been expected to give the account required.[387] It is not clear whether the requirement is nevertheless implicit or whether it will always be presumed to be reasonable to account for suspicious circumstances.[388]

---

[387] See Jackson, [1991] Crim.L.R., at p.408.

[388] As suggested by Peter Mirfield, *Silence, Confessions and Improperly Obtained Evidence*, Oxford 1998, p.262. For the same author's earlier commentary on the 1994 Act see "Two Side-effects of sections 34 to 37 of the Criminal Justice and Public Order Act 1994," [1995] Crim.L.R. 612.

(1) Effect of accused's failure or refusal to account for objects, substances or marks associated with his person

Section 36 of the Act provides:—

"(1) Where—

(a) a person is arrested by a constable, and there is—

(i) on his person; or

(ii) in or on his clothing or footwear; or

(iii) otherwise in his possession; or

(iv) in any place in which he is at the time of his arrest,

any object, substance or mark, or there is any mark on any such object; and

(b) that or another constable investigating the case reasonably believes that the presence of the object, substance or mark may be attributable to the participation of the person arrested in the commission of an offence specified by the constable; and

(c) the constable informs the person arrested that he so believes, and requests him to account for the presence of the object, substance or mark; and

(d) the person fails or refuses to do so,

then if, in any proceedings against the person for the offence so specified, evidence of those matters is given, subsection (2) below applies.

(2) Where this subsection applies—

(a) a magistrates' court inquiring into the offence as examining justices;

(b) a judge, in deciding whether to grant an application made by the accused [for dismissal of charge following notice of transfer in a case of serious fraud or of a violent or sexual offence involving a child under fourteen]; and

(c) the court in determining whether there is a case to answer; and

(d) the court or jury, in determining whether the accused is guilty or the offence charged,

may draw such inferences from the failure or refusal as appear proper.

(3) Subsections (1) and (2) above apply to the condition of clothing or footwear as they apply to a substance or mark thereon.

(4) Subsections (1) and (2) above do not apply unless the accused was told in ordinary language[389] by the constable when making the

[389] Code C10.5B specifies the elements of the warnings required: see p.196, *infra*.

request mentioned in subsection (1)(c) above what the effect of this section would be if he failed or refused to comply with the request.

(5) This section applies in relation to officers of customs and excise as it applies in relation to constables.

(6) This section does not preclude the drawing of any inference from a failure or refusal of the accused to account for the presence of an object, substance or mark or from the condition of clothing or footwear which could properly be drawn apart from this section."

(2) Effect of accused's failure or refusal to account for presence at a particular place

Section 37 of the Act provides—

"(1) Where—

(a) a person arrested by a constable was found by him at a place[390] at or about the time the offence for which he was arrested is alleged to have been committed; and

(b) that or another constable investigating the offence reasonably believes that the presence of the person at that place and at that time may be attributable to his participation in the commission of the offence; and

(c) the constable informs the person that he so believes, and requests him to account for that presence; and

(d) the person fails or refuses to do so,

then if, in any proceedings against the person for the offence, evidence of those matters is given, subsection (2) below applies.

(2) Where this subsection applies—

(a) a magistrates' court inquiring into the offence as examining justices;

(b) a judge, in deciding whether to grant an application made by the accused [for dismissal of charge following notice of transfer in a case of serious fraud or of a violent or sexual offence involving a child under fourteen]; and

(c) the court in determining whether there is a case to answer; and

(d) the court or jury, in determining whether the accused is guilty of the offence charged,

may draw such inferences from the failure or refusal as appear proper.

---

[390] The term "place" includes any building or part of a building, any vehicle, vessel, aircraft or hovercraft and any other place whatsoever: s.38(1).

(3) Subsections (1) and (2) do not apply unless the accused was told in ordinary language by the constable when making the request mentioned in subsection (1)(c) above what the effect of this section would be if he failed or refused to comply with the request.

(4) This section applies in relation to officers of customs and excise as it applies in relation to constables.

(5) This section does not preclude the drawing of any inference from a failure or refusal of the accused to account for his presence at a place which could properly be drawn apart from this section."

(3) Ancilliary provisions

(a) *Committal, transfer and sending forthwith*

The same considerations apply as in relation to section 34, with all amendments being provided for by the same statutory measures.

(b) *The "offence charged"*

Section 38(2) provides that the reference in sections 36(2) and 37(2) to the "offence charged" includes a reference to any other offence of which the accused could lawfully be convicted on that charge. Accordingly, where, for example, a court could determine the validity of a transfer, decide whether a prima facie case has been established, or return a conviction in respect of an offence other than that charged or indicted the failure or refusal in question may be relevant in that particular adjudication.

(c) *Failure or refusal insufficient in itself for a conviction*

Section 38(3) provides that no one may have proceedings against him transferred to the Crown Court for trial, have a case to answer or be convicted of an offence solely on an inference drawn from a failure or refusal to which section 36(2) or 37(2) relates. Similarly, section 38(4) provides that where there has been a notice of transfer in a case of serious fraud or in the case of an offence of violence or sex involving a child under fourteen a judge must not refuse an application for dismissal if the charge is based solely on an inference drawn from such a failure or refusal.

(d) *Sections 36 and 37 do not preclude the operation of existing statutory powers to exclude evidence as inadmissible or of any exclusionary discretion*

Nothing in sections 36 or 37 prejudices the operation of a provision of any enactment which provides (in whatever words) that any answer or evidence given by a person in specified circumstances shall not be admissible in evidence against him or some other person in any proceedings or class of proceedings (however described, and whether civil or criminal).[391] Further, nothing in the section prejudices any power of a court, in any proceedings, to exclude evidence (whether by preventing questions being put or otherwise) at its discretion.[392] The effect of the first of these provisions would seem to be to ensure that sections 36 and 37 place no impediment on the power of any court to invoke section 76 of P.A.C.E. in order to exclude evidence, for example, of an interview containing a relevant failure. The second measure would have the same effect in relation to the discretion under section 78 to exclude an interview containing a relevant failure.

(e) *Refusal of access to a solicitor*

Sections 36 and 37 has been amended from a day yet to be appointed by the insertion of new subsections (4A) and (3A) respectively providing that where the accused was at an authorised place of detention at the time of the failure subsections (1) and (2) of each section do not apply if he had not been allowed an opportunity to consult a solicitor prior to being questioned, charged or officially informed that he might be prosecuted.[393]

(4) The time and place of a significant failure or refusal

It is to be noted that for a failure or refusal by the suspect to be capable of having evidential significance under sections 36 and 37 a request for an explanation must be made by an officer. If this is not done, no adverse inferences may be drawn. The request must be made after the suspect has been arrested. It therefore contrasts with the general failure to mention provision in section 34 which relates to questioning under caution and which may apply to questioning prior to arrest. Such a request would clearly constitute an interview and this is in fact made explicit in the language of C10.5A and C10.5B, which set out the special warnings to be given to the suspect as a condition for the drawing of an adverse inference and which require a record to be made of the interview in which the request is made. It follows that the request can normally only be made at the police station, unless the request is capable of being justified as necessary under the provisions of C11.1 (permitting an interview to take place outside a police station or other authorised place of detention in the special categories of urgency permitted by the provision). Both sections expressly provide that they do not preclude the drawing of inferences from failure or refusal to give

---

[391] s.38(5). The reference to giving evidence is a reference to giving evidence in any manner, whether by furnishing information, making discovery, producing documents or otherwise: *ibid*.

[392] s.38(6).

[393] Inserted by the Youth Justice and Criminal Evidence Act 1999, s.58(1) and (2).The amendments apply only to proceedings instituted on or after the commencement date for the new section but so apply whether the relevant failure or refusal on the part of the accused took place before or after that date: s.67(4) and Sched. 7, para.. 8. For further consideration see, *infra*, p.156. Section 38(2A) provides that in s.36(4A) and s.37(3A) "authorised place of detention" means (a) a police station or (b) any other place prescribed for the purposes of that provision by order made by the Secretary of State, and the power to make an order under s.38(2A) shall be exercisable by statutory isntrument which shall be subject to annulment in pursuance of a resultion of either House of Parliament.

explanations apart from their application. The effect of this is that silence in response to a request made before arrest may give rise to an inference where permitted under Common law. However, whilst a request made after a decision to arrest but before arrival at the police station might under Common law permit an adverse inference to be drawn, such a request would normally constitute an improper interview and the defendant's silence would be open to exclusion.

(5) Application

The working of the special "failure to explain" provisions of the Act is well illustrated by a Northern Ireland case in which inferences were drawn under Article 6 of the Criminal Evidence (Northern Ireland) Order 1988, the equivalent of section 37, dealing with failure to explain presence at a particular place. As triers of fact in non-jury "Diplock" trials[394] judges are required to decide what inferences to draw from silence under the Order and of stating and elaborating on those inferences in their grounds of decision.[395] It has been noted that initially the judges were cautious in the way they applied the new provisions[396] but as time went on they became bolder,[397] as attested by *McCartan and McKay*.[398] The defendants were convicted of illegal possession of firearms on the basis of an inference drawn under Article 6 of the Order from their refusal to explain their presence at a particular place. The defendants, who were charged with possession of firearms, had been arrested in a car park about 15 yards through an alleyway from their homes. They were in the company of a third man who was linked by scientific evidence to rifles and ammunition which, although only 200 to 250 yards away, could not be reached without taking a somewhat circuitous route. They were, therefore, very much closer to their own homes than to the weapons and ammunition and there was nothing unusual about their being in the car park, which was was in an area where people from the local housing estate commonly milled around and walked about. When questioned by the police both defendants remained silent. Non-accidental presence of a person in the company of another person who can be proved guilty of committing an offence at that time is, without further evidence of participatory action, theoretically sufficient to convict of participation in the offence.[399] Yet there

---

394 Suspension of jury trial in cases relating to offences with potential terro rist connections scheduled under the Northern Ireland (Emergency Provisions) Act 1973 was originally enacted by s.2 of that Act and re-enacted in the Northern Ireland (Emergency Provisions) Act 1978, s.7 and Sched. 4.

395 See Jackson, "Curtailing the Right of Silence: lessons from Northern Ireland" [1991] Crim.L.R. 404, at pp.409-410. It has also been observed that the judges were originally "uneasy" about the changes made to the right to silence: Prof. I. Dennis, , "The Criminal Justice and Public Order Act 1994," [1995] Crim.L.R. 4, at p.15.

396 See Jackson, "Inferences from silence: from common law to common sense," (1993) 44 N.I.L.Q. 103.

397 Opinion given in B.B.C. Radio *File on Four* edition of October 26, 1993, transcript, p.12.

398 Cited *ibid*.

399 See *Coney* (1882) 8 Q.B.D. 534; *Wilcox* v. *Jeffrey* [1951] 1 All E.R. 464; *Allan* (1965) 47 Cr.App.R. 243, at pp.246 adn 249; *Clarkson* (1971) 55 Cr.App.R. 445, C.-M.App.Ct.

must be proof that the encounter is not accidental. The defendant must be in the other's company by intent or design. It is not enough to come upon the other by chance or accident. From the proximity of the defendants to their homes, the fact that the location was one of frequent public resort and the distance to the *corpus delicti*, the defence case was that it was not possible to be certain that the defendants had deliberately joined the company of the third man. It seems, therefore, that the deficit of proof of non-accidental presence was made up by the refusal to answer questions.

In *Campbell*[400] the Northern Ireland Court of Appeal upheld the adverse inference drawn by the trial judge sitting without a jury under Article 5 (the Northern Ireland equivalent of section 36) that the defendant's explanation at trial was false and a recent invention. This was clearly a restricted application of the section because an inference may be drawn under both sections whether or not an innocent explanation is subsequently proferred.

It has been argued that the proliferation of inferences which may be permissible under sections 34, 36 and 37 operate unfairly against the accused and that on appeal the availability of an inference under section 36 or 37 handicaps the defence when arguing that the absence of a *McGarry* direction renders the conviction unsafe.[401]

E. *MENTAL INCAPACITY OF THE SILENT SUSPECT*

(1) General considerations

A confession may be excluded in the discretion of the judge where its reliability is likely to be vitiated by the defendant's mental condition.[402] Analagously, it is reasonable to assume that, rather than relying on a favourable direction to the jury, the court may prefer to exclude evidence of the silence of a defendant whose severely restricted cognitive ability, for example, may have prevented him grasping the significance of the new caution and whose silence therefore may well not be a reliable indication of guilt.[403] Discretionary exclusion of silence is available under section 78 of P.A.C.E. and under common law by virtue of the preservation of these discretions for the purposes of the 1994 Act by section 38(6).[404] During the passage of the 1994 Act Lord Taylor C.J. cautioned that the position of the very young and the vulnerable (*i.e.* the mentally disordered and handicapped) had to be "very specially considered."[405] It has been argued that the evidence of silence in the case

---

400 (1993) unreported, N.I.C.A., March 29.

401 Birch, [1999] Crim.L.R., at p.787; *McGarry* [1999] 1 Cr.App.R. 377, C.A.

402 *Stewart* (1972) 56 Cr.App.R. 161, at p.163.

403 In *Martin* [1992] 5 N.I.J.B. 1, at p.41, N.I.C.A., it was said that if a judge, sitting as a tribunal of fact, felt that a defendant had not understood the caution or had some doubt about it, then he should not draw an adverse inference.

404 "Nothing in sections 34, 35, 36 or 37 prejudicies any power of a court, in any proceedings, to exclude evidence (whether by preventing questions being put or otherwise) at its discretion."

405 555 H.L. Deb., col. 520, May 23 (Committee stage).

of a person suffering from a severe mental illness should never be permitted to go before the jury.[406] In *Condron* silence was said to be irrelevant and its admissibility perverse where the accused was of very low intelligence and limited understanding and was advised by his solicitor to say nothing.[407]

Code C of P.A.C.E. contains a comprehensive array of provisions and guidance notes for the detention, treatment and questioning of mentally disordered handicapped detainees. These are found at various points in the code but are also gathered together in summary form under Annex E to the code.[408]

(2) Determination of mental disorder and mental handicap

(a) *Definitions*

The way in which the definitions of mental disorder and mental handicap are addressed in P.A.C.E. is confusing. Note for Guidance C1G in Code C states that the generic term "mental disorder" is used throughout Code C, and reference is made in the Note to the definition of the term given in section 1(2) of the Mental Health Act 1983, that is "mental illness, arrested or incomplete development of mind, psychopathic disorder and any other disorder or disability of mind." The term "mental handicap" is not separately defined in the Code but is defined in section 77(3) of the P.A.C.E. Act, for the purposes of section 77, as "a state of arrested or incomplete development of mind which includes significant impairment of intelligence and social functioning." These two definitions taken together would seem to suggest that mental handicap is subsumed within the meaning of mental disorder and yet mental disorder and mental handicap are obviously distinct concepts, as Note for Guidance C1F indeed stresses. The solution may be that mental handicap is a manifestation of mental disorder. In *Walker*[409] it was said that the court is not restricted to considering a defendant's mental condition where there is a personality disorder but may consider impairment of intelligence.

(b) *Suspicion of mental disorder/handicap to be treated as such in fact*

If an officer has any suspicion, or is told in good faith, that a person of any age may be mentally disordered or mentally handicapped, or mentally incapable of understanding the significance of any questions put ot him or his replies, then that person shall be treated as a mentally disordered or mentally handicapped person.[410] Further, it has been held that an officer's evidence that he concluded that the

---

406 Dennis, "The Criminal Justice and Public Order Act 1994," [1995] Crim.L.R. 4, at p.15.

407 [1997] 1 W.L.R. 827, at p.837.

408 The provisions for interview replace those contained in para. 4A of the *Administrative Directions on Interrogation and the taking of Statements*, re-issued together with the 1964 Judges' Rules in 1978.

409 [1998] Crim.L.R. 211, C.A. See also *Wilkinson* (1996) unreported, C.A., July 24.

410 Code C.1.4. It has been suggested that the lack of any lay definition for the various terms used in this provision may lead custody officers to form their own idiosyncratic intepretation of these concepts and make their own assessments of the suspect's level of understanding: see Palmer, "Still Vulnerable After All These Years," [1996] Crim.L.R., 636, at p.641.

defendant was *not* mentally handicapped is irrelevant since the officer is neither a medical witness nor an expert for this purpose.[411] Where the custody officer has any doubt as to the mental state or capacity of a person detained an appropriate adult should be called.[412]

(c) *Mental handicap defined by reference to I.Q.*

Many factors contribute to learning difficulties but a commonly accepted gauge of mental handicap is intelligence quotient (I.Q.). In one study it was found that the mean average I.Q. of offenders was around 90, while in another it was estimated that the average I.Q. of detained suspects was not likely to exceed 85.[413] On the basis that the mean average I.Q. of the adult population is 100 it is commonly asserted that an I.Q. of 69 or below is an indication of mental handicap. However, the Court of Appeal has said that they were not attracted to the concept that the judicial approach to submissions of inadmissibility under section 76(2)(b) of the P.A.C.E. Act should be governed by which side of an arbitrary line, whether at 69/70 or elsewhere the I.Q. fell.[414]

(d) *Difficulties in recognising symptoms*

One commentator has enumerated a number of problems encountered in recognising symptoms.[415] Some custody officers may wrongly identify symptoms of mental disorder and mental handicap as attributable to drink or drugs and that, equally, intoxicating substances may mask an underlying mental health problem. Again, given that the majority of people with mental illness who are in police custody are detained there under section 136 of the Mental Health Act 1983, there may be a tendency for officers, accustomed to witnessing manifestations of extreme mental illness, to interpret more minor symptoms as "normal." Moreover, many adults with learning difficulties may be motivated to conceal the fact and in a busy custody suite there may be insufficient time to identify either difficulties of that sort or potential mental health problems. She suggests that suspects could be asked specifically if they need special help, that questions about which school they attended can often reveal special needs, and that familiarity with the common types of medication likely to be in a suspect's possession, and the symptoms they repress, may increase awareness amongst custody officers.

(e) *Determination by the jury to be based on expert evidence of handicap*

For the jury to make a valid judgment on the reliability or otherwise of an alleged confession by a defendant who is or may be mentally handicapped, evidence of the

---

411 *Ham* (1995) unreported, C.A. 95/2020/W3.

412 Note for Guidance C1G.

413 See respectively Eysenck and Gudjonsson, *The Causes and Cures of Criminality*, London 1989, and Gudjonsson, Clare, Rutter and Pearse, *Persons at Risk During Interviews in Police Custody: The Identification of Vulnerabilities*, R.C.C.J. Research Study No 12. H.M.S.O. 1993.

414 *Raghip, sub nom. Silcott, Braithwaite and Raghip* (1991) *The Times*, January 9; *Walker* [1998] Crim. L.R. 211.

415 By Palmer, [1996] Crim.L.R., at pp.634-635.

defendant's mental condition should be adduced before them. It is not sufficient for them to be invited to make such an assessment for themselves from observing the defendant giving evidence in court. In *Raghip et al.*[416] the only evidence against the defendant of involvement in the murder of a constable during disturbances at the Broadwater Farm Estate in North London consisted of alleged admissions. At trial the evidence of psychologists was that he was of average intelligence but evidence was subsequently agreed that his I.Q. was in the low 70s, that he was abnormally suggestible and had a level of functioning equivalent to a child of 9¾ and a reading of age 6½. In dismissing the previous application for leave to appeal the Lord Chief Justice had endorsed a "judge for yourself" approach in directing the jury on whether the appellant was sufficiently mentally handicapped for the confession to be rendered unreliable. In appearing to disavow such an approach the court took the view that the jury would have been assisted in assessing the mental condition of the appellant and the consequent reliability or otherwise of the alleged admissions by hearing the psychological evidence. It would be impossible for the lay person to divine the psychological data from an accused's performance in the witness box. By analogy these considerations clearly apply to the evidence of the suspect's silence.

(3) Incidence of mental disorder and handicap amongst suspects

The R.C.C.J. noted that the problems associated with suspects who are or may be mentally disordered are likely to be increasingly encountered as rising numbers of people suffering from mental disorder find themselves living in the community.[417] Accordingly, they commissioned an investigation into the psychological characteristics of adult suspects with a view to identifying those who might require special treatment.[418] The research entailed interviews with, and psychological assessment of, adult suspects detained at two police stations. Interviews were carried out with 173 suspects and complete psychological assessments were obtained of 156 detainees who were subsequently interviewed by the police. The researchers found that the police interviewed many suspects of poor intellectual ability, with 6% having a reading age of below 9 years, that is to say they were illiterate and needed an appropriate adult. Nevertheless, between 80% and 90% understood their basic

416 *supra*.

417 Report, c.3, para. 84.

418 Gudjonsson, Clare, Rutter and Pearse, *Persons at Risk During Interviews in Police Custody: The Identification of Vulnerabilities*, Royal Commission on Criminal Justice Research Study No. 12, London, HMSO 1993. For additional research see, *e.g.*, Gudjonsson, "Confession Evidence, Psychological Vulnerability and Expert Testimony," (1993) 3 *Journal of Community and Applied Social Psychology*, 117; Bean and Nemitz, *Out of Depth and out of Sight*, MENCAP, London 1994; Pearse, "Police Interviewing: The Identification of Vulnerabilities," (1995) 5 *Journal of Community and Applied Social Psychology*, 147; Robertson, Pearson and Gibb, *The Entry of Mentally Disordered People to the Criminal Justice System*, Research Findings no. 21, Home Office Research and Statistics Department, Home Office 1995; Palmer, "Still Vulnerable After All These Years," [1996] Crim.L.R. 633, citing Palmer and Harr, *A PACE in the right direction?* Institute for the Study of the Legal Profession, Faculty of Law, University of Sheffield, 1996 (results of an exploratory empirical study carried out in South Yorkshire between July 1994 and March 1995).

legal rights. The researchers estimated that 7% of suspects were probably suffering from mental illness,[419] 3% from mental handicap and one or two suspects from brain damage. Although the police missed some of these cases, in the view of the researchers they were able to identify the most serious cases and take the necessary steps to ensure that they were appropriately represented. The researchers nevertheless thought, on the basis of their evaluation of the mental state of the suspects in their sample (not only those suffering from a mental disorder), that there was a need for an appropriate adult in between 15% and 20% of the cases. Using the existing guidelines the police requested one in only 4%. They concluded that there must be clearer guidelines for police officers about the criteria to be employed when considering the need for an appropriate adult. The Commission recommended that this be considered by the working party they proposed should be established.

(4) Detention

On the initial detention of a person who is mentally handicapped or appears to be suffering from a mental disorder the custody officer must, as soon as practicable, inform the appropriate adult of the grounds for the detention and the detainee's whereabouts, and ask the adult to come to the police station to see the person.[420] The giving of that information and the request must be recorded.[421] An appropriate adult must be permitted to consult the custody record of a detained juvenile as soon as practicable after arriving at the police station and when the juvenile leaves police detention the appropriate adult must be supplied on request with a copy of it as soon as practicable, an entitlement which lasts for 12 months after the detainee's release.[422] If the appropriate adult is already at the police station when the information required by the code to be given to detained persons at the outset of detention is given then that information must be given to the mentally disordered or handicapped detainee in the presence of the appropriate adult; but if the latter is not at the police station when the information is given then it must be given to the

[419] *Cf.* slightly lower figures recorded in studies by Robertson (*The Role of Police Surgeons*, R.C.C.J. Research Study No. 6, 1992, (4.5 per cent)), and by Robertson, Pearson and Gibb (*supra* (2.1 per cent.). But Palmer, in [1996] Crim.L.R., at p.635, reports that the impression of most of those interviewed in the South Yorkshire study was that many more mentally disordered people were coming into contact with the police than in previous years, an impression which she notes is supported by the N.A.C.R.O. Mental Health Advisory Committee, *Policy Paper I: Community Care and Mentally Disturbed Offenders*, 1993.

[420] C3.9. The *appearance* of mental disorder was new to the code in 1995. Code C9.2, requiring the custody officer to call the police surgeon immediately if a person brought to a police station, or already detained there, appears to be suffering from physical illness or mental disorder, is injured, fails to respond normally to questions or conversation (other than through drunkenness alone), or otherwise appears to need medical attention. It has been pointed out that where there is any suspicion of mental disorder an appropriate adult must be contacted and this must therefore be done at the same time as the police surgeon is called, and not, as may have been the practice in some forces, only after a police surgeon has assessed the person as suffering from a mental disorder: Palmer, [1996] Crim.L.R., at p.638.

[421] C3.18.

[422] C2.4.

detained person in the presence of the appropriate adult once the latter arrives.[423] Whichever is applicable must be recorded.[424] The detained person must be advised by the custody officer that the appropriate adult (where applicable) is there to assist and advise him and that he can consult privately with the appropriate adult at any time.[425] The giving of this advice must be recorded.[426] A Note for Guidance advises that whenever possible juveniles and other persons at risk should be visited in their cells more regularly than at the normal one-hour intervals.[427] It is assumed that this embraces all persons in the category of the mentally disordered or handicapped. Particular care must be taken when deciding whether to use handcuffs on a mentally disordered or handicapped person who is held in a locked cell.[428]

(5) Interviews

Code C[429] stresses that although persons who are mentally disordered or mentally handicapped are often capable of providing reliable evidence, they may, without knowing or wishing to do so, be particularly prone in certain circumstances to provide information which is unreliable, misleading or self-incriminating; special care should therefore always be exercised in questioning such a person and because of the risk of unreliable evidence it is also important to obtain corroboration of any facts admitted whenever possible. In the light of these considerations the general rule is that persons who are mentally disordered or mentally handicapped, whether suspected or not, must not normally be interviewed or asked to provide or sign a written statement in the absence of an appropriate adult.[430] It has been held to be a misdirection to suggest to the jury that the provision is of little importance.[431] The potential difficulty arising out of the applicability of the rule to interviewed persons "whether suspected or not" has already been discussed in the section dealing with the definition of interview. The rule was considered and applied in *Everett*.[432] The appellant was aged 42 but had a mental age of 8 and, in the absence of an appropriate adult, made admissions during an interview conducted in the police car on the way to the police station and then on tape at the police station. It was held that the judge erred in not taking account of the medical evidence as to the defendant's mental condition. The admissions should have been excluded under

423 C3.11.

424 C3.18.

425 C3.12. There is no separate provision in the code enshrining the right of private consultation and there is no obligation on custody officers to explain the facility to the appropriate adult.

426 C3.18.

427 Note C8A.

428 C8.2.

429 Note C11B. See 1964 *Administrative Directions*, para. 4A(c).

430 C11.14.

431 *Lamont* [1989] Crim.L.R. 813.

432 [1988] Crim.L.R. 826, C.A. See also *Kenny* [1994] Crim.L.R. 284; *Wood* (1994) Crim.L.R. 222; *Lewis* (1995) unreported, C.A. 94/1941/X3 (breach but appeal dismissed); *Ham* (1995) unreported, C.A. 95/2020/W3 (appeal allowed); *Manning and Oyelawo* (1995) unreported, C.A. 93/3852//Z2 (breach but appeal allowed).

section 76(2)(b) of the P.A.C.E. Act. But in *Jones (Ronald)*[433] a conviction for manslaughter was upheld even though the mentally sub-normal and highly suggestible appellant was interviewed in the absence of a responsible adult (and was not told, initially, of his right to a solicitor) because the court was impressed by the fact that the alleged admissions "were almost word for word what the pathologist said must have happened so far as the sequence of injuries was concerned." Under section 76(2)(b) this would not have been relevant but it is not clear if exclusion was sought under section 76 or section 78.

(6) Appropriate adult

In the case of mentally disordered or mentally handicapped persons the appropriate adult means (i) a relative, guardian or other person responsible for his care or custody, (ii) someone who has experience of dealing with mentally disordered or mentally handicapped persons but is not a police officer or employed by the police, such as an approved social worker as defined by the Mental Health Act 1983 or a specialist social worker, or (iii) failing either of the above, some other responsible adult aged 18 or over who is not a police officer or employed by the police.[434] The significance of the ostensible distinction between the Code definitions of appropriate adult and that of "independent person" for the purposes of the statutory warning to the jury (see below) is not clear. A Note for Guidance advises that a person should not be an appropriate adult if he is suspected of involvement in the offence in question, is the victim, is a witness, is involved in the investigation of has received admissions prior to attending to act as the appropriate adult.[435] Another Note advises that it may in certain circumstances be more satisfactory for all concerned if the appropriate adult is someone who has experience or training in the care of the mentally disordered or handicapped rather than a relative lacking such qualifications but that if the person himself prefers a relative to a better qualified stranger or objects to a particular person as the appropriate adult, his wishes should if practicable be respected.[436] The R.C.C.J. referred to research findings which indicated that specialist and psychiatric social workers were increasingly being called in as appropriate adults in such cases of mental disorder as were identified (about 1% of the sample, or 110 persons).[437]

---

433 (1990) unreported, C.A. 4654/X3/89.

434 C1.7(b). An approved social worker means an officer of a local social services authority appointed to act as an approved social worker for the purposes of the Act: Mental Health Act 1983, s.145(1).

435 Note C1C.

436 Note C1E.

437 Report, Chap. 3, para. 84; Brown Ellis and Larcombe, *supra*. For additional research material see, *e.g.*, Littlechild, "Reassessing the Rôle of the 'Appropriate Adult'," [1995] Crim.L.R. 540; Robertson, "Police Interviewing and the Use of Appropriate Adults," (1996) 7 *Journal of Forensic Psychiatry*, No.2, 297; Pearse and Gudjonsson, "How appropriate are appropriate adults?" (1996) 7 *Journal of Forensic Psychiatry*, No.3, 570.

A Note for Guidance introduced in 1991 advises that a solicitor who is present at the station in that capacity may not act as the appropriate adult, a prohibition the purpose of which the R.C.C.J. were unable to follow.[438] The Note was expanded in the 1995 edition to advise against lay visitors present at the police station in that capacity from acting as appropriate adults. Where the appropriate adult is present at an interview, he must be informed that he is not expected to act simply as an observer; and also that the purposes of his presence are, first, to advise the person being questioned and to observe whether or not the interview is being conducted properly and fairly, and, secondly, to facilitate communication with the person being interviewed.[439] The interesting point has been made that a more appropriate phrase than "facilitate communication" might be "facilitate understanding, for otherwise there is a danger that apporpirate adults may construe their rôle to include encouraging silent suspects to answer police questions, which is a legal issue and one to be left to the legal adviser.[440] It is precisely because of the difficulties appropriate adults may encounter in determining the need for and importance of legal advice, that the Home Office Working Party on Appropriate Adults, which was set up on the recommendation of the R.C.C.J., proposed that whenever a suspect was identified as requiring an appropriate adult, a legal adviser should also be called.[441]

Expressing dissatisfaction with the present rules and practical arrangements for providing the necessary advice and protection for those who are likely to be particularly vulnerable to pressure while in police custody the R.C.C.J. believed that a more systematic approach was needed to the question of which people are suitable for being called upon to serve as appropriate adults and the training that they should receive.[442] They noted the suggestion for the preparation of a video film to assist in training and for showing to appropriate adults who may be called on without having had any previous experience of the role. They also saw some advantage in the preparation of a leaflet about the role and reponsibilities of appropriate adults which could be handed to them by the police on arrival at the police station. The possibility of establishing local panels of suitable persons seemed to the R.C.C.J. worthy of exploration. But they did not wish to make any specific recommendations connected with appropriate adults because they endorsed the recommendation of various researchers that there should be a comprehensive review (possibly by a Home Office

---

[438] Note for Guidance C1F; Report, Chap. 3, para. 85.

[439] C11.16. Research has revealed that appropriate adults are not always advised of their rôle either before the interview (Brown, Ellis and Larcombe, *Changing the Code: Police Detention under the Revised P.A.C.E. Codes of Pratice*, Home Office Research and Planning Unit, 1993) or during the interview (Evans, *The Conduct of Police Interview with Juveniles*, R.C.C.J. Research Study No. 8, 1993).

[440] See Palmer, [1996] Crim.L.R., at pp.642-643, pointing out that in *Jefferson et al.*, (1994) 99 Cr.App.R. 13, the father's conduct in vociferously exhorting his son to tell the police the truth was held not to have been incompatible with the rôle of appropriate adult.

[441] *Appropriate Adults: Report of Review Group*, Home Office 1995. See R.C.C.J. Report, Chap.3, para. 86.

[442] *ibid.*, para. 85.

chaired multi-disciplinary working party) of the role, function, qualifications, training and availability of appropriate adults.[443]

(7) Statutory caution to the jury: P.A.C.E. Act, section 77

Special considerations apply where (i) the case against the accused depends wholly or substantially on a confession by him, (ii) the court is satisfied that he is mentally handicapped and (iii) the court is satisfied that the confession was not made in the presence of an independent person. Upon a trial on indictment in such circumstances section 77(1) of the P.A.C.E. Act requires the judge to warn the jury that there is a special need for caution before convicting in reliance on the confession and to explain to them that the need arises because of those circumstances. It has been stressed that the judge should actually use the phrase "special need for caution" and should explain why a confession from a mentally handicapped person may be unreliable.[444] For the case against the defendant to depend substantially on the confession it need not be the only evidence or even most of the evidence.[445] The warning is such an essential part of a fair summing up that failure to adminster it warrants the quashing of a conviction.[446] Where the three factors apply in a summary trial the court must treat the case as one in which there is a special need for caution before convicting the accused on his confession.[447] For the purposes of these provisions the term 'mentally handicapped' and 'independent person' have specific meanings: the former means that the person is in a state of arrested or incomplete development of mind which includes significant impairment of intelligence and social functioning and the latter does not include a police officer or a person employed for, or engaged on, police purposes.[448]

It is arguable that the requirements of section 77(1) ought to apply by analogy to cases in which the defendant's silence forms a significant component of the prosecution case, so that, even if in the case of some mental impairment the evidence of silence is not excluded by the trial judge, nevertheless there should be a warning of the kind required by the subsection.

---

443 *ibid.*, para. 86.

444 *Bailey* [1995] Crim.L.R. 723 (severe personality disorder; mild mental handicap; I.Q. 65).

445 *ibid.*

446 *Lamont* [1989] Crim.L.R. 813; *Jones (Ronald)* (1990) unreported, C.A. 4654/X3/89; *Bailey, supra.*

447 s.77(2).

448 s.77(3). The term "police purposes" has the meaning assigned to it by s.64 of the Police Act 1964: *ibid*. Whether lay persons to whom the accused confessed were independent was considered in *Bailey, supra.*

(8) Rôle of police surgeons in assessing mental disorder and fitness for interview

Where a defendant was interviewed but answered no questions and by reason of his mental disorder or handicap it is found that he was in fact, or may have been, unfit to be interviewed the court will be expected to rule that no inferences can be drawn from his silence and that consequently the interview will be excluded. However, the defence will rarely find it easy to establish unfitness through *post facto* assessment. By far the best hope for them is that a police surgeon, called in to examine the suspect, certifies him unfit to be interviewed, an end to the issue. Where a suspect is legally represented in the police station the solicitor will have the opportunity to confer with the doctor and the custody officer and this may produce a consensus against interview. On the other hand, it may involve a clash of opinion between a general physician with no specialist knowledge of clinical psychiatry or educational psychology and a solicitor with no formal training in those discliplines but many years practical experience "at the coal face" in dealing with the mentally ill and handicapped.[449] Confronted with a difference of opinion between two non-experts the custody officer may prefer to let the interview proceed and leave the decision to be vetted by the court.

The precise rôle of police surgeons in assessing mental disorder is unclear. No statement is given in Code C of the purpose behind the requirement for calling out the police surgeon in cases of apparent mental disorder. There would be three broad aspects to a strictly medical role: (a) to examine for the purpose of confirming the existence and form of mental disorder; (b) to administer appropriate medication; and (c) to determine whether hospital admission is necessary. It is noteworthy that the code makes no separate express provision for call-out of a police surgeon in cases of mental *handicap*. But there is ambiguity as between Code C and the P.A.C.E. Act over whether mental handicap is embraced within the definition of mental disorder, a question discussed earlier.[450] If mental disorder does include mental handicap, it would mean that a police surgeon would have to be called in a case of learning difficulties, to use the presently more preferred nomenclature, in spite of the fact that they can hardly be regarded as constituting a medical condition. Yet since medical practitioners, even those with psychiatric training or experience, are clearly not qualified *per se* in the assessment of impairment of intellectual or educational potential, it might be asked what purpose could be regarded as being served by calling out a police surgeon in cases of mental handicap. The answer may lie in the problems which often arise in distinguishing symptoms of mental disorder from impairment of intelligence or social functioning, a recognition exercise which is arguably more appropriately undertaken by a medical practitioner than a custody officer. The inclusion of mental handicap within the definition of mental disorder would mean that in cases of suspected mental handicap it would be obligatory to refer the issue to a police surgeon for the very purpose of determining whether the

---

449 Such a dispute occurred in *Condron* [1997] 1 Cr.App.R. 185.

450 See, *supra*, p.133.

symptoms exhibited are in fact those of low intelligence or poor social functioning (neither of which by definition require medical attention or treatment), as against those of mental ill health, which may well require it.

The confirmatory function may have an additional purpose beyond that of a purely medical one. In cases of doubt it may be desirable for the custody officer to obtain a professional opinion on the existence of mental disorder (including, arguably, mental handicap) in order to determine whether there will ultimately be any need for the attendance of an appropriate adult at the police station. But that purpose is not permitted to justify delaying compliance with the obligation under the code to begin the process of contacting and securing the attendance of an appropriate adult where a newly detained person appears to be suffering from mental disorder. The code is quite clear that in cases of suspected mental disorder the twin requirements of calling the police surgeon and contacting the appropriate adult arise, and must be pursued, in unison.[451] Yet it has been reported that in some forces the incorrect practice may have been followed of postponing contact with the appropriate adult pending an asssessment by the police surgeon.[452]

In contrast with the failure to contact the appropriate adult until after the police surgeon has seen the suspect, custody officers have sometimes contacted an appropriate adult whilst refraining from the code obligation to call out the police surgeon in a case of suspected mental disorder; this is in spite of the fact that police surgeons operate on a rota basis and are mostly in general practice and that there is therefore rarely any obstacle to their swift attendance. Apart from cases where the offence is minor and the suspect is released without interview, some custody officers may be so confident in their assessment that mental disorder exists that they regard a medical opinion as unnecessary. This brings the topic to consideration of the police surgeon's role as an arbiter of whether the mentally disordered suspect is fit to be interviewed. It may be that a police surgeon had found the suspect fit to be interviewed in the past, but the risk of relying on that earlier opinion is that it does not necessarily mean that the suspect is fit to be interviewed on the present occasion.[453]

The only reference in Code C to the police surgeon's role in assessing fitness of suspects for interview is in relation to drink or drugs.[454] There is no reference in the code to such a function in cases of suspected mental disorder or mental handicap. Yet there is no doubt that this constitutes a significant part of their role. Research conducted on behalf of the R.C.C.J. reveals that although 89 per cent of a sample of prisoner examinations were for physical illness or injury, alcohol and drug related

[451] C3..9 and C1.4.

[452] Palmer, [1996] "Still Vulnerable After All These Years," Crim.L.R. 636, at p.638. Bean and Nemitz consider that police surgeons should play no part in the decision to call on an appropriate adult: *Out of depth and out of sight*, Midlands Centre for Criminology, University of Loughborough. *Cf.* Clarke "Fit for Interview?" (1991) *The Police Surgeon*, p.40.

[453] Palmer, [1996] Crim.L.R., at pp.636-637, citing Bean and Nemitz, *supra,* and Palmer and Hart, *A PACE in the right direction?* Institute for the Study of the Legal Profession, Faculty of Law, University of Sheffield, 1996 (results of an exploratory empirical study carried out in South Yorkshire between July 1994 and March 1995).

[454] Note C12B.

matters or forensic examination and sampling matters, almost 10 per cent concerned assessments of mental disorder and mental handicap.[455] The same research found that police surgeons considered their main function in cases involving mental disorder concerned determinations on fitness for detention and interview, with occasional input in decisions on fitness to charge or the need for an appropriate adult. Exactly what considerations are relevant in determining fitness for interview is debateable. Most police surgeons polled in one study thought that assessments should take account of orientation and mental state but there is evidence that opinions may be based simply on physical fitness to be interviewed.[456] The shortcomings of such an approach were highlighted in one typical view in which it was observed that whilst a "florid schizophrenic" might be said to be physically fit to be interviewed in the sense of being able to sit down, listen, hear and speak, whether any credence could attach to such an interview, and therefore whether an interview would have any useful point, was doubtful.

The special reference of the study commissioned for the R.C.C.J. on the work of police surgeons was their role in assessing and treating detainees who might be considered unfit for interview on grounds of mental health.[457] It was found that there was a difference between London and elsewhere. Outside London, it was more frequently the case that suspects were considered unfit for interview but it less frequently happened that an appropriate adult was called. In London, by contrast, few of those detained were declared unfit for interview but doctors advised the police to call an appropriate adult in almost a quarter of the cases referred to them for assessment of possible mental disorder. The criteria used to assess fitness for interview varied with the doctor. The R.C.C.J. were concerned by suggestions they received that the work of police surgeons lacked any central co-ordination and quality control.[458] General practitioners received little or no training in police work, nor did their training include psychiatry, in spite of the fact that a significant number of those detained by the police may be suffering from mental disorder. The universities were not involved to the extent that they might be in the training of police surgeons. Whilst the Metropolitan Police require aspiring force medical examiners (as police surgeons are known in London) to undertake some specialist training for their role as a pre-condition to appointment, there is no such requirement in other police areas, where attendance at various training courses is purely voluntary.[459] The Commission recommended the setting up of a Home Office working party to consider the need for a central co-ordinating body, the need for "centres of excellence" at universities, the appropriate training and standards for police surgeons, the role of psychiatry, the fees payable, the availability and use of psychiatric nursing staff and other relevant matters. The working party would need

---

[455] Robertson, *The Rôle of Police Surgeons*, R.C.C.J. Research Study No. 6, 1992.

[456] Palmer and Hart, *supra*.

[457] Robertson, *The Role of Police Surgeons,* cited in the report, Chap. 3, para. 89.

[458] *ibid.*, para. 90.

[459] See Palmer, [1996] Crim.L.R., at p.637. The Association of Police Surgeons en courage greater participa-tion in training amongst members: *ibid.*

to include appropriate representatives from the police, the psychiatric bodies, police surgeons and lawyers among others. Such a working party was established in the autumn of 1995 and the hope has been expressed that it will give serious thought to whether or not police surgeons are the appropriate personnel for mental health assessments or whether the whole system ought to be remodelled.[460]

The R.C.C.J. also considered there was a need for improved training and guidelines for the police on how to decide when to call out police surgeons and welcomed the fact that this was already being addressed by the police service in collaboration with the medical profession.[461]

(9) Duty psychiatrist schemes

The R.C.C.J. further recommended that experiments be conducted to determine whether duty psychiatrist schemes, similar to those in existence at certain magistrates' courts, might be introduced at busy police stations in city centres.[462] They further recommended that every police station should in any event have arrangements for calling upon psychiatric held in any cases where this was needed, with police surgeons being able to obtain advice from a psychiatrist about cases in which they have doubts about the mental state of the suspect and they suggested that duty solicitors should be involved as far as possible in consultations between police surgeons, suspects, and the psychiatrist.[463] In the view of the R.C.C.J. legal aid funds ought to be available to cover the costs of exceptional consultations by psychiatrists at police stations if authorised by a police surgeon in cases where the transport of the suspect to the hospital was not practicable for legal or security reasons.

F. *JUVENILES*

(1) Persons who must be treated as juveniles

Anyone who appears to be under the age of 17 must be treated as a juvenile for the purposes of Code C in the absence of clear evidence to show that he is older.[464]

---

[460] *ibid.*, p.639.

[461] Report, Chap. 3, para. 91.

[462] *ibid.*, para. 92.

[463] *ibid.* Palmer has suggested that community psychiatric nurses might be better suited to the role of assessing detainees' mental health than medical doctors who have not been psychiatrically trained and she suggests various duty scheme arrangements: [1996] Crim.L.R., at p. 639.

[464] C1.5.

(2) Detention

Other than in respect of cases of homicide Part IV of the P.A.C.E. Act (dealing with detention) does not apply to a child (defined as a person under 14) who has been arrested without warrant.[465] Upon the initial detention of a child or young person (hereafter referred to as a "juvenile"), including detention under the terrorism provisions, the custody officer must, if it is practicable, ascertain the identity of a person responsible for his welfare (for example, his parent or guardian or, if he is in care, the care authority or voluntary organisation, or any other person who has, for the time being, assumed responsibility for his welfare) and that person must be informed as soon as practicable that the juvenile has been arrested, why he has been arrested and where he is detained.[466] All this must be recorded.[467] The special obligation to notify the fact of the juvenile's detention to the person responsible for his welfare is in addition to the right not to be held incommunicado.[468] A Note for Guidance[469] advises that if the juvenile is in the care of a local authority or voluntary organisation but is living with his parents or other adults responsible for his welfare then, although there is no legal obligation on the police to inform them, they as well as the authority or organisation should normally be contacted unless suspected of involvement in the offence concerned; even if a juvenile in care is not living with his parents, consideration should be given to informing them as well. In the case of a juvenile who is known to be subject to a supervision order, reasonable steps must also be taken to notify the person supervising him[470] and this must be recorded.[471] The custody officer must, as soon as practicable, inform the appropriate adult (who may or may not be a person responsible for his welfare) of the grounds for his detention and his whereabouts, and ask the adult to come to the police station to see the person.[472] This must be recorded.[473] An appropriate adult must be permitted to consult the custody record of a detained juvenile as soon as practicable after arriving at the police station and when the juvenile leaves police detention the appropriate adult must be supplied on request with a copy of it as soon as practicable, an entitlement which lasts for 12 months after the detainee's release.[474]

If the appropriate adult is already at the police station then the information required by the code to be given to the detained juvenile at the outset of detention must be given to the juvenile in his presence but if the appropriate adult is not at the

465 s.52, referrring to the definition of a "child" in the Children and Young Persons Act 1969, s.70(1).

466 Children and Young Persons Act 1933, ss.34(2),(3),(4),(5),(6),(8),(10) and (11) as substituted for original s.34(2) by P.A.C.E. Act, s.57; and Code C3.7.

467 C3.18.

468 Children and Young Persons Act 1933, s.34(9), incorporated by P.A.C.E. Act, s.57 and C3.7.

469 Note C3C.

470 Children and Young Persons Act 1933, s.34(7), incorporated by P.A.C.E. Act, s.57 and C3.8.

471 C3.18.

472 C3..9.

473 C3.18.

474 C2.4. The obligation to furnish the appropriate adult with a copy of the custody record is an innovation of the 1995 edition.

police station when the information is given then it must be given to the detained juvenile in the presence of the appropriate adult once that person arrives.[475] Whichever applies must be recorded.[476] The R.C.C.J. cited the findings of research that before the revision of Code C in 1991 the appropriate adult was informed of the juvenile's right to consult a solicitor in about half the cases but that this rose to over three-quarters afterwards.[477] The significance of this change in the context of the revision is obscure, since no relevant alteration in the code was effected by the revision.

Code C makes it clear that juveniles must be informed of their rights and entitlements, including the right to access to legal advice, on arrival at the police station in the same way as adult suspects. But the R.C.C.J. cited research findings indicating that information about these rights was invariably deferred until the appropriate adult arrived.[478]

The custody officer must advise the juvenile detainee that the appropriate adult is there to assist and advise the detainee and that he can consult the appropriate adult privately at any time.[479] The giving of this advice must be recorded.[480]

Accommodation

Juveniles must not be placed in a police cell "unless no other secure accommodation is available and the custody officer considers that it is not practicable to supervise him if he is not placed in a cell or the custody officer considers that a cell provides more comfortable accommodation than other secure accommodation in the police station."[481] The alternative of using a cell if it provides more comfortable accommodation than other secure accommodation in the police station was an innovation of the 1995 revision. In any event, he may not be placed in a cell with a detained adult.[482] If a juvenile is placed in a cell, the reason must be recorded.[483] A Note for Guidance advises that whenever possible juveniles should be visited more regularly than at the normal one-hour intervals.[484]

(3) Interviews in general

In 1929 the Royal Commission on Police Powers and Procedure recommended that some person other than a police officer should always be present with any child

---

475 C3.11, referring to information required to be given by C3.1-C3.4.

476 C3.18.

477 Report, Cm. 2263, c.3, para. 82, citing Brown, Ellis and Larcombe, *Changing the Code: Police Detention under the Revised PACE Codes of Practice*, Home Office Research and Planning Unit, London, HMSO 1993.

478 Report, c.3, para. 82, citing *ibid*.

479 C3.12.

480 C3.18.

481 C8.8.

482 *ibid*.

483 C8.12.

484 Note C8A.

under 16 from whom a statement was being taken.[485] The 1964 Administrative Directions stated that "[a]s far as practicable children and young persons under the age of 17 years (whether suspected of crime or not) should only be interviewed in the presence of a parent or guardian, or in their absence, some person who is not a police officer and is of the same sex as the child."[486] There was no provision for urgent interviews, although the consideration of practicability may have been intended to allow for them.

In contrast with the terse statement of principle under the 1964 régîme Code C provides a comprehensive structure of rules for the interviewing of juveniles. The code stresses the importance of remembering that although juveniles are often capable of providing reliable evidence, they may, without knowing or wishing to do so, be particularly prone in certain circumstances to provide information which is unreliable, misleading or self-incriminating.[487] Special care should therefore always be exercised in questioning juveniles and because of the risk of unreliable evidence it is also important to obtain corroboration of any facts admitted whenever possible. In the light of these considerations the general rule on the questioning of juveniles is that, whether suspected or not, they must not normally be interviewed or asked to provide or sign a written statement in the absence of an appropriate adult.[488] The potential difficulties involved in the application of this rule were discussed in the section dealing with the definition of an interview. The rule was applied in *Fogah (Delroy)*[489] in which a confession to robbery, obtained by questioning the 16-year-old defendant in the street after arrest was excluded because of the absence of an appropriate adult. In *Gleaves*[490] the appellant, aged 16, was interviewed in the presence of a solicitor but not an appropriate adult and made admissions. The interview was excluded by the trial judge but it was held that other admissions made 8 days later in the presence of a solicitor should also have been excluded.

The requirement for an appropriate adult is mandatory under the code and the absence of any qualification based on practicability gives the police no latitude as they enjoyed under the previous, 1964, regime. Thus, rulings of the kind in *Roberts*[491] would no longer be permissible, however sympathetic the court might be to the quandry the police face with a juvenile who thinks he is too "grown-up" to have a parent or independent adult present. The defendant, a young person, was questioned in the absence of his mother, but this was excused on the grounds that he had particularly asked that she should not be present. The more rigorous approach under P.A.C.E. was anticipated in the first instance case of *Glyde*,[492] in which, understandably perhaps, the police were treated with less indulgence. A 16-year-old youth was arrested at his home at breakfast time on suspicion of involvement in a

[485] Report para. 96.
[486] para. 4.
[487] Note C11B.
[488] C11.14.
[489] [1989] Crim.L.R. 141, Snaresbrook Crown Court, ruling given November 3, 1988.
[490] [1993] Crim.L.R. 685, C.A.
[491] [1970] Crim. L.R. 464, C.A. See also *Willoughby* (1978) unreported, C.A. 4354/A/77.
[492] [1979] Crim.L.R. 985.

burglary. His mother, a single parent, could not accompany him to the police station as she had to see off her younger children to school. On the way to the station the police drove by way of the burgled premises and asked him if he had committed it and he admitted that he had. The defence elected not to seek a *voir dire* and in the presence of the jury the officer was asked under cross-examination why he had not waited until he could question the defendant in the presence of a responsible adult. He purported to explain that he had encountered the defendant in the past and knew that he would not have wanted to be interviewed in the presence either of his mother or of a social worker. As the confession constituted the only evidence against the defendant the judge directed the jury to acquit at the close of the prosecution case.

Urgent interviews

The special circumstances of urgency or emergency which, exceptionally, allow the interviewing outside police stations of normal adult suspects whom the police have decided to arrest have been applied in the 1995 revision to allow the interviewing outside police stations of juveniles (and mentally disordered or handicapped persons) whether or not suspected (and, therefore, whether or not under arrest, pending or actual). Thus, a juvenile may be interviewed in the absence of the appropriate adult outside a police station or other authorised place of detention if the consequent delay before the presence of an appropriate adult can be arranged would be likely to lead to interference with or harm to evidence connected with an offence or interference with or physical harm to other people, or to the alerting of other people suspected of having committed an offence but not yet arrested for it, or would be likely to hinder the recovery of property obtained in consequence of the commission of an offence.[493] There appears to be no requirement to record the grounds for conducting an interview in any of these circumstances. When an interview is to take place in a police station or other authorised place of detention a juvenile may be interviewed in the absence of the appropriate adult if, and only if, an officer of the rank of superintendent or above considers that any of the above consequences would otherwise follow[494] and a record must be kept of the grounds for any decision to interview a juvenile in these circumstances.[495] Questioning of a juvenile where, exceptionally, it is allowed in the absence of an appropriate adult may not continue once sufficient information to avert the relevant risk has been obtained.[496] Juveniles are one of the special groups which it is observed in a Note for Guidance are regarded as particularly vulnerable and the Note explains that the provisions allowing the overriding of the usual safeguards for juveniles in the case of police station interviews (or those in other authorised places of detention) are designed to protect them and to minimise the risk of interviews producing unreliable evidence and should be applied only in exceptional cases of need.[497] The

493 C11.14 and C11.1.
494 C11.14 and Annex C1.
495 *ibid.*, para. 3.
496 C11.14, C11.1 and Annex C3.
497 Annex C, Note C1.

circumstances which under the 1995 code exceptionally permit an interview of a juvenile in the absence of an appropriate adult may be compared with the formulation in the previous edition. The 1991 code provided that an *arrested* juvenile might be interviewed in the absence of an appropriate adult if, and only if, an officer of the rank of superintendent or above considered that delay would involve an immediate risk of harm to persons or serious loss or damage to property. The permitting circumstances have therefore been broadened for interviews both outside and inside the police station (or other authorised place of detention). Moreover, interviews with arrested juveniles outside the police station in the absence of an appropriate adult no longer require the imprimatur of a high ranking officer. It is noteworthy that under the 1991 edition the exception would not seem to have applied in the case of a suspected juvenile whom the police wished to interview but had not yet arrested, even if it had been decided to make an arrest.

(4) Appropriate adult

An "appropriate adult" in the case of a juvenile means his parent or guardian or, if he is in care, the care authority or voluntary organisation, his social worker, or failing any of those, another responsible adult aged 18 or over who is not a police officer or employed by the police.[498] The term "in care" is used in Code C to cover all cases in which a juvenile is "looked after" by a local authority under the terms of the Children Act 1989.[499] A Note for Guidance[500] advises that a person, including a parent or guardian, should not be an appropriate adult if he is suspected of involvement in the offence in question, is the victim, is a witness, is involved in the investigation or has received admissions prior to attending as the appropriate adult. If the parent of a juvenile is estranged from the juvenile, he should not be asked to act as the appropriate adult if the juvenile expressly and specifically objects to his presence.[501] Another Note advises that if a juvenile admits an offence to or in the presence of a social worker other than during the time that the social worker is acting as the appropriate adult for that juvenile, another social worker should be the appropriate adult in the interests of fairness.[502] A notable innovation of the 1991 revision was a Note for Guidance stating that a solicitor who is present at the police station in that capacity may not act as the appropriate adult.[503] The 1995 revision adds to the Note that a lay visitor who is present at the police station in that capacity may also not act as the appropriate adult. The purpose of the 1991 innovation was not clear to the R.C.C.J.[504] but it was introduced in response to a submission that

---

498 C1.7(a). Under the original code (C1.7) there was no age qualification for the responsible adult required in the absence of parent, guardian, care official or social worker.
499 C1.7(a).
500 Note C1C.
501 *ibid.*
502 Note C1D.
503 Note C1F.
504 Report, c.3, para. 85.

where the police treated the solicitor as the appropriate adult this was liable to provoke a conflict of interest.[505]

Apart from the designated exceptions given by the code when parents ought not to act as the appropriate adult there will be other, less clearly defined, instances when a parent may be deemed unsuitable to be employed as such. This issue arose in the appeal case of *W*[506] in which it was submitted that the mother of the appellant, a juvenile, should not have been used as the appropriate adult. It was held, dismissing the appeal, that the judge had not been wrong in principle in ruling that although psychotic at the time and suffering from some form of intellectual deficit, her paranoid delusions were confined to her neighbours, her thought processes were rational in discussing her family, she was perfectly capable of dealing with current events and was not unsuitable.

The question of whether a parent is always suitable to act as the appropriate adult formed the subject of research conducted on behalf of the R.C.C.J.[507] The findings suggest that in many cases juvenile suspects need independent assistance in their dealings with the police and that this is not always best provided by a parent. The research was based on an analysis of taped interviews with juvenile suspects and involved the examination of a total of 164 taped interviews in which the police record of interview revealed either that the suspect had made a full confession or that the outcome of the interview was unclear from the record. The interviews took place during 1990 at police stations in one police force. It was suggested that parents may find it difficult to remain objective and it was found not uncommon for them to take the side of the police and assist the process of obtaining a confession. (In *Jefferson et al.*[508] it was unsuccessfully contended on appeal that appellant's father had been inclined to side with the police and should not have acted as the appropriate adult.) On the other hand, the R.C.C.J. noted that there were doubtless instances of parents being too defensive.[509] They rightly recognised that although some parents may not be suitable to act as appropriate adults it is difficult to be prescriptive about this,[510] and, indeed, even if it were possible to lay down criteria for determining suitability it is difficult to see how they might be validly applied. Other research cited by the R.C.C.J.[511] revealed that local authority social services departments are increasingly being asked to provide the appropriate adult in cases of juveniles.

Where the appropriate adult is present at an interview, he should be informed that he is not expected to act simply as an observer; and also that the purposes of his

---

505 Submission by the Legal Action Group, see *Bulletin*, November 1989, reported in *The Times*, November 6, 1989 and see [1991] Crim.L.R., at 245, note 45.

506 [1994] Crim.L.R. 593, C.A.

507 Evans, *The Conduct of Police Interviews with Juveniles*, Royal Commission on Criminal Justice Research Study No. 8, London, HMSO 1993, cited in the main report, para. 83.

508 (1994) 99 Cr.App.R. 13; [1993] Crim.L.R. 881.

509 Report, Cm. 2263, c.3, para. 81, citing Brown, Ellis and Larcombe, *Changing the Code: Police Detention under the Revised PACE Codes of Practice*, Home Office Research and Planning Unit, London, HMSO 1993.

510 Report, c.3, para. 85.

511 *ibid.*, para. 81.

presence are, first, to advise the person being questioned and to observe whether or not the interview is being conducted properly and fairly, and secondly, to facilitate communication with the person being interviewed.[512] A Note for Guidance advises that because juveniles are prone to provide information which is unreliable the appropriate adult should be involved in any questioning if there is any doubt about a person's age.[513]

Expressing dissatisfaction with the present rules and practical arrangements for providing the necessary advice and protection for those who are likely to be particularly vulnerable to pressure while in police custody the R.C.C.J. believed that a more systematic approach was needed to the question of which people are suitable for being called upon to serve as appropriate adults and the training that they should receive.[514] They noted the suggestion for the preparation of a video film to assist in training and for showing to appropriate adults who may be called on without having had any previous experience of the role. They also saw some advantage in the preparation of a leaflet about the role and reponsibilities of appropriate adults which could be handed to them by the police on arrival at the police station. The possibility of establishing local panels of suitable persons seemed to the R.C.C.J. worthy of exploration. But they did not wish to make any specific recommendations connected with appropriate adults because they endorsed the recommendation of various researchers that there should be a comprehensive review (possibly by a Home Office chaired multi-disciplinary working party) of the role, function, qualifications, training and availability of appropriate adults.[515]

The advice of the Note for Guidance referred to above that parents should not act as an appropriate adult if, *inter alia*, they have received admissions focuses attention on the question addressed by the Runciman Commission as to what rules should apply when information is passed by a suspect to an appropriate adult.[516] Whether the principle of absolute confidentiality ought to be invoked as it is for lawyer-client communications the R.C.C.J. were uncertain, although they acknowledged the argument that it undermined the whole purpose of the role. However, if the appropriate adult could be required by a court to give evidence of any incriminating material, they believed that this needed to be clearly stated and that suspects should not be given the impression that whatever they said to the appropriate adult was entirely in confidence if that was not to be the case. They recommended the formulation of an unambiguous rule.

---

[512] C11.16.
[513] Note C11A.
[514] Report, c.3, para. 85.
[515] *ibid.*, para. 86.
[516] *ibid.*, para. 87.

(5) Interviews at school[517]

Juveniles may only be interviewed at their places of education in exceptional circumstances and then only where the principal or his nominee agrees. Every effort should be made to notify both the parents or other person responsible for the juvenile's welfare and the appropriate adult (if this is a different person) that the police want to interview the juvenile and reasonable time should be allowed to enable he appropriate adult to be present at the interview. Where awaiting the appropriate would cause unreasonable delay and unless the interviewee is suspected of an offence against the educational establishment, the principal or his nominee can act as the appropriate adult for the purposes of the interview. A Note for Guidance advises that it is preferable that a juvenile is not arrested at his place of education unless this is unavoidable in which case the principal or his nominee must be informed.[518]

G. *PERSONS UNDER THE INFLUENCE OF DRINK OR DRUGS*

No person who is unfit through drink or drugs to the extent that he is unable to appreciate the significance of questions put to him and his answers may normally be questioned about an alleged offence in that condition.[519] There is no exception for interviews outside the police station but where an interview is to take place in a police station or other authorised place of detention a person heavily under the influence of drink or drugs may be interviewed in that state if, and only if, an officer of the rank of superintendent or above considers that delay will lead to interference with or harm to evidence connected with an offence or interference with or physical harm to other people, or to the alerting of other people suspected of having committed an offence but not yet arrested for it, or will hinder the recovery of property obtained in consequence of the commission of an offence.[520] In such circumstances a record must be made of the grounds for any decision to interview a person[521] and questioning must cease once sufficient information to avert the immediate risk has been obtained.[522] A Note for Guidance stresses that in view of the risk of unreliability persons in this category should only be interviewed in exceptional cases of need.[523] As in the case of juveniles and the mentally disordered and handicapped the above criteria for permitting interviews with those heavily under the influence of drink or drugs were introduced by the 1995 revision and

517 C11.15, replacing para. 4 of the *Administrative Directions* 1964.

518 Note C11C.

519 C12.3.

520 Annex C1. Note for Guidance C12B states that the police surgeon can give advice about whether or not a person is fit to be interviewed in accordance with C12.3.

521 Annex C2.

522 Annex C3.

523 Annex C, Note C1.

enlarge the circumstances in which such interviews could be conducted under the 1991 code.

H. *LEGAL ADVICE*

(1) Circumstances when inferences are conditional on access to a solicitor

The drawing of an adverse inference in failure to mention cases under section 34 or in failure to account cases under sections 36 and 37 has not been made subject to any express condition requiring that the defendant must have had an opportunity to consult with a solicitor at the time of questioning, charge or request. The "even terms" principle approved in *Chandler*[524] as a condition for inferring a tacit admission has therefore not been *expressly* imported into the statute to cover failure to mention and failure to account. In the wake of the enactment of P.A.C.E. exchange abolitionists had largely justified their case on the two most prominent provisions of the new regime: the requirement which would eventually be achieved for all interviews at the police station to be tape-recorded and the guarantee of the right of suspects to have a solicitor in the police station. In keeping with the latter the Working Group's recommended guidelines for the drawing of adverse inferences included the question whether in the particular case the suspect had enjoyed access to a solicitor prior to being questioned.[525]

The situations in relation to which inferences may be permissible under the Act are as follows—

- **Questioning of detained suspects at the police station:** *i.e.*, where the suspect has been brought to a police station under arrest, detained for inquiries under P.A.C.E. and is formally interviewed under caution.
- **Post-arrest questioning outside the police station in emergency cases:** *i.e.*, where the police have decided to arrest the suspect or where they have actually arrested him and they ask such questions under caution outside the police station (or other authorised place of detention) as are permitted in the circumstances of exceptional urgency defined by Code C.11.1.[526]
- **Pre-arrest questioning under caution outside the police station:** *i.e.*, where the police have not yet arrested the suspect and no decision to arrest

[524] [1976] 1 W.L.R. 585.

[525] *Report*, para. 65.

[526] Code C11.1: "Following a decision to arrest a suspect he must not be interviewed about the relevant offence except at a police station (or other authorised place of detention) unless the consequent delay would be likely (a) to lead to interference with or harm to evidence connected with an offence or interference with or physical harm to other persons suspected of having committed an offence but not yet arrested for it; or (c) to hinder the recovery of property obtained in consequence of the commission of an offence. Interviewing in any of these circumstances shall cease once the relevant risk has been averted or the necessary questions have been put in order to attempt to avert that risk."

has yet been made and questioning is conducted under caution outside a police station.

- **Pre-arrest questioning under caution at the police station:** *i.e.*, where the suspect attends the police station voluntarily and is not placed under arrest before being questioned.

(a) *Questioning of detained suspects at the police station*

Subject to the extensive regulatory provisions contained in the P.A.C.E. Act and in Code C the police are empowered to question suspects in detention at the police station. It is laid down in the Act that "[a] person arrested and held in custody at a police station or other premises shall be entitled, if he so requests, to consult a solicitor privately at any time."[527] One of the principal reasons for consulting a solicitor while in custody at the police station is to obtain advice in relation to any questioning the police may conduct and the chief limitation on the power to question suspects in detention at the police station is the fundamental provision of Code C that normally no one who has requested, and has not thereafter waived, legal advice may be interviewed or continue to be interviewed until he has had the opportunity to receive it.[528] The detainee may have his solicitor present during questioning to advise and support him.[529] The product of an interview conducted in breach of these rules, whether an admission or significant silence, would be liable to be excluded under section 78 of P.A.C.E., possibly also under section 76. Similarly, an admission or significant silence at the point of charge would be liable to exclusion if access to a solicitor had been wrongly denied. If, then, the requirement for "even terms" is satisfied by police compliance with the duty of granting the suspect an *opportunity* to have a solicitor present (and not exclusively by actual presence) that condition for drawing an adverse inference in cases of failure to mention and failure to account, although not expressly incorporated in the 1994 Act, applies by virtue of P.A.C.E. where the suspect is under arrest and is in detention at the police station.

(i) Statutory delay of access for security reasons. P.A.C.E. empowers the police to delay access to a solicitor in the case of detention for a serious arrestable offence where an officer of superintendent's rank or above has reasonable grounds for believing that the exercise of the right to consult a solicitor (a) will lead to interference with or harm to evidence connected with a serious arrestable offence or interference with or physical injury to other persons; or (b) will lead to the alerting of other persons suspected of having committed such an offence but not yet arrested for it; or (c) will hinder the recovery of any property obtained as a result of such an

---

[527] s.58(1).

[528] C6.6. The paragraph sets out exceptions to the rule, see *infra*. The procedure to be followed in cases of waiver after a change of mind is set out in C6.6(d). For change of heart on waiver, see *Wolchover and Heaton Armstrong on Confession Evidence*, paras. 2-339 and 2-340.

[529] This is the implication of the provision for private consultation "at any time" (s.58(1)). Moreover, "[w]here a person has been permitted to consult a solicitor and the solicitor is available (*i.e.* present at the station or easily contactable by telephone) at the time the interview begins or is in progress, he must be allowed to have his solicitor present while he is interviewed." (C.6.8.)

offence.[530] A person who has requested legal advice may not be interviewed or continue to be interviewed until he has received it unless any of these circumstances apply or the officer of superintendent's rank or above has reasonable grounds for believing that delay will involve an immediate risk of harm to persons or serious loss of, or damage to, property.[531]

(ii) Solicitor delayed or unavailable. Additionally, an interview may proceed without prior consultation with a solicitor, in spite of a request for a solicitor, (1) if the superintendent or officer of higher rank has reasonable grounds for believing that where a solicitor, including a duty solicitor, has been contacted and has agreed to attend, awaiting his arrival would cause unreasonable delay to the process of investigation, or (2) if the solicitor nominated by the person or selected by him from a list cannot be contacted, or has previous indicated that he does not wish to be contacted, or having been contacted, has declined to attend, and the detained person has been advised of the Duty Solicitor Scheme but has declined to ask for the duty solicitor, or the duty solicitor is unavailable.[532] Although these provisions appear to give some latitude to the police to proceed in the absence of an unavailable solicitor the effect of an associated *Note for Guidance* is to oblige the police to exhaust almost every endeavour in arranging for the attendance of an alternative solicitor.[533]

(iii) *Murray v. U.K.* (European Court of Human Rights). Although the police retain a nominal discretion to proceed with an interview in the absence of a solicitor where security reasons or the solicitor's unavailability factor apply, the effect of the landmark decision in *Samuel*[534] was that the power of such refusal, particularly in relation to security reasons, is now largely academic and that there will be few if any conceivable opportunities in practice for the police to invoke delay legitimately. The proof of this is that since *Samuel* there have been no reported cases in which refusal of access has been upheld.[535] The question whether an adverse inference may properly be drawn against a defendant who, having been deprived of access to a solicitor in accordance with statute, stands on his silence when interviewed, was the subject of a ruling by the European Court of Human Rights in the Northern Ireland

---

[530] P.A.C.E., s.58(6) and (8) and Code C, Annex B(1). Authorisation must be confirmed in writing as soon as practicable: s.58(7).

[531] Code C.6.6(a) and (b)(i).

[532] Code C.6.6(b)(ii) and (c). In any of the circumstances in (2) the interview may be started or continued without further delay provided that an officer of the rank of Inspector or above has given agreement for the interview to proceed in those circumstances: C.6.6(c).

[533] Note C6B advises: "A person who asks for legal adv ice should be given an opportunity to consult a specific solicitor or another solicitor from that solicitor's firm of the duty solicitor. If advice is not available by these means, or he does not wish to consult the duty solicitor, the person should be given an opportunity to choose a solicitor from a list of those willing to provide legal advice. If this solicitor is unavailable, he may choose up to two alternatives. If these attempts to secure legal advice are unsuccessful, the custody officer has discretion to allow further attempts until a solicitor has been contacted and agrees to provide legal advice. Apart from carrying out his duties under Note C6B, a police officer must not advise the suspect about any particular firm of solicitors."

[534] (1987) 87 Cr.App.R. 232.

[535] See *Wolchover and Heaton-Armstrong on Confession Evidence*, para. 2-410. *Cf. Alladice* (1988) 87 Cr.App.R. 380, C.A., in which Lord Lane C.J. remained permissive of the police and dismissive of *Samuel* and see *Dunn* (1990) 91 Cr.App.R. 150 (breach upheld but appeal dismissed because appellant very experienced and not disadvantaged).

case of *Murray (John)* v. *U.K.*[536] The defendant was arrested at a house where an informer against the I.R.A. was being held captive and for 48 hours denied access to a solicitor under statutory provision. He was questioned 12 times during that period and the trial judge drew very strong inferences from his consistent refusal to account to the police for his presence at the house and from his refusal to give evidence. The Court found no violation of Articles 6.1 and 6.2 of the European Convention on Human Rights arising from the application of the silence provisions of the 1988 Order, so did not directly make the drawing of an adverse inference conditional on an accused's access to a solicitor.[537] However, such a result was achieved by the Court in a different way. By 12 votes to 5 they held that there had been a breach of Article 6.1 taken in conjunction with the Convention guarantee of the right of access to a lawyer provided by Article 6.3(c).[538] Adopting the opinion of the European Commission the Court took the view that the scheme contained in the 1988 Order was such that it was of "paramount importance" for the rights of the defence that an accused had access to a lawyer from the outset of interrogation. They pointed out that, under the Order, at the beginning of police interrogation, the accused was confronted with a fundamental dilemma relating to his defence. If he chose to remain silent adverse inferences might be drawn against him in accordance with the provisions of the Order. On the other hand, if he opted to break his silence during the course of interrogation, he ran the risk of prejudicing his defence without necessarily removing the possibility of inferences being drawn against him. Under such conditions, the concept of fairness enshrined in the Article 6 required that the accused had the benefit of the assistance of a lawyer already at the initial stages of police interrogation. To deny access to a lawyer for the first 48 hours of police questioning, in a situation where the rights of the defence might well be irretrievably prejudiced, was, whatever the justification for such denial, incompatible with the rights of the accused under Article 6.

(iv) H.O. circular guidance in England and Wales consequent on *Murray*. Following the decision in *Murray* v. *U.K.* the Home Office issued a circular to the police in England and Wales advising that the usual practice will be for suspects to have access to legal advice before being interviewed at the police station, but encouraging the police, where access is denied, to put inference-bearing questions again after the suspect has been given the opportunity to obtain such advice.[539] In parallel the Attorney-General issued guidance to prosecutors in England and Wales advising them not to seek to rely on inferences drawn from silence before an accused had been granted access to legal advice.[540]

---

536 (1996) 22 E.H.R.R. 29; *The Times*, February 9, 1996. See also now *Averill* v. *U.K.*, E.C.H.R. application no. 36408/97, June 6, 2000, *The Times*, June 20, 2000; and *Magee* v. *U.K.*, EC.H.R. application no. 28135/95, June 6, 2000, *The Times* June 20, 2000.

537 See Chapter 4, for the terms of Art. 6.1 and 6.2.

538 "Everyone charged with a criminal offence has the . . . the right to defend himself in person or through legal assistance of his own choosing or, if he has not sufficient means to pay for legal assistance, to be given it free when the interests of justice so require."

539 H.O. 53/1998., set out in 163 J.P.N. 18. The Northern Ireland Office issued corresponding guidance.

540 Circular 40/1998, similarly set out in *ibid.*, see 327 H.C. Deb., cols. 130-131, December 1, 1998.

(v) Legislation consequent on *Murray*. In consequence of *Murray* v. *U.K.* a new subsection, (2A), was inserted in section 34 by section 58(1) and (2) of the Youth Justice and Criminal Evidence Act 1999, enacting that the provisions of subsections (1) and (2) of section 34 do not apply where the accused was at an authorised place of detention at the time of the failure if he had not been allowed an opportunity to consult a solicitor prior to being questioned, charged or officially informed that he might be prosecuted, as mentioned in section 34(1).[541] New subsection (4A) was inserted in sections 36 of the 1994 Act by section 58(1) and (3) of the 1999 Act and new subsection (3A) was inserted in section 37 of the 1994 Act by section 58(1) and (4).[542] In the light of the impact of the decision in *Samuel*, *supra*, on the application of P.A.C.E. the new subsections afford little practical benefit in relation to the trial of ordinary criminal offences, since the police do not now ever officially deprive defendants in custody at the police station of the right of access to legal advice.

(b) *Custodial questioning outside the police station*

The prohibition on normal questioning under caution of arrested persons outside the police station, introduced for the first time in 1991, reflects the principle that where a suspect has been arrested questioning in normal circumstances should only take place at the police station (or other authorised place of detention[543]) where the full range of protective P.A.C.E. facilities are available. Questioning of suspects under arrest or those whom it is intended to arrest must routinely await their detention at the police station. They must not normally be questioned before that stage. The circumstances of exceptional urgency in which it is likely to be sanctioned outside the police station will be extremely rare. Thus, any question of a failure during post-arrest questioning to mention a fact relied on at trial will almost always arise only after the stage at which the entitlement to a solicitor and to notice of that right has begun to run. (A request to account for any of the circumstances in sections 36 and 37 will necessarily constitute an interview. Such requests are unlikely to be made before arrival of the suspect at the police station, as it is difficult to envisage circumstances in which they could ever be justified as so urgent as to come within the exceptions to C.11.1.[544])

---

541 Section 58(1) and (5) of the 1999 Act inserts s.38(2A) in the 1994 Act, providing that "authorised place of detention" means a police station or any other place prescribed for the purposes of s.34(2A) by order by the Secretary of State and the power to make such an order shall be exercisable by statutory instrument which shall be subject to annulment in pursuance of a resolution of either House of Parliament. By s.68(3) and (4)(d) of the 1999 Act the insertion of s.34(2A) takes effect as from a day to be appointed, save that it came into force on July 27, 1999, for the purpose only of the exercise of the power to make an order.

542 New s. 38(2A) inserted by s.58(1) and (5) of the 1999 Act, also applies to ss. 36 and 37, as does s.68(3) and (4)(d) of the 1999 Act.

543 The term "other authorised place of detention" in C11.1 is not defined in the Act or the Code but logically refers to any premises designated for the detention of arrested suspects under P.A.C.E., for example, an office with detention facilities used by customs investigators.

544 Thus although the guidance in circulars 40/1998 and H.O. 53/1998 acknowledges that questioning under the two sections might occur in exceptional circumstances prior to arrival at the police station or other authorised place of detention, it states that the effect of the code is an expectation that such questioning would not occur.

It would appear that inferences may be drawn from silence in response to emergency (C.11.1) questioning outside the police station in spite of the fact that there is no right of access to a solicitor at this stage. Section 58(1) of the P.A.C.E. Act enacts: "A person arrested and held in custody at a police station or other premises shall be entitled, if he so requests, to consult a solicitor privately at any time." Although the term "premises" includes any place and, in particular, *inter alia*, any vehicle[545] it is now settled that suspects who have been arrested only enjoy the right of access to a solicitor after the stage has been reached at which their detention in custody has been authorised, that is after they have been brought to a designated police station (or other authorised place of detention) and the custody officer has satisfied himself that the statutory detention conditions have been met.[546] Thus an arrested person will not enjoy the benefit of the section at the place of his arrest (not being a police station), nor in a police vehicle on the way to the police station. The rule is only logical. It would be absurd and an impediment on the rule that an arrested person must be brought to a police station as soon as practicable[547] if the police had to allow the arrested person the facility of a private telephone call to his solicitor from a pay-phone or mobile telephone or otherwise a visit to the solicitor's office on the way to the police station. Quite apart from the delay there might be security implications in allowing a telephone call to a number which had not first been screened in the way that this is usually carried out by the custody officer. Since a person who has been arrested must not normally be questioned before being brought to the police station or other authorised place of detention it hardly matters that the person will have no right to consult a solicitor before arriving at the police station. However, C.11.1 permits questioning of arrested suspects outside the police station in cases of exceptional urgency listed in the paragraph. It is in this very rare situation[548] that the arrested suspect may be questioned under caution without having the right to consult a solicitor but the need to ask questions because of the emergency would be defeated if the suspect had first of all to be allowed to consult a solicitor.

On the face of it where such emergency questioning outside the police station is permissible the police would appear to be under no Code obligation to postpone the interview if the suspect requests a solicitor[549] and any evidence of significant silence obtained by such questioning may presumably be deployed for the purposes of sections 34, 36 or 37, as the case may be, and inferences appropriately authorised, provided that that silence was put to the suspect at the beginning of any interview carried out at the police station.[550] The guidance issued by the Attorney-General and by the Home Office in the light of *Murray* assumes that the decision applies only to

---

545 P.A.C.E., s.23; s.118(1).

546 *Kerawalla* [1991] Crim.L.R. 451, C.A. For a discussion of the decision see *Wolchover and Heaton-Armstrong on Confession Evidence*, paras. 2-295 to 2-298.

547 P.A.C.E., s.30.

548 So rare that there are no reported or otherwise known recorded cases of officers cla iming such an exception.

549 *Kerawalla, supra.*

550 C11.2A.

interviews at a police station or other authorised place of detention, since suspects under arrest outside a police station have no right of access to a solicitor.[551] However, whether it is correct that *Murray* does not or should not apply to custodial questioning outside the police station has been called into doubt.[552] Although the E.C.H.R. were considering denial of access to legal advice at the police station, they stressed the benefit of legal advice "at the initial stages of police interrogation" when silence can lead to irretrievable prejudice, the potential effect of which gives rise to the paramount importance of access to legal advice. In amending the 1994 Act to take account of *Murray* the Government have declined to extend its application to questioning under caution outside the police station. However, as already noted, the E.C.H.R. stated in *Condron* v. *U.K.*[553] that "the physical presence of a solicitor during police interview [was] a particularly important safeguard for dispelling any compulsion to speak which may be inherent in the terms of the caution" and the fact that a person has remained silent following legal advice was to be given appropriate weight by the domestic court as there might be good reason why such advice was given. It has been suggested that this observation "seals the fate" of the legitimacy of drawing an adverse inference from an interview conducted outside the police station and before access to legal advice.[554] On the other hand, the E.C.H.R. were referring to the failure to provide "detailed responses," not normally a consideration in questioning conducted outside police stations. Moreover, the scope of urgent interviewing is so narrow that the point is of little more than theoretical interest.

(c) *Pre-arrest questioning under caution outside the police station.*

There is one situation in which there is undoubted potential scope for section 34(1) and (2) to bite where the police are permitted to conduct an interview with a suspect despite his expressed wish to defer answering questions until after he has consulted a solicitor. This is in the case of questioning under caution outside the police station prior to arrest. Such questioning is permitted unless the officer intends to make an arrest in any event. Suspects who are not under arrest obviously enjoy an absolute entitlement to have a solicitor present when questioned but where they request a solicitor P.A.C.E. places no prohibition on questioning or further questioning until the solicitor has been consulted, as it does in the case of detained suspects under Code C6.6. Outside the police station the police may properly therefore put questions to a suspect whom they do not yet intend to arrest despite his

[551] As already mentioned, the guidance accepts that requests under sections 36 or 37 might be made in exceptional circumstances prior to arrival at the police station or authorised place of detention, but states that the effect of Code C is an expectation that they would not be made in this situation. As distinct from ordinary questioning it is difficult to conceive of circumstances in which section 36 and 37 requests might need to be made in Code C11.1 emergencies.

[552] Jennings, "Resounding Silence," *New Law Journal*, May 17, 1996, 725; May 24, 764; May 31, 821, at p.864.

[553] para. 60.

[554] Jennings, Ashworth and Emmerson, [2000] Crim.L.R., at p.882, note. 27.

expressed wish to wait for a solicitor. In other words they may legitimately ignore the free suspect's request to speak to a solicitor.

As in the case of (urgent) custodial questioning outside the police station, the importance place in *Condron* v. *U.K.* on access to legal advice as condition for drawing an adverse inference may have rendered such inferences impermissible in the context of pre-arrest questioning under caution. Whether such a prognosis is warranted, the reality is that it is almost inconceivable that any tribunal of fact would find that a defendant had acted unreasonably in opting for silence at this stage where the police brushed aside his request for a postponement of questioning pending his having an opportunity to consult a solicitor.

A suspect whom the police seek to question under caution outside a police station cannot, if he is not under arrest, be refused access to a solicitor, since by virtue of his being a free person there will be no power to prevent access. If he is stopped from trying to contact a solicitor that would be evidence of his being under *de facto* arrest and non-urgent interviewing would be impermissible outside the police station under Code C11.1. (It is noted below that a free suspect's silence in the face of questions asked of him despite his expression of a wish to speak to a solicitor first would not be likely to be regarded as unreasonable.)

(d) *Pre-arrest questioning at the police station*

Anyone present at a police station voluntarily, whether as a potential witness or under suspicion of having committed an offence, enjoys an absolute right to obtain legal advice. This is an implicit attribute of freedom and is recognised in a *Note for Guidance* to Code C which advises that persons present at a police station "voluntarily to assist with an investigation should be treated with no less consideration" than people in custody at the police station and "enjoy an absolute right to obtain legal advice."[555] Refusal to allow access would be evidence that the person was not free to go, but was actually under restraint and held improperly, and this would pose obvious implications for the admissibility of any questioning and its product. Riding rough shod over the request of a free person to contact or secure a solicitor by ignoring the request and conducting questions in the face of it would be tantamount to a refusal of the request and thus evidence that the person was *de facto* in custody. If the person objected to being questioned under caution in these circumstances and was allowed to walk out it is inconceivable that his response could provide any basis for an inference.

[555] Note C1A.

(2) Interview without a solicitor

(a) *Replies withheld pending legal advice following declined request for a solicitor*

As already indicated, from a day yet to be appointed no inference will be permissible under sections 34, 36 or 37, in relation to questioning of a suspect in detention at the police station (or other authorised place of detention) where the suspect was refused access to a solicitor. On the other hand, where a suspect is questioned under caution outside the police station prior to arrest or where an emergency interview takes place outside the police station under C.11.1 the police are not obliged to desist from questioning if the suspect requests a solicitor. If, then, on being questioning the suspect maintains his silence on the professed ground that he wants to speak to a solicitor before answering any questions the court may have to consider whether it would be reasonable to draw an adverse inference or whether it would be unreasonable to hold his silence against him. Here there is no bar against an adverse inference referable to any impropriety in the interview and the issue whether or not it is fair and reasonable to draw such an inference will devolve on whether the supposed desire for a solicitor was a reasonable one in the circumstances. The R.C.C.J. acknowledged as one of a number of possible innocent explanations for silence a reasoned decision to wait until the allegation has been set out in detail and the suspect has had the benefit of legal advice.[556] Admittedly this is not quite the same thing as a deliberate decision to await a consultation before answering questions but in *Argent*[557] Lord Bingham C.J. acknowledged that good reasons for making no comment might be the fear that what was said would not be fairly recorded or a desire to say nothing before taking legal advice.

Whether such an explanation was reasonable (and therefore credible) was considered in the Northern Ireland appeal of *Quinn*,[558] although a detailed scrutiny of the facts shows that the defendant was not actually deprived of his right of access before interview. He was interviewed about various scheduled offences arising from an incident for which he had been arrested under the emergency provisions but declined to say anything to the police. In evidence at his trial he offered by way of defence a straightforward explanation of the suspicious circumstances implicating him in involvement and purported to attribute his silence at interview to the fact that he wanted to speak to a solicitor before answering any questions. But the Court of Appeal agreed with the trial judge's view that since at the time of his arrest the appellant had full notice of the case against him his account was one for which he did not need the advice of a solicitor before giving it to the police and that his silence was a deliberate tactic which would not have been adopted by someone who had a truthful explanation. This calls to mind *Tune*, *supra*, and although it seems to fly in the face of the very purpose of having legal advice the case was not in fact one in which the defendant had actually been deprived of a solicitor before interview. He

---

556 Report, chap. 4, para. 13.

557 [1997] 2 Cr.App.R., at p.33.

558 (1993) unreported, N.I.C.A. September 17, cited in Jackson, [1995] Crim.L.R., at pp.592-593.

had asked for one on arriving at the police station, but the P.A.C.E. rule prohibiting an interview after a request for legal advice until the advice has been given had no application in cases under the emergency legislation and this apparently allowed the police to take him for interview before he could speak to a solicitor. However, he made no renewal of his request at the outset of the interview and, significantly, the defence never challenged the interviewing officer's evidence that the right to a solicitor had not been deferred and that if the request had been repeated the interview would have been immediately suspended. In effect, the defendant had not pursued his original request and had waived his right to a solicitor. It is perhaps not surprising, therefore, that his attempt to explain away his silence by reference to a desire to seek legal advice before speaking to the police was disbelieved.

(b) *Right to legal advice waived*

Where a defendant has waived his right to consult a solicitor the court will need to give very close attention to whether the caution were satisfactorily explained by the police, whether he understood its terms and whether, in short, he fully appreciated the implications of silence. This will call for a careful investigation of the defendant's state of mind, the evidence of the interview and the circumstances as a whole and the jury will need to be given careful directions[559]

(3) Legal and practical effects of solicitor's advice to say nothing

(a) *Fundamental tension between the assumption that the innocent always want to speak and the presumption that it is reasonable to follow a solicitor's advice to say nothing*

Before the 1994 Act there was a strong correlation between suspects exercising their right to silence and representation by a legal adviser at the police station.[560] The Act by no means eradicated the practice of advising silence, although obviously it was bound to diminish, and its continued incidence has given rise to a number of appellate decisions concerning the impact of such advice on the operation of the Act.

When curtailment of the right to silence was mooted towards the end of the 1980s it was quickly perceived that any legislation might be rendered inherently unworkable by the mere factor of solicitors advising their clients to say nothing.[561] If the suspect's silence could always be conclusively explained away on the basis that he was simply following legal advice it would never be possible to draw an adverse inference from his silence whenever the legal representative had given such advice. When the C.L.R.C. published their scheme in 1972 this problem was not voiced,

---

559 See D. Roberts, "Legal Advice, the Unrepresented Suspect and the Courts: Inferences from Silence under the Criminal Justice and Public Order Act 1994," [1995] Crim.L.R.; H. Fenwick, "Curtailing the Right to Silence, Access to Legal Advice and Section 78," [1995] Crim.L.R. 132; A. Jennings, "Resounding Silence," *supra,* p.764.

560 See the various studies cited, *supra*, at p.28.

561 See *e.g.* Wolchover, "Guilt and the Silent Suspect," *New Law Journal*, April 14, 1989, p.501.

perhaps because prior to P.A.C.E. suspects were commonly denied access to a solicitor before charge[562] and the possibility that solicitors, on the rare occasions that they were granted access, might advise the defendant to say nothing was probably not seen as a potentially significant spoke in the wheel of the committee's scheme. In contrast, by the late 1980s free representation by a solicitor in the police station was available to all who requested it and every suspect had to be informed of the right to request a solicitor. (After 1991, they had to be told that such representation would be free.) In the light of that change, it was now a fundamental and real issue whether it could still be reasonable to expect a suspect to answer police questions even though he had been advised by his solicitor not to do so.

Sanctioning adverse inferences gives rise to a difficult conundrum arising out of the basic right of detained suspects to enjoy access to the advice of a solicitor in the police station. The condundrum is this. On the one hand the sanctioning of adverse inferences from silence is supposedly based on common sense. Conversely, if suspects are given the right to take legal advice in the police station it must surely, as a matter of common sense, be reasonable to expect them to follow such advice as it is their right to receive. Otherwise, what would be the purpose of bestowing the right? It was the very basis of the logic of permitting adverse inferences—that as a matter of common sense it is reasonable to assume that the innocent will want to answer questions—which ought to have been its own undoing. Just as an adverse inference is driven by common sense, so equally if a solicitor advises silence it can hardly be common sense to expect the suspect to be the arbiter of that advice by rejecting it. The fundamental flaw in the legislation was that a solicitor only had to give that advice in order to stave off an adverse inference.

It cannot be both reasonable to expect the suspect to answer questions and at the same time reasonable for the suspect to follow advice to say nothing. One of these propositions must surrender to the other. In *Connolly and McCartney*,[563] a decision on the counterpart Northern Ireland provisions, it was suggested that the second might well be expendable. Giving the judgment of the Northern Ireland Court of Appeal, Carswell J. suggested that if the failure to mention facts was "objectively unreasonable" it did "not become reasonable merely because a solicitor gave his client ill-judged advice." The implications of this observation may be far-reaching. There may be any one of a number of reasons why a solicitor would be exercising good judgment in advising his client to say nothing. However, it should presumably always be coupled with a warning that although it may be safer to say nothing than to speak there will be a risk that the court might attribute silence not to the advice to say nothing but to the use of it as a pretext for concealing the lack of a plausible story or the weaknesses in a fabricated one. Without such a rider an unqualified exhortation to say nothing would be misleading and therefore incompetent. However, to draw an adverse inference against a defendant who had received such

562 See Zander, "Access to a Solicitor in the Police Station," [1972] Crim.L.R. 342; "Informing the Suspect of his Rights in the Police Station," (1972) 69 *Law Soc.Gaz.*, 1238.

563 (1992) unreported, cited in Pattenden, "Inferences from Silence," [1995] Crim.L.R. 602, at p.609.

misleading advice it would surely be necessary to demonstrate that he must have known that advice lacking the requisite rider was misleading. Supposing the solicitor baldly urges the client to say nothing and wrongly assures him, in contradistinction to the authorities, that in view of the advice there can be no possibility of prejudice at all and that the words of the caution are no more than a mere formality having no application to the position where a solicitor has advised silence. In other words, the solicitor tells his client, take no notice of the words of the caution when it is given, they don't mean you. If the advice is followed it could hardly be reasonable to hold the accused's silence against him unless the client happened to enjoy a thorough working intimacy with the intricacies of the 1994 Act. In the absence of such insight it is difficult to see how it could be reasonable to draw an inference against the defendant who had been advised to say nothing on this misconceived basis, since his silence might well be attributable to that advice.[564] As a matter of common fairness no adverse inference could be drawn from his silence and the solicitor would as it turns out have been correct therefore to tell his client that no inference could be drawn. In effect bad advice becomes good advice by the simple act of giving it. It would in short be self-justifying or self-fulfilling.

There is more than one escape route from the circularity of this argument. The first involves a practical saving. It is almost inconceivable that any solicitor or accredited representative would ever be prepared to admit in the witness box having given such defective advice and the defence would be faced with the problem that in the absence from court of the supposedly inept solicitor the accused would be exposed to sceptical cross-examination if he claimed to have been given it. The consequence might be the jury's disbelief in the defendant's evidence that he was given this advice. (On the other hand, although the jury are exhorted not to speculate on evidence they haven't heard, they would not be able to judge whether the solicitor is absent because he would only deny giving the advice, which would hardly help the defendant, or conversely because he did give the advice and was ashamed to admit it.) The second possible escape route argues that even if the jury accept that the defective advice was given this would not necessarily preclude them from finding that the defendant knew it was unsound but that he used it as a convenient shield either for concocting a false story later or blocking awkward scrutiny of a false story already concocted.[565] The objection to this, however, is that it involves an assumption about the extent of the accused's legal knowledge which it can hardly be realistic to make.

An equally difficult question concerns advice to be silent which, although coupled with a rider cannot be related to any of the standard criteria for advising silence, and which, even if it is not based on whim, may be attributable to the solicitor's laziness and an unwillingness to spend time and effort on taking proper

---

564 "[T]he public interest cannot be served by an adverse inference being drawn against a defendant who has genuinely followed what is subsequently judged to be bad advice": Jennings, "Resounding Silence," *supra*, p.765.

565 See *Martin, Morrison and others* (1991) unreported, Belfast Crown Court, May 8, cited in Jackson, [1995] Crim.L.R., at p.597.

instructions in uncomfortable conditions at the police station. The giving of the rider means that the suspect is alerted to the risk of an inference and is not misled in that way. But there remains the problem that he must still make a value judgment on the advice and, if the solicitor had no rational basis for giving it, the accused can hardly be expected to have discerned this.

There are two alternative implications, then, of the thinking in *Connolly* that defendants cannot automatically excuse their silence by reference to bad legal advice. On the one hand it imputes to the suspect an awareness of the deficiency in the lawyer's advice and therefore flies in the face of the assumption implied in the right to legal advice conferred by P.A.C.E. that a suspect will not enjoy a better view of his legal position than his lawyer.[566] On the other hand, it makes no such assumption but, as a matter of policy, simply punishes defendants for the failings of their lawyers. Since it is unlikely that Carswell J. can have intended either of these possibilities to apply it is difficult to avoid the suspicion that his attitude was tempered more by a belief in the endemic nature of non-coöperation in Northern Ireland than by any question of professional incompetence.

An even sterner regime of approach than *Connolly* may have been intended in the assumption made by McDermott L.J. in *Kinsella*,[567] another Northern Ireland appeal, that "an experienced solicitor" would not generally advise silence. This may have meant no more than that a defendant will much more effectively advance his case by disclosing it at the first opportunity. But, equally, it may have been intended to mean that solicitors usually advise their clients to answer questions because of the risk that if they were to advise silence and the advice were taken, the court might impute bad motive to the client all the same (*Martin, Morrison*). If advising the suspect to say nothing is ill-judged because it is the contrary of what experienced solicitors would do, then, under *Connolly,* defendants will always be acting unreasonably in not rejecting that advice.

(b) *Solicitor's advice to be silent cannot pre-empt an adverse inference as a matter of law*

Abolitionists of the right to silence were not put off by the obstacles identified in the previous section and, as noted by the R.C.C.J., believed nonetheless "that the prosecution should be able to comment at trial on the refusal of any persons against whom there [was] a *prima facie* case to explain their conduct, *whether or not such a refusal was based on legal advice.*"[568] During Commons consideration of the measure the Home Secretary rejected a suggestion that no inference would be drawn if a solicitor had advised silence[569] and in Commons Committee the Government spokesman said, "Nothing in the Bill would bar a court from drawing an adverse inference just because the defendant acted or said that he had acted on legal advice.

---

566 See Pattenden, [1995] Crim.L.R., at p.609.

567 (1993) unreported, Belfast Crown Court, cited in E. Rees, *Counsel* March/April 1995. For consideration of the Nothern Ireland authorities on the topic see Jackson, "Interpreting the Silence Provisions: the Northern Ireland Cases," [1995 Crim.L.R. 587, at pp.592-594.

568 Report, chap. 4, para.8, emphasis supplied.

569 235 H.C. Deb., col. 26, January 11, 1994.

It will be for the courts to decide what, if any inferences to draw . . ."[570] The common sense notion that it is reasonable to expect defendants to follow legal advice they have requested was therefore sacrificed on the alter of policy, the real purpose of the proposed rule evidently being to defeat the anticipated ploy of "experienced professional criminals" who might need to justify a decision to remain silent by representing that their solicitors had advised them to say nothing at least until the allegations against them had been fully disclosed.[571]

At the time of the English legislation this issue was a path already well trodden by the courts of Northern Ireland. Under the Criminal Evidence (Northern Ireland) Order 1988 dictates of policy, perhaps driven in part by the extreme conditions prevailing in the province (where silence was pursued in the vast majority of scheduled cases), gave an answer to the question whether inferences could be pre-empted by the fact of legal advice in favour of silence. In *Quinn*[572] Hutton L.C.J. observed that "the drawing of a common sense inference in an appropriate case" was not to be "stultified by the existence of a right to legal advice." But here, as has already been seen, a different point was before the court, in that the accused's attempt to explain away his silence by reference to a wish to take legal advice before answering any questions was directly contradicted by the fact that he had effectively waived his right to legal advice in the first place.

The issue received rather more salient attention in *Martin, Morrison and others* [573] where the defendant stated in interview that on legal advice he would be answering no questions and did not do so. On appeal it was held that the trial judge (again, Hutton L.C.J.) was right to draw an adverse inference based on interpreting the defendant's ostensible attribution of his silence to legal advice as "a tactical desire not to reveal his line of defence at that stage." The effect of this decision was that the tribunal of fact would not be bound to attribute silence to legal advice *merely because the advice preceded it.* Instead it was open to tribunals to infer that advice to say nothing was used by the defendant in order to facilitate a dishonest defence. The silence might be a cover for gaining time to invent a false defence later, or to avoid detailed interrogation on a false story already fabricated but perhaps not yet honed to perfection or otherwise checked for watertightness against other information or evidence. Advice to say nothing tendered in good faith may be acted on in bad faith. Conversely, it is in theory conceivable that whilst it is tendered in bad faith it is acted on in good faith, although it is likely that where the solicitor is acting with dishonest intent it is because he is conniving with the accused. But it is assumed that the prosecution would rarely be suggesting that the advice was tendered by the lawyer other than in good faith and the only issue would be whether it was exploited by the defendant in bad faith.

---

570 *Select Committee B 1993-94,* vol. 2, col. 407, February 1, 1994.

571 R.C.C.J. report, chap. 4, para. 8.

572 (1991) unreported, N.I.C.A., September 17, cited on the point by E. Rees, *Counsel*, March/April 1995.

573 (1991) unreported, Belfast Crown Court, May 8; N.I.C.A., cited in Jackson, [1995] Crim. L.R., at p.597.

That a solicitor's advice to say nothing will not under the English legislation conclusively avert an adverse inference was affirmed in *Condron and Condron*[574] the facts and decision in which were set out earlier. On appeal the defence had initially sought to argue that in any case in which a solicitor advised the defendant not to answer questions the judge should exclude a "no comment" interview. However, counsel subsequently resiled from that position, recognising, in anticipation of the court's view, that it would render section 34 wholly nugatory.

(c) *Prediction that defence will need to adduce evidence explaining reasons for advising silence in order to avert an adverse inference*

Not only would a solicitor's advice to remain silent not preclude an adverse inference as a matter of law but in *Condron* Stuart-Smith L.J. stated that if the accused gave as a reason for not answering questions that he had been advised by his solicitor not to do so, that bare assertion was unlikely by itself to be regarded as a sufficient reason for not mentioning matters relevant to the defence. It is assumed that the court was predicting the view fact-finders would be likely to take, not the unlikelihood of trial judges in such a case excluding evidence of silence or otherwise directing juries not to draw an adverse inference, since *Condron* is also authority for the proposition that such courses would be exceptional.

Stuart-Smith L.J. went on to say that if the accused wished to invite the court not to draw an adverse inference it would be necessary to go further than merely asserting that he was silent on legal advice. The accused would have to explain the basis and reason for the advice. This would be necessary, it was suggested, to enable the jury to assess whether the defendant was acting reasonably in remaining silent. The explanation might come from the accused himself or it might come from the solicitor. If without calling the solicitor the defendant attempted to articulate the reasons the solicitor gave him for advising silence this might breach the rule against hearsay or involve inadmissible conjecture, but would not necessarily do so. (The hearsay question is considered later.) Even if there was no infringement of hearsay or the rule against conjecture it would certainly amount to the waiver of lawyer-client privilege, entitling the Crown to cross-examine on the reasons given.[575] Quite apart from any question of hearsay it may be observed that few defendants would be capable of repeating coherently the reasons they were given for being advised to remain silent. In the case of those who were able the reason would hardly be inarticulacy.

It is far from clear why, according to *Condron*, it will be necessary to state the reasons for *giving* the advice to remain silent in order for the jury to be able to make a valid assessment of whether the defendant was acting reasonably in *accepting* it. It is the defendant's reasons for remaining silent which are at issue, not whether the solicitor's advice was sound or ill-judged.[576] How might the basis for the advice be

---

574 [1997] 1 Cr.App.R. 185, at p.191.

575 See also *Bowden* [1999] 1 W.L.R. 823, p.831.

576 Philip Plowden, "Silence at the police station," *New Law Journal,* October 30, 1998, 1598, at p.1599.

material? It might be argued that the stronger the reason for advising silence so the stronger might be the terms of the solicitor's advice to say nothing; the stronger the terms of that advice so the stronger the impact on him and therefore the more reasonable would it have been to follow the advice.[577] Conversely, if the reason was weak the advice may have been lukewarm, making it less reasonable for the defendant to have followed it. In fact the argument is tenuous. It is hardly the correctness of the advice which determines the conviction with which it is delivered. Bad advice can be given in confident tones, good advice in tentative ones.)

It might, on the other hand, be argued that if the suspect is told the reasons and they are good ones, this would make it more reasonable for him to follow the advice. So the solicitor's reasons would be relevant in that they influenced the defendant's decision. This would require the reasons to be explained to the defendant and would make the assessment of the suspect's reasonableness in choosing silence dependent on his powers of comprehension. The more intelligent the suspect, the more likely would he be to understand the reasons given to him for saying nothing and so the more reasonable the decision to follow the advice. Yet the manifest absurdity of such an approach is demonstrated by the converse: the weaker the suspect's intellect the less reasonable would it be for him to say nothing. However, in most cases it is the very backwardness of the suspect which is likely to be seen as justifying advice to say nothing. In any event, making reasonableness dependent on intelligence would be inconsistent with the principle established in *Argent* that the test is not that of some hypothetical reasonable man but of the defendant with all his foibles.

In *Van Bokkum and others* the Court of Appeal on the face of it appeared to go further than *Condron* in stating that the trial judge "correctly said that it was no answer for the defendant simply to say that he was acting on his solicitor's advice."[578] However, it seems probable that what was meant was no more than that the bare assertion would be unlikely to oust the risk of an adverse inference, a restatement of *Condron*. This is to be deduced from the fact that the court went on to observe that the judge was not saying that the jury should ignore the fact that the appellants had been given legal advice to say nothing.[579] The decision is noteworthy for the fact that the convictions were upheld notwithstanding the judge had apparently invited the jury to speculate on what the appellants had told their solicitors in the absence of any evidence of this. In the presence of their solicitors and on their advice the appellants gave no comment interviews in relation to drugs allegations. The solicitors were not called to state their reasons and in giving directions under section 34 the judge pointed out that there was therefore no independent evidence as to what the solicitor knew of the case and he invited the jury to consider what the basis was for the advice, how much the solicitors had been told of their clients' cases and what their understanding was of the strength of the case against their clients. Following on from that, he said, the question had to be asked whether in the face of a simple, innocent and complete explanation would any

[577] *ibid*.
[578] (2000) unreported, C.A. 199900333/Z3 *et seq*., March 7, transcript, para. 37.
[579] *ibid*., para. 47.

solicitor advise silence? When looking at a solicitor the test was not was he good or bad, experienced or inexperienced, not even what advice he actually gave, but whether the jury were of the view that in the circumstances which obtained at the time it was reasonable to have expected disclosure. Objection was immediately taken by the first appellant's counsel to this direction on the basis *inter alia* that it invited the jury to speculate as to what the appellant had told his solicitor and the Crown conceded that there was a danger that it did invite such speculation.[580] The same observations were made in relation to all appellants and on appeal the Crown conceded that the comments complained of were unhelpful.[581] In giving judgment the court said:

> "There can be no criticism of the fact that the judge reminded the jury that they had not heard evidence from the solicitors. His comments did not suggest that he was critical of this. The essence of the criticism against the judge is that he should not have invited the jury to consider what advice the solicitors would have given if they had been given the explanations which the jury had heard. He should not have done this since it invited the jury to consider whether the appellants had told their solicitors the truth when there was no evidence or suggestion that they had not done so."[582]

It is not completely clear whether the last sentence in this passage implies agreement with the appellants or whether it simply continues the summary of the ground of complaint. That the point appears to have been conceded by the Crown suggests the former, more particularly as the complaint is not otherwise adjudicated upon. Since the judge reminded the jury of the correct test five times in the course of summing up the court were of the view that the comment did not cast doubt on the overall safety of the convictions.

(d) *"Tactical" reasons for silence*

Possibly the real relevance of the soundness or otherwise of the advice is that if the reasons are good ones this might tend to lessen any risk of the jury reaching the conclusion that it was given and received as a pretext for disguising the fact that the defendant had no defence or none that would stand up to scrutiny under police questioning. This seems to have been the purpose which the court had in mind in *Condron.* There Stuart-Smith L.J. said that where the solicitor was called to explain the reasons for advising silence and this amounted to a waiver of privilege the solicitor could be asked—

---

580 *ibid.*, paras 39-40.
581 *ibid.*, para. 46.
582 *ibid.*, para. 47.

> "... whether there were any other reasons for the advice, and the nature of the advice given, so as to explore whether the advice may also have been given for tactical reasons."[583]

The word "tactics" is usually understood as the art of manoeuvring towards a particular objective in some competitive or combative pursuit. The court was in fact rejecting an argument put forward by the appellants that, for the purpose of ruling on exclusion, a distinction ought to be made between tactical and non-tactical reasons for advising silence. The purport of the phrase tactical reasons in the context is unclear but seems to convey something disingenuous and manipulative, as distinct from pure or innocent. So an example of non-tactical advice in that sense might be where the solicitor believes in all sincerity that since his client is of low intelligence, inarticulate and repressed, he would cut a poor figure in interview and might give a misleading impression of guilt. Conversely, the extreme example of advice which is tactical in the sense that it is impelled by underhand motives is advising silence with the deliberate intent that the defendant who has no answer may gain time to think up a plausible story later. But between these opposite ends of the spectrum it may be meaningless to attempt to categorise advice as either tactical or non-tactical. Advice may be tactical without involving improper motives. An example, *par excellence* of this is where in an assault case the accused tells the solicitor that he is claiming self-defence and the solicitor anticipates that the evidence of identity may turn out to be too weak to sustain the prosecution case in court. He will not want to prejudice a defence based on putting the prosecution to proof on that issue by allowing his client to make a confession and avoidance. If at trial the identification evidence proves to be adequate and the accused elects to run self-defence, the solicitor can pre-empt an inference of late fabrication by revealing his instructions at the police station and can explain why he advised his client to say nothing at that stage. The advice to be silent was plainly tactical in the sense of involving the deployment of skill to achieve an advantage in the contest, but for all that it is eminently reasonable. So merely because advice was tactical is no reason in itself to disparage it as warranting an adverse inference. Another example is where the solicitor advises silence in the belief that the police have not been forthcoming enough in their disclosure of the evidence for him to be able to give his client proper advice. Is this tactical or "innocent" advice and what does it matter? In fact, in the example given above of the client of low intelligence, it might be said that the advice to be silent is tactical in the sense that it is designed to save the client from falling into a trap. In the end the term affords little assistance.

---

583 [1997] 1 Cr.App.R. 185, at p.197.

(e) *Appellate suggestion that unexplained advice to say nothing should not be left to the jury*

The prediction in *Condron* was adopted in *Roble*[584] in which the appellant's solicitor was called to confirm that she had advised silence but did not give her reasons for doing so, and it was further adopted in *Daniel*.[585] However, in contrast with merely predicting how juries might be likely to view silence in the absence of an explanation given for advising such a response, a régîme rather more restrictive for defendants was proposed by the Court of Appeal in *Beckles*.[586] In the interview the appellant's solicitor stated that after a lengthy private consultation the appellant was being advised not to answer questions "at the present time," since, on the basis of what had been said about the allegations, it was not reasonable for him to do so. The statement did not reveal what the solicitor had been told about the allegations, nor why the solicitor believed that it was unreasonable for the appellant to answer questions. At trial the appellant did not volunteer the substance of the consultations and the solicitor was not called to give evidence. The Court of Appeal referred with approval to *Roble* but expressed the perhaps surprising notion that the trial judge had been "over-lenient" *in even leaving to the jury* whether the solicitor's advice "was capable of providing a reason for not disclosing the facts in question." This view represents a significant departure from the previous position in which it had been predicted that a jury would be unlikely, as a matter of fact, to fail to draw adverse inferences when no testimony had been given of the essence of the private consultation between a suspect and solicitor. It involves a shift to the position that as a matter of law a jury should ignore the factor of legal advice when considering adverse inferences, unless the substance of that advice is disclosed to the trial court.[587]

Whilst the court's opinion may be discouraging for those who would wish to see the ambit of the Act circumscribed in favour of defendants, it is very far from imposing a binding principle on the courts. In the first place, it was plainly *obiter*, since the *ratio* of the appeal concerned the question whether inferences were restricted to those of subsequent fabrication of the fact mentioned in proceedings but not in interview or whether a permissible inference was that the accused wished not to be questioned. As already stated, the Court of Appeal had already held, in *Daniel*, that permissible inferences were not restricted to the first kind but included the second.

The second and more important reason for disavowing the dictum in *Beckles* is that it would arbitrarily exclude relevant evidence going to an issue in the case. That issue is the question whether it would have been reasonable to expect the defendant to talk to the police. If it be the case that the defendant genuinely believed he had a valid reason for not doing so then it can hardly be reasonable to expect him to have

---

584 [1997] Crim.L.R. 449.

585 [1998] Crim.L.R. 818.

586 (1998) unreported, C.A. 97/4261/Z4, May 7.

587 See Sybil Sharpe, "No Comment Interviews on Legal Advice: Defence before Charge," *Archbold News*, October 28, 1998, 8.

talked all the same. The test of whether the defendant's reason for choosing silence is valid and credible is subjective. If the defendant tells the jury that he was advised by his solicitor to say nothing that is relevant evidence as to his state of mind. Since it is relevant it is admissible evidence for the jury to consider. (Indeed, it is difficult to imagine evidence more relevant to his thinking than his own account of it.) The dictum was plainly thrown in almost as an aside, evidently in order to demonstrate that insofar as the summing up erred, it did so in the appellant's favour. Had the court considered the implications of their remark in greater depth (which they would have done had it been central to their decision) it is likely they would have come to a very different view.

(f) *The problem of hearsay*

(i) Defendant's evidence of solicitor's advice. The admissibility of evidence given by the defendant as to his solicitor's advice to say nothing in interview was considered in *Davis*.[588] The appellant had been stopped from giving evidence of the advice his solicitor gave him, where that advice had resulted in him making no comment in interview, on the ground that such evidence would be hearsay. The Court of Appeal pointed out that an accused is free to give evidence about his reasons for deciding not to answer questions provided the hearsay rule is not breached. In giving such an explanation, he may wish to repeat a statement of fact made by his solicitor. That may or may not be hearsay. It would not be hearsay if the purpose were not to prove the truth of the solicitor's statement, but merely to demonstrate that the words were said. It follows that a judge who has to rule on the admissibility of evidence of what was said between an accused and his solicitor must be told in advance what the evidence will be, and if need be conduct a *voir dire*. Since the purpose of adducing evidence of the solicitor's words will almost invariably be to establish their effect on the defendant's mind and not whether such advice was reasonable or justified, there will in this situation be no encroachment into hearsay. *Davis* is to be contrasted with *Daniel*[589] in which the appellant was prevented from telling the jury the reasons his solicitor had given for advising silence and, as in *Davis*, it was held that he had misapplied the hearsay rule. However, the appeal was dismissed because it was held that if the appellant had truly told his solicitor what he had claimed to have told him the solicitor would not have advised silence and the court would have expected at least an affidavit from the solicitor in support of the appellant's assertion.[590]

(ii) Solicitor's confirmation on tape of advice to say nothing. It is the common practice for solicitors who have advised the client to give a "no comment" interview to announce on tape during the preliminaries of the interview the fact that they that have given that advice. Sometimes they refer to their reasons. On basic principles such a declaration would be admissible as a statement made in the defendant's

588 (1998) Crim.L.R. 659 (97/06301/W5, February 20, 1998).

589 [1998] Crim.L.R. 818.

590 Birch suggests that whilst these may be respectable reasons for inferring that the reasons are false it is unclear how a jury would have been supposed to come to them: [1999] Crim.L.R., at p.786.

presence during an interview by police and explaining his reaction as a whole.[591] It is assumed that the confirmation of prior advice will not amount to waiver of privilege (see below). Where a defendant who has evinced an initial intent to a give a "no comment" interview falters and begins to give substantive replies it is sensible practice to interrupt the questioning by reminding the client of the previous advice and of the client's decision to follow it, and then to ask if the client now wishes to change his mind or to have a further consultation in private.[592] This formality may be contrasted with a stratagem alleged by the defendant in a trial at first instance, when it was claimed that the solicitor's accredited representative, having forcefully advised the defendant to say nothing against her expressed wish to speak, had told her that he would tread on her foot under the table to remind her to be quiet.[593] Apart from avoiding embarrassment and prejudice if the interviewing officer becomes aware of such literally *sub rosa* communication the open approach has several benefits. (1) It reinforces the advice previously given and strengthens the client's resolve. (2) It reinforces the message to the jury that the decision is the solicitor's and absolves the defendant from responsibility. (3) It re-affirms the impression that the client would dearly love to answer but for the advice from the solicitor.

(iii) Solicitor's damaging statement of advice announced at beginning of interview. The admissibility of a potentially damaging statement made by a solicitor at the outset of an interview by way of explaining the defendant's proposed silence was considered in *Fitzgerald.* At the commencement of the interview with the police, the appellant's solicitor made a statement to explain his client's decision to remain silent, saying that having discussed it with him he was "concerned that the possible involvement of other parties . . . may prevent him from putting his defence fully and frankly." At trial, his evidence was that he was completely uninvolved

---

[591] The admissibility of the solicitor's on-tape advice was affirmed in *Fitzgerald* [1994] 4 *Archbold News* 2.

[592] See Eric Shepherd, *Becoming Skilled: A Resource Book*, Police Station Skills for Legal Advisers series, Law Society Criminal Law Committee, 1st ed. 1994, para. 9.3.5, on action where the client changes tack on silence (reissued unchanged on the point in 1997). The manual advises, at para. 8.3.2, that prior to interview clients should be alerted to the risks and pitfalls involved in a "no comment" interview. The client should be alerted to the fact that that replying "no comment" or giving some other stereotyped response to the same effect throughout an interview obviously feels unnatural, sounds inherently ill-mannered and may well be provocative. It is pointed out that this is an unavoidable consequence of opting to exercise the right to silence, saps good humour and goodwill, causes cumulative strain and increases conversational pressure to "come back" with a positive response to counter what is being asserted by the questioner. Making no substantive reply can lead both parties to burn emotionally inside and the attempt to keep calm also uses up emotional energy. The suspect becomes progressivley tired and less able to maintain a no comment response. To persist with a no comment approach requires grit, doggedness, self-control and single-mindedness. The client should be exhorted not to lose heart if a lapse should occur but to return to exercising the right to silence. The interviewer may attempt to use various arguments to undermine that resolve. The manual recommends, at para. 8.3.6, that the suspect should be reasssured that if this happens the legal adviser will intervene immediately to admonish the officer with a reminder that it is for the suspect's legal representative to give legal advice and improper for the police to give alternative advice. For exhaustive treatment of the ambit of the solicitor's interventionist discretion in police interviews see *Wolchover and Heaton-Armstrong on Confession Evidence*, pp. 295-302.

[593] *Abbott* (2001) unreported, Wood Green Crown Court, T2000-0783, January 15. When proofed the representative denied the allegation and was not called by the defence and, prosecuting counsel taking a neutral position, the judge acceded to a defence submission that the jury be directed to draw no adverse inference from the silence.

with the offence, a robbery, and just happened to be innocently in the area. It was held that the judge was right to conclude that the solicitor's statement was admissible. There was no application to call explanatory evidence in relation to the advice given either on the *voir dire* or before the jury. The statement was relevant because it gave a reason for the appellant's silence in interview, and whether or not inferences should be drawn was an issue in the case. If a solicitor, following consultation with his client, chooses in the presence and hearing of his client to say something expressly for the record as to why his client is going to remain silent in intervew, it would be a negation of common sense if such a statement were not admissible. The solicitor's reason could be said to be the appellant's reason, either because it was a statement expressly made by the appellant's agent on his behalf or because it was made in his presence and he did not resile from it as might have been expected had he not concurred in it.

(g) *The problem of legal professional privilege*

(i) Conflicts of principle. The tabling of the silence provisions of what became the Criminal Justice and Public Order Act 1994 occasioned considerable anxiety that the measures would force defendants to waive the privilege of lawyer-client confidentiality.[594] In the wake of the Act the issue first received judicial attention in *Condron*,[595] in which the Court of Appeal said that if the accused wished to avoid the drawing of an adverse inference he would need to adduce the basis or reason for the advice not to answer questions and that once that was done it might well amount to a waiver of legal professional privilege. This attitude provides a stark contrast with the earlier decision of the House of Lords in *R.* v. *Derby Magistrates' Courts, ex parte B*[596], that the free exchange of information between client and lawyer is so vital to the operation of the administration of justice that legal professional privilege must be absolute. The two approaches can be reconciled only on the basis of an assumption on the part of the Court of Appeal that uninhibited consultation with a legal adviser would not be deterred by the prospect that what was said might one day have to be revealed, technically with the accused's consent but in circumstances in which this could not be refused, at trial.[597] It is difficult to see such a view being advanced with much conviction. The European Court of Human Rights would appear to have remained unmoved by the dilemma posed for accused persons as a result of the decision of the Court of Appeal in *Condron*. In *Condron* v. *U.K.* the Court observed that the fact that the applicants were subjected to cross-examination on the contents of their solicitor's advice could not be said to raise an issue of fairness under Article 6 of the European Convention on Human Rights:[598]

---

594 See *e.g.* Christopher Sallon, "Turning a Dear Ear on the Right of Silence," *Counsel*, January/February 1994, p.13.

595 [1997] 1 Cr.App.R. 185.

596 [1996] A.C. 487.

597 See R. Pattenden, (1998) 2 E. & P.142, at p.156.

598 Application no. 35718/97, May 2, 2000, para. 60.

> "They were under no compulsion to disclose the advice given, other than the indirect compulsion to avoid the reason for their silence remaining at the level of a bare explanation."

(ii) Simple statement by accused in evidence that solicitor advised silence is not waiver of privilege. In *Condron*[599] it was held that if an accused person gives as a reason for not answering questions, that he has been advised by his solicitor not to do so, that advice does not amount to a waiver of privilege on the substance of communications between the solicitor and client.

(iii) Confirmation by solicitor that accused was advised to be silent. Presumably, if the accused calls his solicitor to the witness box simply to confirm that he was given such advice, this will similarly involve no waiver.

(iv) Waiver. It has already been noted that faced with cross-examination on the reasons for having advised the defendant not to answer questions the solicitor in *Condron* had claimed privilege and the trial judge had upheld his objection. The Court of Appeal doubted whether he had been right to do so. Although, as the court pointed out, the issue has not been fully argued before them, Stuart-Smith L.J. expressed the view that if the accused wished to invite the court of trial not to draw an adverse inference it would be necessary to state the basis or reason for the advice and that once that was done it might well amount to a waiver of privilege. Once privilege was waived, the accused, or the solicitor if called, might be asked whether there were any other reasons for the advice and the nature of the advice given, so as to explore whether the advice might also have been given for tactical reasons. In other words, once privilege is waived the defence are bound to disclose everything that the accused told the solicitor. This was affirmed in *Roble*,[600] and in *Moore*.[601] If the judge declines to hold a voir dire, the defence will be unable to prevent the jury learning what the accused told his solicitor and what the solicitor told him, a state of affairs which could prove embarrassing for the defence.[602]

(v) Reliance by defendant on reasons given by solicitor in interview for advising silence. It may be envisaged that to give credence to the solicitor's reasons for advising silence the defence will normally call the solicitor to explain those reasons to the court. However, it may be that at the beginning of the interview the solicitor gave his reasons for advising the defendant not to answer questions and that the accused chooses not to call the solicitor to reiterate them but merely states in evidence that those were the reasons for his acceptance of the advice. In *Bowden*,[603] Lord Bingham C.J. stipulated that if a defendant sought to rely on reasons for the advice expressed during the interview, without calling the solicitor, this would not avoid a waiver of privilege.

---

599 [1997] 1 Cr.App.R., at p.197. See also *Van Bui* [2001] All E.R. (D) 41(judge in error but conviction not unsafe).
600 [1997] Crim.L.R. 449.
601 (1998) unreported C.A. No. 96/5760/Z5.
602 See *Kavanagh*, (1997) unreported, C.A. 9503897/Z2, February 7.
603 [1999] 1 W.L.R. 823, at p.829.

(vi) Effect of relying on reasons during voir dire. In *Bowden*,[604] Lord Bingham C.J. stated that if the reasons for advising silence are elicited during the course of a *voir dire* the outcome of which is a ruling not disallowing adverse inferences, and the defence then repeat those reasons in the course of the trial, privilege is deemed to have been waived: "The defendant cannot at any stage have his cake and eat it."

(vii) Desirability of judge giving a warning as to waiver. In *Condron* the court took the view that it was probably desirable that the judge should warn counsel, or the accused, that the privilege might be taken to have been waived, if the accused gave evidence of the nature of the advice.

(viii) No waiver where solicitor confirms defendant's private disclosure of trial account. In *Condron*[605] the Court of Appeal observed that whilst a solicitor may well be able to give a satisfactory explanation for having advised the defendant not to answer police questions, it will avail a defendant little if he failed to tell his solicitor the fact on which he is now relying as part of his case. If therefore he did convey that fact to the solicitor it will clearly help the defence case if the jury can be told that he did so. On this point the court declared an important principle relating to privilege. It was always open to a party to rebut the inference that facts have been subsequently fabricated by showing that the relevant facts were communicated to a third party. This would not involve waiver of privilege if it is the solicitor to whom the fact is communicated. The solicitor, for this purpose, is in the same position as anyone else. The court relied for this point on *Wilmot*,[606] and *dicta* in that case were approved in *Bowden*[607] in which the Court of Appeal said that the 1994 Act had not been intended to modify the existing law on legal professional privilege. In the unlikely event, as the court put it in *Condron*, that the solicitor advised his client to say nothing, even though the client has given him information which amounts to a defence, or affords an innocent explanation of otherwise incriminating evidence, the solicitor can be called to say that he was given this information and this, if accepted, will rebut the inference of subsequent fabrication.

(ix) Ambit of waiver and inspection of the file. It has not been pronounced whether, on the waiving of privilege, the prosecution are entitled to inspect all the solicitor's notes from the time of the interview including any passages noting the defendant's account of the offence. It has been observed that cases in civil law suggest that if a witness is examined on part of a document he may not be cross-examined on other parts of it unless they clearly relate to the relevant material.[608] Whilst this saving may be applicable to the law on criminal evidence, it is difficult to see how notes of what the defendant told the solicitor about the offence could be less relevant to the advice to be silent.

---

604 *ibid.*, at p.831.
605 [1997] 1 Cr.App.R. 185, at p.197.
606 89 Cr.App.R. 341.
607 [1999] 1 W.L.R. 823, at p.827. See also *Van Bui* [2001] All E.R. (D.) 41.
608 See Anthony Jennings, *Archbold News*, June 9, 1999, 5 at p.7, and cases cited there.

(4) Officially sanctioned reasons for advising silence

(a) *Good reasons for advising silence*

In spite of clear evidence that a silent defendant was advised by his solicitor to answer no questions (and despite the standard direction approved by Lord Bingham in *Argent*[609]) they may nevertheless harbour sinister thoughts about the advice, suspecting that it was given in order to gain a delay for the defendant either to concoct a false defence or otherwise to avoid interrogation until he had had time to prepare himself and his story for cross-examination at trial. Such suspicions might be allayed if the jury were to be informed that the advice enjoyed the imprimatur of official approval. The Law Society, for example, have issued guidelines, which are considered below, setting out various reasons why it may be right and proper to advise a client not to answer police questions. Informing the jury via a declaration at the outset of the police interview that, in accordance with criteria contained in those guidelines, the defendant has been advised to say nothing, might well persuade them that the advice had been tendered on a sound and proper footing and not as a pretext for concealment. It may be enough to refer to the guidelines without necessarily reading the relevant criteria into the record. This may be a satisfactory way of avoiding the need to call the solicitor to explain the reasons in the witness box. It is proposed to set out here an exposition of some of the criteria which underpin the guidelines.[610]

Perhaps the most fundamental reason for advising the client to say nothing is that however frank and forthcoming the police may be in disclosing the details of the evidence they have in their possession *now* there will be no way of knowing how strong the case is likely to stand *at the point of trial*. An explanation by way of denial may involve an assertion which closes a hiatus in the prosecution case. The classic example is an allegation of assault in which by the time of the trial the evidence, including that of identification, may be too weak for the case to stand up. The defendant would say that he was only defending himself but to make this assertion to the police would involve an admission that he was the person involved in the incident in question and would supply all that was needed for the case to go forward. In such a case the solicitor, not knowing how strong the case *is likely to be in the future*, would advise silence in order to avoid any risk that an answer will take the form of a decisive confession and avoidance. (If the identification evidence at trial proves adequate and the defendant chooses to run self-defence the solicitor can always be called to confirm that the defendant disclosed that the defence to him at the police station and to explain why advise was given to answer no questions.) The more complicated a case the more difficult it will be to assess in the absence of a considered scrutiny of the evidence whether an explained denial will prove to be

609 See *infra*, p.186.

610 These were originally propounded in Wolchover, "Guilt and the Silent Suspect," *New Law Journal*, April 14, 1989, pp.501-502 and subsequently developed in *Wolchover and Heaton-Armstrong on Confession Evidence*, London: Sweet and Maxwell's Criminal Law Library, 1996, pp.694-698.

decisive in making up any deficit in the prosecution's case. Closely related to this ground for advising silence is that where even the police do not yet know the direction which their suspicions will take them. Providing truthful answers by way of denial may permit the prosecution to tailor the charges against the accused. The solicitor may legitimately wish to protect his client from a "fishing expedition."[611]

In stark contrast with the situation in which silence may be the only defence against an inadequate case becoming a sufficient one is the situation in which the considerable strength of the case emerges at a very early stage. Thus, often at the point of interrogation it is already known that the case against the suspect is a strong and reliable one and it can be safely anticipated that it will remain so up to the trial and through to the completion of the prosecution evidence. The situation is manifestly not one in which the police need the suspect's explained denial in order to ensure that at trial a *prima facie* case is sustained. Here the solicitor's decision whether to encourage the client to get his defence on record at the earliest opportunity may be an easy one.

However, between the two extremes of weak and strong cases lies a no man's land of uncertainty and unpredictability. Most interrogations take place following an arrest on suspicion and in many such cases the evidence is neither very strong nor particularly weak. Although solicitors will enjoy a reasonable opportunity for private consultation before any questioning proceeds, it will necessarily be subject to the constraints of urgency. In any case of complexity the solicitor will know very little of the details and such facts as the police do possess may not be revealed until the interview is well under way and then only in a piecemeal fashion which gives no flavour of the case as a whole. Importantly, the "legal" representative will often be an unqualified member of staff whose skill in comprehending the issues and giving needed advice at short notice will be relatively limited. Against that background there may be compelling and wholly proper reasons why solicitors (or their clerks) will advise their clients to remain silent, instead of agreeing to answer questions or otherwise to give an account of themselves.

The facts may be complex, the sequence confused, the lapse of time since relevant events occurred substantial. The defendant's mental and linguistic resources may be limited, making it difficult for him to articulate his account clearly. In performing their proper advisory role in preparation of the defence lawyers can rarely avoid a sustained effort of scrutiny of the prosecution case, working with the client, if the client's narrative is to be brought out in a way that does full justice to his defence. Practitioners often find their clients quite unable to achieve an ordered and coherent recollection of details without resort to the prosecution statements as the effective trigger to memory. But these are the tools of pre-trial preparation, not briefing for police interrogation. At that stage suspects have very little material to help them with their memory. They may be confused and liable to make mistakes of fact which at trial could be interpreted as lies. They may forget important details and when they remember them at trial are liable to be accused of late invention. They

[611] See S. Greer, "The Right to Silence: A Review of the Current Debate," (1990) 53 M.L.R. 709, at p.728.

may be unaware of some vital fact which explains away otherwise suspicious circumstances and the failure to mention it may similarly lead to the suggestion of late invention. They may express themselves loosely without appreciating how the nuances of interpretation can shift dramatically across even slight variations of language. They may not understand, or may even mishear, a particular question and the reply may give a misleading impression. Most dangerous of all is the possibility that they may feel guilty when in fact they have done nothing criminal; in an emotional and suggestible frame of mind they may make untrue admissions which even the most vigilant solicitor might be hard pressed to prevent. To collect his thoughts the client should be calm and composed. To engender the necessary relaxed milieu for this takes sympathy and gentle encouragement. It is not the job of defending lawyers to jump on the client's every ill-considered word, turning it round against him and using it as a lever to extract a confession. Rather, it is to help clients concentrate on the issues and express themselves in a way which, within their capabilities, most felicitously represents the essence of their defence.

By contrast with the defending lawyer's approach to the client and the concept of the neutral, or "cognitive," interview nowadays encouraged in fashionable police circles, questioning of suspects is often still practised along traditional adversarial lines, is often hostile, conducted with an edge of incredulity designed to induce anxiety and ill-judgment, perfunctory and shallow. Without proper guidance and consideration of the details, the suspect may be tempted in such circumstances to have resort to expedient lies, or otherwise to oversimplify his explanation in a way which distorts his true position. The result may be an embarrassment of inconsistency. Moreover, in questioning the suspect, the police will not necessarily reveal the full picture; their reticence may be deliberate in the hope of catching him out or it may be that the interrogator does not himself know all the circumstances. Presented with a distorted or misleading resume of the allegation, one short on key details, the suspect may be tempted to leave out potentially damaging or embarrassing facts in the short-sighted belief that "what the police don't know they won't grieve over." He forgets that the police may well discover those facts later. It may even be on the advice of the solicitor that where the prosecution case is relatively weak it is better to keep back an unlikely although true defence in order to avoid shifting the focus of the trial from the credibility of the prosecution to the credibility of the defence.

Whilst it is true that the interrogation is not the trial, the suspect's utterances under questioning may prove crucial to the outcome of the case. That this important encounter should involve no opportunity for the suspect to consult at length beforehand with a lawyer will be aggravated by an inquisitorial procedure which is alien to the format of trial. The suspect will not be questioned in the first instance by his own advocate from a proof, to be followed, only when the advocate has exhausted the subject-matter, by prosecutorial cross-examination. The argument—

> ". . . that at the interrogation stage it is not necessary to offer the suspect a fair opportunity to defend himself because at this stage the police are

not concerned to try him but only to gather evidence . . . ignores the fact that the investigatory stage is more than an evidence-gathering exercise. It is designed to build up the case against the suspect. . . . It is no exaggeration to say that the prosecution's case is often won during the interrogation. Once an inculpatory case has been erected, it places the accused at enormous procedural disadvantage. . . . The procedural safeguards afforded to the accused at the trial become hollow, if a conviction can in effect be secured during the interrogation and if at that stage the suspect lacks comparable safeguards."[612]

These, then, are arguments which might be advanced for a decision to shield the client from the consequences of a failure by the police to probe his position in a way that does full justice to his case and before the solicitor has enjoyed a proper opportunity of doing so. They are arguments for advising the client to defer offering his account until he can be advised on how to present it in its most persuasive form.

The uncharitable view is to interpret the description given above of the advisory or consultative process as coded language, in effect, for "helping the client to concoct a story." At the very least, it may be said, the arguments for delay predicated on them are rationalisations for gaining the client a breathing space in which to think out a plausible defence or to prepare for cross-examination on a story already invented. Such a view is to apply a label of institutional dishonesty to a role of the defending advocate which is generally regarded as falling within the proper margins of professional integrity. It is to assume that the conventional function of the defence lawyer is based on an unholy alliance with the client. In fact, there is no rule against asking even leading questions in consultation or conference and one can certainly do that without necessarily suggesting a false story for the client to latch on to. It is all a matter of discretion. There is an obvious difference between making up a defence—putting a story into the client's mouth which does not belong there—and providing him with words which naturally articulate thoughts that are clearly discernible but which he lacks the command of language to express himself unaided. (The use of the term "coaching" is usually meant perjoratively in the present context, but it can describe what lawyers habitually do without the slightest taint of impropriety.) Lawyers with any experience develop in practice an almost unerring sense of knowing where the line must be drawn.[613] With all these considerations it is no wonder, as Mackenzie has stated, that—

"... [i]t is the received understanding among criminal practitioners—both solicitors and barristers—that in the case of 90% of suspects under

---

612 A. Zuckerman, "Trial by Unfair Means—The Report of the Working Group on the Right of Silence" [1989] Crim.L.R. 855, at pp.860-861.

613 See generally Prof. Richard Wydich, "The Ethics of Witness Coaching," 17 Cardoza Law Review, No. 1, Yeshiva University of New York, September 1995.

> investigation the only safe advice for a solicitor to give is for the suspect to decline to answer any question."[614]

Above the desire to protect the client from what may quite genuinely and professionally be judged an unsatisfactory means of discovering his side of the matter—police interrogation—there is another consideration. This is the classic dilemma of deciding which horse to ride. If the case ultimately proves to be a strong one, making it difficult for the defendant to escape conviction, an early confession will gain him full credit in mitigation. On the other hand, the materials which the police are eventually able to mount against him may turn out to be insufficient even for a case to answer. It goes against the grain in a state of such uncertainty to refrain from exhorting silence. The benefit to be gained later from a confession forthwith may be minute compared with that of acquittal on the grounds of inadequate proof. The solicitor is not a priest, whose duty it is to unburden the client's soul.

(b) *Official guidance from the Criminal Law Committee of the Law Society*

A concise counterpart of the detailed arguments expounded in the previous section on why it may be justifiable for legal advisers to urge their clients to remain silent has been incorporated in a guidance circular issued by the Law Society's Criminal Law Committee.[615]

The Committee advise that where a suspect admits guilt to a solicitor who is unsure whether the police have sufficient and strong evidence on which the Crown Prosecution Service would decide to prosecute or a court would convict, the safest advice remains unchanged: the client should remain silent. The Committee go on to suggest that answering police questions may pose a greater risk of wrongful conviction than in the case of silence if the client:— (a) is in an emotional, highly compliant and highly suggestible state of mind at the time of the interview; (b) is confused and liable to make mistakes which could be subsequently interpreted incorrectly as deliberate lies; (c) has forgotten important details and distrusts his or her memory; (d) responds inappropriately to negative feedback by the police and may tend to go along with their suggestive questioning; (e) uses loose expressions and is unaware of the possible adverse intepretations which can be placed on them; (f) for some psychological reason may perform badly during interview and not do

---

614 "Silence in Hampshire," *New Law Journal*, May 18, 1990, p.696.

615 *Changes in the Law Relating to Silence*, summarised in *Criminal Practitioner's Newsletter*, vol. 20, Law Society, October 1994. See also Roger Ede, (Secretary of the Committee), "Why shouldn't a client stay silent?" *The Times*, March 12, 1995, and leader in *ibid.*, March 14, 1995. In the light of then recent authority the guidelines were revised in 1997 (see *Criminal Practitioner's Newsletter*, July 1997, recommending that solicitors hand in a written statement during the interview). The 1994 guidance superceded advice previously given in the Committee's booklet *Advising a Suspect in the Police Station*, first published in 1985. See Mackenzie, "Silence in Hampshire," *supra*, for a vexed account of how the Hampshire police made it an official practice, where suspects exercised their right to silence in an interview, to quote various passages from the booklet out of context in order to create the impression that the Law Society's policy was to encourage suspects to answer police questions. For a detailed treatment of the solicitor's function in advising suspects as to silence in the police station, see *Wolchover and Heaton-Armstrong on Confession Evidence*, pp. 287-303 and 698-701.

justice to his or her case.[616] In addition, the Committee acknowledge as legitimate a decision to advise silence based on inadequate disclosure of relevant information, previous experience of the police using unfair pressure during questioning or the client's fear of reprisal. In the Committee's special guidance the Committee refer to and reiterate advice they have previously published in their manual *Becoming Skilled*, in which detailed reasons are given for advising in favour of silence as a response to deficient or inappropriate police methods of interview.[617]

In their guidance circular, the L.S.C.L.C. stress the need for the advice on silence to be properly recorded. If the client remains silent on the adviser's recommendation it will be necessary to ensure that the court understands the reason for the advice, and this is achieved by putting it on record at the police station. It is pointed out that police interviewers are now enjoined to invite legal advisers at the start of the taped interviewer to explain their advisory rôle to the client and that when so invited the adviser should make an opening statement in the form recommended in *Becoming Skilled*.[618] The circular advises practitioners to take this opportunity to explain on tape the client's chosen response to questioning, to record that the client has chosen to remain silent on the adviser's recommendation if that is the case, and the reason why that advice has been given. Although the circular does not say so, representatives at the police station would do well to state on tape that their reasons for recommending silence are in accordance with Law Society guidelines. That the advice has the backing of the Law Society is likely to strengthen the impact on the jury of the statement of reasons and reduce still further the chances of their drawing an adverse inference.

The L.S.C.L.C. circular suggests that practitioners keep full, clear notes of the advice they give their clients in order to "guard against the danger of a silent client, who would not accept a recommendation to answer questions, alleging later that by remaining silent, he or she was merely following bad legal advice." This is presumably intended to protect the solicitor where the defendant in evidence dishonestly wishes to "blame" his solicitor for the advice he was given, saying "I wanted to speak but my solicitor would not let me." In unusual circumstances such

---

616 In the light of this guidance it has followed that in order to assess whether there are proper grounds for advising in favour of a "no comment" interview legal representatives have had to spend much longer with their clients in consultation than prior to the Act and have had to give more considered thought to the question. It will no longer do to give a perfunctory exhortation to say nothing. Indeed, in the experience of practitioners, the average duration of consulations has been increasing significantly since 1995 and this is borne out by recent research which also reveals that more care is being taken in formulating the advice: see study by Bucke and Brown, cited *supra*, at p.27, note 105.

617 Eric Shepherd, *Becoming Skilled: A Resource Book*, Police Station Skills for Legal Advisers series, Law Society Criminal Law Committee, 1st ed. 1994, para. 9.3.6, reissued unchanged on the point in 1997. In *Advising a Suspect in the Police Station*, *supra*, para. 5.3.4(h) the Committee warn of the special risks involved in intimating an alibi defence. They advise that it may be better to say nothing of an alibi than to intimate such a defence but then to refuse to disclose the details of supporting witnesses, which may be suspicious. The risk of disclosing such witnesses is that they are often reluctant to give information to police officers arriving unannounced, or if not first seen by a defence solicitor are more susceptible to being intimidated or pressured by police into denying the alibi.

618 See the national model for police investigative interviewing in a *Guide to Interviewing*, Home Office Central Planning Unit, 1992; *Becoming Skilled*, para. 9.3.6.

as these the solicitor might feel compelled mid-trial to cease acting for the defendant. Much more common would be the situation where the defendant is given advice to stay silent, follows the advice and then at trial volunteers that he was only only doing what he was advised. Even if there is the slight suggestion of the client "blaming" his solicitor for his silence there will be no reason for lawyer and client to break ranks over this. If the jury are led to suppose that the original advice was "bad" that cannot be the defendant's fault, an adverse inference against the client would be entirely unreasonable, and placing responsibility on to the solicitor ought to be an end of the matter. It is not the lawyer who is on trial and, in any event, an order against him for costs would be indefensible.

(c) *Reasons endorsed by the Court of Appeal*

In *Roble*[619] the Court of Appeal set out examples of the sort of considerations which might warrant a solicitor advising a client to refrain from answering questions. The appellant's solicitor had given evidence on the *voir dire* explaining her advice to her client not to answer police questions. She conceded that the appellant, a Somali, was conversant in English and that she had advised him on past occasions to answer questions in interview, which he had done without an interpreter. But in her view he lacked a sufficient understanding of English to deal with the difficult legal concepts involved in the present case. Her opinion was that the appellant's instructions to her were unclear, not because he was guilty and was hedging his bets, but because she could not tell whether they amounted to self-defence or merely to a denial of the requisite intent. She therefore believed that he would be unable to give a coherent account and should remain silent in interview. The trial judge allowed in the evidence of the interview but the solicitor was not recalled before the jury and the only evidence they heard had come from the defendant, namely that he had been advised to say nothing. It was submitted that both the ruling and the summing up on the inferences to be drawn from the appellant's silence in interview were defective. It was held, following *Condron*, that whether the accused could reasonably have been expected to mention facts upon which he relied on in his defence was for the jury to decide. In giving the judgment of the court, Rose L.J. indicated that good reasons for advice to remain silent might be that the interviewing officer has disclosed little or nothing of the nature of the case against the defendant, so that the solicitor cannot usefully advise his client or, where the nature of the offence, or the material in the hands of the police is so complex, or relates to matters so long ago, that no sensible immediate response is feasible. Such considerations, the court stated, did not arise in the present case.

---

[619] [1997] Crim.L.R. 449.

(5) Have the provisions on pre-trial silence been marginalized on the highest authority?

It was related earlier how in *Condron and Condron*[620] Stuart-Smith L.J. arguably sought to restrict the nature of the proper inference which could be drawn under section 34 to late fabrication. The implications of this were that it might have ensured that a damaging inference could be averted simply by evidence from the solicitor confirming that the accused had disclosed to him at the police station the account tendered at trial. So saying the court stressed that this would not amount to a waiver of privilege. Had the restriction been maintained across the judicial board this might well have put paid to any possibility of an adverse inference where the defendant had disclosed his account to the solicitor at the police station. However, as has been seen, in subsequent decisions it was held that an alternative inference, equally valid, might be that the suspect feared to subject his account to scrutiny, knowing that it was false. Was the omission by Stuart-Smith L.J. to include the alternative inference merely an oversight, attributable to the fact that the decision concerned the issue of possible late fabrication, or, for all his strictures on the need for evidence from the solicitor, did *Condron* represent a deliberate and subtle attempt to do precisely what was said might not be done, namely to drive a coach and horses through section 34? The answer will perhaps never be known. However, a more permanent injury to the statute would appear to have been done, perhaps by sleight of hand, on somewhat higher authority than that of Stuart-Smith L.J.

Contrary to the obiter dictum in *Beckles*,[621] referred to earlier, it is unlikely that adducment of the reasons for advising silence will ever become a legal pre-condition for admissibility of the fact of that advice. In other words, the dictum is sure to be sidelined, not to say forgotten. It is manifestly in conflict with a clear statement by no less an authority than Lord Bingham C.J. in *Argent* that the fact of such advice is a "very relevant" consideration in determining whether an adverse inference should be drawn.[622] Lord Bingham was not saying that the advice had to be explained by a solicitor in order to qualify as relevant and therefore admissible.

Quite the contrary, Lord Bingham's pronouncement may be regarded, *and utilised* (by the defence), as a key signal to juries to find that where a solicitor advised the defendant to say nothing, the defendant's silence may be attributed to that advice (rather than to any sinister alternative). Indeed, it is the good sense of juries which may ultimately be the saving which protects defendants from the potential harshness of the 1994 Act, for as Dr Pattenden suggests:

> "In practice we may find that jurors are less critical than judges of defendants who remained silent on their solicitor's advice. Jurors may

---

620 [1997] 1 Cr.App.R. 185.

621 (1998) unreported C.A., 97/4261/Z4, May 7, 1998

622 [1997] 2 Cr.App.R. 27, at p.36.

think that if they were arrested they would not try to second guess their lawyer."[623]

It has been observed that although Lord Bingham's pronouncement may offer an attractive argument to a jury the Court of Appeal has given insufficient consideration to the position of inexperienced defendants who have done no more than follow what they thought to be good legal advice.[624] This criticism should be measured against another statement by Lord Bingham, again in *Argent*,[625] cautioning juries not to ignore the vulnerability of suspects. In deciding whether silence was a reasonable response to police questioning the jury are to be instructed to use as their yardstick—

"... the actual accused with such qualities, apprehensions, knowledge and advice as he is shown to have had at the time [and not] some hypothetical, reasonable accused of ordinary phlegm and fortitude."

Whilst a jury might well find helpful the defence solicitor's assessment of those of the accused's personal characteristics which caused the advice to be tendered, such assistance is not an essential prerequisite for them to find on the point in favour of the defendant, despite the prediction by Stuart-Smith L.J. in *Condron*. The primary issue for them is not the solicitor's assessment of the defendant. The question for the jury is what caused the defendant to accept the advice. This the jury will glean not principally from the solicitor's view of his client's personality but from their own assessment of the defendant, perhaps from his performance and demeanour in the witness box if he gives evidence. The question they will need to ask themselves is whether the defendant was genuinely adopting the advice or merely using it as a pretext for concealing the lack of a defence or avoiding an awkward interrogation. Whatever reasons a solicitor might offer the jury for having given the advice in good faith this will help them little in determining the defendant's true reasons for having adopted it. The existence of secret reasons for silence associated with a guilty conscience is in its nature capable of being determined only on the basis of conjecture and presupposition. By contrast, legal advice to say nothing offers a positive and readily identifiable explanation of the defendant's silence. Forced to choose between barren speculation and the acceptance at face value of a perfectly feasible reason for the accused's silence it will not be difficult to predict the outcome of an exercise in common sense.

Here, again, an authoritative pronouncement by Lord Bingham in *Argent*[626] may well serve, *as it was arguably intended to do*, as a strong hint to the jury in favour of

---

[623] (1998) 2 E & P 141, at. p.152.

[624] Mansfield and Jennings, "The Right to Silence in Criminal Proceedings," Practical Research Papers series, Sweet and Maxwell, London, 1997, 5.

[625] [1997] 2 Cr.App.R. 27, at p.33.

[626] *ibid*., at p.34.

defendants. This was through the approval the Lord Chief Justice gave to the following passage from the Recorder of the City of London's summing-up:

> "He has told you why he chose to be silent. That was the advice that he received from his solicitor. You will consider whether or not he is able to decide for himself what he should do or whether having asked for a solicitor to advise him he would not challenge that advice."

This was part of a direction which Lord Bingham described as "a model of succinctness and also . . . of comprehensiveness" which the court could "see no ground for criticising . . . in any way." Read literally the passage quoted poses a choice offered in insouciant terms. However, it is not difficult to discern where Lord Bingham's preference lay. It is not simply a question of assuming that in keeping with rhetorical method the preferred of two options will always be expressed last for emphasis, though this is perhaps a helpful pointer. More substantially, the plain and most obvious meaning of the passage is to contrast those who would seek legal advice from those who can decide for themselves and do not need a solicitor. The simple and straightforward message of the direction is clear: those who request advice may normally be expected to follow it, otherwise why ask for a solicitor? It is, of course, always possible that a person who is perfectly "able to decide for himself" might purport to request a solicitor with the secret intent of securing validation for a pre-formed decision to be silent. To suggest that in a given case the solicitor may have been doing the client's bidding is clearly to presume too much but there is no warrant either for imputing to the direction that it had in contemplation the possibility that the defendant "latched on"[627] to advice. There is nothing about the context in which the direction was approved from which it can be argued to have been intended to refer *inter alia* to a person who though able to decide for himself what he should do might ask for a solicitor in order to obtain cosmetic ratification for a decision already reached. It might be added that the original terms of the Recorder's direction would hardly have been approved for general use without careful consideration of their meaning.

Through the medium of the approved direction the good sense of the uncomplicated notion that a person who asks for legal advice may be expected not to "challenge that advice" is conveyed to juries. It has already been observed that Lord Bingham undoubtedly signalled where his sympathies lay in relation to the Act when he spoke of Parliament having "in its wisdom . . . seen fit to enact section 34."[628] The approved direction in *Argent* arguably reflects his stratagem for neutralising its impact. Defending counsel will find it useful in their speeches to quote the passage ahead of the judge, reading it with doubtless intended emphasis, explaining its meaning (in terms of the above intepretation) and telling the jury that it derives from Lord Bingham, the "Lord Chief Justice of England and Wales," and

---

627 Jennings, Ashworth and Emmerson, [2000] Crim.L.R., at p.883.

628 *Argent* [1997] 2 Cr.App.R. 27, at p.32.

that the judge will repeat it to them in his summing up. This should give authority to counsel in arguing against an adverse inference.

If the defendant testifies in chief that he gave a no comment interview on his solicitor's advice the prosecution will want, if they can, to probe whether that was his true reason. If the defendant has not been asked in chief to develop the reasons why he was given that advice the prosecution will make little progress without straying into the forbidden territory of privilege. The defence must be alert to intervene, in bland terms, asking to raise a matter in the absence of the jury, before voicing their objecting to the prosecution ploy. If the defendant's previous convictions have come out the prosecution may well seek to ask him if he had not sufficient experience to make up his own mind perfectly well. Provided he stolidly maintains (as in conference he should have been forewarned to do) that having asked for a solicitor he was doing no more than following his solicitor's advice it is difficult to see what further questions can properly be asked, without the prosecution trespassing into privilege. In short they will be bound by the answer.

In the light of *Argent* the strategy of the defence, where the defendant is advised to answer no questions at interview, should in future be to steer clear of calling the solicitor to give evidence of his reasons for the advice. Those reasons are largely irrelevant and unnecessarily waive privilege with all the risks so entailed. All that the solicitor need do, is to confirm at the beginning of the interview that he has advised his client to answer no questions. To establish a causal link and for the avoidance of any doubt the client should, as previously advised, confirm on tape that he is answering no questions on legal advice. Then, whether or not the client gives evidence, the fact of the advice will be on record. The curtain stays firmly in place, neither the prosecution nor the judge or jury can peek behind it, and the court is bound to accept that the defendant was silent for the very good reason that he was simply doing as he was advised by his solictor.

The jury will of course have to be given Lord Bingham's *Argent* direction in conjunction with a statement of the "fifth essential," namely a direction that if, despite any evidence relied upon to explain the defendant's silence or in the absence of any such evidence, they were to conclude that the silence could only sensibly be attributed to his having no answer or none that would stand up to scrutiny in cross-examination they might draw an adverse inference. Therefore, if the silence can sensibly—or plausibly—be attributed to the solicitor's advice to maintain silence there must be no adverse inference. In the face of the undeniable fact of the solicitor's advice to be silent and the defendant's claim that he was acting on that advice it is difficult to see how the prosecution could possibly hope to succeed in contending that the silence could not sensibly be attributed to the advice (as opposed to the absence of an answer or none that would stand up in cross-examination). Provided the defence resist the temptation to call evidence explaining the reasons for the solicitor's advice and given the unlikelihood therefore of the prosecution being able to establish any evidential basis for asserting that the silence was not attributable to the advice Lord Bingham's *Argent* direction and the "fifth essential" will be reinforced by *Mountford*[629] considered earlier. There it was held that the judge should not have left the jury "to make what they could" of the effect of section 34 on the defendant's silence because there was no evidence on which they could rationally reject the appellant's reason for not mentioning his defence without first rejecting the truth of the defence itself. Thus, to the *Argent* and "fifth essential" directions there will need to added a direction that there being no evidence rationally justifying rejection of the defendant's assertion that he was silent because that was what he was advised by his solicitor, there can be no basis for drawing any inference against him from his silence. This would certainly have to be made clear if the prosecution sought to invite the jury to conjecture whether the request for the solicitor was made in order to disguise the existence of a prior intent to say nothing in any event. Against the totality of these directions any prospect of an adverse inference would seem to be remote.

In commentaries on the E.C.H.R. decision in *Condron* v. *U.K.*[630] it has been suggested that the effect of the judgment on domestic law may be to require the incorporation in the J.S.B. specimen directions of a two-stage formulation requiring the jury to be directed (a) that legal advice to be silent must be taken into account and (b) that "if the reason for such silence is the reason given and not because the defendant had no explanation, then no adverse inference should be drawn."[631] Even assuming that the decision will require amendment to the specimen directions (although it is unclear why this is the case) it is difficult to see why the first proposed "stage" would add anything to what on time-honoured principles is already required in the summing up. Where the defence raise legal advice as the reason for silence the jury must be told it is an issue for them to consider. Failure to do so will assuredly amount to misdirection. In the interests of facilitating efficient summings up standardised directions are of course always useful but it is not clear why the E.C.H.R. judgment renders inclusion of the specific direction in the list of specimens any more "necessary" than do previously enunciated dicta in the Court of Appeal. As to the second "stage," this appears to involve stating that if the jury accept the solicitor's advice as the reason for silence, then that will be the reason for silence, which is hardly saying anything. The fault is probably not intentional tautology but hasty journalism, although repeated in a second article.[632] It is assumed that what the commentators meant to say was that the jury must be directed that if they find that the reason for silence is *or may be* the reason given and not because the defendant has no explanation, then no adverse inference should be drawn—the fifth essential in effect. Here again, the direction is already required, although still inexplicably absent from the current specimen directions. In *Condron* the Court of Appeal purported to demote it from an "essential" to merely "desirable" but this was because they held that the evidence apart from the issue of silence was

629 [1999] Crim.L.R. 575.

630 Application no. 35718/97, May 2, 2000.

631 A. Jennings, "The death of silence or safety?" C.B.A. newsletter, June 2000; A. Jennings and E. Rees Q.C., "Is silence still golden?" *Archbold News*, June 14, 2000.

632 Jennings, Ashworth and Emmerson, *Silence and Safety: The Impact of the Human Rights Law*, [2000] Crim.L.R. 879, at p.882.

overwhelming, that the omission of the direction did not mean that possibly innocent defendants had lost the chance of a deserved acquittal, and that it was not therefore fatal to their convictions. In *Condron* v. *U.K.* the court were not convinced of the overwhelming nature of the evidence apart from silence and it followed, in their view, that the omission may have resulted in innocent defendants being convicted. Had the E.C.H.R. agreed with the Court of Appeal that the evidence apart from silence was indeed overwhelming it remains unclear whether they would have found in favour of the applicants. The stress which the court laid on the state of the evidence suggests that they were not considering the omission as an issue of fairness in isolation of the issue of culpability.

In short, it would appear that although acclaimed by the commentaries'authors as likely to have a "profound" effect on domestic law it is tolerably clear that the text of *Condron* v. *U.K.* will have produced no more momentous an impact on the application of the silence provisions of the 1994 Act than our own judiciary have already achieved. It is actually rather surprising that in *Condron* the Court of Appeal failed to hold that the omission to give the "fifth essential" rendered the convictions unsafe, a shortcoming the rectification of which was really all that *Condron* v. *U.K.* brought about, although, coming down to basics, very little more. In contrast, the combined effect of *Cowan, Condron, Argent* and *Mountford* may have been quietly to have administered section 34 its *coup de gràce*.

I. *CAUTIONS UNDER P.A.C.E.*

The pre-P.A.C.E. history of the caution to suspects was set out earlier. This section deals with the procedural requirements for administering cautions to suspects as provided in the 1995 edition of P.A.C.E. Code C, section 10. In discussing its provisions extensive reference is made to the two previous editions, as well as to the Judges' Rules.

(1) The preface to questioning suspects

(a) *The requisite of objective grounds for suspicion*

Code C10.1 provides that a person whom there are grounds to suspect of an offence must be cautioned before he is asked any questions about it (or further questions if it his answers to previous questions that provide the grounds for suspicion) where the questions are of a kind which the paragraph requires to be prefaced by a caution.[633]

It is interesting to compare this requirement with Rule 2 of the Judges' Rules 1964: "As soon as a police officer has evidence which would afford *reasonable* grounds for suspecting that "a person has committed an offence, he shall caution

[633] It has now been held that although the code spoke merely of "a person whom there are grounds to suspect of an offence" it was implicit that the grounds be reasonable: *James* [1997] Crim.L.R. 650.

that person or cause him to be cautioned before putting to him any questions, or further questions, relating to that offence." It is not clear why the Code dispensed with the adjective "reasonable." Whilst, on one view, the epithet may be regarded as implicit in the term "grounds," it may be that omission of the word as contrasted with the Judges' Rules was intended to impose on the interviewer an obligation to caution if he subjectively believed that there were grounds for suspicion, even though his belief could not be justified objectively.

If the subjective option is to be preferred the code would seen to signal a return to a form of test not seen since Rule 2 of the 1912 Rules. But it will be a subjective test imposing a more rigorous obligation on the officer than an objective test. This contrasts with the pre-1964 regime which allowed a subjective discretion *less* rigorous than an objective test would have been. The old rule had provided: "Whenever a police officer has made up his mind to charge a person with a crime, he should first caution such person before asking any questions, or any further questions, as the case may be." There was no counterpart of the 1964 rule in the 1912 Rules. The difference between the two regimes was striking. Under the old regime a caution was required only if there was a subjective intention to charge. It was never clear if there was any significance in the use of the word "charge" as distinct from "arrest" or whether the term was meant as synonym for arrest. It was assumed that there had been no arrest because questioning after arrest was prohibited. But did the rule contemplate that the officer need not caution if although he fully intended to make an arrest he had not yet decided to follow through with charging the suspect in due course? This seems unlikely; charge and arrest were probably treated as synonymous. In any event even if reasonable grounds for suspicion existed there was no requirement to caution as a condition precedent for asking questions in the absence of a decision to charge. Conversely, under the 1964 rule the concern was not—

> ". . . with the subjective and elusive, with the private thoughts of an officer who may or may not have made up his mind to make a charge, but with a more objective state of affairs. . . . Obviously some subjective element will be relevant, such as the officer's assessment of the personality of the suspect, the officer's view as to whether the person is lying or not. But these factors will be insufficient without relation to more concrete evidence."[634]

It is not clear from such decisions on the code as have dealt with the question of the caution whether the test is grounds objectively considered or those subjectively conceived. In *De Sayrah*[635] it was said not to be "the requisite for a caution that you

---

634 The judges had usually applied an objective test: see Patrick Devlin, *The Criminal Prosecution in England*, Oxford 1960, pp.29-30, and see Gerald Abrahams, *Police Questioning and the Judges' Rules*, London: Oyez 1964, pp.44-45.

635 (1990) unreported, C.A. 89/5270/Y3 (fraudulent evations of general betting duty; questions asked by customs officers during search for documents at appellant's home address).

should have hard and fast evidence but that you should have grounds to suspect." In *Nesbeth*[636] the appellant, not yet a suspect, was questioned about a car alarm and then, still not a suspect, was subsequently questioned again, whereupon he changed his original story. It was held that no caution was required because the opportunity to steal was not sufficient to furnish a ground for suspicion. These throw no light on the particular point raised here.

(b) *Purpose of questions requiring a prefatory caution*

(i) Questions requiring a caution. Code C10.1 goes on to provide that questions which the paragraph requires to be prefaced with a caution are those put to the suspect—

> ". . . regarding his involvement or suspected involvement in th[e] offence [of which he is suspected] if his answers or his silence (i.e. failure or refusal to answer a question or to answer satisfactorily) may be given in evidence to a court in a prosecution."

This is the P.A.C.E. definition of "interview" originally set out in Note for Guidance C11A of the 1991 revision of Code C. The Note has been deleted in the 1995 edition and new paragraph C11.1A defines the term by reference to C10.1. The definition of interview and questions requiring a caution have now been brought together. This was not the position under the 1991 edition of the code. Confusingly, paragraph 10.1 provided that questions required to be prefaced with a caution were those "put to the suspect for the purpose of obtaining evidence which [might] be given to a court in a prosecution." This was distinct from the defintion of interview given in old Note for Guidance 11A. If the test of when to caution is now when the officer believes that there are grounds for suspicion (even if his belief is not justifiable objectively) this represents a widening of the ambit of the definition of interview in favour of defendants. The decision in *Purcell*,[637] would now have to be decided the other way. The appellant whilst in custody for other matters became hysterical and volunteered that he was wanted for something very bad. Without cautioning him the officer asked him what it was to which he confessed to a rape some 12 months earlier. During a *voir dire* the officer stated that he was not seeking to obtain evidence but that he was "more interested in finding out what had disturbed this man." It was submitted that there should have been a caution after the appellant said he was wanted for something very bad but it was held that there had been no breach of paragraph 10.1 because the question had not been put "for the purpose of obtaining evidence which may be given to a court in a prosecution."

(ii) Questions not requiring a caution. Paragraph 10.1 excludes from questions requiring a caution those—

---

[636] (1991) unreported, C.A. 336/Y3/90. See also *Mellor* (1996) unreported, C.A. 95/1734/Y5.

[637] [1992] Crim.L.R. 806, C.A.

> ". . . put for other purposes, for example, solely to establish his identity or his ownership of any vehicle or to obtain information in accordance with any relevant statutory requirement . . . or in furtherance of the proper and effective conduct of a search, (for example to determine the need to search in the exercise of powers of stop and search or to seek cooperation while carrying out a search) or to seek verification of a written record in accordance with paragraph 11.13."

In conjunction with new paragraph 11.1A this effectively upgrades the definition of an interview into a code provision. In the 1991 edition the definition merely enjoyed the status of a Note for Guidance.[638]

(c) *Extended caution where suspects are not under arrest when questioned*

Whenever a person who is not under arrest is initially cautioned before or during an interview he has at the same time to be told that he is not under arrest and is not obliged to remain with the officer.[639]

(d) *Breaks in questioning*

Where there is a break in questioning under caution the interviewing officer must ensure that the person being questioned is aware that he remains under caution and if there is any doubt the caution should be given again in full when the interview resumes.[640] In *Bryce*[641] the appellant was interviewed on tape and said nothing to incriminate himself. After the taped interview had concluded he was questioned further without being cautioned (and without any contemporaneous record being kept). It was held that this amounted to more than a technical breach. The court warned that if it were possible for an officer simply to assert that, after a properly conducted interview producing nil return, the suspect confessed off the record and for that confession to be admitted, then the safeguards of the Code could readily be bypassed.

In considering whether or not to caution again after a break officers are advised to bear in mind that they may have to satisfy a court that the person understood that he was still under caution when the interview resumed.[642]

(e) *Documentation*

A record must be made required when a caution is given under paragraph 10 of the Code, either in the officer's pocket book or in the interview record as appropriate.[643]

---

638 Note C11A.
639 C10.2. *Cf.* the original (1985) code.
640 C10.5.
641 (1992) 95 Cr.App.R. 320. See also *Doran* (1990) unreported, C.A. 88/7185/Y2.
642 Note for Guidance C10A.
643 C10.7, broadly replicating a provision in r.2 of the 1964 Rules.

(f) *Juveniles, the mentally disordered and the mentally handicapped*

If a juvenile or a person who is mentally disordered or mentally handicapped is cautioned in the absence of the appropriate adult, the caution must be repeated in the adult's presence.[644]

(2) The terms of the caution

(a) *Incompatibility of the old caution and the drawing of adverse inferences*

Broadly following the time-honoured pattern the wording of the caution prescribed by the 1st and 2nd editions of Code C was this: "You do not have to say anything unless you wish to do so, but what you say may be given in evidence."[645] An unqualified notice signalling that there is no *duty* to speak does not necessarily imply that an innocent person may not reasonably be expected to do so. But it might have tended to convey the impression that the law would never permit an inference to be drawn against a defendant who failed to answer police questions and it would therefore be misleading if such an inference could properly be drawn. Consequently, administering the traditional form of caution would have rendered it unfair to draw such an inference because an innocent defendant whose urge to proclaim his innocence was outweighed by extraneous motives for staying silent might have felt that he could indulge those motives at no cost in terms of the repercussions at trial. The traditional caution was therefore an obstacle to the licensing of adverse inferences from silence. But it was necessary to decide whether to abolish it outright and not replace it with any form of caution, or to substitute a modified caution warning of the risks involved in holding back a defence (or a fact material to it). On the natural impulse theory there was no *need* for any such warning since the innocent hardly need to be reminded of an urge which comes naturally. But some innocent defendants might have remained silent for extraneous motives and might thereby have unwittingly incurred the risk of an unwarranted inference being drawn against them. Some form of warning was therefore clearly necessary.

(b) *The current (new) version*

As part of their general scheme the C.L.R.C. had proposed abolition of the caution altogether and its replacement by an appropriate warning to be given not at the outset of any interview but at the stage when defendants were charged or officially informed that they might be prosecuted.[646] But the traditional form of caution served to assure suspects that it was no offence to stay silent and that they could not be detained in custody until they gave satisfactory replies. Its retention in some form was clearly desirable. Therefore, although the provisions of the Criminal Evidence (Northern Ireland) Order 1988 broadly followed the C.L.R.C. proposals,

---

644 C10.6.

645 C.10.4. *Cf.* terms of the caution under r.2 of the 1964 Rules: "You are not obliged to say anything unless you wish to do so but what you say may be put into writing and given in evidence."

646 11th report, para. 43.

the new regime in the province differed from the Eleventh Report in that it did not abolish the traditional form of caution outright. Instead, the revised Code of Practice on Police Detention and Questioning made under the Northern Ireland Police and Criminal Evidence Order 1989[647] introduced an amalgam of the traditional caution and the C.L.R.C. warning. This was adopted by the Working Group and became the model for the 1995 edition of Code C, revised in order to take account of the 1994 Act. The original text of the modified caution incorporated in the 1994 draft was criticised as cumbersome and confusing[648] and was reworked for the draft code approved by Parliament. The approved form now reads:

> "You do not have to say anything. But it may harm your defence if you do not mention when questioned something which you later rely on in court. Anything you do say may be given in evidence."[649]

According to the Working Group, this combination is aimed at being "powerful enough to act as a warning" without at the same time "being seen as an implied threat."[650] They stressed that the suspect was not to be made to feel that he had to speak, but he had to be made fully aware of the consequences of not speaking. It has been suggested that this is an empty distinction since to tell a suspect that failure to speak here and now may undermine his defence is to put pressure on him here and now.[651] In a psychological assessment of the approved version it was found that 60 per cent of a sample of 109 members of the general public randomly selected in London perceived it as "pressuring" or "a threat."[652] It is true that the Working Group themselves gave application of pressure as the avowed purpose of their caution, aiming as they did to "persuade guilty people to talk more."[653] But the Group's apparent inconsistency does not diminish the validity of the fundamental premise supposedly underlying the whole scheme that to encourage an innocent suspect to do what comes naturally is not to apply pressure. Most of the 109 members of the public canvassed in the study cited above stated that they were unable to understand the second limb.[654] Its poor comprehensibility has been explained at least in part by the fact that the phrase "when questioned" is an

---

647 Police and Criminal Evidence (N.I.) Order 1989, article 65; Codes of Practice, H.M.S.O. 1989, Code C, section 10; and *A Guide to the Exercise by Police Officers and Members of Her Majesty's Forces of Certain Powers Conferred by the Northern Ireland (Emergency Provisions) Acts 1978 and 1987, and the Prevention of Terrorism (Temporary Provisions) Act 1989*, H.M.S.O. 1990, Part IV, paras. 49-59. See Jackson, [1991] Crim.L.R., at p.407, note 14.

648 See *The Times*, August 29, 1994. For a psychological assessment of the draft version see Gudjonsson and Clare, "The proposed new police caution (England and Wales): How easy is it to understand?" (1994) 3 *Expert Evidence* 109-112.

649 C10.4.

650 Report, para. 69. In order lessen any element of compulsion some solicitors make a practice of stressing on tape that although silence *may* harm the defence, "then again it may not."

651 See Zuckerman, [1989] Crim.L.R., at p.860.

652 Shepherd and Mortimer, "The police caution: Comprehension and perceptions in the general population," (1996) 4 *Expert Evidence* 60-67.

653 Report, para. 69.

654 Shepherd and Mortimer, *supra*.

embedded adverbial clause, the placing of which interrupts the main part of the sentence, separates the verb "mention" from its object "something which you later rely on in court," and so throws the attention of the listener off the track of the main idea.[655] The adopted version has also been criticised on the basis that to tell the suspect that the relevant silence "may harm your defence" may be misleading in the sense that it appears to imply that the fact relied on can be supplied at any time before trial without harm being done and that it fails to warn the suspect that silence can form part of the prosecution case.[656] The point behind the first part of this critique is obscure but is perhaps intended to suggest that the suspect may be induced by the wording to assume that failure to mention the relevant fact *now* can always be rectified by mentioning it "when questioned" by a solicitor preparing the defence later or by a police officer coming back to the accused with further questions from time to time up to the trial. There may be some theoretical merit in this concern but whether such a possibility would in actuality occur to any suspect, as against the more obvious meaning that the present questioning is the last chance to mention the fact before trial, is perhaps remote, especially if the suspect is represented by a solicitor in the police station and will receive advice on the purport of the caution. The second part of the critique is little better than a quibble, since to the lay mind at least harm to the defence case is synonymous with the building of the prosecution case. In any event, there is barely any scope for failure to mention a relevant fact under section 34 to form a constituent part of the prima facie case. Rightly enough, the E.C.H.R. in *Condron* v. *U.K.* rejected the argument of the applicants that the caution was ambiguous or unclear as to the consequences of their refusal to answer police questions, in that its terms never put them on clear notice of the full legal implications of remaining silent during interview, in particular that their silence could contribute to the prosecution case against them.[657]

(c) *Minor deviations*

Minor deviations from the prescribed terms of the caution do not constitute a breach of the requirement to administer a caution provided that the sense of the caution is preserved.[658] A caution which omitted the words "unless you wish to do so" was held to be a minor deviation.[659]

(d) *Clarification*

If it appears that the person does not understand what the caution means, the officer who has given it is advised to go on to explain it in his own words.[660]

---

[655] See Michèle Asprey, *Clarity*, No. 41, April 1998, pp.11-15.

[656] By Jennings, "Resounding Silence," *New Law Journal*, May 24, 1996, at p.766, also suggesting that it fails to warn that the silence "may provide the main basis upon which guilt is based." Yet it is doubtful if s.34 failure can have this effect.

[657] E.C.H.R., application no. 35718/97, May 2, 2000, paras. 47 and 59. It may be noted that Jennings was second counsel for the applicants.

[658] C10.4.

[659] *Makuch and Dhainant* (1988) unreported, C.A. No. 4291/E1/87. See also *Saunders* [1988] Crim.L.R. 521.

[660] Note for Guidance C10C.

(3) Requirement for appropriate warning where failure to co-operate may effect immediate treatment

The code provides that where, despite the fact that a person has been cautioned, failure to co-operate may have an effect on his immediate treatment, he should be informed of any relevant consequences and that they are not affected by the caution.[661] Examples given are when his refusal to provide his name and address when charged may render him liable to detention, or when his refusal to provide particulars and information in accordance with a statutory provision, for example, under the Road Traffic Act 1988, may amount to an offence or may make him liable to arrest.

(4) Caution on arrest

(a) *Caution on arrest an innovation of P.A.C.E.*

The Judges' Rules had included no requirement for a caution to be given on arrest. The caution had been a condition precedent for questioning on suspicion. In contrast, Code C introduced a requirement that a person must be cautioned on arrest for an offence unless (a) it is impracticable to do so by reason of his condition or behaviour at the time, or (b) he has already been cautioned immediately prior to arrest in accordance with the requirement for administering a caution to a suspect prior to putting any questions to him about the offence of which he is suspected.[662] The issue of immediacy arose in a slightly different context in *Oni*.[663] The appellant was driving a car from which his co-accused was seen by police to throw a cannabis cigarette. The appellant was asked if the cigarette was cannabis and when he said it was he was cautioned. A very short time afterwards the officer, without again cautioning him asked him questions about a quantity of heroin which the police had found in the car. His answers revealed that he knew that the passenger, his co-accused, was trafficking. The trial judge found as a fact that no more than two minutes had passed between the first caution and the caution which accompanied the arrest. It was held that the caution during the questioning about the cannabis cigarrette was apt to cover the later questions and that there was no code breach but that even if there had been the judge in considering unfairness under P.A.C.E. section 78 rightly took into account that there was no evidence of prejudice on the appellant's part from the lack of a second caution.

(b) *Purpose of new caution on arrest*

At first blush the new form of caution would seem to be inappropriate and out of place as a concomitant of arrest. No inference can be draw under the new Act from the failure of a defendant on arrest to mention some fact later relied on in

[661] C10.5C. This first appeared in the 1994 draft revision as proposed Note for Guidance C10D.
[662] C10.3.
[663] [1992] Crim.L.R. 183, C.A.

proceedings. It is only from such a failure when the arrested suspect is subsequently questioned that such an inference may properly be drawn. It may therefore be asked why it is necessary to warn a person *on arrest* about the possible consequences of a failure *later* (*i.e.* when questioned) to mention a fact relied on in subsequent proceedings? The intention can hardly be to put pressure on the suspect to mention at arrest a fact to be relied on at trial because it is expressly not the purpose of the new Act to permit inferences to be drawn from failure at arrest. (It may be that the intention is to put the arrested suspect on notice at arrest about the importance of mentioning significant facts when questioned in due course but it is far from clear why this should have been considered necessary.) What can be the point of belabouring a suspect *at the point of arrest* with a warning about a failure which can only happen *later*? It might be thought to have been far better for suspects at the point of arrest simply to be told that they needn't say anything (the old caution) or alternatively to have done away with the caution at that stage altogether. (Before PACE there was no obligation to caution on arrest; it was only necessary to administer one if it was intended to ask the suspect questions at that stage.) However, it would probably have been politically impossible to abolish the caution on arrest required by Code C10.3. The reference to the failure when questioned was no doubt incorporated into the caution on arrest partly to cover rare instances of extreme urgency where it was necessary to question arrested suspects before they could be brought to the police station (Code C11.1). Partly also incorporation may have been considered necessary to avoid a disparity between forms of caution at different stages, for otherwise officers might often find themselves confounding or misapplying two different versions. This meant that the caution on arrest had to refer to a "failure when questioned" (since there could be no failure *now*). With the constraints involved in making an arrest the caution at that stage necessarily had to be in terms which were terse, if not perfunctory. Out of the need for consistency the same cumbersome and tongue-twisting "failure when questioned" form had to be applied redundantly at the beginning of normal interviews at the police station. Yet there could be no consistency with the terms of the new caution given at charge stage which necessarily replaced the phrase "when questioned" with the preposition "now". Although the arrest and interview cautions necessarily had to differ in form from that at charge stage, the distinction was tolerable in practical terms because the first two would generally be administered by investigating officers whereas the caution at charge would be given by custody officers. The scope for inadvertant cross-misapplication of the two forms would thus be very limited.

In fact, there was no need for the caution at interview to be in the telegraphic terms necessary at arrest. At interview the explanation involved in the caution could have been made more expansive. Code C10.4 concedes that minor deviations from the wording do not constitute a code breach provided that the sense of the caution is preserved. Yet the wording has in practice proved problematical. Prudence dictates that after administering the caution the interviewing officer should ask suspects what they understand by the caution and this is now frequently done. The common reaction provides an everyday demonstration of the unintelligibility of the caution in its present form to a great many defendants. Officers exhaust themselves trying to explain it and defendants waste valuable mental energy trying to absorb the explanation and then trying to explain back their understanding to the officer.

It was argued earlier that but for the giving of the traditional caution an inference of tacit acceptance of the truth of an allegation would have been capable under Common law of being drawn from the silence of the person when informed by a police officer of the existence of the allegation. However, the officer and the accused had to be on even terms and they could not normally be on even terms unless the suspect had a lawyer present representing him. The new Act preserves the Common law. Since in the vast majority of cases suspects will not have their lawyers with them when they are arrested it can rarely happen that under Common law silence on arrest may give rise to an inference of tacit acceptance of the allegation. It is, however, possible that the new caution was intended for those rare occasions when a suspect is arrested in the presence of his solicitor. The traditional "absolute" form of caution would have prevented an inference of tacit acceptance from the silence of the suspect on being arrested in the company of his lawyer. The new form removes any obstacle to this.

(5) Special warnings relevant to sections 36 and 37 of the Criminal Justice and Public Order Act 1994

The code makes provision for any suspect interviewed after arrest by a constable to be warned as to the evidential consequences under sections 36 and 37 of the Criminal Justice and Public Order Act 1994 of failing or refusing to account (1) for objects, marks or substances or marks of such objects, found on or about his person, or in or on his clothing or footwear, or otherwise in his possession, or in the place where he was arrested or (2) for his presence at the place where he was arrested, at or about the time when the offence for which he was arrested is alleged to have been committed.[664] For an inference to be drawn from a suspect's failure or refusal to answer a question about one of these matters, the interviewing officer must first tell him in ordinary language: (a) what offence he is investigating; (b) what fact he is asking the suspect to account for; (c) that he believes this fact may be due to the suspect's taking part in the commission of the offence in question; (d) that a court may draw a proper inference from his silence if he fails or refused to account for the fact about which he is being questioned; and (e) that a record is being made of the interview and that it may be given in evidence if he is brought to trial.[665]

(a) *Reference to "inference" in the prescribed warning*

The Working Group wished to avoid specific references in the warning to the possibility of inferences, and thought that the word would not always be

---

[664] C10.5A.
[665] C10.5B.

understood.[666] In response to a submission that the use of the word "inference" does not constitute ordinary language the Northern Ireland Court of Appeal have held that the word is commonplace in the vocabulary of the community and that it would be difficult to find a synonym or an equivalent phrase which did not lose of its precision and clarity of meaning.[667] However, the court went on to express confidence that a judge who accepted that an accused did not understand the warning given in a caution, or who had doubts about it, would not draw an adverse inference.

(b) *Juvenile and mentally impaired suspects*

The provision under paragraph C10 relating to juveniles and the mentally disordered and handicapped referring to "cautions," cannot apply to special warnings because these can only be given in the course of questioning after arrest and there can be no questioning of such persons in the absence of an appropriate adult.

(6) Effect of the failure to caution

(a) *Exclusion of admissions*

The absence of a caution is regarded as in most circumstances bound to be a significant and substantial breach of the Code[668] even if neither deliberate nor flagrant.[669] In *Doolan*[670] the court took the view that a failure to caution coupled with breaches of other interview provisions were sufficient to render the evidence of admissions unreliable, with the result that it should have been excluded under section 76(2)(b). But in *Weekes*,[671] in which the court rejected the trial judge's description of the officer's failure to caution after seeing the appellant drop a packet on the ground as "technical and peripheral," and described the breach as regrettable and going to the officer's credibility, it was nevertheless held not such as to render the verdict unsafe. Awareness of the right to silence in spite of the omission to administer a caution is a relevant factor in determining whether the omission had prejudiced the accused. In *Allison and Murray* there were breaches of paragraphs 10.1 and 10.5 but it was considered relevant that both appellants admitted during the *voir dire* that they knew they did not have to answer questions.[672] Whilst an

---

666 Report, para. 70.

667 *Martin* [1992] 5 N.I.J.B. 40.

668 See, *e.g., Sparks* [1991] Crim.L.R. 128, C.A., *Pall* [1992] Crim.L.R. 126, C.A; *Hunt* [1992] Crim.L.R. 582, C.A.; *Hanamoonsing* (1991) unreported, C.A. 5450/W4/90. For other cases considered on appeal see *Shah* (1993) unreported, C.A. no. 92/2635/Z4; *Oransaye* [1993] Crim.L.R. 722; *Konscol* (1993) unreported, C.A. 92/1352/Z2; *Gizzi* (1993) unreported, C.A. 92/5227/Y5; *Park* (1993) *The Times*, July 30; *Hoyte* [1994] Crim.L.R. 215; *Okafor* [1994] Crim.L.R. 221; *Weerdesteyn* (1994) *The Times*, March 17.

669 *Sparks, supra*.

670 [1988] Crim.L.R. 747, C.A. (3852/A2/87).

671 (1993) 97 Cr.App.R. 222.

672 (1988) unreported, C.A. 1731/A1/88. See also *Campbell* (1991) unreported, C.A. 4048/W3/89.

admission obtained by questioning in the absence of a necessary caution may lead to its exclusion this will not necessarily vitiate the admissibility of subsequent replies properly prefaced by a curative caution.[673]

Evidence of admissions obtained by questioning in breach of the requirement to give a caution may well be regarded as warranting exclusion by virtue of the general discretion under section 78 of P.A.C.E.

(b) *Exclusion of evidence of silence*

The failure to administer the new form of caution would not *ipso facto* preclude the operation of the 1994 Act and the drawing thereunder of on inference against the accused from his silence. The Act is not triggered by the caution. On the other hand, the failure to caution might be deemed to render unfair the adducing of evidence of silence and hence to warrant excluding that evidence under section 78. An admission by the accused on the *voir dire* that he knew that his silence could be held against him might result in a ruling that since the breach had not resulted in any disadvantage evidence of the silence should not be excluded.

---

673 *Hanamoonsing, supra*.

CHAPTER THREE

SILENCE AT TRIAL

I. THE OLD LAW

A. *PRACTICE BEFORE THE CRIMINAL EVIDENCE ACT 1898*

The history of the spoken participation of defendants in their own trial has already been covered in Chapter 1. Judicial questioning of the prisoner at the bar had died out by the early 18th century. However, even when later in the century it became permissible for felony prisoners to be represented by counsel for all purposes except the making of a closing speech to the jury, few such prisoners were ever actually represented and this majority therefore must necessarily have continued to speak from the dock, cross-examining, asserting facts in doing so, and dealing with any questions from the bench asked by way of clarification. Unrepresented, they were certainly allowed to address the jury at the end of the trial but it is not clear if, when they were represented, they were allowed to do what their counsel could not. In 1836 Parliament bestowed on counsel defending in trials for felony the right to make a closing speech.[1] Whether or not represented defendants had prior to 1836 been allowed to make an unsworn statement to the jury, towards the end of the century represented defendants were occasionally allowed to make an unsworn statement from the dock.[2] Full participation of the defendant as a witness in all cases was permitted by section 1 of the Criminal Evidence Act 1898, when defendants and their spouses became competent witnesses for the defence but not compellable witnesses for the prosecution.[3] Prior to the general legislation of 1898 Parliament had already enacted some 26 statutes which allowed the accused and spouse to give evidence in specific cases.[4]

---

[1] 6 & 7 Geo. IV c.114, s.1.

[2] Sir James Stephen reports Cave J. permitting this in the winter circuit of 1882 and recalls that he himself had permitted it: *History of the Criminal Law of England*, vol. 1 at p.440.

[3] For a first-hand account of the practical effects of the Act see Sir T. Humphreys, *Criminal Days*, London 1945, pp.44-47.

[4] See Lord Lowry, 554 H.L. Deb., col. 398, April 25, 1994.

B. *PRACTICE UNDER SECTION 1(b) OF THE CRIMINAL EVIDENCE ACT 1898*

(1) The effect of the Act

The Act placed defending counsel in a difficult dilemma. On the one hand, the defendant who exercised the right to give evidence might prove a disaster in the box. Conversely, if the defendant declined to give evidence there was the risk that the jury might assume that he had something to his discredit to hide, namely his guilt. The dilemma was aggravated if the defendant had a criminal record and the the defence case involved "casting imputations" on the character of prosecution witnesses. The loss of credit was likely to prove fatal. Eventually, long after the Act was passed, it seemed that defending counsel might be saved from this dilemma by a somewhat eccentric line of thinking enunciated in the following passage from the judgment of Lord Goddard C.J. in *O'Neill*:[5]

> "In this case a violent attack was made on the police. It was suggested that they had done improper things . . . The applicants had the opportunity of going into the box at the trial and explaining and supporting what they had instructed their counsel to say. They did not dare go into the box and therefore counsel, who knew that they were not going into the box, ought not to have made these suggestions against the police . . . It is . . . entirely wrong to make suggestions as were made in this case, namely that the police beat the prisoners until they made confessions, and then, when there is a chance for the prisoners to substantiate what has been said by going into the box, for counsel not to call them."

In contrast with this, it was stressed in the later case of *Brigden*[6] that strong comment in the summing-up was the appropriate deterrent against defendants casting serious imputations and then not substantiating them in the witness box. However, in *Callaghan*[7] the Court of Appeal preferred the approach of Lord Goddard C.J., and although this may have saved counsel from a difficult dilemma it offered a very serious challenge to the independence of the Bar and the traditional duty of counsel to act fearlessly on behalf of clients. Representations were made by the Professional Conduct Committee of the Senate of the Inns of Court and Waller L.J., who had presided in *Callaghan*, issued a statement on behalf of the Court of Appeal effectively abandoning their original position and restoring *Brigden*. It was declared that where a client requires the police evidence to be challenged in the manner considered in *Callaghan* and *O'Neill*, but he nonetheless refuses to go into the witness box because of his very bad record, it is counsel's duty to warn his client

---

[5] (1950) 34 Cr.App.R. 108.
[6] [1973] Crim.L.R. 579.
[7] (1979) 69 Cr.App.R. 88.

that the judge will probably make a very strong comment on his failure to support the allegations on oath. If the client persists with his instructions counsel must carry them out despite the fact that he knows that his client will not be supporting the allegations by going into the witness box.[8]

When Parliament was debating what became section 1 of the Criminal Evidence Act 1898, allowing defendants to give evidence on oath, it was recognised that this would necessarily exert pressure on them to go into the witness box and the question arose whether that inherent compulsion ought to be compounded by allowing comment to be made on a defendant's refusal. At Committee stage in the Commons, therefore, a private member moved an amendment prohibiting comment by both the prosecution and the judge. The amendment was at first resisted altogether by the Government but the Solicitor-General eventually agreed that the prosecution should be forbidden to comment.[9] But he insisted that judges should not be included in the prohibition in order to allow them a discretion to comment in exceptional cases such as where the defence involved "grievous reflections" on the character of the prosecutor. It was argued that the limitation would show that it was only in "special circumstances" that comment might be made.[10]

Shortly after the 1898 Act came into force and, in spite of the Parliamentary history, it was argued, in *Rhodes*,[11] that the judge had no right to comment. But although the section made no express reference to the judge it was held, on the principle *expressio unius est exclusio alterius*,[12] that the question whether to comment was one "entirely for the discretion of the judge." It was assumed thereafter that the discretion was entirely unfettered[13] but it later became clear, from *Waugh* v. *R.*,[14] that there were limits and a conviction might be quashed where the comment was unjustified or excessive. In the latter decision Lord Oaksey (in effect adopting the argument of the Solicitor-General in the Commons in 1898) observed that the very fact that the prosecution was not permitted to comment on the prisoner electing not to give evidence showed how careful a judge ought to be in making comment. (By contrast with the prosecution, counsel for a co-accused enjoyed the right to comment on the defendant's failure to give evidence and the judge had no discretion to prevent it.[15] This was consistent with the general judicial intepretation of the 1898 Act which distinguished the rights of co-accused from those of the Crown.[16])

---

8 *The Times*, February 20, 1980.

9 Accordingly s.1(b) stated: "The failure of any person charged with an offence, or of the wife or husband, as the case may be of the person so charged, to give evidence shall not be made the subject of any comment by the prosecution." The words "or of the wife or husband, as the case may be, of the person so charged" were removed by Sched. 7, Part V, to the Police and Criminal Act 1984. The section was repealed by Sched. 10, paras. 2 and 11, to the Criminal Justice and Public Order Act 1994.

10 60 H.C. Deb., cols. 662-674, June 30, 1898. See also 11th report, para. 108.

11 [1899] 1 Q.B. 77.

12 See *Cross on Evidence*, 6th ed., p.350.

13 See *Voisin* [1918] 1 K.B. 531, at p.536.

14 [1950] A.C. 203.

15 *Wickham* (1971) 55 Cr.App.R. 199.

16 See *Murdoch* v. *Taylor* [1965] 1 All E.R. 406.

(2) Permissible comment at Common law

To prohibit comment is not necessarily an advantage for the accused. In a dissenting opinion in the American case of *Griffin* v. *California*[17] it was asked:

> "How can it be said that the inferences drawn by a jury will be more detrimental to a defendant under the limiting and carefully controlling language of the instruction here involved than would result if the jury were left to roam at large with only its untutored instinct to guide it, to draw from the defendant's silence broad inferences of guilt?"

In the view of the majority, on the other hand, damage limitation was no justification for the sacrifice of principle:

> "What the jury may infer [from the accused's silence], given no help from the court, is one thing. What it may infer when the court solemnises the silence of the accused into evidence against him is quite another."

According to *Cross*,[18] "[t]he reported decisions most certainly do not suggest any tendency on the part of English judges to 'solemnise the silence of the accused into evidence against him.'" Yet in spite of the exalted authority of the textbook's author this is hardly an accurate statement. Whilst the precise ambit of permissible judicial comment on the refusal to testify was for a long period time uncertain[19] it was eventually settled that a direct invitation to infer guilt was permissible in very strong prosecution cases where the facts in issue were peculiarly within the defendant's knowledge and clearly called for an explanation.[20]

(a) *Criticism without direct invitation to infer guilt*

Apart from very strong cases, for many years adverse comment appears to have been regarded as permissible provided it was restricted to a decently veiled insinuation and the jury were not invited in direct language to conclude that refusal was indicative of guilt. In *Pratt*,[21] decided after *Waugh* v. *R*., a conviction was quashed where, in summing up, the judge had said, "You might have thought that P would have gone into the witness box and told you what he had been doing and explained [his actions] and seen fit to give his version on oath and to allow you to have the opportunity of seeing him cross-examined so that you could assess his evidence . . . He has not chosen to do so. So you have not heard from P and he has not seen fit to answer the evidence in this case. It is a matter for you as to what

---

17 380 U.S. 609 (1965), at p.621.
18 6th ed., at p.350.
19 See C.L.R.C., 11th Report, para. 309.
20 *Mutch* [1973] 1 All E.R. 178.
21 [1971] Crim.L.R. 234.

inference you draw." Although these remarks did not *in precise terms* express an invitation to infer guilt, in the court's view that was their unequivocal meaning.

The point at which insinuation becomes an invitation to convict may be difficult to discern but any early diffidence engendered by an initial wariness of the 1898 Act eventually gave way, with familiarity, to a more robust view. In *Jackson* Lord Goddard C.J. said that "whatever may have been the position very soon after the Criminal Evidence Act 1898 came into operation . . . everybody now knows that absence from the witness-box requires a very considerable amount of explanation."[22] In their 11th report the C.L.R.C. cited a case dating back to 1937 (*Jackson* was decided in 1953) and suggested that comment was made much more sparingly than it had been in the past, sometimes almost apologetically and with an increasing tendency to stress the right of the accused not to give evidence.[23] Shortly after the report it was held to be mandatory to balance such adverse comment as was proper with a direction that the defendant was not obliged to give evidence[24] and in another a decision soon after the report it was said that the judge should not seek to bolster up a weak case by strong comments.[25] Not many years before the 11th report Lord Parker C.J. sought in *Bathurst*[26] to achieve a uniformity of approach with a model direction pointing out that—

> ". . . the accused is not bound to give evidence, that he can sit back and see if the prosecution have proved their case, and that while the jury have been deprived of the opportunity of hearing his story tested in cross-examination, the one thing that they must not do is to assume that he is guilty because he has not gone into the witness box."

The editors of *Archbold*[27] submitted that in referring to "the jury having been deprived of the opportunity of hearing the defendant's story tested in cross-examination," Lord Parker must have had in mind cases where the defendant had made a statement from the dock; if he had neither done that nor given evidence he can have put forward no story, apart from an admission. This was to give too narrow a meaning to "story," a term which, in the sense intended by Lord Parker, must surely have embraced the defendant's case as advanced in cross-examination. The *Bathurst* formula was adopted by the Judicial Studies Board as a model direction minus the remark about depriving the jury of the opportunity to hear the defendant's story tested in cross-examination but with the addition of the direction that—

---

22 (1953) 37 Cr.App.R. 43. *Cf.* the stout defence by Devlin J. of the accused's right not to give evidence in *Bodkin Adams* (1957): see Bedford, *The Best We Can Do*, Penguin 1958, p.217.

23 11th report, para. 109, referring to *Nodder* (1937) unreported, see Glanville Williams, *The Proof of Guilt*, 3rd ed., pp.59-60.

24 *Mutch* [1973] 1 All E.R. 178.

25 *Sparrow* (1973) 57 Cr.App.R. 352.

26 [1968] 1 All E.R. 1175, at p.1178.

27 See less recent editions, para. 4-431.

> ". . . [t]he fact that the defendant has not give evidence proves nothing one way or the other. It does nothing to establish guilt. On the other hand, it means that there is no evidence from the defendant to undermine, contradict or explain the evidence put before you by the prosecution."

The last sentence has never been very satisfactory, suggesting as it does that the evidence for the prosecution had not been disproved. Yet where evidence is *challenged* it must be proved and proof may be thwarted without defence evidence. A particular piece of prosecution evidence may be demonstrably contradicted by other prosecution evidence, or may be shown by reasoning and argument to be unconvincing.

(b) *Cases where an invitation to infer guilt became permissible*

At the time of the 11th report, then, comment, was permissible provided it was held not to have invited an inference of guilt. But comment on silence which is adverse implies suspicion of guilt no matter how it is couched; where to draw the line between permissible insinuation and "encouraging the assumption" that the accused had not gone into the witness box because he was guilty was likely to be almost arbitrary. That the difference was a matter of word-play having little real significance was recognised by Salmon L.J. in *Sullivan*[28] when he said: "The line dividing what may be said and what may not be said is a very fine one, and it is perhaps doubtful whether in a case like the present it would be even perceptible to the members of any ordinary jury." It is little wonder that, in a now celebrated remark, the wholly artificial distinction was described by Sir Rupert Cross as "gibberish."[29]

It was doubtless an acceptance of the validity of these criticisms that led the Court of Appeal in *Mutch*[30] to authorise the drawing of an inference of guilt from the defendant's refusal to give evidence, although only in appropriate cases. After stressing the defendant's right not to give evidence the trial judge had gone on to direct the jury that they were entitled to draw inferences unfavourable to the defendant where he was not called to establish an innocent explanation of facts proved by the prosecution "which, without such explanation, tell for his guilt." This was held to be "very near to encouraging th[e] assumption" that the defendant was guilty and the court had to decide whether the legal concept expressed in the direction was applicable in the circumstances of the case. In applying that concept in his summing-up the trial judge had read from a passage in the then current edition of *Archbold* which, from the two cases cited there in support of the concept, it was clear to the Court of Appeal was applicable only if the evidence had established a

[28] (1966) 51 Cr.App.R. 102, at p.105.
[29] [1973] Crim.L.R. 329, at pp. 332-333.
[30] [1973] 1 All E.R. 178.

situation calling for "confession and avoidance."[31] (This would be where the defence admit an incriminating fact and seek to offer an innocent gloss on it, for example, absence of *mens rea*.) But it is evident from the emphasised words in the following passage of the judgment of Lawton L.J. that the licence to draw an adverse inference was not confined to such cases:

> ". . . an inference [can] be drawn from uncontested *or clearly established facts* which point so strongly to guilt as to call for an explanation; if no explanation is given when the circumstances are such that an innocent man would be expected either to give an explanation *or deny the basic facts*, this is a factor that can be taken into consideration."[32]

The disjunction is not intended to express "clearly established" and "uncontested" as synonyms. The passage does not mean facts clearly established by virtue of being uncontested. The expression "clearly established facts" here simply means those which, although based on disputed evidence, would be clearly established if the disputed evidence were accepted by the tribunal. They are distinct from uncontested facts pointing so strongly to guilt that they need to be explained if the defendant is to escape conviction (confession and avoidance). The distinction is made plain by the alternatives of giving an explanation and "denying the basic facts," the second of which is inapplicable to confession and avoidance. The clear sense of the passage is that where evidence points strongly to guilt if not disputed, the failure of the defendant to dispute it from the witness box will warrant an adverse inference which may tilt the case into a conviction.

In *Mutch* itself the nature of the defence was confined to putting the prosecution to strict proof on identification. The sole issue was whether the undisputed evidence clearly established an identification. As the case did not turn on an identification accepted by the defence as clearly established if the supporting evidence were not disputed it did not fall within Lawton L.J.'s dictum. It was therefore apparent that the jury should not have been directed that they could impute guilt to the appellant from the fact that he chose not to give evidence. This contrasts with *Brigden*,[33] an appeal decided in the same year. There the issue was whether incriminating articles attributed to the appellant had in fact been planted on him by the police and the court upheld a comment that the appellant's absence from the witness box "may help you in deciding whether there is a ha'porth of truth in that allegation about this police officer." This was not therefore a case of putting the prosecution to proof. The defence were not arguing that the evidence of the finding of the articles was not "clearly established" if the witnesses were to be believed. The evidence of the finding of the articles was obviously regarded as being of a kind which, if true, was

---

31 37th ed., 1969, para. 1308, citing *Corrie and Watson* (1904) 68 J.P. 294; 20 T.L.R. 315, and *Bernard* (1908) 1 Cr.App.R. 218.

32 [1973] 1 All E.R., at pp.180-181.

33 [1973] Crim.L.R. 579.

so clear-cut and certain and pointed so strongly to guilt, that it called for a denial or explanation from an innocent person.

Shortly before Parliament debated what became section 35 of the 1994 Act its enactment was pre-empted in a decision which assimilated the common law with recent interpretation of the equivalent Northern Ireland measure, Article 4 of the Criminal Evidence (Northerrn Ireland) Order 1988. In *Martinez-Tobon*[34] the Court of Appeal approved of the Judicial Studies Board direction based on *Bathurst* but sanctioned stronger comment where the defence case involves alleged facts which (i) are at variance with prosecution evidence or additional to it and exculpatory and (ii) must, if true, be within the knowledge of the defendant. In so far as "stronger comment" meant an invitation to infer guilt, the effect of the decision was to relax the principle in *Mutch*. Now, the level of strength of the prosecution case at which an inference of guilt might be drawn from the defendant's refusal to give evidence was the mere adducement of a bare *prima facie* case. For the assertion by the defence of an exculpatory fact at variance with the prosecution or additional to it is an implicit feature of every criminal trial in which the prosecution adduce a *prima facie* case and the defence do more than merely put the prosecution to proof. Again, the type of fact in requirement (ii) is distinct from a fact *peculiarly* within the defendant's knowledge (*e.g.* his intent) and is of such broad application as to be almost ubiquitous. In all cases therefore in which the defence did not restrict themselves to putting the prosecution to proof judges would seem under common law to have acquired a discretion to depart from the Judicial Studies Board *Bathurst* direction and to invite the jury to infer guilt.

II. THE CRIMINAL JUSTICE AND PUBLIC ORDER ACT 1994

A. *THE ACT FORESHADOWED*

(1) Eleventh Report of the Criminal Law Revision Committee

Together with their proposals for the abolition of the right to silence at the investigative stage the C.L.R.C. proposed in their 11th report that it should become permissible to draw appropriate inferences from a defendant's refusal at trial to give sworn evidence and, "without good cause," to answer questions.[35] They proposed that silence in the courtroom should be capable of amounting to corroboration of other evidence.[36] The Committee recognised that the law provided much greater scope for judicial comment on the failure of defendants to give evidence than it did

[34] [1994] 2 All E.R. 90.

[35] Report, paras. 110-113; draft Criminal Evidence Bill, cl. 5. The draft clause is conveniently set out in *Murray* v. *D.P.P.* (1993) 97 Cr.App.R. 151, H.L., at p.153-154.

[36] Report, para. 111.

on suspects' refusal to answer police questions. In their opinion this was because in court there was less chance of being misreported or misunderstood; there was less liklihood of panic, confusion and inadequate preparation; and when the time came for the accused to testify if he chose, a *prima facie* case would already have been established against him. In the opinion of the C.L.R.C. the then current state of the law was much too favourable to the defence. They believed that when a *prima facie* case had been made against the accused it should be regarded as incumbent on him to give evidence in all ordinary cases. They had no doubt that the prosecution should be entitled, like the judge, to comment on failure to do so and that the prohibition on comment by the prosecution was wrong in principle and entirely illogical. Defending counsel in his speech would always be in a position to reply to comment by the prosecution. The Committee's scheme was enacted in Singapore in 1976[37] and enacted for Northern Ireland in Article 4 of the Criminal Evidence (Northern Ireland) Order 1988.

(2) The Home Office Working Group

The Working Group thought that the existing judicial discretion to comment was sufficient to indicate to the jury the significance of the defendant's failure to testify but that it was desirable that judges should make more frequent and robust use of their existing right to comment.[38] They recommended that the prosecution should be permitted to comment on the failure in similar terms and suggested that this would "give the defence the opportunity to explain the defendant's reasons."[39] They gave no indication as to who might give such an explanation but presumably they envisaged it would be proffered by counsel since this had been the view of the C.L.R.C. They recommended[40] that the General Council of the Bar and the Law Society should include provision in their codes of conduct for it to be the duty of a lawyer to warn the client of the consequences of silence.

(3) Northern Ireland

Enacting the scheme of the C.L.R.C., Article 4 of the Criminal Evidence (Northern Ireland) Order 1988 provides that a court of jury may draw such inferences from an accused's refusal to give sworn evidence or to answer questions as appear proper. In addition, section 1(b) of the Criminal Evidence Act (N.I.) 1923 has been repealed with the result that the prosecution as well as the judge may now apparently comment on the accused's silence at trial. Since the language of the Order is

---

37 Enacted by the Criminal Procedure Code (Amendment) Act 1976. See Meng Heong Yeo, "Diminishing the Right of Silence: The Singapore Experience," [1983] Crim.L.R. 89.

38 para. 114.

39 *ibid.*

40 *ibid.*, para. 115.

virtually identical to the Criminal Justice and Public Order Act 1994, Northern Ireland case law may properly be regarded as relevant in the application of the English Act, which therefore came complete with an appendix of judicial annotation covering five years of intepretation.[41]

B. *THE ACT*

(1) The terms of section 35

(a) *The text of the section*

Section 35 of the Criminal Justice and Public Order Act 1994 follows in broad structure the scheme of clause 5 of the C.L.R.C.'s draft Criminal Evidence Bill, although with no provision for a ritual invitation to the accused to give evidence of for corroboration. The section provides:—

> "(1) At the trial of any person[42] for an offence subsections (2) to (7) below apply unless—
> (a) the accused's guilt is not in issue; or
> (b) it appears to the court that the physical or mental condition of the accused makes it undesirable for him to be called upon to give evidence;
>
> but subsection (2) below does not apply if, at the conclusion of the evidence for the prosecution, his legal representative informs the court that the accused will give evidence, or where he is unrepresented, the court ascertains from him that he will give evidence.
>
> (2) Where this subsection applies, the court shall, at the conclusion of the evidence for the prosecution, satisfy itself (in the case of proceedings on indictment, in the presence of the jury) that the accused is aware that the stage has been reached at which evidence can be given for the defence and that he can, if he wishes, give evidence and that, if he chooses not to give evidence, or having been sworn, without good cause refuses to answer any question,[43] it will be permissible for the court or jury to draw such inferences as appear proper from his failure to give evidence or his refusal, without good cause, to answer any question.
>
> (3) Where this subsection applies, the court or jury, in determining whether the accused is guilty of the offence charged, may draw

---

[41] Edward Rees, "The Irish Experience of Silence in Court," *Counsel*, November/December 1994.

[42] As originally enacted the words "who has attained the age of fourteen years" were contained in the text at this point. They were removed by s.35 of the Crime and Disorder Act 1998.

[43] As to the position where the accused refuses, without good cause, to answer a particular question see *Ackinclose* [1996] Crim.L.R. 747, C.A.

such inferences as appear proper from the failure of the accused to give evidence or his refusal, without good cause, to answer any question.

(4) This section does not render the accused compellable to give evidence on his own behalf, and he shall accordingly not be guilty of contempt of court by reason of a refusal to do so.

(5) For the purposes of this section a person who, having been sworn, refuses to answer any question shall be taken to do so without good cause unless—

   (a) he is entitled to refuse to answer the question by virtue of any enactment,[44] whenever passed or made, or on the ground of privilege;[45] or

   (b) the court in the exercise of its general discretion excuses him from answering it.

(6) [Repealed].[46]

(7) This section applies—

   (a) in relation to proceedings on indictment for an offence, only if the person charged with the offence is arraigned on or after the commencement of this section;

   (b) in relation to proceedings in a magistrates' court, only if the time when the court begins to receive evidence in the proceedings falls after the commencement of this section."

(b) *Ancillary provisions*

(i) Legal representative. The expression "legal representative" means an authorised advocate or authorised litigator, as defined by the Courts and Legal Services Act 1990.[47]

(ii) Offence charged. The reference to offence charged in section 35(3) includes a reference to any other offence of which the accused could lawfully be convicted on that charge.[48]

(iii) Section 35 does not preclude the operation of existing statutory powers to exclude evidence as inadmissible or of any exclusionary discretion. Nothing in section 35 prejudices the operation of a provision of any enactment which provides (in whatever words) that any answer or evidence given by a person in specified circumstances shall not be admissible in evidence against him or some other person in any proceedings or class of proceedings (however described, and whether civil or

---

44 *E.g.* Criminal Evidence Act 1898, s.1(f).

45 *E.g.* legal professional privilege.

46 As originally enacted sub-section (6), in keeping with subs.(1), provided: "Where the age of any person is material for the purposes of subsection (1) above, his age shall for those purposes be taken to be that which appears to the court to be his age." The subsection has been repealed by s.35 of the Crime and Disorder Act 1998.

47 CJPOA, s.38(1) referring to s.119(1).

48 s.38(2).

criminal).[49] Further, nothing in the section prejudices any power of a court, in any proceedings, to exclude evidence (whether by preventing questions being put or otherwise) at its discretion.[50]

(c) *Erstwhile restriction to persons of 14 years of age and over*

In contrast with the provisions on investigative stage silence, those relating to silence at trial were initially restricted to defendants over the age of fourteen, a restriction which was removed by section 35 of the Crime and Disorder Act 1998.

(2) Strength of evidence impelling an inference of guilt from courtroom silence

(a) *Initial cautious phase in Northern Ireland: the brink of proof test*

The commentator Jackson has pointed out that before the Criminal Evidence (Northern Ireland) Order 1988 judges in the province tended to refrain both from making any adverse comments to juries about the failure to testify and from drawing adverse inferences in cases where they sat as a tribunal of fact.[51] With such a tradition as this (in contrast to England and Wales) it was perhaps not suprising that initial judicial response to Article 4 was cautious. Jackson has also noted[52] that in a number of scheduled cases the prosecution were unsuccessful in inviting inferences to be drawn under the article and there was a tendency for judges, following *Sparrow*,[53] to deprecate use of the article in order to bolster up a weak case. He further notes that cases in which judges adopted such a position notably included some involving possession of firearms and explosives, that is in precisely the sort of case in which the habitual silence of defendants was claimed to be a serious problem. The cautious attitude was exemplified in *Smyth*,[54] in which Kelly L.J. said of the refusal of the trial judge to apply the Order where there was some scientific and identification evidence to link the defendant with the murder:

> "It seems to me that in some cases the failure of an accused to give evidence may justify a finding of guilt where the weight of the prosecution evidence just rests on the brink of the necessary standard of proof. In other cases the failure to give evidence may merely heighten suspicion."

---

[49] s.38(5). The refeerence to giving evidence is a reference to giving evidence in any manner, whether by furnishing information, making discovery, producing documents or otherwise: *ibid.*

[50] s.38(6).

[51] Viscount Colville, *Review of the Northern Ireland (Emergency Provisions) Acts 1978 and 1987*, Cmnd. 1115, 1990, p.40, cited in Jackson, [1991] Crim.L.R. at p.410.

[52] *ibid.*

[53] (1973) 57 Cr.App.R. 352, C.A.

[54] (1989) Extempore judgment, October 20, cited in Jackson, [1991] Crim.L.R., at pp.410-411.

This appeared to be saying that the defendant's refusal to give evidence could only nudge the case over into a conviction where the evidence was already so strong as to be very close to achieving proof beyond reasonable doubt. Where the evidence was weaker than being on the brink a refusal to give evidence could raise no inference capable of making up the deficit. *Smyth* appeared to follow the pronouncement of Lawton L.J. in *Mutch* and interpreted the Order as merely declaratory of the common law. But the language was admittedly tentative, which allowed for later adjustment. Such caution as was evinced in *Smyth* initially meant few cases in which inferences were drawn from silence which made a decisive difference between acquittal and conviction.[55] In one indictment for murder and conspiracy to cause grievous bodily harm, it was ruled that the defendant's refusal to give evidence entitled the court to discount the exculpatory part of an admission to the police, rather than to go towards proving matters that were not ever admitted.[56] In the event the judge was not satisfied beyond reasonable doubt that the defendant had had murder in his mind.

(b) *The move to a robust "common sense" approach*

Although the initial approach of the courts was one of caution there was a gradual tendency to reduce the strength of other evidence before invoking the defendant's refusal to enter the witness box as a makeweight for conviction. *McCartan and McKay*,[57] already discussed in relation to investigative stage silence, is a case in point. In an earlier case, *McDonnell*,[58] Nicholson J. stated that "the refusal to give evidence may be used by the court as supportive of other evidence from which at least the accused's probable guilt can be inferred or as corroborative of such other evidence and thus enable the court to conclude beyond reasonable doubt that the accused is guilty." It has been suggested that this was to apply a legal equation for conviction made up of the civil standard of proof plus silence, a standard substantively lower than that of brink level.[59] In keeping with the drift away from the threshold of proof as the standard for invoking the defendant's courtroom silence Kelly L.J. himself clearly had second thoughts. In *McLernon*[60] he stated that when referring in *Smyth* to the brink of reasonable doubt he had never intended to limit the application of the Order in such a way and he went on:

> "The Article is in the widest terms. It imposes no limitation as to when [the inference] may be invoked or what result may follow if it is invoked .... [T]he court has ... a complete discretion as to whether

---

55 See *e.g. O'Neill* (1990) unreported, May 17, Sheil J., cited *ibid*, p.411.

56 *Gamble* (1989) unreported, October 27, Carswell J., cited *ibid*.

57 B.B.C. Radio Four, *File on Four*, October 26, 1993, transcript p.12. See also *Kane, Kelly and others* (1989) unreported, March 30, Carswell J., cited in Jackson, [1991] Crim.L.R., at p.412, and *Martin, Morrison* et al. (1991) Belfast Crown Court, May 8, cited by Jackson, [1995] Crim.L.R., at p.597.

58 (1989) unreported, Belfast Crown Court, March 13.

59 E. Rees, *Counsel*, November/December 1994.

60 [1992] N.I.J.B. 41, N.I.C.A., April 1, cited in Jackson, [1995] Crim.L.R., at p.596.

> inferences should be drawn or not...and...if it decides to draw inferences what their nature, extent and degree of adversity may be . . . . In [*Smyth*] I gave such instances in broad and general terms . . . but I add . . . that in certain cases a refusal to give evidence . . . may well in itself with nothing more increase the weight of a *prima facie* case to the weight of proof beyond reasonable doubt."

Kelly L.J. therefore reconciles the apparent self-contradiction by stating in effect that whilst *usually* it requires evidence close to proof beyond reasonable doubt for absence from the witness box to make up the small deficit, *exceptionally* there need only be a bare *prima facie* case for a refusal to give evidence to be capable of bridging the gap. The language of Article 4 certainly imposes no restriction on the latter approach.

It was clear, as Jackson argued[61] that the question as to which approach was the proper one needed to be resolved and this the House of Lords was asked to do in *Murray* v. *D.P.P.*, an indictment for attempted murder.[62] Thumb prints matching the appellant's were found on the car used in the attempt, fibres matching a balaclava from the car were found in the appellant's hair combing, and fibres matching the upholstery and recent firearms residue particles were found on his jeans which were damp and muddy when seized on the morning after the offence. The only account given by the appellant before his arrest was that he had been at a friend's house during the night and that his jeans were muddy because he had been out hunting two days previously. The trial judge directed himself that he would have been entitled under common law to draw an inference against the defendant from his failure to give evidence. This, he held, was because the case was one in which the forensic findings were admitted but the defendant sought to rely on innocent explanations for them, the confession and avoidance situation. He therefore appears to have made the assumption that the licence to draw an adverse inference under common law was restricted to cases in which the defence involved confession and avoidance, whereas in *Mutch* Lawton L.J. had in fact allowed for such an inference where the evidence pointed so strongly to guilt as to require a denial of the evidence or an explanation of it—the more general brink of proof situation. But although he ruled that he would have been entitled to draw a decisive inference against the accused under common law he held that there was no impediment on invoking Article 4 to convict, whatever the common law position had been.

On appeal it was contended (i) that the judge had been wrong to hold that the defence involved confession and avoidance permitting an adverse inference to be drawn at common law "from the accused's failure to give sworn factual foundation to the innocent alternatives which he allege[d] counter[ed] the prosecution case of the forensic findings," (ii) that no inference of guilt would therefore in the circumstances have been allowed under common law, (iii) that Article 4 was merely declaratory of the common law and did not allow a judge trying a criminal case

---

61 Jackson, [1991] Crim.L.R., at p.413.
62 (1993) 97 Cr.App.R. 151.

without a jury to draw inferences from the refusal of the accused to give evidence which he would not have been permitted by common law to invite the jury to consider if the case had been tried with a jury, and (iv) that Article 4 therefore afforded no basis on the facts for drawing an inference of guilt from the defendant's refusal to give evidence.

The Court of Appeal upheld the second submission but also held that Article 4 afforded wider powers than the common law to draw an inference of guilt and there did not need to be a defence of confession and avoidance for the article to be invoked. The erroneous assumption that *Mutch* only allowed an adverse inference in cases where the defence involved confession and avoidance was not apparently questioned. In upholding the decision of the Court of Appeal the House of Lords noted that the Article closely followed the proposal in the 11th report, and that the C.L.R.C. had plainly expressed an intent to change the law. Whether the law at the time of the report restricted inferences of guilt to cases involving confession and avoidance or, not so narrowly, to brink cases—the position which it is submitted was settled in *Mutch* after the 11th report—is not clear. But, either way, the C.L.R.C. evidently intended their scheme to have a broader application than in brink cases. The 11th report had clearly indicated the starting point at which it *might* be open to a court under their scheme to infer guilt from a refusal of the defendant to give evidence.[63] This was to be at the stage where the prosecution had established a *prima facie* case and it is apparent in particular from the following important passage of Lord Mustill's speech that this was the view of the House of Lords:[64]

> "At this stage the trial is in a state of balance. The fact-finder waits to see whether in relation to each essential ingredient of the offence the direct evidence, which it is at least possible to believe, should in the event be believed, and whether inferences that might be drawn from such evidence should actually be drawn. Usually, the most important of the events for which the fact finder is keeping his judgment is suspense will be the evidence of the accused himself, for most prosecutions depend upon witnesses who speak directly to the participation of the defendant, who knows very well where the truth lies. So also with many of the inferences which the prosecutor seeks to draw from facts which are directly proved. If in such circumstances the defendant does not go on oath to say that the witnesses who have spoken to his actions are untruthful or unreliable, or that an inference which appears on its face to be plausible is in reality unsound for reasons within his personal knowledge, the fact-finder may suspect that the defendant does not tell his story because he has no story to tell, or none which will stand up to scrutiny; and this suspicion may be sufficient to convert a provable prosecution case into one which is actually proved. This is not of course because a silent defendant is presumed to be guilty, or because silence

[63] para. 10.

[64] (1993) 97 Cr.App.R., at pp. 154-155.

> converts a case which is too weak to call for an answer into one which justifies a conviction. Rather, the fact-finder is entitled as a matter of common sense to draw his own conclusions if a defendant who is faced with evidence which does call for an answer fails to come forward and provide it. So also if the defendant seeks to outflank the case for the prosecution by means of a 'positive' defence—as for example where he replies in relation to a charge of murder that although he did kill the deceased he acted under provocation. If he does not give evidence in support of this allegation there will in very many cases be a legitimate inference that the defence is untrue."

The test of a *prima facie* case is whether the evidence called by the prosecution is capable of persuading a reasonably minded jury properly directed that the case is proved beyond reasonable doubt. Traditionally, the expression commonly used to describe such evidence, a "case to answer," has never meant a case literally requiring an answer in the sense of counter-evidence from the defence on pain of an inference of guilt. It has merely meant a case for which the defendant will have to answer to the tribunal of fact, that is be subject to a verdict. But the context of Lord Mustill's discourse would seem to suggest a novel conflation of the traditional meaning of the phrase and a new meaning, the idea that a *prima facie* case is by definition one which an innocent person would naturally feel impelled to answer in the witness box, such that a refusal is *potentially* capable of warranting an inference of guilt. Whether a *prima facie* case is *actually* strong enough to warrant such an inference will be decided by the tribunal of fact on the basis of common sense. (The "common sense" approach follows the lead of the C.L.R.C.[65] and the Judicial Committee of the Privy Council in adjudicating on an appeal involving the equivalent Singapore provision.[66]) Such an analysis of the effect of Article 4 is consistent with the fact that the C.L.R.C. never envisaged that a case to answer *would necessarily* warrant the drawing of an inference of guilt from the refusal to give evidence. Whilst the Committee took the view that a refusal to give evidence would be more significant as the case was stronger, they stressed that it would be of little or no significance if the case against the defendant was weak.[67] In his speech in *Murray* Lord Slynn of Hadley stated that there must be a "clear" *prima facie* case if an inference of guilt is to be drawn from the defendant's refusal to give evidence.[68] If this means that in general a case should be reasonably firm (not shaky but not necessarily on the brink of proof) before such an inference can reasonably be drawn it would be entirely consistent with the view of the C.L.R.C. Although it is for the tribunal of fact in the first instance to determine whether a *prima facie* case is strong enough to warrant an adverse inference from the defendant's refusal to answer it in

---

65 11th report, para. 110.
66 *Haw Tua Tau* v. *Public Prosecutor* [1982] A.C. 136, at p.153, *per* Lord Diplock.
67 11th report, para. 110.
68 (1993) 97 Cr.App.R., at p.161

the witness box the determination is justiciable on appeal.[69] In the case of judge-only "Diplock" trials the appellate court will know from the reasoned verdict whether an adverse inference was drawn. In jury trials the summing-up will disclose whether a jury were authorised in the particular case to infer guilt from the defendant's refusal to give evidence.

Against the backdrop of the development of case law interpreting Article 4 it is clear that in relaxing the principle in *Mutch* to the extent that they did in *Martinez-Tobon* the English Court of Appeal effectively pre-empted not only enactment of the section but also its interpretation in accordance with that of Article 4. In short, the Common law caught up with section 35 before it became law and it is therefore codified in England and Wales rather than changed by the Act.

(c) *Judge ought not to direct the jury not to draw an adverse inference merely because the prosecution case is weak*

In *Byrne* the Court of Appeal rejected the suggestion that a judge ought to direct the jury not to draw an adverse inference where the prosecution case was weak.[70]

(3) The general application of section 35

In *Cowan*[71] it was submitted that section 35 was so at variance with established principle that its operation should be reduced and marginalised as far as possible. Rejecting the argument[72] the Court of Appeal held that the plain words of the section do not justify confining its operation to exceptional cases. Apart from the special circumstances set out in section 35(1) in which no adverse inferences were to be drawn the section was otherwise in terms of general application.

(4) Implied condition for inference that it must be reasonable to expect the accused to give evidence

Unlike section 34(1), section 35 imposes no express requirement for it to have been reasonable to expect the accused to give evidence. However, this is presumably implied.

---

69 *Muckian* (1994) unreported, N.I.C.A., December 2, *per* MacDermott L.J., cited in Pattenden, [1995] Crim.L.R., at p.606.

70 (1996) unreported, C.A. 95/4159/W4, November 21, *per* Lord Taylor C.J.

71 [1996] Q.B. 373; [1995] 4 All E.R. 939.

72 *ibid.*, at pp.943-945.

(5) Specific factual inferences and general inferences of guilt

It was stressed in *Murray*[73] that whilst in all but the simplest cases the permissible adverse inferences from courtroom silence may have to be considered separately in relation to each particular issue the inferences which may be drawn are not merely specific inferences drawn from specific facts. Although the refusal of the accused to give evidence would not by itself necessarily indicate guilt the inferences which might be drawn *include, in an appropriate case, an inference that the defendant is guilty of the offence with which he is charged.* According to Lord Slynn the inferential process would involve reasoning that—

> ". . . if aspects of the evidence taken alone or in combination with other facts clearly call for an explanation which the accused ought to be in a position to give, if an explanation exists, then a failure to give any explanation may as a matter of common sense allow the drawing of an inference that there is no explanation and that the accused is guilty."[74]

If the true reason for the defendant declining to give evidence is that he is guilty and has no answer to the charge normally the only basis for a plea of not guilty will be that the prosecution case is so weak as to require no other approach than that of simply putting the prosecution to proof. Where the case is so evidently weak that the rationale of this approach is palpable and justified it will clearly be inappropriate to draw an adverse inference from his silence. But if the case is reasonably strong it is most unlikely that the defence approach would be one of simply putting the prosecution to proof. If the defendant does not plead guilty he will have to run a positive defence involving the averment of exculpatory facts. If then he declines to give evidence it can hardly be said that he has "no explanation." His defence may be false but it is not non-existent. So on the face of it an inference that he is silent because he has no explanation would, in strict semantic terms, be illogical. But the reference by Lord Slynn to the accused having "no explanation" may be shorthand conveying the idea that even where a positive defence is run it may be inferred from the defendant's refusal to go into the witness box that he has no explanation *which would be capable of standing up under cross-examination.* The steps in the process of reasoning would be—

(i) the accused is absent from the witness box because he fears that under testing his proferred defence will be exposed as false;
(ii) he is likely to know better than anyone the strengths or weaknesses of his defence;
(iii) his fear is therefore based on a keen awareness that his defence is weak;

[73] (1993) 97 Cr.App.R., at p.155, *per* Lord Mustill.
[74] *ibid.*, pp. 160-161.

(iv) it is likely that he knows this to be the case because his defence *actually is* false.

A particular problem in using silence to furnish a decisive element in the proof of guilt is that it necessitates the assumption that the accused is silent because he is guilty. Yet, as Jackson has argued, this begs the question of why he is silent, for if without the evidence of silence the evidence falls short of furnishing the necessary standard of proof there can be no basis for a belief that the silence is attributable to the accused's guilt:

> "It is difficult to see how a case which falls short of proof beyond reasonable doubt can be raised up to the standard of proof beyond reasonable doubt by the equivocal fact of an accused's failure to testify. . . . It may be that the stronger the case is, the harder it is to rebut. But no matter how strong the evidence, the court or jury is in a position to draw the 'proper' inference from silence only where it knows the reason for silence. Without knowledge of the reason, it would only seem safe to draw an inference of guilt when the trier of fact is already convinced of guilt on the basis of existing proof beyond reasonable doubt. But the inference then becomes merely an *ex post facto* rationalisation of what the trier of fact is already convinced of and the provision becomes redundant. If the trier of fact has become convinced on the basis of lesser proof than this, then the provision is being used to do what in many cases it cannot do, namely provide the necessary evidence to bring the proof up to the standard."[75]

Jackson's argument is that silence is necessarily equivocal, for there can never be certain knowledge of the reason why a person declines to give evidence. It is therefore unsafe to assume that the defendant is silent because he is guilty. But this is precisely the point about section 35, which is based on the supposition that, even where the evidence apart from the refusal to testify might not by itself furnish proof to the necessary standard, as a matter of common sense it may in a given case be safe to conjecture that silence points to guilt. This arises from the axiom that "innocence always wants to declare itself." On the other hand, the problem with assessment by reference to common sense has been well expressed in the comment that "the subjectivity of the individual juror coping with an undefined system of measurement is an uncertain framework for criminal justice."[76]

---

[75] [1995] Crim.L.R., at p.600.
[76] E. Rees, *Counsel*, November/December 1994.

(6) Directions to the jury

(a) *Judicial Studies Board specimen direction*

In *Cowan* the Court of Appeal considered that the following specimen direction suggested by the Judicial Studies Board was in general terms a sound guide, subject to the possible need to adapt it to the particular circumstances of an individual case:

> "The defendant has not given evidence. That is his right. But, as he has been told, the law is that you may draw such inferences as appear proper from his failure to do so. Failure on its own cannot prove guilt but, depending on the circumstances, you may hold his failure against him when deciding whether he is guilty. [There is evidence before you on the basis of which the defendant's advocate invites you not to hold it against the defendant that he has not given evidence before you, namely . . . If you think that because of this evidence you should not hold it against the defendant that he has not given evidence, do not do so. But if the evidence he relies on present no adequate explanation for his absence from the witness box then you may hold his failure to give evidence against him. You do not have to do so.] What proper inferences can you draw from the defendant's decision not to give evidence before you? If you conclude that there is a case for him to answer, you may think that the defendant would have gone into the witness box to give you an explanation for or an answer to the case against him. If the only sensible explanation for his decision not to give evidence is that he has no answer to the case against him, or none that could have stood up to cross-examination, then it would be open to you to hold against him his failure to give evidence. It is for you to decide whether it is fair to do so."[77]

(b) *The five essentials*

In addition to the specimen direction the Court of Appeal in *Cowan* considered it necessary, additionally, to highlight the following essentials:—

(1) The burden of proof remains on the prosecution throughout to the standard required.

(2) The defendant is entitled to remain silent as of right and by choice and the right to silence remains.

(3) An inference from failure to give evidence cannot on its own prove guilt.

(4) Since the jury might not believe the witnesses whose evidence the judge considers sufficient to raise a prima facie case it must be made clear to the jury that they have to find a case to answer on the prosecution evidence before drawing an adverse inference from the defendant's trial silence.

---

[77] The words in brackets were to be used only where there was evidence.

(5) If, despite any evidence relied on to expalin his silence or in the absence of any such evidence, the jury conclude the silence can only be attributed to the defendant's having no answer, or none that would stand up to cross-examination, they may draw an adverse inference.[78]

(7) Jury must be satisfied that a prima facie case exists before drawing an adverse inference

The "fourth essential" was deduced by the Court of Appeal from the terms of section 38(3), which provides that a person may not be convicted of an offence solely on an inference drawn from a failure or refusal by the defendant to give evidence. Since by definition the accused's absence from the witness box can have relevance to the trial only after the judge has determined that a *prima facie* case has been established, section 38(3) is plainly intended to control the use made by the jury of the defendant's refusal to give evidence. In *Cowan* Lord Taylor C.J., giving the judgment of the Court of Appeal, explained the relevance and impact of the subsection in that context:

> "[T]he jury must be satisfied that the prosecution have established a case to answer before drawing any inference from silence. Of course, the judge must have thought so or the question whether the defendant was to give evidence would not have arisen. But the jury may not believe the witnesses whose evidence the judge considered sufficient to raise a *prima facie* case. It must therefore be made clear to them that they must find there to be a case to answer on the prosecution evidence before drawing an adverse inference from the defendant's silence."[79]

This is to construe section 38(3) as meaning that where the jury find that the evidence adduced by the prosecution is insufficient to raise a *prima facie* case they may not deploy an adverse inference from the defendant's trial silence to make up the deficit. The construction equates an insufficiency of evidence with there being "no evidence," the phrase commonly used to describe the position when evidence is insufficient. On the basis of that equation it follows that if an adverse inference from trial silence could, but for section 38(3), make up the deficit in evidence otherwise insufficient to establish a *prima facie* case it would be furnishing the "sole" material of proof.

---

[78] The importance of these directions was reiterated in *Byrne* (1996) unreported C.A. no. 95/4159/W4, November 21.

[79] [1996] Q.B. 373, at p.381. In *Argent* [1997] 2 Cr.App.R. 27, at p.35, the trial judge had assumed that an inference from pre-trial silence was not proper unless the jury first found a case to answer. As Pattenden observes (2 E. & P., at p.149, note) this is not supported by anything the Court of Appeal has said and is difficult to reconcile with the express words of the statute, which permit pre-trial silence to be taken into account by the court in determining the existence of a case to answer.

Dr Pattenden has queried whether Lord Taylor considered the full implications of requiring the jury to be instructed that they had to be satisfied that a *prima facie* case had been adduced before they could draw an inference from the fact that the accused has elected not to give evidence.[80] She observes:

> "The accepted test of a *prima facie* case is whether there is prosecution evidence, assumed to be true and uncontradicted, upon which a reasonable jury could convict. What test is the jury to apply? The passage [in *Cowan*] supposes that the jury, unlike the judge, will consider the credibility of the prosecution witnesses. If so, how does a finding of a *prima facie* case differ from a finding of guilt? Is it a case of concentrating exclusively on the prosecution evidence, other than any inferences arising from the accused's in-court silence? Are jurors capable of this? Must the judge direct them as to the nature of a case to answer? As yet the Court of Appeal has provided no answers."

The fourth essential was the subject of an appeal in *Birchall*[81] against a conviction for murder, in which it was referred to as "essential (4)." It was held that the failure to direct the jury on that precondition, either in the terms of the standard direction or in similar terms, posed a clear risk of injustice and that the omission to give that direction together with new evidence admitted on the appeal rendered the conviction unsafe. The Crown had submitted that the omission was immaterial because there was plainly a prima facie case. Giving judgment and in apparent response to this contention, Lord Bingham C.J. said that the court was reluctant to countenance the view that direction of a jury called for the mouthing of a number of mandatory formulae and departure by a trial judge from a prescribed form of words would by no means always justify the upsetting of a verdict. Standard directions, were, however, devised to serve the ends of justice and the court had to be astute to ensure that those ends were not jeopardised by failure to give directions where they were called for. The drawing of inferences from silence was a particularly sensitive area. Many respected authorities had voiced the fear that section 35 and its sister sections might lead to wrongful convictions. It seemed possible that the application of those provisions could lead to decisions adverse to the United Kingdom at Strasbourg under Articles 6.1 and 6.2 of the European Convention on Human Rights unless those provisions were the subject of carefully framed directions to juries. Inescapable logic demanded that a jury should not start to consider whether to draw inferences from a defendant's failure to give oral evidence at trial until they had concluded that the Crown's case was sufficiently compelling to call for an answer from the defendant. In the light of the court's decision the Crown did not seek a retrial.

80 (1998) 2 E. & P. at p.149.
81 (1998) *The Times*, February 10; [1999] Crim.L.R. 311.

(8) Adverse inference may be inappropriate

(a) *Broad discretion to direct or advise the jury not to draw an adverse inference*

In *Cowan* the Court of Appeal had no doubt that as section 35 only permits such inferences "as appear proper," use of that phrase was intended to leave a broad discretion to a trial judge to decide in all the circumstances whether any proper inference was capable of being drawn by the jury.[82] If not, the judge should tell them so; otherwise it was for the jury to decide whether in fact an inference should properly be drawn. In appropriate circumstances a court may decline to draw an adverse inference from trial silence and a judge may direct or advise a jury against doing so. It has been pointed out[83] that the Court of Appeal has not said when a judge should "direct," as opposed merely to "advise," against a negative inference.

(b) *Appellate interference with discretion will be unusual*

It is implicit in the awarding of a "broad discretion" that interference with the exercise of the discretion would be unusual and, indeed, this was the expressed intention of the Court of Appeal. Giving the judgment of the court, Lord Taylor C.J. stated:

> "We wish to stress, moreover, that this court will not lightly interfere with a judge's discretion to direct or advise a jury as to the drawing of inferences from silence and as to the nature, extent and degree of such inferences. He is the best person to have the feel of the case, and so long as he gives the jury adequate directions of law as indicated above and leaves the decision to them, this court will be slow to substitute its view for his."[84]

(c) *Defendant's physical or mental condition precluding an adverse inference*

Section 35(1) is precluded from applying if it appears to the court that the accused's physical or mental condition makes it undesirable for him to be called upon to give evidence. The C.L.R.C. primarily intended the exemption to apply in cases of insanity and diminished responsibility[85] but the expression "undesirable" clearly implies a wider embrace. In the Commons the Home Secretary envisaged that defendants who were "unwell," "confused," or "not in a position to give a proper account" would come within the subsection.[86] In *Harkin and Gordon*,[87] a Northern Ireland case, the trial judge ruled on the basis of medical evidence that the accused was not mentally handicapped but on appeal further medical evidence

---

[82] [1996] Q.B. 373, at p.380.

[83] Pattenden, 2 E. & P., at p.148.

[84] [1996] Q.B., at p.382. Sybil Sharpe has observed that this non-interventionist approach maintains the rheteric of fairness whilst at the same time stultifying its application: "Vulnerable defendants and inferences from silence," *New Law Journal,* June 6, 1997, 842, at p.843 (2nd part, June 13, 897).

[85] 11th report, para. 113.

[86] 241 H.C. Deb., col. 277, April 13, 1994.

[87] (1995) N.I.C.A. January 16, cited in Jackson, [1995] Crim.L.R., at p.595.

revealed that he was suffering from schizophrenia at the time of his trial. It was held that in the light of this evidence the judge might well have considered it undesirable to call upon the accused to give evidence as his condition could have impaired his fitness to perform competently as a witness.[88]

The exception was considered in some depth in *Friend*,[89] an appeal against conviction for murder. The appellant, 14 at the time of his arrest and 15 by the time of his trial, was assessed by a leading consultant forensic psychologist[90] who gave evidence of tests administered after arrest which indicated a very low IQ of 56, and although his mental age at that stage was difficult to assess it equated approximately to that of a child of 9 years. Shortly before the trial his I.Q. was measured at 63, giving a mental age of between 9 and 10 years, the improvement probably being related to an increased ability to concentrate. He remained "within the handicapped bracket,"[91] was "educationally disadvantaged," which meant that his potential had not been fully developed, was "virtually illiterate," with reading skills of a boy of six years, and his powers of concentration and self-expression were poor. He was tested for suggestibility in order to establish whether he might agree with what the police put to him in interview and was found to be less suggestible than other average people. Although he was "limited" in his ability to comprehend and to give an account of himself it was considered that when allowed plenty of time during a clinical consultation or in an interview to settle down and to concentrate, and so long as time and care were taken to ensure that he understood, he could give a coherent account. However, the consultant's concern was that, as the appellant was restless, tense and anxious, under the stress of giving evidence in the witness box he would be prone to distraction, would find it more difficult to listen to questions and to concentrate, could not command the same intellectual resources and might not do justice to himself. In short whilst he might be able to give a very coherent account of himself in an inteview; it might be quite another matter to cope with questioning in the witness box.

The judge ruled that the appellant's mental condition was not such as to make it undesirable to give evidence and he therefore exercised his discretion to allow an adverse inference under section 35. In doing so he took into account the following matters: the psychologist's assessment; the fact that the appellant was able to give a very coherent (if not true) account in the police interview, when he was accompanied by his mother and represented by a solicitor; the fact that his lower

---

[88] In *Friend* [1997] 2 Cr.App.R. 231, at p.242, the Court of Appeal cited schizophrenia as a possible reason for invoking the subsection.

[89] *supra*, discussed in Sharpe, "Vulnerable defendants and inferences from silence" *supra*. For other consideration of the possibly disabling effect of the defendant's mental condition on the court's power to permit inferences to be drawn from the defendant's decision not to give evidence see Grubin, "Silence in court: psychiatry and the Criminal Justice and Public Order Act 1994," *The Journal of Forensic Psychiatry*, Vol. 7, No. 3, December 1996, 647. In *Stone (Michael),* a notable trial for murder, the accused was exempted from the operation of section 35 on the grounds of his psychiatric history: see *The Guardian*, October 21, 1998.

[90] Dr Gisli Gudjonsson, whose findings are referred to in [1997] 2 Cr.App.R., at pp.234 and 238.

[91] In the words of the trial judge, H.H. Judge Michael Combe, he was "to some degree mentally retarded": [1997] 2 Cr.App.R., at p.237.

than average suggestibility score meant that he was not going to agree very easily to questions by counsel for the co-defendants or the Crown; his behaviour soon after the offence in helping to dispose of murder weapons (although not his alleged behaviour at the time of the offence); that it was within the judge's own powers to mitigate the stress of giving evidence by ensuring that the appellant, as in the case of all witnesses, was treated fairly and courteously, not bullied in cross-examination, understood every question and took time to answer, and that there would be breaks. In effect, the trial judge was saying, this supervisory duty met the psychologist's concern about the appellant's potential "distractability" if he gave evidence; the fact that children as young as eight gave evidence in Crown Court trials was "accommodated by the trial judge ensuring that no undue pressure was put upon a child witness."[92]

It was submitted that the judge had erred in the exercise of his discretion in failing to take sufficient account of the psychologist's assessment that the appellant could not do himself justice in giving evidence because of his poor ability to concentrate and express himself[93] and instead gave disproportionate weight to the appellant's interview, his lack of suggestibility and to the fact that after the offence he had gone with a co-defendant to dispose of a knife.[94] However, it was held that in exercising his discretion the judge had not "applied the wrong test if only because there [was] no right test" and it was not "appropriate to spell out a test to be applied in such a situation . . ."[95] In applying the section no formal guidelines were called for.[96] It was held that the judge's ruling was not an unreasonable exercise of his discretion within the *Wednesbury* criteria.[97] In the view of the Court of Appeal the trial judge reached his conclusion in a proper and balanced manner and did not exercise his discretion capriciously; he took account of relevant matters and did not consider those which were irrelevant; it was open to him on the evidence before him to arrive at the conclusion he reached; and it could not be said that no judge could rationally have reached the same conclusion.

In giving the judgment of the Court of Appeal Otton L.J. made clear that the issue of whether the defendant was suffering from a mental condition vitiating his fitness to give evidence was distinct from the more fundamental issue of fitness to plead.[98] Between fitness to plead on the authorities regulating that topic and fitness to testify within the meaning of section 35, there was perceived to be, in the words

---

92 [1997] 2 Cr.App.R., at p.239, apparently quoting the trial judge.

93 The Court of Appeal dismissed the consultant psychologist's assessment of the appellant's "poor ability to concentrate and express himself" as "somewhat vague": [1997] 2 Cr.App.R., at p.242.

94 In rejecting the submission the court held that the judge was fully entitled to consider the appellant's conduct "before and after" the offence: [1997] 2 Cr.App.R., at p.241. It has been argued that conduct immediately before and after an offence demonstrates guilty knowledge, not a level of comprehension relevant to questioning, nor to communication skills: Sharpe, *New Law Journal,* June 13, 1997, at p.897.

95 [1997] 2 Cr.App.R., at p.242.

96 *ibid.*

97 *ibid.*, at p.243; *Associated Provincial Picture Houses Ltd.* v. *Wednesbury Corporation* [1948] 1 K.B. 233, at p.229.

98 [1997] 2 Cr.App.R., at p.241.

of the trial judge, a "grey area"[99] in which the accused's mental (or physical) condition made it undesirable for him to give evidence. In the court"s view the issue of the desirability of giving evidence will be considered only very rarely because in the majority of cases in which the issue of disabling mental condition is raised there will be evidence that the accused is unfit to plead.[100]

Although the court considered it inappropriate to supplement section 35 with any test or guidelines they did offer examples of the sort of physical and mental conditions which might make it undesirable for the accused to give evidence.[101] Thus, they stated that a "physical condition might include a risk of an epileptic attack; a mental condition, latent schizophrenia where the experience of giving evidence might trigger a florid state." Whilst these illustrations are hardly exhaustive, Pattenden has suggested that they indicate that the court perceived the subsection in terms of the risk to the accused's health in giving evidence.[102]

It has already been mentioned that as originally enacted section 35 applied to defendants who had reached the age of 14 years but that the restriction was removed by the Crime and Disorder Act 1998. In *Friend* the point was taken on appeal that it was the appellant's mental, rather than his chronological, age, which should have been the relevant criterion.[103] Rejecting the argument the Court of Appeal derived support from the fact that s.9 of the Family Law Reform Act 1969 defined the attainment of age as the "commencement of the relevant anniversary" of the date of birth and they made the assumption that when using the expression "attained the age of 14 years" in the 1994 Act the draftsman had in mind the definition used in the 1969 Act. It has been argued that there is no evidence on which to base such an assumption and that the importing of a definition from a civil law statute into the criminal law was *in pari materia and* unwarranted.[104] But even though the appellant in *Friend* may technically have come within the section, the decision shows, as Pattenden has pointed out, that—

> ". . . [t]here is little prospect that the judge will direct a jury not to draw an adverse inference from the accused's failure to testify if the Court of Appeal did not require this in a case where the silent accused was just 13 months above the mimimum age necessary for section 35 to apply and had an actual mental age of nine. If this is not the kind of

---

[99] *ibid.*, at p.237.

[100] *ibid.*, at pp.239-240. Sharpe has argued that since the fitness to plead issue has nothing to do with a capacity to testify but concerns the issue of whether the accused has sufficient intellect to comprehend the course of the proceedings and to make a proper defence "both the trial judge and the Appeal Court allowed [the] extraneous issue [of fitness to plead] to cloud the assessment of whether it was undesirable for [the appellant] to testify": *New Law Journal*, June 6, 1997, at p.843. The rationale of this criticism remains obscure to the present writer.

[101] [1997] 2 Cr.App.R., at p.242.

[102] (1998) 2 E. & P., at p.150.

[103] [1997] 2 Cr.App.R., at pp. 239 and 241.

[104] Sharpe, *New Law Journal,* June 6, 1997, at p.843.

vulnerable defendant whom Lord Taylor predicted in his *Tom Sargent Memorial Lecture* would be protected, who is?" [105]

In that lecture Lord Taylor suggested that cases in which the judge will direct the jury, or the jury may decide of their own accord, that an adverse inference ought not to be drawn would include those "where there is a very young defendant or one with low intelligence or one, who for some other reason, is peculiarly vulnerable."[106] It was the absurdity highlighted by *Friend* in having a statutory rule excluding inferences on the basis of an arbitrary chronological age cut-off at the same time as a discretion allowing inferences where the defendant's mental age was well below the cut-off which inspired the repeal of the age condition by the Crime and Disorder Act 1998.

(d) *Instances where discretion will not be exercised in favour of defendants*

(i) Weak prosecution case. As stated earlier the Court of Appeal has indicated that there is no basis for exercising discretion in directing the jury not to draw an adverse inference where the case for the prosecution is weak.[107]

(ii) Defendant not interviewed by police. In *Napper*[108] the appellant had been interviewed about various transactions and had provided detailed answers but had not been interviewed about certain other matters for which he was ultimately charged fifteen months later. The Court of Appeal held that although the jury were entitled, in determining whether or not to draw an adverse inference, to take into account the fact that the appellant had furnished full answers to all the matters about which he was interviewed, it was not a reason for the trial judge not to invoke section 35 that the police had omitted to interview the appellant about the additional matters at a time when his memory of all the details would have been reasonably fresh. In the court's view the additional matters would not have been difficult to recall fifteen months later and "it would have been open to the appellant, when charged . . . to have voluntarily given his account . . . There was nothing to prevent him . . . recording in a statement to his legal advisers, from which he could have refreshed his memory, all the matters which related to the offences charged . . ."

(iii) Impact on silence at trial of explanation given to the police. It has been suggested that where the accused has given an explanation to the police but has then elected not to give evidence at his trial the tendency of the Northern Ireland courts has been not to allow the giving of the earlier explanation to lessen the likelihood of an inference being drawn.[109] In *Gamble*[110] the refusal of the defendant to give evidence was treated by Carswell J. as justifying his discounting altogether the

---

105 (1998) 2 E. & P., at p.165.

106 Reported in *New Law Journal*, January 28, 1994, 125, at p.126.

107 *Byrne* (1996) unreported, C.A. 95/4159/W4, November 21.

108 [1996] Crim.L.R. 591; (1996) 161 J.P.R. 16, at p.21, *per* Lord Taylor C.J. See also *Norton* (1996) unreported, C.A. 96/0319/X2, April 29.

109 Edward Rees, *Counsel*, March/April 1995, pp.20-22.

110 *supra*, note 33.

exculpatory part of an explanation given to the police. The same thinking clearly underlies the following statement by Kerr J. in *Gallen*:[111]

> "The purpose [of the provisions] is to require an accused to submit his explanation to the test of presentation and cross-examination in the witness box or alternatively face the consequence that the failure to do so may allow the court to draw an adverse inference against him. It would be wholly incongruous if he could escape these consequences by the recital of an exculpatory explanation in interview."

(e) *Innocent reasons for silence must be canvassed evidentially*

It was submitted in *Cowan* that without the need for evidence defending counsel could properly advance reasons or excuses for trial silence which might justify the court not drawing or the jury being directed not to draw an adverse inference. Rejecting this argument it was held that for a court to decline to draw an adverse inference from the defendant's trial silence or for a judge to direct the jury to decline to do so, there had to be some evidential basis or some exceptional factors in the case making that a fair course to take. In developing the submission it had been suggested[112] that where the defence case involved an attack on prosecution witnesses and counsel informed the court that the defendant declined to give evidence because of the risk of retaliatory cross-examination on his record pursuant to section 1(f)(ii) of the Criminal Evidence Act 1898, the judge might discourage the jury from making a section 35 inference. In the view of the court this would lead to a bizarre result in that a defendant with convictions would be in a more privileged position than one with a clean record. The former could avoid submitting himself to cross-examination with impunity; the latter could not. It might also be said that the suggestion appears to fly in the face of the amended judgment in *Callaghan* in which the Court of Appeal held that where a defence involved attacking the police and the defendant was reluctant to give evidence for fear of retaliation under the 1898 Act defending counsel's duty was to warn the client that the court would probably make strong comment.

In stressing that there had to be an evidential basis or some exceptional factors in the case for not drawing an adverse inference from silence the court warned that the rule against advocates giving evidence dressed up as a submission applied in the present context to make it improper for a defence advocate to provide the jury with reasons for the client's silence at trial in the absence of evidence to support such reasons. But whether in fact a submission is a genuine argument or, on the other hand, evidence dressed up as a submission may be extremely difficult to determine and may be a matter of presentation and degree. For example, defending counsel might wish to implant in the jury's mind the suggestion that the reason why the client has not been called to give evidence is that his lawyers consider he will make

[111] (1993) unreported, Belfast Crown Court, November, cited by E.Rees, *Counsel*, March/April 1995, at p.22.

[112] Clearly following Pattenden, [1995] Crim.L.R., at p.607.

a poor witness of whom a "very clever prosecuting barrister such as my learned friend" would take advantage by leading him into giving confused answers and making him appear untruthful. Counsel obviously cannot assert this evidentially but with diffidence it may be feasible to make the point without offending the general rule. Would it be giving evidence to refer as a matter of generality to the self-evident fact that the defending lawyer's rôle is to give advice on such disparate aspects of the conduct of the defence as whether to call the defendant, and to the critera for making that decision? Such an argument might be evidentially based if reference could be made to the tape of the defendant's police interview revealing his woeful performance as a witness.[113]

Evidence that the defendant is too afraid for his personal safety to give evidence. In a Northern Ireland trial the judge decided not to use against the defendant his refusal to give evidence after it was suggested that he feared for his personal safety if he went into the witness box to denounce his co-accused.[114] This would only be permitted in England if the trial judge could be persuaded to accept that the defendant's fear was an "exceptional factor," and the issue would presumably have to be resolved on a *voir dire* by calling the defendant to attest to his fear. However, in *Chadwick*[115] it was held that there was no obligation on a judge to conduct a *voir dire* to determine whether a defendant is not giving evidence through fear or duress.

(9) Procedure to be followed at the end of the prosecution case

(a) *Original proposal for calling on the defendant to give evidence*

The original scheme proposed by the C.L.R.C. involved the performance of a ritual in which the accused, in the presence of the jury, was to be called upon by the court to give evidence and to be warned of the effect of refusing to give evidence. This procedure was adopted by Singapore, incorporated into the Northern Ireland legislation and originally proposed in the Criminal Justice and Public Order Bill. The terms of the address to the defendant in Northern Ireland were formulated the Lord Chief Justice and approved by the Supreme Court judges.[116] The defendant was to be warned that the effect of refusing to give evidence or, having gone into the witness box, refusing without good reason to answer any question, was that the court or jury, in deciding whether or not to convict, could take the refusal into account to the extent that it considered proper. A more comprehensive warning is used in Singapore where defendants are additionally to be told that they are not

[113] For suggested defence submissions to the jury as a tactical means of ameliorating anticipated adverse comment by the judge under the former régîme see Wolchover, "Spiking the judge's guns when defendants are silent" *Law Soc. Gaz.*, November 11, 1987, 3233, December 2, 3487.

[114] *Barkley* (1992) N.I.C.R. November 27, cited in *ibid.*

[115] [1998] 7 *Archbold News* 3.

[116] See Jackson, [1991] Crim.L.R., at p.410.

compelled to give evidence on their own behalf, that they shall not be guilty of contempt of court by reason of a refusal to be sworn and that they may consult counsel in deciding whether or not to give evidence.[117]

(b) *Proposal abandoned in favour of mere warning of the potential effect of refusing to give evidence*

In the event the proposed requirement for a ritual invitation to the accused to give evidence was dropped by the Government after intervention by the Lord Chief Justice, Lord Taylor of Gosforth,[118] and the requirement has been deleted from the Criminal Evidence (Northern Ireland) Order 1988, which has been brought into line with the English statute.[119] However, section 35(2) retains the provision for the court to satisfy itself in the presence of the jury that the accused is aware that such inferences as appear proper may be drawn from a refusal to give evidence. On April 10, 1995 Lord Taylor C.J. sitting in the Supreme Court of Judicature, issued *Practice Direction: Crown Court (Defendant's Evidence)* on the procedure by which a Crown Court was to satisfy itself that the accused was aware of the opportunity to give evidence and of the effect of choosing not to do so:[120]

> "*Form of words to be used pursuant to section 35 of the Criminal Justice and Public Order Act 1994*
>
> 1. At the conclusion of the evidence for the prosecution, section 35(2) of the Criminal Justice and Public Order Act 1994 requires the court to satisfy itself that the accused is aware that the stage has been reached at which evidence could be given for the defence and that he can, if he wishes, give evidence and that, if he chooses not to give evidence, or having been sworn, without good cause refused to answer any question, it will be permissible for the jury to draw such inferences as appeared proper from his failure, without good cause, to answer any question.
>
> *If the accused is legally represented.*
>
> 2. Section 35(1) provides that section 35(2) does not apply if at the conclusion of the evidence for the prosecution the accused's legal representative informed the court that the accused will give evidence. That should be done in the presence of the jury. If the representative indicates that the accused will give evidence, the case should proceed in the usual way.
>
> 3. If the court is not so informed, or if the court is informed that the accused does not intend to give evidence, the judge should in the presence of the jury inquire of the representative in these terms: 'Have you advised your client that the stage has now been reached at which he may give evidence and, if he chooses not to do so or, having been sworn,

[117] *ibid.*, citing *Haw Tua Tau* [1981] 3 All E.R. 14, at p..18-19.
[118] See 554 H.L. Deb., col. 443, April 25, 1994.
[119] By Sched. 10, para. 61(3), to the 1994 Act.
[120] [1995] 2 Cr.App.R. 192.

without good cause refuses to answer any questions, the jury may draw such inferences from his failure to do so?'

4. If the representative replies to the judge that the accused has been so advised, then the case would proceed. If counsel replies that the accused has not been so advised then the judge should direct the representative to advise his client of the consequences set out in paragraph 3 and should adjourn briefly for that purpose before proceeding further.

If the accused is not legally represented.

5. If the accused is not represented the judge should at the conclusion of the evidence for the prosecution and in the presence of the jury say to the accused: 'You have heard the evidence against you. Now is the time for you to make your defence. You may give evidence on oath, and be cross-examined like any other witness. If you do not give evidence, or having been sworn, without good cause refuse to answer any question the jury may draw such inferences as appear proper. That means they may hold it against you. You may also call any witness or witnesses whom you have arranged to attend court. 'Afterwards you may also, if you wish, address the jury by arguing your case from the dock. But you cannot at that stage give evidence. Do you now intend to give evidence.'"

(c) *Continued right of defence to submit no case*

The draft Bill originally proposed by the C.L.R.C. provided that before the accused could be warned that he would be called upon to give evidence, the court was to be required to have ruled against there being no case to answer. Neither Section 35 nor Article 4 of the Northern Ireland Order contain any such express provision and in *Murray* v. *D.P.P.*[121] it was suggested that the only reason why Article 4 contained no such requirement must have been that the continued right of the accused to submit that there was no case to answer and of the judge's duty to consider whether a sufficient case had been made out (even if the point was not raised by the defence) was regarded as too obvious to call for expression.

(10) Effect of cumulative silence

Even if the evidence for the prosecution apart from that of the accused's behaviour during the investigation is less than adequate for a *prima facie* case, when evidence of the silence of the accused *qua* suspect is added on it may be enough to erect a case to answer. If the *prima facie* case so made out is reasonably firm the further silence of the accused at trial may be enough to build on the earlier silence to achieve proof of guilt.

---

[121] (1993) 97 Cr.App.R., at p.154, *per* Lord Mustill.

CHAPTER FOUR

IMPACT OF THE EUROPEAN CONVENTION ON HUMAN RIGHTS

I. THE RIGHT TO SILENCE AND ADVERSE INFERENCES: *MURRAY (JOHN) v. UNITED KINGDOM*

The European Court of Human Rights (E.C.H.R.) has declared that the right not to incriminate oneself, like the right to silence, is an implicit element of the right to a fair trial guaranteed by Article 6.1 of the European Convention for the Protection of Human Rights and Fundamental Freedoms 1950, generally referred to by its abbreviated title of the European Convention on Human Rights.[1] In *Funke* v. *France*[2] it was held that the Applicant's right to silence had been infringed when he was compelled to produce bank statements which may have been relevant to customs investigations into offences of which he was suspected. Such coercion to co-operate with the authorities in the pre-trial process violates the privilege against self-incriinination and jeopardises the fairness of any subsequent hearing. Subsequently, in *Saunders* v. *U.K.* the court held that the use at the defendant's criminal trial of admissions obtained from him under the provisions for compulsory powers of interrogation in serious fraud investigations had contravened his right to a fair trial under the Article.[3]

Before the case was referred to the E.C.H.R. by the European Commission of Human Rights the European Human Rights forum was asked to decide whether the risk of the drawing of an adverse inference from the accused's silence amounted to

---

[1] Cmnd. 8969, 1953. Art. 6(1) provides: "In the determi nation of . . . any criminal charge against him, everyone is entitled to a fair and public hearing within a reasonable time by an independent and impartial tribunal established by law."

[2] (1993) 16 E.H.R.R. 297. See also *Miailhe* v. *France* (1993) 16 E.H.R.R. 332; *Cremieux* v. *France* (1993) 16 E.H.R.R. 357. For consideration of the impact of Article 6 on s.172 of the Road Traffic Act 1988 empowering a police constable to require the owner of a road vehicle to disclose the identity of the driver at a particular time and place, in the wake of *Brown* v. *Procurator Fiscal, Dunfermline* [2000] U.K.H.R.R. 239, see Jennings, Ashworth and Emmerson, *Silence and Safety: The Impact of the Human Rights Law*, [2000] Crim.L.R. 879, at pp.884-885.

[3] (1997) 23 E.H.R.R. 313, judgment given December 17, 1996; followed in applications by the other three defendants (Lyons, Ronson and Parnes) involved in the Guinness trial: *I.J.L., G.M.R. and A.K.P* v. *United Kingdom*, E.C.H.R. Application Nos. 29522/95, 30056/96 and 30574/96, judgment September 19, 2000. Following the E.C.H.R. judgments the Criminal Cases Review Commission has given priority to the Guinness defendants' cases in view of the appellant Lyons' age and deteriorating health and the Court of Appeal is expediting the appeal process for the same reason: see *The Times*, January 26, and February 28, 2001.

the compelling of self-incrimination. In *Murray (John)* v. *U.K.*[4] it was contended that Articles 6.1 and 6.2[5] were violated by the provisions of the Criminal Evidence (Northern Ireland) Order 1988 permitting adverse inferences to be drawn from the failure of an accused both to give an explanation to the police of his presence at a particular place in suspicious circumstances and to give evidence at trial. Giving judgment, the E.C.H.R. by 14 votes to 5 agreed with the opinion of the Commission that legislation permitting the drawing of an adverse inference to be drawn against the accused from his failure to answer police questions and from his refusal to give evidence at trial violated neither Article 6.1, entitling the accused to a fair and open trial by an independent and impartial tribunal established by law, nor Article 6.2, guaranteeing the presumption of innocence. The E.C.H.R. attached importance to the fact that the complainant was tried by an experienced judge whose reasons could be examined by an appeal court[6] and the judgment by no means guarantees a decision for the U.K. in any case in which adverse inferences may have been drawn from silence by a jury or lay judges, who do not give reasons.[7] Furthermore, the judgment contains propositions which may render the silence provisions of the 1994 Act invalid on other grounds.[8]

II. *MURRAY v. U.K.*: THE FACTS

The complainant was found by police in a house in which an informer against the Provisional I.R.A. was being held captive. He was arrested and at the police station a detective superintendent, pursuant to the Northern Ireland (Emergency Provisions) Act 1987 authorised delay of the defendant's access to a solicitor for 48 hours on the grounds that access would interefere with operations against terrorism. Under the 1988 Order he was cautioned that adverse inferences might be drawn if he failed to answer questions and over a period of two days was interviewed 12 times. Before each interview he was either cautioned or reminded that he was under caution and remained silent throughout the interviews. He saw a solicitor before the final two interviews but the solicitor was not allowed to be present at the interviews. Evidence given at trial by the defendant's co-accused that the defendant had recently arrived

---

[4] Original trial concluded May 8, 1991; appeal dismissed by the Northern Ireland Court of Appeal, July 1991; application lodged with the Commission August 16, 1991, as No. 4018731/91; declared admissible January 18, 1994 (see 5 *Human Rights Case Digest* 40); Commission report issued June 27, 1994 (see (1994) E.Comm.H.R.R., 1873/91), reported as (1994) E.H.H.R. C.D. 1; referred to the Court by the Commission September 9, 1994, and by the U.K. Government October 11, 1994; judgment given February 8, 1996 (No. 41/1994/488/570), reported as (1996) 22 E.H.R.R. 29. See Roderick Munday, "Inferences from silence and European Human Rights Law," [1996] Crim.L.R. 370.

[5] "Everyone charged with a criminal offence shall be presumed innocent until proved guilty according to law."

[6] (1996) 22 E.H.R.R., at p.62.

[7] See Pattenden, 2 E. & P., at p.161, and Munday, *supra*, [1996] Crim.L.R., at p.381.

[8] Pattenden, 2 E. & P., at p.161.

at the house when the police arrived was discounted as not being credible. The trial judge, the Lord Chief Justice of Northern Ireland, sitting without a jury in a "Diplock court," drew strong inferences against the defendant under Article 6 of the 1988 Order from his failure, when arrested and interrogated, to account for his presence in the house, and, under Article 4 of the Order, from his refusal to give evidence, and the defendant was convicted of aiding and abetting the false imprisonment of the informer.

III. *MURRAY v. U.K.*: THE JUDGMENT OF THE EUROPEAN COURT OF HUMAN RIGHTS.

In its judgment the E.C.H.R. stated that although not specifically mentioned in Article 6 of the Convention there could be no doubt that the right to remain silent under police questioning and the privilege against self-incrimination were generally recognised international standards which lay at the heart of the notion of fair trial as envisaged in the Convention. By providing the accused with protection against improper compulsion by the authorities those immunities contributed to the avoidance of miscarriage of justice and to the securing of fair trial. The E.C.H.R. did not consider that it was called upon to give an abstract analysis of the scope of those immunities and, in particular, of what constituted in that context "improper compulsion." What was at stake in the case was whether those immunities were absolute in the sense that the exercise by an accused of the right to silence could not under any circumstances be used against him at trial or, alternatively, whether informing him in advance that, under certain conditions, his silence might be so used, was always to be regarded as "improper compulsion."

On the one hand, the E.C.H.R. noted, it was self-evident that it was incompatible with the immunities under consideration to base a conviction solely or mainly on the accused's silence or on a refusal to answer questions or to give evidence himself. However, the E.C.H.R. deemed it equally obvious that those immunities could not and should not prevent the accused's silence, in situations which clearly called for an explanation, from being taken into account in assessing the persuasiveness of the evidence adduced by the prosecution.[9] The right to silence was therefore not an absolute right and it could not be said that the accused's decision to remain silent throughout criminal proceedings should necessarily have no implications when the trial court sought to evaluate the evidence against him.

Whether the drawing of adverse inferences from the accused's silence infringed the Convention was a matter to be determined in the light of all the circumstances of the case, having particular regard to the situations where inferences might be drawn, the weight attached to them by the national courts in their assessment of the

---

[9] (1996) 22 E.H.R.R., at p.60.

evidence and the degree of compulsion inherent in the situation. In examining the degree of compulsion involved in the present case the applicant was in fact able to remain silent and, despite the repeated warnings as to the possibility that inferences might be drawn from his silence, he did not make any statements to the police, did not give evidence, and remained a non-compellable witness whose insistence on maintaining silence throughout the proceedings did not amount to a criminal offence or a contempt of court. Furthermore, silence in itself could not be regarded as an indication of guilt.[10]

The E.C.H.R. conceded that a system which warned the accused, who was possibly without legal assistance (as was the defendant in the present case) that adverse inferences might be drawn from a refusal to provide an explanation to the police for his presence at the scene of a crime or to testify during his trial, when taken in conjunction with the weight of the case against him, did involve a certain level of indirect compulsion. Since, however, the defendant could not be compelled to speak or to testify, that factor on its own could not be decisive. In the opinion of the Court the drawing of inferences under the 1988 Order was subject to an important series of safeguards designed to respect the rights of the defence and limit the extent to which reliance could be placed on inferences. In the first place, before inferences could be drawn under Articles 4 and 6 of the 1988 Order appropriate warnings had to be given to the accused as to the legal effects of maintaining silence. Again, as indicated by the House of Lords in *Murray* v. *D.P.P.*,[11] the prosecutor had to establish a *prima facie* case against the accused. The question in each particular case was whether the evidence adduced by the prosecution was sufficiently strong to require an answer. The national court could not conclude that the accused was guilty merely because he chose to remain silent. It was only if the evidence against the accused called for an explanation which the accused ought to be in a position to give that a failure to give any explanation "may as a matter of common sense allow the drawing of an inference that there is no explanation and that the accused is guilty."[12] Conversely if the case presented by the prosecution has so little evidential value that it calls for no answer, a failure to provide one could not justify an inference of guilt.

Although the Court found no violation of Articles 6.1 and 6.2 arising from the silence provisions of the 1988 Order they did hold, by 12 votes to 5, that there was a breach of Article 6.1 taken in conjunction with Article 6.3(c) as regards the denial of

---

10 *ibid.*, at p.61. Pattenden, 2 E.&P., at p.162, suggests that this comment may also be directed against the use of silence as substantive evidence; alternatively, she argues (n.157), it may be a reference to the fact that the accused cannot be convicted solely on the basis of his silence).

11 (1992) 97 Cr.App.R. 151.

12 (1996) 22 E.H.R.R. at p.62. In their report to the E.C.H.R the European Commission observed that "the 1988 Order constituted a formalised system which aims at allowing common sense implications to play an open role in the assessment of evidence." See A. Jennings and E. Rees, Q.C., "Is silence still golden?" *Archbold News*, June 14, 2000, 5, at p.6: "Arguably, there is an internal tension, even irrationality, in the principle that the right of silence is an internationally recognised standard of fairness that simultaneously permits an inference of guilt from the exercise of that right. The Court has found a point of equilibrium in the view that such inferences are 'proper' in the language of the Act and, therefore, fair in the language of Article 6 when, in the circumstances, guilt is the only 'common sense' conclusion."

the defendant's access to a lawyer during the first 48 hours of his detention. That aspect of the judgment has already been discussed.[13]

IV. GROUNDS UPON WHICH THE U.K. LAW ON SILENCE MAY VIOLATE THE CONVENTION

There are at least four grounds upon which it has been predicted that the investigative stage silence provisions of the 1994 Act might fall foul of the Convention:

- unsuitability of the tribunal of fact
- substantive use of evidence as direct evidence of guilt
- no inference without a prima facie case
- no conviction based solely or mainly on the accused's silence.

The first in order of these is considered under a heading of its own. The others are listed under other possible Convention challenges.

A. *UNSUITABLE TRIBUNAL*

(1) Reasoning involved in inference must be susceptible to review on appeal

In *Murray* v. *U.K.*[14] the European Commission of Human Rights drew a decisive distinction between trial of a scheduled offence in Northern Ireland by a judge sitting alone without a jury and, on the other hand, trial by jury. At the time this was of potential significance for the future of the provisions on silence in the Criminal Justice and Public Order Act 1994. The crux of the difference was that a judge sitting alone gives a reasoned judgment as to the basis on which he decides to draw adverse inferences and the weight he gives to them. The correctness of that reasoning process is thus rendered justiciable on appeal. This point was elaborated upon in the opinion of Mr. N. Bratza (as he then was), the U.K. member:

> "I attach considerable importance to the fact that adverse inferences . . . are drawn by a judge sitting without a jury. Not only is a judge, by his training and legal experience, likely to be better equipped than a lay juryman to draw only such inferences as are justified from a defendant's

[13] See *supra*, at pp.155-157.
[14] (1994) E.H.H.R. C.D.1.

> silence but, as pointed out by the Commission, a judge in Northern Ireland gives a reasoned judgment as to the grounds on which he decides to draw inferences and the weight which he gives to such inferences in any particular case: whether the inferences can be properly drawn in all the circumstances and whether proper weight has been given to them by the trial judge is then open to review by the Court of Appeal in Northern Ireland. The same safeguards against unfairness do not appear to me to exist in the case of a jury trial. When it is a jury which must decide, without giving reasons, what adverse inferences, if any, to draw against an accused from his silence and what weight to attach to such inferences in arriving at a verdict, the risk of unfairness occurring appears to me to be substantially increased, however carefully formulated a judge's direction to the jury might be."[15]

Although this point was only referred to in an abbreviated form in the judgment of the European Court of Human Rights there are indications that the court may have also been concerned about the suitability of jury trial as forum for the drawing of adverse inferences from silence. Significantly the court stressed that in the present case the trier of fact was an experienced judge, that in Northern Ireland trial judges sat without a jury, and that in exercising the discretion as to whether, on the facts of the particular case, an adverse inference should be drawn from the defendant's silence the judge had to explain the reasons for the decision to draw inferences and the weight to attach to them. The exercise of the discretion in that regard was, the Court said, subject to review by the appellate courts. The implicit suggestion seemed to be that since jury verdicts "are presented in the form of inscrutable dooms which do not reveal the intellectual process leading to a conclusion of guilt" there can be no such review in the case of jury trials.[16] Thus the licensing of adverse inferences in the context of a jury system would be inherently unfair and would constitute a violation of Article 6(1).

Whether the distinction drawn by the E.C.H.R. between trials by judge alone and those by jury seemed to be heralding a general disavowal of the evidential silence provisions of the 1994 Act in the context of English jury trials was not clear. In the first place, as Roderick Munday argued, given the disparate composition of the Court and the fluid nature of some of its jurisprudence, it was no easy matter to predict the course of future litigation.[17] More fundamentally, as Munday pointed out, the Court had repeatedly interpreted its rôle as not being to judge the fundamental compatibility of the legislation of signatory states with Articles of the Convention, but merely that of determining whether the effect of applying the national law in the particular case violates the Convention.[18] Yet a ruling which, on the basis of the impossibility of review argument, held that permitting a jury to draw

---

[15] *ibid.*, at p. C.D.16.
[16] Munday, [1996] Crim.L.R., at p.381. See *ibid.*, at p.382, for discussion of the review question.
[17] *ibid.*, at p.371.
[18] *ibid.*

an adverse inference from the defendant's silence violated the Convention would have had a significant impact on the generality of trials for serious crime in the United Kingdom. (It would remain permissible to draw an adverse inference in trials by stipendiary magistrates or in Crown court appeals against conviction.)

(2) Review argument undermined by its generality of application

In spite of *Murray v. U.K.* it was by no means certain that the English silence provisions would ultimately be in peril from the E.C.H.R. or from the English Court of Appeal applying the Human Rights Act 1998. The problem with an objection based on the absence of any realistic means of monitoring the jury's reasoning is one which could be taken against the very nature of English jury trial. If a judge misdirects a jury in summing up, or fails to give adequate directions, the verdict may be set aside because it is assumed that, as laymen, they were or may have been misled. Conversely, it is inherent in the traditional concept of jury trial that if directions are correct and coherently explained it is presumed that the jury must have applied them, however complex in reality the legal principles involved. To contend that the jury should not be let loose on a defendant's silence because the possible reasons for it are peculiarly elusive, because the analytical process of identifying those reasons demands an especially rigorous calibre of intellect, and because the jury's thinking is not susceptible to review on appeal, is an objection which could be taken on a vast array of topics that juries are customarily required to address.

(3) Recognition by the E.C.H.R. that the jury is not an intrinsically unsuitable tribunal for adjudicating on the silence provisions

(a) *Requirement for proper directions*

In the event, the E.C.H.R. has now concluded that the silence provisions of the 1994 Act do not violate the convention where jury trial is concerned. In *Condron* v. *U.K.*,[19] the facts and judgment in which were reviewed in Chapter 2, the applicants did not seek to argue that the right to silence was an absolute right in the context of a jury trial and conceded that provided there were proper safeguards, including, most importantly, adequate directions given to the jury on the relevance and potential significance of the accused's silence section 34 did not by itself violate the applicants' human rights.

For its part, the court held that section 34 of the 1994 Act specifically entrusted to the jury, properly directed, the task of deciding whether or not to draw an adverse inference from an accused's silence as part of a legislative scheme designed to

[19] Application no. 35718/97, May 2, 2000. See in particular paras. 55 to 68 of the judgment.

confine the use at trial which could be made of that silence.[20] Accordingly, the court held, the fact that the issue of the applicants' silence was left to the jury could not of itself be considered incompatible with the requirements of a fair trial.[21] It was essential to ensure that the jury received adequate directions and the court upheld the argument that because it was impossible to ascertain the extent to which the silence of the applicants at the police station played a part in the jury's decision to convict, the verdict not being accompanied by reasons which were amenable to review on appeal, the trial judge was obligated to approach the issue with the utmost caution.[22] The trial judge had omitted to direct the jury that if they were not satisfied that the applicants' silence at the police interview could not sensibly be attributed to their having no answer or none that would stand up to cross-examination they should not draw an adverse inference. The Court of Appeal had taken the view that such a direction would have been "desirable" but held that because the evidence of guilt was overwhelming the convictions were not unsafe. The United Kingdom Government argued that the fairness of the trial was secured by the domestic appeal proceedings. However, the E.C.H.R. held[23] that the failure to give the necessary direction could not be remedied on appeal because—

(a) the Court of Appeal had no means of ascertaining whether or not the applicants' silence played a significant role in the jury's decision to convict (*i.e.* it was impossible to ascertain what weight, if any, was given to their silence);
(b) in having regard to the weight of the evidence against the applicants the Court of Appeal were in no position to assess properly whether the jury considered the evidence [apart from silence[24]] to be conclusive of guilt;
(c) they did not accept that the evidence against the applicants' was as overhelming as the Court of Appeal considered it to be.

Since the imperfection in the direction to the jury could not be remedied on appeal it was incompatible with the exercise by the applicants of their right to silence at the police station and they were therefore deprived of the right to receive a fair hearing within the meaning of Article 6 of the Convention.

---

20 para. 66.

21 para. 57. The court went on to state: "It is, rather, another relevant consi deration to be weighed in the balance when assessing whether or not it is fair to do so in the circumstances." This seems to be saying that the fact that the issue of the applicants' silence was left to the jury was a relevant consideration to be weighed in the balance when assessing whether or not it was fair to do so —an odd tautology if ever there was one and yet one further solecism in the text of the judgment.

22 See paras. 46 and 47 for the applicants' argument on the point.

23 See paras. 62-64.

24 It is presumed that the court was referring to the evidence apart from silence, although they did not say so in terms, because the jury obviously did consider the totality of the evidence as furnishing conclusive proof of guilt.

(b) *The appellate tests of safety and fairness harmonised*

In ruling in *Condron* v *U.K.* that the failure to give the jury adequate directions had deprived the appellants of a fair trial in accordance with Article 6 the E.C.H.R. considered itself bound to—

> ". . . have regard to the fact that the Court of Appeal was concerned with the safety of the applicant's conviction, not whether they had in the circumstances received a fair trial. In the [Strasbourg] Court's opinion, the question whether or not the rights of the defence guaranteed to an accused under Article 6 of the Convention were secured in any given case cannot be assimilated to a finding that his conviction was safe in the absence of any enquiry into the issue of fairness."[25]

This passage was described as being likely to have "profound consequences" for the approach of the Court of Appeal in determining appeals against conviction, a prediction which in the event proved most prescient.[26] Replacement of the original "unsafe and unsatisfactory" test by the "unsafe" test for the determination of appeals against conviction[27] had resulted in uncertainty as to whether a conviction could be safe despite procedural irregularity or unfairness in the trial, the key question being "whether the word 'unsatisfactory' signified an additional and independent ground for quashing a conviction or merely another way of saying 'unsafe.'"[28] In *Francom and others*[29] the judge had agreed to direct the jury to draw no adverse inferences from the omission of the appellants to mention matters relied in the trial and gving judgment, the Court of Appeal pointed out that the statutory test of "unsafeness" in section 2(1) of the Criminal Appeal Act 1968, as amended by section 2(1) of the Criminal Appeal Act 1995, was not identical to the issue of unfairness in Article 6

---

25 *ibid*., para. 65.

26 See A. Jennings, "The death of silence or safety?" C.B.A. newsletter June 2000; A. Jennings and E. Rees, Q.C., "Is silence still golden?" *Archbold News*, June 14. 2000, 5, at p.7. For a recent analysis of the issue see Jennings, Ashworth and Emmerson, *Silence and Safety: The Impact of the Human Rights Law*, [2000] Crim.L.R. 879, at pp. 888-894.

27 Amendment of the Criminal Appeal Act 1968, s.2(1), by the Criminal Appeal Act 1995, s.2(1), recom-mended by the Royal Commission on Criminal Justice in order to provide "a single broad ground which would give the court sufficient flexibility to consider all categories of appeal": Cmnd. 2633, June 1993, Chap. 10, para. 32. A minority considered that the new test gave insufficient guidance towards adopting "the less restrictive approach of which all of us are in favour": para. 34.

28 *Chalkley and Jeffries* [1998] 2 Cr.App.R. 79, *per* Auld L.J., adopting a narrow approach but acknowled-ging that this would be subject to the view of the E.C.H.R. A broad approach had been favoured in *Graham* [1997] 1 Cr.App.R. 302 but subsequently eschewed in *Kennedy* [1999] 1 Cr.App.R. 54, *Callaghan* [1999] 5 *Archbold News* 2; C.A. 97/08628/X4, and *Rajcoomar* [1999] Crim.L.R 728. In *Macdonald* [1998] Crim.L.R. 806, Auld L.J. left the question open, from which the Court of Appeal in *Mullen* [1999] 2 Cr.App.R. 143 (*per* Rose L.J.) deduced that *Chalkley* had not concluded the construction of "unsafe." Since the term therefore remained ambiguous a reference was permitted in *Mullen* to the intention of Parliament, which, supported by the opinion of the Lord Chief Justice and senior judiciary, had been to restate the then existing practice of the Court of Appeal: 256 H.C. Deb. col. 24; Standing Committee B, *Official Report*, March 21, 1995, col. 26. (See Prof. J.C. Smith in [1999] Crim.L.R. 215, suggesting that Parliament was "unwittingly, but seriously, misled" by the opinion of the judges.) Having referred to *Hansard* the court opted for a broad meaning but without fully considering the relationship between unfairness and safety.

29 [2000] 9 *Archbold News*, 3 *The Times*, October 24; C.A. 99/3936/W5, *et seq*.

of the Convention,[30] a distinction which the court noted had been recognised by the E.H.C.R. in *Condron* v. *U.K.* and by the Court of Appeal in *Davis, Rowe and Johnson*.[31] However, in the court's view, following variously *Condron* v. *U.K.*, *Mullen*[32] and *Davis,Rowe and Johnson*, the term "unfair" was—

> ". . . to be given a broad meaning favourable to the defendants. It is not limited to the safety of the conviction itself, but encompasses the entire prosecution process. The Court of Appeal looks at all the circumstances of the case, including questions of law, abuse of process and questions of evidence and procedure. . . . A misdirection of the jury can result in a breach of Article 6. But it may not do so. In the same way it may not make a conviction unsafe. It all depends on the circumstances of the case. . . . In a case such as the present, we would expect this court to be approaching the issue of lack of safety in exactly the same way as the [E.C.H.R.] approaches lack of fairness. The directions which a judge gives at a trial are designed to achieve the very fairness required by Article 6.1. As we understand the jurisprudence of the [E.C.H.R.] that court does not adopt a technical approach to the question of unfairness. . . . Approaching the present case, we therefore . . . ask ourselves whether the omission of the required direction by the judge has in fact achieved unfairness, focusing on the importance of the right to silence, or impaired the safety of the conviction, in the proecss not drawing any distinction between the two tests.[33]

It had been urged for the appellants that the position in *Francom* was exactly the same as that considered in *Condron* v. *U.K.* because the court did not know what could have influenced the jury's decision.[34] In the judgment of the court, the test which had to be applied was—

> ". . . whether, notwithstanding what is, in this case, a non-direction, we are satisfied that no reasonable jury could have come to a different conclusion from that which was reached by this jury if they were properly directed. This approach not only means that there must be a lack of safety, it also means there must be no unfairness because the non-direction or misdirection must not affect the defendant's right to a fair trial."[35]

---

30 *ibid.*, para. 43.

31 (2000) *The Times*, July 17; C.A. 99/2239/41/S3.

32 [1999] 2 Cr.App.R. 143.

33 paras. 43, 47 and 48, *per* Lord Woolf, C.J.

34 para. 45.

35 para. 50, following an interpretation of *Condron* v. *U.K.* originally suggested by Jennings, "The death of silence or safety?" C.B.A. newsletter June 2000, 3, at p.4.

In *Togher*[36] Lord Woolf C.J., giving the judgment of the Court of Appeal, pointed out that with the incorporation of the Convention into domestic law occasioned by the Human Rights Act 1998 there was a need for consistency with the approach in *Condron* v. *U.K.* The requirement of fairness in the criminal process had always been a common law tenet of the greatest importance. Fairness in both jurisdictions was not an abstract concept. It was not concerned with technicalities. Applying the broader approach identified in *Mullen*, if a defendant had been denied a fair trial it would almost be inevitable that the conviction would be regarded as unsafe. This meant, following *Mullen*, that a conviction could be unsafe even if there was no doubt that the defendant had committed the offence of which he had been found guilty.

It should, however, be emphasised that the actual decision of the E.C.H.R. in *Condron* v. *U.K.* was firmly rooted in its judgment that the failure to direct the jury properly meant not simply that justice was not seen to be done but that the particular procedural failure had led to a real risk that innocent persons were convicted as a result of the misdirection.

B. *OTHER POSSIBLE CONVENTION CHALLENGES TO THE SILENCE PROVISIONS*

(1) Substantive use of evidence as direct evidence of guilt

In *Murray* v. *U.K.* the E.C.H.R. conceded that the Convention immunity from improper compulsion could not prevent "the accused's silence, in situations which clearly called for an explanation, from being taken into account in assessing the persuasiveness of the evidence adduced by the prosecution"[37] It has been argued that by this the court was intending to restrict the use of silence by preventing it from serving as substantive evidence of guilt, or evidence having "force in its own right," to coin a phrase employed by one commentator.[38] This may be assuming too much. The only way in which failure by the defendant to account for objects, substances, marks associated with his person (section 36 of the 1994 Act) or for his presence at a particular place (section 37) can "be taken into account in assessing," *i.e.*, can strengthen, the incriminatory effect of the objects, etc, or the presence, is if the failure is taken as evidence of a tacit admission that there is no innocent explanation to be offered. No other interpretation of the failure can have such an effect. It lends persuasive support precisely and exclusively because of its substantive quality as evidence of a tacit admission of guilt. If it is not evidence of an admission it does not strengthen the evidence for which an explanation is called for.

---

[36] *R.* v. *Topher*, *R.* v. *Doran*, *R.* v. *Parsons* (2000) *The Times*, November 21 (judgment, October 12; reasons November 9).

[37] (1996) 22 E.H.R.R., para. 47, at p.60.

[38] Peter Mirfield, *Silence, Confessions and Improperly Obtained Evidence*, Oxford University Press, 1997, p.215. See also Pattenden, 2 E. & P., at p.162.

As to section 34, the failure to mention a fact relied upon in proceedings, the same basic principle may apply, though necessarily tacit admission is far from being the only interpretation of the failure. If a vital exculpatory fact is relied upon by the defence which was not mentioned by the defendant when interviewed as a suspect, the effect of the failure *may be* to increase the persuasive quality of the existing evidence adduced by the prosecution by virtue of the inference drawn from the defendant's silence that he was not then relying on that fact because he was accepting the validity of the allegation.

The E.C.H.R. stipulated that "silence, in itself, cannot be regarded as an indication of guilt."[39] Although Pattenden suggests that this is a stricture which may be directed against the use of silence as substantive evidence, she concedes that, alternatively, it may have been no more than a reference to the principle that the accused cannot be convicted solely on the basis of his silence.[40] This interpretation is preferable because it coheres with the argument that silence increases the persuasive quality of incriminating evidence only insofar as it can be taken as an acknowledgment that there is no innocent explanation.

(2) No inference without a *prima facie* case

In *Murray* v *U.K.* the E.C.H.R. held that "the prosecutor must first establish a *prima facie* case against the accused" before any inference is drawn from silence and they drew no distinction between the equivalent of section 35 (Northern Ireland Article 4) and section 37 (Article 6).[41] Three of the dissenting judges made the same point as to the equivalent of section 34 (Article 3).[42] Section 35 is not affected since as enacted, and applied in *Cowan*, it does not operate until there is a *prima facie* case. However, the judgment plainly restricts the use which can be made of silence under sections 34, 36 and 37 to make up any deficit in establishing a *prima facie* case.

It has already been mentioned that in *Condron* v. *U.K.*[43] the applicants, relying on *Murray* v.*U.K.*, sought to challenge the trial judge's direction on the ground that it omitted a reference to the requirement that the prosecution must establish a *prima facie* case before an adverse inference might be drawn. The applicants conceded that the point had not been taken before the Court of Appeal, maintaining that they would have stood little prospect of success. The U.K. Government argued that having regard to the facts that the Court of Appeal accepted the main ground for challenging the direction and that the law in this area was evolving at the time of the appeal, the applicants should have included the issue in their grounds of appeal. The E.C.H.R. considered that it did not have to take a stand on the issue having regard to its finding on the main defect relied on by the applicants. In any event, it has been

39 (1996) 22 E.H.R.R., at p.61.
40 2 E. & P., at p.162.
41 (1996) 22 E.H.R.R., at p.62.
42 (1996) 22 E.H.R.R., at p.75, *per* Judge Walsh, joined by Judges Makarczyk and Lohmus.
43 E.C.H.R., application no. 35718/97, May 2, 2000.

suggested that the point is academic because the current J.S.B. specimen direction requires that there should be a case to meet before an adverse inference can be drawn under section 34.[44] Yet, as was noted earlier, the validity of the specimen direction is plainly at odds with *Doldur*,[45] although the latter is in conflict with *Murray* v. *U.K.*.

(3) No conviction based solely or mainly on the accused's silence

In *Murray* v. *U.K.* the E.C.H.R. stressed that since the right to silence like the privilege against self-incimination, lay at the heart of the notion of a fair procedure under Article 6, "particular caution" was required before a domestic court could invoke an accused's silence against him.[46] Thus, the court would disallow convictions based "solely or mainly on the accused's silence or on a refusal to answer questions or to give evidence . . ."[47] The prohibition on convictions based solely on silence is met by section 38(3), according to which a defendant will not have a case to answer or be convicted on an inference drawn solely from a failure or refusal to which sections 34, 36 or 37 relate.[48] It has already been pointed out in the discussion on section 38(3) that the subsection is of little practical benefit and in the majority of cases, the E.C.H.R. ban on convictions based mainly on the accused's silence is also unlikely to have much practical significance. In most of the English appeal cases the prosecution case was already a strong one without silence,[49] and in Northern Ireland Diplock court judges frequently stress the same point when giving their reasons for conviction.[50] However, in a minority of cases, the prohibition of convictions based mainly on silence is likely to have real impact on the operation of the 1994 legislation because the Act—

> ". . . permits multiple inferences without in any way restricting the weight to be placed on each inference. Legislation [subsequently enacted] additionally allows the jury to draw an inference from the accused's failure to disclose to the prosecution before trial the nature of his defence and the matters on which he takes issue with the

---

[44] See Jennings, Ashworth and Emmerson, *Silence and Safety: The Impact of the Human Rights Law*, [2000] Crim.L.R. 879, at p. 882, note 27.

[45] [2000] Crim.L.R. 178, C.A. See *supra* p. 109-110.

[46] (1996) 22 E.H.R.R., para. 47, at p.60. Similarly, in *Averill* v. *U.K.*, E.C.H.R. application no. 36408/97, June 6, 2000, *The Times*, June 20, 2000, para. 47, the court stated that the extent to which adverse inferences might be drawn from an accused's failure to respond to police questining "must be necessarily limited."

[47] (1996) 22 E.H.R.R., para. 47, at p.60.

[48] Replicating Art. 2(4) of the Northern Ireland Order.

[49] See, *e.g. Condron* [1997] 1 W.L.R. 827; *Argent* [1997] 2 Cr.App.R. 27; *Bowers* [1998] Crim.L.R. 817; *Daniel* [1998] Crim.L.R. 818; *Taylor* [1999] Crim.L.R. 77.

[50] See, *e.g. Mathers and Hillen* (1993) unreported, N.I.C.A., September 1; *McKee* (1991) unreported, Crown Court in Northern Ireland, October 14, both cases cited by Birch, [1999] Crim.L.R., at p.774, n.30.

> prosecution.[51] As a result the prosecution can rely, in part, on pre-trial silence(s) to make out a case to answer and the jury, in order to convict, may combine the same pre-trial inference(s) with an inference from in-court silence and the accused's omission to tender a defence statement."[52]

In other words, "the adverse inference is permitted, jurisprudentially, to run free."[53] In *Murray* v. *U.K.* the accumulation of a Northern Ireland Article 4 (section 35) inference and an Article 6 (section 37) inference at the conviction stage was tolerated because the prosecution without reference to the accused's silence already had a "formidable" case.[54] It has been suggested[55] that the E.C.H.R. would have been unlikely to find that there had been a fair trial had the prosecution relied upon the accused's refusal to explain to police why he was at the scene of the crime to bolster a weak prosecution case sufficiently to avoid a submission of no case, and had the judge then relied upon the accused's pre-trial silence, his failure to deliver a defence statement, and his absence from the witness box to be convinced of his guilt beyond reasonable doubt.

In *Condron* v. *U.K.*[56] the applicants, relying on *Murray* v.*U.K.*, sought to challenge the trial judge's direction on the ground that he failed to state that the silence of the applicants could not constitute the "main" basis for their conviction. As in the case of their argument that the summing up should also have laid down a requirement for the establishment of a *prima facie* case, the applicants conceded that the point had not been taken before the Court of Appeal, maintaining that they would have stood little prospect of success. The U.K. Government argued that having regard to the facts that the Court of Appeal accepted the main ground for challenging the direction and that the law in this area was evolving at the time of the appeal, the applicants should have included the issue in their grounds of appeal. The E.C.H.R. considered that it did not have to take a stand on the issue having regard to its finding on the main defect relied on by the applicants. Presumably to establish compatibility with *Murray* v. *U.K.* it has been urged that the J.S.B. specimen direction should be amended to embrace the principle that an adverse inference cannot be the main basis for a conviction.[57]

---

51 Criminal Procedure and Investigations Act 1996, s.5(11)(3)(b).

52 Pattenden, 2 E. & P., at pp.162-163. See also R. Munday, "Inferences from silence and the European Human Rights Law," [1996] Crim.L.R. 370; and Prof. A. Ashworth, "Article 6 and the Fairness of Trials," [1999] Crim.L.R. 261.

53 Jennings, "Recent developments in the law relating to the right to silence," *Archbold News*, June 9, 1999.

54 (1996) 22 E.H.R.R., at p.62.

55 Pattenden, 2 E. & P., at pp.163.

56 E.C.H.R., application no. 35718/97, May 2, 2000.

57 Jennings, Ashworth and Emmerson, [2000] Crim.L.R., at pp. 881-882.

V. POSSIBLE EFFECTS OF ADVERSE FINDINGS ON U.K. LAW

A. *IMPACT OF THE CONVENTION ON DOMESTIC COURTS PRIOR TO THE COMING INTO FORCE OF THE HUMAN RIGHTS ACT 1998*

In *Cowan*,[58] decided by the Court of Appeal before the E.C.H.R. gave judgment in *Murray* v. *U.K.*, Lord Taylor C.J., giving judgment, stressed that decisions of the Commission and of the European Court on Human Rights were not binding on the Court of Appeal but were merely of assistance in resolving any ambiguity in domestic law. It was held that there was no ambiguity in section 35. Lord Taylor predicted that if the E.C.H.R. upheld the opinion of the Commission treaty obligations might require amending action by Parliament. Commenting also on the Commission opinion of Mr Nicholas Bratza that adverse inferences might be peculiarly incompatible with jury trial he said that juries in criminal trials were often required to draw inferences in a number of circumstances and provided they were properly directed there was no reason why they should not be permitted also to draw inferences from silence.[59] Any potential clash between the Convention and domestic law was in the event averted by the concession on the part of the applicants in *Condron* v. *U.K.* that the drawing of adverse inferences was not necessarily incompatible with trial by jury.

It has already been mentioned that in *Birchall*[60] Lord Bingham C.J. acknowledged the possibility that the application of the silence provisions of the 1994 Act could lead to decisions adverse to the United Kingdom at Strasbourg under Articles 6.1 and 6.2 unless those provisions were the subject of carefully framed directions to juries, a prediction entirely borne out by the decision in *Condron* v. *U.K.*

B. *HUMAN RIGHTS ACT 1998*

The Human Rights Act 1998 imposes a general obligation to interpret legislation in a way that is compatible with the Convention "[s]o far as it is possible to do."[61] Decisions of the E.C.H.R. and opinions of the European Commission of Human Rights must be taken into account by a court or tribunal in determining any question arising in connection with a Convention right.[62] If satisfied that a provision of legislation is incompatible with a Convention right an eligible court may make a

58 [1996] Q.B. 373.
59 *ibid.*, at p.382.
60 (1998) *The Times*, February 10; [1999] Crim.L.R. 311.
61 s.3.
62 s.2.

declaration of incompatibility,[63] but a declaration will not affect the validity, continuing operation or enforcement of the provision in respect of which it is given and is not binding on the parties to the proceedings in which it is made.[64] Where such a declaration has been made a Minister of the Crown may by order make such amendments to the particular legislation as he considers necessary to remove the incompatibility, if he considers that there are compelling reasons for doing so.[65] Aggrieved individuals may still pursue Convention remedies in the E.C.H.R.

It will be interesting to see whether the Court of Appeal uses its interpretive power under the 1998 Act to invoke *Murray* v. *U.K.* by quashing convictions based mainly on the evidence of silence, and to make a declaration of incompatibility (similarly invoking *Murray* v. *U.K.*) in any case in which a trial court has used the evidence of silence under sections 34, 36 or 37 to uphold the existence of a prima facie case. Hitherto the Government has not sought to amend the Criminal Justice and Public Order Act 1994 in order to achieve consistency with Convention rights as enunciated in *Murray* v. *U.K.* but with the intercession of our own judges it may be more willing to do so.

---

[63] s.4. Eligible courts in England and Wales are the House of Lords, the Judicial Committee of the Privy Council, the Courts-Martial Appeal Court, the High Court or the Court of Appeal: s.4(5).

[64] s.4(6).

[65] s.10.